4231

The County Books Series
GENERAL EDITOR : BRIAN VESEY-FITZGERALD

MIDDLESEX

THE COUNTY BOOKS SERIES

A series comprising 57 Volumes. It covers every county in England and there will be five books on Scotland, two on Ireland, two on the Hebrides, and one each on Orkney, Shetland, Wales, the Isle of Man and the Channel Islands

THE FOLLOWING FORTY-FOUR VOLUMES
HAVE NOW BEEN PUBLISHED

PLEASE WRITE TO THE PUBLISHERS
FOR FULL DESCRIPTIVE PROSPECTUS

MIDDLESEX

by

NORMAN G. BRETT-JAMES
M.A., B.LITT., F.S.A.

Illustrated and with a Map

London
Robert Hale Limited
18 Bedford Square WC1

By the same Author

Mill Hill School (1807-1907)
The Charm of Switzerland
My Term Off
War Record of Mill Hill School (1914-18)
Modern Essays
The Life of Peter Collinson
Mill Hill School, 1807-1922
A London Anthology
The Story of Mill Hill Village
The Story of Hendon
The Growth of Stuart London
Some Extents and Surveys of Hendon
English Public Schools : Mill Hill
Walking in the Welsh Border
Introducing Chaucer
War Record of Mill Hill School (1939-45)

First published . . 1951

CONTENTS

v

CONTENTS

vi

LIST OF ILLUSTRATIONS

LIST OF ILLUSTRATIONS

Present-day difficulties do not permit of a comprehensive map of the area being included in this book. For more detailed information readers are referred to the respective Ordnance Survey sheets.

ACKNOWLEDGMENTS

The illustrations above numbered 1 and 22 are reproduced from photographs supplied by Staniland Pugh of Amersham, Nos. 18 and 27 by Gerald Wilson of Ilford, and Nos. 38 and 46 by D. W. Gardner of London, N.W.10. The remaining forty-three are reproduced from photographs supplied by Geoffrey Dempsey of London, S.W.1.

FOREWORD

MIDDLESEX, as we know it today, is just 60 years old; a reasonably good record for a man, a trifle for a county. It finds some difficulty in securing recognition, perhaps because of its inadequate capital, and many, perhaps most, who live within its confines call themselves Londoners and not Middle Saxons.

It is not strictly true to say that "Middlesex once had as a capital the greatest city in the world, London; and that a single stroke of the axe of Parliament robbed it of the proud distinction." True, most of the London suburban areas were in Middlesex, but not the City of London. In fact the City exercised very definite rights over the county, which in a sense was its property. However, strict historical accuracy insists today that the real capital of England is, and for many centuries has been, Westminster; and that was definitely in Middlesex until the formation of county councils in 1888. But the traditional capital of Middlesex is Brentford, though much of the county's business is still carried on in that small enclave of Middlesex, the Westminster Guildhall. And the strenuous and successful efforts of the men and women of this very small county to save for posterity a green girdle of open woods and fields; the success of Middlesex in many fields of sport; the magnificent achievements on every battlefield in the two World Wars of the men of the County Regiment (The Die-Hards); the way in which all the varied activities, which played so big a part in civil defence, were taken up by the folk of every walk of life in the Axis War; and many other signs of local patriotism—all these have kindled a very keen county spirit perhaps unknown before. And it will be a source of great satisfaction to all concerned in its production if this volume should prove to be a cause of renewed interest in Middlesex among many of its two million inhabitants.

The thanks of the author are due, and are hereby tendered to his predecessors in the study of Middlesex history, some of whom are mentioned in the list of authorities; to the

ix

County Archæological and the district Historical Societies for much co-operation and support in many county projects; to his son, Antony Brett-James, for conspicuous help in the chapters on cricket and on the County Regiment; to Colonel Maurice Browne, M.C., D.L., J.P., and Major H. Marsh, Captain R. W. T. Smith and others of the "Die-Hards," who have co-operated so willingly; to Sir Frederick Handley-Page, Sir Geoffrey de Havilland and other pioneers in aviation; and to all who have helped in various ways to bring the book to a definite and, it is hoped, a successful conclusion.

There is much discussion today about the future frontiers of adjacent counties, but so far our postal address is still Hertfordshire, and we still live in Middlesex! A record time of service at Mill Hill, 42 years boy and master, and more than half a century in the same county tends to make one, as the old Greek historian put it, her lover.

NORMAN G. BRETT-JAMES.

RIDGEWAY,
ELSTREE, HERTS.

CHAPTER I

THE COUNTY OF MIDDLESEX

MIDDLESEX is, with the single exception of Rutland, the
smallest of all the English counties. It is situated on the left
bank of the Thames, which forms its southern boundary and
separates it from Surrey. Two other rivers, the Colne and
the Lea, separate it from Buckinghamshire and from Essex,
while its northern boundary, which it shares with Hertfordshire, is possibly the ancient artificial limit of Grimsdyke.

From a geographical point of view it contains the greater
part of the County of London, but politically this is nowadays
entirely separate. Owing to the original connection between
the two, Middlesex has not received from historians the
attention it deserves; and frequently an author has started out
to write the story of Middlesex, including London, and has
gossiped so fully about the latter as to leave only a last
chapter or two for the ancient county and its interesting towns
and villages.

But without mentioning London there is an immense
amount of history and romance in the strictly limited area,
whose greatest length from east to west is only 19 miles,
though from corner to corner—that is, from Shepperton to
Waltham—it measures 28 miles. It varies in width from north
to south between 11 and 19 miles. Before 1888 its area was
roughly 283 square miles, or 180,000 acres; nowadays it is
only 234 square miles and has lost 30,000 acres to the County
of London. Population increases very fast in most parts of
Middlesex, and but for the green belt it might well have
developed into a mere suburb of London in the true sense of
the word—that is, an area outside a city to which business folk
resort for rest and recreation, and where many of them sleep
and live. In 1801 the population of Middlesex was only
70,000. By 1901 it had increased to nearly 800,000, and in
1938 the population served by the County Drainage Scheme
was over a million, and was increasing at the rate of 50,000
a year.

11

To anyone who has lived for more than half a century in Middlesex it has been a source of genuine sadness to see "picturesque, quiet lanes and elm shaded hay fields such as Birket Foster loved to paint" gradually disappear. Every year, as the fields vanish, bricks and mortar advance, lanes become streets and highways, and one more beauty spot has yielded to suburbia. As far back as 1709 a writer remarked that Middlesex was "in effect but the suburbs at large of London, replenished with the retiring houses of the gentry and citizens thereof." But the real country lingered for a long time to come, and it is mainly the twentieth century that has made such irremediable inroads. Someone in 1904 published a description of *Picturesque Middlesex* with many delightful sketches, purposely selected from outside the London area. He rejoices that "much that is picturesque still exists unspoilt by the ever-increasing influence of London and the onslaught of the Jerry-builder," and he hopes that the sketches may in the future have value as records of rustic scenery which by that time will have hopelessly disappeared.

Almost forty years ago another writer claimed that within an hour from the City "the lover of solitude may be in wooded lanes about the Buckinghamshire border, north of Uxbridge among the woodlands of Harrow Weald and Stanmore, or in unfrequented by-ways beyond Barnet." Wise foresight on the part of local authorities, and the efforts made over three decades, and at last successful, to establish a green girdle and thus to stop further urbanisation, have helped to preserve these last vestiges of country. The three great plans for the City of London, the County of London and for Greater London have revived the hopes of all lovers of Middlesex, and the magnificent volume of the Royal Commission of Ancient Monuments showed what treasures this county still possessed.

At the moment many Middlesex authorities and responsible individuals are torn between two loyalties—the wish to preserve all the open country that the county still possesses, and the duty of finding house room for the thousands of families who wish to go on living in Middlesex, but for whom no adequate accommodation exists. This problem occurs in no other county on anything like the same scale, and can perhaps only be solved by the satellite town which must live strictly up to its name, and never become a mere London dormitory.

Though Middlesex has as remarkable a story to tell as any other English county, it has limitations which no other county shares. In few counties does change occur so rapidly. Forty years ago a historian remarked that "the placid attraction of Kingsbury Church lies in its loneliness among pleasant fields on a low ridge above the Brent Reservoir; that of Northolt that it has escaped restoration, just as the village has hitherto escaped development." The words were hardly printed before change began, and today Kingsbury is a crowded, busy suburb, and Northolt Aerodrome is the terminus of the British European Airways.

We must recognise that Middlesex cannot hope to vie with most, if not all, of the other English counties by reason of its small size, comparative flatness and its inevitable association with London. A formidable list of scenic beauties could be catalogued which it is impossible to find anywhere in the county. The proximity of the capital has destroyed its local patriotism in a manner quite unique. Centuries ago, in rivalry to Devonians or Yorkshiremen, Kentishmen or men of Kent, a "Middlesex Clown" could hold his own, and, according to Thomas Fuller, of the *Worthies,* "clown" was a term of praise, not of contempt. He quotes other words which have lost their original significance—villain—a dweller in a village; and churl—a strong, stout husbandman; and he might have mentioned hussy—a hard-working housewife; and he insists that clown is derived from *colonus*—"one that plougheth the ground (without which neither King nor Kingdom can be maintained)."

But in spite of Fuller, we do not find many people proud or even conscious of being Middlesex folk, though the type of Cockney Londoner is quite recognisable. When the county plays cricket it is at Lord's, where it is a guest of the M.C.C., whose initial letter does not stand for Middlesex but for Marylebone. When the County Council meets it is at Westminster, where its County Hall is miles outside the county boundary. When Middlesex stores its archives, this is done at Osterley Park, and its county town is nominally Brentford, one of the most unsuitable places for such an honour. A very recent scheme to transfer the county activities to a large open space where the North Circular Road crosses Hendon Way, not far from Watling Street and the Welsh Harp, might give Middlesex a much-needed county centre and provide a visible, tangible object for county loyalty.

CHAPTER II

MIDDLESEX IN THE MAKING

THE earth, as we know it today, is not the same as it was even thousands of years ago. Still vaster are the changes when one reckons years by millions. Even now it is possible to see changes taking place on the sea coast or near a river mouth. At Lowestoft the water is encroaching on the land, while in Romney Marsh the sea has receded in historic memory several miles. Reculver (the Roman Regulbium), at the north end of the Wansum Channel that separates Thanet from the mainland, has within living memory all but fallen into the sea; whereas Richborough (Rutupiæ), at the southern end, is getting farther inland every year. On a larger scale the River Mississippi brings down a great volume of silt annually into the Gulf of Mexico, showing the power of water; and the destruction of Pompeii nearly two thousand years ago, and of Messina only half a century back, provide some notion of the drastic changes wrought by earthquake. Nothing so dramatic is to be found in Middlesex, but there are obvious examples of the influence of rivers, glaciers and rain, and some more remote and less important traces of the action of volcanoes in a very far-off age.

The greater part of Middlesex is covered with London clay, a thick layer of soil which makes the county productive but stiff for digging. This is one of the water-formed layers which are found as a rule lying on the top of earlier rocks, whereas in fire-formed rocks the layers are frequently tilted up on one side. In still earlier eras a large tableland of chalk was laid down over the whole of South-eastern England, formed by small microscopic animals, which gradually got piled up one on top of the other, as is happening today at the bottom of the Atlantic Ocean. Each of these creatures lived in a very small shell, and sometimes one can see, with the aid of a microscope, the little animal in its shell, but now turned to chalk. The sea must have washed over South-eastern England to have produced this layer of chalk, and the great

15

stretch of time during which chalk was forming is indicated by its depth. The syncline of chalk slopes down from the escarpment of the Chilterns on the north and rises up to the outstanding range of the North Downs, and this great dip was probably produced partly by volcanic action far below the chalk surface. The chalk varies in depth, but is homogeneous in content, and it reaches a depth of almost 1,000 feet in the South Downs; but the maximum recorded in the London area is 655 feet at Meux's Brewery in Tottenham Court Road, 590 feet at the White Heather boring at Willesden, and 702 feet in a digging at Southall. Underneath the chalk, Devonian strata, which are Palæozoic or Primary rocks, were reached in each of the three borings mentioned, at just about 1,000 feet down, as well as at Kentish Town, under the Bull Dog Brewery, and at Chiswick.

The chalk of the London Basin was not exposed for a very long geological period, but was depressed below the level of the sea in the Lower Eocene era some millions of years ago. In this period Lower London Tertiaries, including the Thanet sands, were laid down in shallow water, and they run in thin strata (not more than 40 feet) through Hendon, Ealing, Sunbury and Weybridge.

A later submersion brought about the laying down of the Woolwich and Reading beds over the whole of our area, mainly the latter, which are partly marine, partly estuarine. These beds consist of sands, clays, pebbles, sarsen and puddingstone, but at Ickenham, Ruislip and Pinner they appear as a mass of mottled clay, as may be seen in Ruislip Reservoir, and at Harefield and in the northern portion of the Colne Valley, close to the Buckinghamshire border. Above these Tertiaries is the London clay, formed when the whole of South-eastern England was sunk below the level of a warm sea whose shores were covered with sub-tropical vegetation. This clay varies in thickness—some 400 feet in Essex and Surrey, to 353 feet in Hampstead, 135 in Covent Garden, 64 in Tottenham Court Road, and only 18½ feet in Enfield. On the top of the London clay was a thin coating of gravel, formed by the grinding together of stones, while the sand is the accumulation of small particles formed by constant rubbing together.

16

When the sea again subsided there were main rivers left flowing down from the high chalk hills near Marlborough towards the spot where the mouth of the Thames now is. Several smaller streams wound their way where the soil was softer, and washed away trenches which developed into the considerable valleys of Northern Middlesex.

The original Thames was clearly much wider than it is today, and it washed out a broad plain at the foot of the Middlesex hills. So the heights to the north of the county are not so much the result of piling up, but are more probably the remnants of a large plateau, which has been gradually denuded, while the pockets of sand and gravel, whose excavation has furnished our hill-top ponds, are the sole survivors of the layer of Bagshot Sands which originally covered the whole surface of the clay before rain and streams swept so much of it away.

It is not easy to separate these Bagshot Sands from the Claygate Beds, so named in the Geological Survey of 1912 by Henry Dewey, and found in Hampstead with a thickness of almost 100 feet, and immediately underneath the Bagshot Sands at Harrow, where they are only half as thick. Hampstead, Highgate and Harrow have layers of Bagshot Sands, which act as filters and give a good water supply, which has been responsible for the development of all three as important residential centres.

In other nearby counties the chalk is almost everywhere visible, notably in Kent, Surrey, Berkshire and Sussex. Only in two places in Middlesex does the chalk come to the surface —at Harefield and at South Mimms.

The subsequent geological history of the county includes subsidences and re-elevations, and a Pliocene period with following erosions and scourings, which may be responsible for the pebble-gravels found on the heights of Stanmore and Mill Hill, prior to the Ice Age. This very vital epoch did not concern Middlesex quite so much as more northerly areas, but a thrust of ice did penetrate as far as Finchley, but not over much of Hendon. The glacial age brought heavy boulder clay over most of Finchley and as far south as Marylebone and Islington, carrying stones and fossils and some chalk from Lincolnshire. Scandinavian erratics are to be found in the

Swakeleys

Brent Valley, and the glacial gravels occur, but only with a thickness of a few feet. By this time a river was carving out the Thames Valley and there were evidences of the existence of Palæolithic man.

Mention may be made of several deep borings which have penetrated below the chalk. The deepest of all was at White Heather, Willesden, which reached 2,000 feet, including 902 feet of Devonian Rock. Another of 1,146 feet gave the following layers : gravel and clay mixed together 21 feet down, London Clay 64 feet, Reading Beds 51 feet, Thanet Sand 21 feet, chalk 655 feet, Upper Greensand 28 feet, Gault 160 feet, Lower Greensand 64 feet, and Devonian 80 feet.

The heavy nature of the clay has its bearing on sporting facilities for the county. Drainage of fields is not easy, as the disposal of superfluous water presents such difficult problems. Schools and clubs have great difficulty in certain areas in securing satisfactory playing fields; cricket grounds are often unfit for play in the first few weeks of the season; while golf courses do not, as a rule, compare favourably with those in Surrey.

By this time the Thames Valley was beginning to be associated with the Palæolithic men, while the river was laying down deposits in the form of terraces, at one time thought to be four in number, now usually accepted as three. These are the Boyn Hill gravels high up, the Taplow or Middle Terrace, and the Low or Flood Plain gravels. But it is obvious that in the course of centuries soils do not remain stationary, and this fact, combined with man's activities, has obscured the line of the terraces. The river gravels in Middlesex are mainly composed of flints with glacial erratics and some fine Sarsens found here and there, notably at Hanwell and at Hounslow. These Middle Terrace gravels are very important archæologically, and in the rebuilding of destroyed houses and the need for building materials there is serious danger that many important remains will be destroyed. The usual thickness is not great—12 feet at Acton, twice as much at Hanwell, and perhaps a maximum of 40 feet.

The brick-earth which has proved so useful in the making of bricks and tiles is an alluvial soil of various depths—

5-20 feet at Ealing, 10 feet at Acton, 14 feet at Enfield, and up to 30 feet in some areas of North-eastern Middlesex. Of the Boyn Hill Terrace much has been swept away by erosion, and only outliers are to be found scattered all over the county, at Hillingdon, Castlebar Hill in Ealing, Kingsbury, Bush Hill, near Enfield, and at Wood Green and Palmer's Green.

The Middle Taplow Terraces of gravel and brick-earth, which stretch across the southern part of Middlesex, have revealed many Palæolithic flint implements and fossil remains of animals, but curiously enough no fossil remains of man, though there is clear evidence of human settlements.

The Low Terrace or Flood Plain gravels are found in the basin of the Thames and at Ponder's End by the River Lea. Research into the climate in this latter era reveals "a bleak, almost treeless region, largely covered by moss when not under snow, and with little more considerable in the way of vegetation than the stunted bushes of the Arctic Willow and Arctic Birch, even these being half hidden in the growth of moss."

Most of the Taplow, brick-earth and Flood Plain deposits are in that part of Middlesex included in the L.C.C. area, but there is Middle Terrace gravel in Ealing and Acton, overlaid here and there by brick-earth. A big area of brick-earth is to be found in Hounslow Heath, Hayes and Harlington (where London Airport is being developed) to Harmondsworth and Yiewsley and at the Colne Valley to Uxbridge. Gravels are found in the area from Staines and Longford to Hampton, and then up the Brent Valley.

These three terraces have given up remains of all sorts of prehistoric animals indicative of the variety of climates that prevailed there from era to era. In the Boyne deposits have been found remains of the mammoth and of the elephant, of the ancient ox, horse, red deer, reindeer, rhinoceros, boar, wolf, beaver, vole, field mouse; while in the Taplow Terrace, in addition to many of these, were the grizzly bear, hippopotamus and rhinoceros, and the mammoth. On the lower level of the Flood Plain are to be found traces of the lion, hyena, elk, aurochs, reindeer and again the mammoth. Important finds in Middlesex have been made in Staines and Twickenham, Ealing and Acton, Hounslow and Southall.

19

Some idea of the length of time with which we are dealing is evidenced by the estimate that the laying down of these three terraces must have taken at least one hundred thousand years, during which the climate varied from an ice age to a period when jungle and forest covered the whole of Middlesex. Whether the changes came rapidly or gradually it is difficult to say; we find zones of lion and reindeer in the same terrace deposits as if it was possible to have a mixed fauna with animals of both kinds alive at the same time.

Palæolithic man, whose story must next be essayed, lived first in a sub-tropical climate, but after some thousands of years the climate changed. Jungle of Central Africa gave way to tundra of Northern Asia, and between were periods of temperate climate, much as we enjoy or suffer here today.

CHAPTER III

THE GEOGRAPHY OF MIDDLESEX

A CONSIDERABLE portion of Middlesex is flat, more especially the districts which lie near the Thames. If a line be drawn from Brentford to Colnbrook, roughly the Bath Road, all the land to the south is only a few feet above river level. More to the north the country becomes higher, and Uxbridge and Ealing are on obvious ridges. Still farther north there are two distinct systems of high ground, the central containing the heights of Hampstead, Highgate, Crouch and Muswell Hills and the North Middlesex highlands, separated from the other by the Brent river basin. The formation of these highlands includes a long ridge from Potters Bar and High Barnet, passing through Barnet Gate, Woodcock Hill and Elstree, past Brockley Hill and Stanmore Common (505 feet) through Northwood to Harefield. From Barnet Gate two cross-ridges jut out, one that of Totteridge, the other running through Highwood Hill and ending in the mile-long stretch of Mill Hill. Barnet is 435 feet up, Totteridge 455, Mill Hill 409 and Highwood Hill 455. These ridges are separated by valleys, from 100 to 200 feet deep, formed by small streams which run to the north and south of Totteridge, joining up and crossing the road between Mill Hill and Finchley under the name of Dollis Brook, now bridged over, flowing into the Welsh Harp Reservoir by Kingsbury. Another stream, called the Brook, at Edgware unites with the Silk stream and also flows into the Welsh Harp.

From Stanmore the country slopes down through Harrow Weald, and again rises into the isolated spur of Harrow-on-the-Hill, overlooking the Brent Valley. At intervals along the side of this valley are Uxendon Hill, Dudding Hill and Dollis Hill, parted by small streams. The hilly country to the north-west by Harefield overlooks the valley of the Colne, while the high ground in the north-east has a small branch to the south called Winchmore Hill.

21

All the streams of Middlesex naturally flow into the Thames, which forms the county boundary from Staines to Fulham, with a number of interesting towns and villages along its northern bank—Laleham, Shepperton, Upper and Lower Halliford, Sunbury, Hampton, Teddington, Twickenham, Isleworth and Brentford. The Colne rises near Tittenhanger in Herts, enters Middlesex near Harefield, and was at one time called the Ux. It is the western boundary with Buckinghamshire, and in the course of its thirty-five miles it is joined by the Ruislip Brook from Stanmore, Pinner and Yiewsley. At West Drayton the "crystal Colne" divides into three—the Colnbrook, Wraysbury Stream and the Colne proper, reading from west to east. Milton writes :

> "Most transparent Colne
> Feels with excessive joy her amorous bosom swollen."

Its three streams enter the Thames near Staines.

Next comes the Crane or Yedding Brook, which rises near Pinner, and collects several small streams before it flows past Northolt Aerodrome, then close to Heathrow, London Airport, under Cranford Bridge, past Hounslow Heath and Twickenham to join the Thames near Isleworth.

The Brent leaves its reservoir of more than half a square mile, still the home of fish and water birds, flows past Osterley Park and Sion House to join the Thames at Brentford by Old England, immediately opposite Kew Gardens.

There are also two artificial rivers in Middlesex, one, the King's or Cardinal's River, constructed by King Charles I to supply water to Wolsey's Palace at Hampton Court; hence the double name. It was taken out of the River Colne at Harmondsworth, flows through the parishes of Stanwell, West and East Bedfont, past London Airport to Hampton, where it joins the Thames. The other is the Duke of Northumberland's River, constructed by Henry VII to serve the Abbess of Syon House (later the Duke's property) with water for a mill at Twickenham, and also for another convent mill at Isleworth, now called Kidd's Mill. The Duke's river joins the Crane at Bedfont, and all rights in its use were acquired by the Middlesex County Council in 1930.

The last Middlesex river is the Lea, which forms the

county's eastern boundary with Essex from Waltham to Tottenham. It has been made navigable by the cutting of a fresh channel, which has seriously curtailed the fishing on the Lea, once so loved by Izaac Walton. This Lea Navigation runs from Enfield Lock to Tottenham, and between the two streams and north of Ponders End there are the two huge King George the Fifth Reservoirs. The Lea has one tributary, Pymmes Brook, which rises in Hadley Woods, flows through Southgate to Edmonton, where it is called the Wash, made famous by John Gilpin.

The canals of Middlesex have suffered in much the same way as elsewhere, first through the immediate challenge of the railways and later on through improved roads and the introduction of the motor-car. The Grand Junction, now incorporated in the Grand Union Canal, dates from 1805, to link up the Midlands and London. Near Yiewsley and West Drayton it is joined by a branch from the west and goes on to Hanwell and Brentford. The old Paddington Canal branches off at Bull's Bridge on the Crane, runs to Paddington and Regent's Park to the Thames at Limehouse. The prospects which the promoters of canals expected are shown by the announcement in *The Times* for December 19, 1806, that troops destined for service in Ireland would be carried from London to Liverpool by canal boats pulled by relays of horses, taking seven days instead of the usual fourteen by road.

The New River enters the county just between Theobald's Park and Turkey Street, having come from the springs of Amwell and Chadwell. It took five years to construct, cost Sir Hugh Myddelton, King James I and other sympathisers half a million of money, and did as much as the Great Fire of 1666 to make London a reasonably healthy place in which to live. As it passes through Clissold Park it is a most attractive stretch of water.

Chapter IV

EARLY MEN IN MIDDLESEX

THE earliest men of whom we have any historic record lived in the Thames Valley and nearby more than 2,000 years ago. But there must have been inhabitants long before then, and all over the county, particularly near the beds of the streams, we find traces of them. Man's thumb enables him to be a tool-maker, and the weapons and implements he has left behind give us some idea of his life and habits. It is less than a century since the discovery of flint implements in the valley of the Somme, near Abbeville, opened the door to a study of prehistoric archæology. John Evans in 1859 reported the news to the Society of Antiquaries, and claimed that a new field with immense possibilities for antiquarian research had been found. For several years scientists were divided, and some refused to believe that men and the mammoth might be contemporaries, preferring to attribute the stone weapons to the Romans. The study of Palæolithic man might have begun far earlier, seeing that a famous hand-axe had been dug up in the Gray's Inn Lane area late in the seventeenth century. It was discovered by an apothecary, John Conyers, who was digging for gravel in a field near to the Sign of Sir John Oldcastle in the Fields, not far from Battlebridge and the River of Wells. Quite close at hand was Black Mary's Hole, where one of the Parliamentary forts had been built in 1642-3. Not only did Conyers unearth this Palæolithic hand-axe which he called a "British" weapon, but he also dug up a skeleton. "How this elephant came?" is the question he naturally asked, and almost two centuries were to elapse before an answer was forthcoming.

The digging up at Brentford of bones of the elephant, hippopotamus and large deer, and the elk horns at Chelsea, and fossil fish at Highgate, give us some idea of the type of animal that Palæolithic men killed for food. He did very little, if anything, to cultivate the soil. Very valuable dis-coveries of early flint implements have been made in the Lea

Valley by Mr. Greenhill and Sir John Evans, by Mr. Allen Brown near Acton, by Mr. Worthington Smith at Stoke Newington, and near Ealing in the Thames Valley by General Pitt Rivers.

When the development of London and its suburbs forged ahead, there was much digging for drainage, for foundations, and to provide gravels and brick-earth. In most of the big streets of the West End of London Palæolithic flints have been discovered as well as in the north-eastern areas, while in Middlesex itself important finds have been made at Acton, Dawley, Ealing, Hanwell, Hayes, Southall, West Drayton and Yiewsley, and others in the River Thames. One large discovery was made of 600 implements and many flints cut from the stones while they were being fashioned into shape. Allen Brown's invaluable finds in 1885 were not confined to Ealing and Acton; they were extended to Dawley, Hanwell, Hillingdon and Yiewsley. Most of his discoveries, along with those made by Worthington Smith, were bought by Dr. Allen Sturge and presented to the British Museum.

A fine collection is preserved at Gunnersbury House, and good Palæolithics are also to be seen in the London Museum and in the Public Library at Brentford. The British Museum Guide to the Stone Age is a very admirable piece of work. The Stoke Newington discoveries were particularly important, as there seemed to be evidence of a very swift flight from this area and the abandonment of many implements of real value. This is sometimes attributed to the Trail, a drift which brought down semi-liquid, partially thawed masses of material over the Terrace Gravels, especially in the Lea Valley. The Stoke Newington floor was completely overlaid, and it is just possible that the disaster came suddenly, but the evidence does not seem to support that explanation. These early inhabitants of Britain seem to have developed skill in hunting, some knowledge of the use of fire, and gradually a respect for the dead. The fact that the dead were latterly buried with care and provided with food and weapons suggests a belief in continued existence after death.

Long ages passed on and the climate became warmer. Probably in Palæolithic days England was linked up with Europe, as Kipling suggests in discussing the Thames :

"When hundreds of miles to the East I went
And England was joined to the Continent."

It seems to have become an island in Neolithic days, and
these newer folk may have come across the Channel in rough
rafts or canoes. Their weapons were better made, more useful
and more highly polished. Relics of these men have been
found at Northwood and Twickenham near the surface of
the ground as well as in the bed of the Thames. These people
had an increased veneration for the dead, whom they buried
under long barrows of earth. They seem to have been bigger
and stronger than the old Stone men, and were able to clear
away some of the forest that covered most of Middlesex,
and so we sometimes find their remains away from the river
beds. It is suggested that they were Iberian in race, rather
like the Basques in Northern Spain, and were later almost
destroyed by a new set of invaders.

The problem of deciding how long these various eras lasted
is so difficult and complex of solution that some years ago
there was considerable support for the notion that there have
been four epochs instead of two : Eolithic, or Early Stone
men, and Mesolithic, or Middle Stone men, as well as the
better-known types. But these sub-divisions have not been
generally accepted. One may perhaps assume, very tentatively,
that Neolithic man begins in the Thames area, as in Western
Europe generally, about 8,000 B.C.

As we examine the evidence we find that he differed from
his predecessors in having a more settled existence, more
advanced methods of agriculture, and some skill in the
domestication of animals and in the use of pottery. It seems
that most of the Neolithic men in Middlesex lived in the
dense woods near the four main rivers, and they used what
are called "Thames picks" for a series of purposes. These
are longer weapons than the older axe, and they may have
been employed for simple digging, the hollowing out of
canoes, and possibly for attack and defence. There are some
splendid examples of these Thames picks in the British
Museum from the river at Isleworth and Teddington, and a
particularly good specimen in the Brentford Library. The
Neolithic axe is another development, and it is found either
chipped or polished. Specimens have been dug up at Chis-

wick, Harefield, Harlington, Hounslow, Pinner, Teddington and Yiewsley. Great numbers have been discovered in the Thames, and they are to be seen in the various local museums as well as in private collections. Further developments are circular mace-heads, with a hole for a shaft to be inserted, and implements of bone and horn have been found, indicating progress in the use of animals. Pottery of the later Neolithic period shows marked progress, and some very interesting specimens with simple primitive decorations have been dredged up in the river between Mortlake and Chiswick.

CHAPTER V

THE BRONZE AGE

ONE of Kipling's *Puck of Pook's Hill* stories refers to the man who gained the mastery over flint-folk by receiving from the fairies the gift of iron at the cost of losing an eye : "Iron, cold iron is master of them all." Apparently Kipling was moving too quickly forward, seeing that the archæologists tell us that between the Neolithic and the Iron Age there are the Beaker-folk, contemporaries with or followed by the Age of Bronze.

The gradual arrival in Britain of a new folk from Europe, beginning about 2000 B.C. or rather less, brought in a new type of pottery, the beaker, a clay vessel of a far more graceful design than the Neolithic types. Curiously enough, a Neolithic vase, with its rough markings made on the wet clay, already mentioned, was discovered in the Thames close to the very graceful beaker of a new shape which shows such marked progress in design and execution. Both are decorated with simple patterns produced in the moist clay by the use of a stick, small bones, twisted cord or even the finger-nail, and the patterns consist mainly of short lines cut round the bowl in diagonal fashion or chevrons or lozenges. The stretch of Thames from Hammersmith to Brentford and Mortlake has been very productive of beakers and other pottery of the Bronze Age.

This age is marked by the cremation of dead bodies, when the ashes were placed in cinerary urns made of pottery. These vessels vary a great deal in size, from 6 to 24 inches in height, and have been found in Teddington, Ashford, Yiewsley and in Acton. The Sunbury Common Cemetery, near Ashford, discovered in 1870, revealed thirty-two urns deposited on the gravel a foot or so below the surface; and the experts who examined this find decided that the cremation must have taken place in the actual burial pits. Twenty-six of these cinerary urns are to be seen in the British Museum.

Another find was made at Mill Hill Park, Acton, while

digging for house foundations in 1883. A number of the urns are in the British Museum, and one had been cracked before use and mended by the drilling of two holes near the top through which cord might be threaded and fastened. Other specimens of this bucket type were discovered in the Brent Reservoir, or Welsh Harp, at Kingsbury and in gravel pits at Yiewsley.

The Bronze Age barrow at Teddington was excavated in 1854, but some amateur work had been done on it during road construction twenty years earlier. Popular rumour attributed the bodies of man and horse to the Great Plague of 1665, but when experts examined it they came to the conclusion that the barrow was prehistoric. They discovered calcined bones, small fragments of urns, a flint hatchet head and a bronze dagger, a picture of which was reproduced in the first volume of the *London and Middlesex Archæological Society's Transactions*.

The name Tothill is significant, and is found both in Westminster and at the top of Bittacy Hill, Mill Hill. In each case there was a mound of some kind, possibly a burial-place or perhaps one of the "Tots" with their groups of pines or isolated trees, of which Alfred Watkins in his fascinating book, *The Old Straight Track,* has made so much. His piece of country is, of course, the Welsh Border, where he finds very many indications of old straight tracks, of sighting marks, sight notches and marked trees, which the early Christians seem to have discovered and borrowed from paganism. Stukely's Barrow on Brockley Hill, several on Primrose Hill and Hampstead Heath, and Barrow Point at Pinner may perhaps belong to the Bronze Age, but the authorities are very uncertain on this point.

Progress is to be seen in the improved type of bronze axe and dagger, and these have been dug up in the river at Hammersmith, Kew and Mortlake, as well as at Hounslow and Enfield Marsh. The Layton Collection at Brentford, as well as the British and London Museums, has splendid specimens of varying grades of workmanship. These daggers slowly develop into the rapier or Bronze Age sword, about 1000 B.C., and there are many specimens which have been found in the Thames from Staines to Brentford and farther east, and

29

thirty-three of them are preserved in the Layton Collection. This remarkable collection was bequeathed by Thomas Layton, F.S.A., to the Library at Brentford on his death in 1911 at the age of ninety-two, and the prehistoric relics are a really remarkable contribution to our knowledge of early man in Middlesex. They include more than a thousand relics of the Stone Ages, more than a hundred of horn, bone and wood, and five hundred of the Bronze Age; flint daggers, mace-heads made of deer antler, and others made of stone; palstaves or socketed celts, rapiers, swords, daggers, bronze sickles, probably unrivalled save by the British Museum collections. Bronze bucklers found in the river are early examples of defensive weapons, with studs hammered out of the metal, and with handles sometimes still intact. Greater variety of tools begin to be found, including chisels, drills, awls, hammers and even fish-hooks.

A very few personal ornaments have been found in Middlesex, bracelets and pins being the only specimens recorded. A bronze cauldron or two have been dredged out of the river, and all the specimens discovered show increasing perfection on the earlier types. These periods into which the history of early man is divided cannot, of course, be exactly indicated, but the end of the Bronze Age may be dated somewhere about 600 B.C.

CHAPTER VI

THE EARLY IRON AGE

WESTERN EUROPE has two main periods in the development of the use of iron, dividing the thousand years B.C. almost exactly in two. The Celtic language may have reached this country in the later Bronze Age, but there is not much left of it in our Middlesex county place names. "Brent" is one of the most important survivals, and may date from the Hallstatt period on the Continent, so called from a Tyrolese cemetery. There is very little of that earlier time to be traced in this country, but the second period, called La Tine, after a pile station on Lake Neuchatel in Switzerland, is represented by the magnificent Battersea Shield, evidence of a far higher state of civilisation than the Romans would admit. This shield is the outer covering and was probably built up on wood or leather. It consists of a bronze plate with three decorated plates fastened by two dozen rivets, of which eighteen remain in position. There are twenty-seven studs of bright red enamel fastened to the shield by swastikas, with pins to hold them tight. Other specimens have been found in various parts of the Thames, and swords and scabbards of this same period have been discovered, with daggers and spearheads, well designed and executed. One iron spearhead was dug up far away from the Thames at Harefield. Almost as fine as the Battersea Shield, though considerably later, is the horned helmet from the Thames at Waterloo Bridge, probably intended for ceremonial use and only large enough for a child to wear. There are also axe-heads and iron currency bars, possibly alluded to by Cæsar. Knives and keys, axle-ends and a bucket are among the treasures dredged up from time to time, and a series of spoons, whose use has puzzled archæologists not a little.

Near the bronze horde mentioned earlier in connection with Hounslow there was discovered a small horde of small animals dating probably from shortly before the Roman invasion. A good deal of pottery has been recovered from the

31

Thames at Wandsworth, Twickenham and Mortlake, Strand-on-the-Green and Old England, near Brentford.

Bone plates and combs, evidently intended for the use of weavers, have been found, and a feeling of modernity is aroused by the discovery of rather crude coins dating from just before and just after Cæsar's first invasion. These tin or rough silver coins have been found in Gunnersbury Lane, at Eelpie Island, Twickenham and at Hammersmith. But some gold coins, of better quality and design, one with a chariot, charioteer and horses imitated from Macedonian coins, have appeared in Enfield Chase, Southgate and Harlington, and one is recorded with CUN on the obverse, for Cunobelinus, or Shakespeare's Cymbeline.

In the last five hundred years Goidels, Britons and Belgic tribes were moving into this country, settling in the river valleys, especially in the Middlesex and Surrey parts of the Thames, and we are by now in historic times.

It seems that, in spite of much wishful thinking, there is really no archæological or historical evidence for the existence of a Celtic settlement at a bridgehead on the Thames where London stands today.

East Bedfont Church

CHAPTER VII

GRIM'S DYKE

VARIOUS dates have at different times been assigned to this interesting survival, and it may quite suitably be discussed at this juncture.

The northern boundary of Middlesex is more difficult to define than the river fringes of south, east and west. An earthwork runs for four miles close to the Herts border from Pinner Green across Oxhey Lane and Harrow Weald Common to Bentley Priory in Stanmore, and it consists of a vallum and fosse, possibly to mark the limits of the Catuvellauni. The first portion, called "Pinner Grim's Dyke," runs from Cuckoo Hill by Eastcote across the railway to Pinner Green, past Pinner to Woodridings Farm across the railway to Grim's Dyke Golf Course, where there is a finely preserved section. It was described in 1911 as being 63 feet wide at the base with an escarpment of 12 feet into the fosse, which is 5 feet deep and 15 feet across. There is a fine section in the late Sir W. S. Gilbert's property of the same name, and not far from the dam which formed the artificial lake, where Gilbert met with his death, the earthwork makes a rectangular bend. H. J. W. Stone, in an important paper in the *London and Middlesex Transactions* for 1935, shows that geology has determined its position, as it is just on the fringe of gravel and clay and encloses the head waters of all streams flowing north-west. He claims that its layout makes it clear that it was for agricultural and not military purposes, and Brigadier Mortimer Wheeler concurs.

Near Pinner the builders became aware of a covetous tribe which might encroach on their land, and so constructed the Dyke across the watershed which divides the northward from the southward flowing streams. The Dyke would not seem to be Roman nor late Saxon in design, but was probably built soon after the end of Roman rule, possibly by post-Roman Londoners just before the emergence of the kingdom of the East Saxons.

33   c

Major Hugh Braun, writing in 1936, is prepared to agree that the Dyke extended farther east, and in this he agrees with the late G. E. Cruickshank and the late Sir Montague Sharp. A rental of 1306 quoted by him speaks of "Gryms-dich" on the ridge of Brockley Hill near the mill in Little Stanmore, and in a valuation of 1535 there are two fields of the same name. The bank may well lie along Barnet Lane, Woodcock Hill, Boys Hill to Grim's or Grendel's Gate, not far from Scratch Wood, and the names all refer to the Devil, to whose efforts the Saxons seem to have ascribed the Dyke. Farther east in Arkley, near Barnet Gate Windmill, there seem to be further traces; and the Dyke may well have been the northern boundary of Middlesex Forest, and a ditch and rampart to assist in hunting wild beasts. The huntsmen, it is suggested, could drive the beasts towards the Dyke, thus eliminating beaters, and hunt them on the recoil. Wings turning back at the ends of the Dyke, and parks at Pinner, Ruislip, Bentley and Enfield, tend to confirm the hunting explanation. *The Antiquaries Journal* lends support to the extension of the Dyke eastwards as far as Potters Bar, and it is possible that aerial photography might reveal the secret.

In his *Origines Celticæ* (1883) Dr. Guest regarded Grimsdyke as part of the protective earthworks of the British town of Sulloniacæ, and claimed that Middlesex in early Roman times was "merely a march of the Catuvellanni, a common through which ran a wide track way, but in which there was neither town village nor inhabited house . . . between Brockley Hill and the Thames all was wilderness to the Brent." He suggested a pre-Roman origin for Grimsdyke, for whose name A. Hadrian Allcroft suggested another possible derivation from *gruma,* a boundary, rather than *grim,* a goblin. It seems a reasonable conjecture that at some unspecified date a barrier was set up and that Britons, Romans, post-Romans, early and later Saxons all found it useful for hunting, boundary or defence; altered it to suit their needs; used it as a tribal limit; and left it for modern folk to develop parts of the area near it as building estates or to preserve it as an appropriate addition to London's Green Girdle.

CHAPTER VIII

ROMAN MIDDLESEX

THE interest in historic characters with actual names is for
most of us greater than that aroused by Neolithic or Palæolithic man. The first man who came to Britain and left an
account of his travels was a Greek named Pytheas, who came
from Marseilles and opened up trade in tin. But it was not
until 300 years later that the Romans invaded this country,
fifty-five years before the birth of Christ. The Romans had
begun as a small inland tribe, but had in 700 years of fighting
and development conquered almost all the then known world.
Julius Cæsar was angry with the Britons for helping their
friends in Gaul whom he was engaged in trying to conquer.
To stop this aid he made two expeditions across to Britain,
admirably recounted in his *De Bello Gallico,* with which so
many classical scholars have begun their Latin studies. The
first expedition in 55 B.C. was hardly a success, but in the next
year he advanced from somewhere near the modern town of
Deal through Kent to the Thames. There seems to be good
reason for thinking that at this time there was no London in
existence at all. The late Sir Halford Mackinder's theory,
which has gained considerable support from experts, is that
London started life as a port of Verulamium and was placed
just where the Lea flows into the Thames. It was at a settlement later called Verulamium that Cæsar was aiming, and
the road which he had followed from the coast, and the one
he would take after crossing the stream, were both parts of
an ancient British trackway from the Channel across Britain
to North Wales and thus by sea to Ireland.

Cassivellaunus was King of the Catuvellauni, and it was
Cæsar's aim to strike at his well-defended capital as quickly
as possible. To do this it was essential to cross the Thames
with as much speed as possible, and Cæsar tells us that "the
river was passable on foot at one place only and that with
difficulty." When he arrived there he observed a large force
of the enemy drawn up on the opposite bank. "This bank was

also defended with sharpened stakes fixed outwards, and similar stakes were placed under water and concealed by the river." The fact that Cæsar was aiming at Verulamium or nearer Wheathampstead and makes no mention of London suggests that the site of the Metropolis was not yet occupied. What fresh discoveries the excavations made possible by the German bombing reveal cannot yet be fully known, but so far it seems that the wishful thinking of a pre-Roman London of any importance has little foundation in fact. Little has been found of the prehistoric period, and the general impression seems among experts to be that the two hills, divided by the Walbrook, on which London stands were not seriously settled before the later conquest in the time of the Emperor Claudius.

But meantime Cæsar's troops are preparing to cross the Thames somewhere west of modern London, and ingenious explanations have been published to justify the claims of Westminster, Chelsea, Kingston, Brentford, Petersham or Coway Stakes. The stakes at Coway seem to justify its claim to be the site of Cæsar's crossing, but the weight of opinion leans towards Brentford. In the 1880's some hundreds of stakes were discovered in the bed of the river between Isleworth Ait and Brentford Ait, opposite to Kew Gardens, and Sir Montagu Sharp's claim that Cæsar crossed the Thames by Old England, the island to the north of the river between the two mouths of the Brent, seems justified. There is an old trackway running northwards past an alleged British camp at the Butts, and a Roman camp a mile farther north, and the track may lead to Kingsbury and so to Verulamium, nineteen miles from the Ford. To clinch the matter, a granite monument was erected by public subscription at the Ferry Head to record Cæsar's crossing of the Thames and other important happenings at Brentford, and the Duke of Northumberland, K.G., probably the most distinguished landowner in Middlesex, unveiled the memorial in May, 1909.

So let us allow that Cæsar came from the Kentish coast by an old British trackway to the banks of the Thames, crossed with his army of 24,000 men to the Brent Valley, and utilised an existing trackway in his advance against Cassivellaunus. It is of considerable interest to note that William Camden gives his authority to Coway Stakes as the scene of Cæsar's crossing, and explained the stakes as a British attempt to prevent his passing.

The later attack on London by Aulus Plautius was checked on the Medway by the vigorous Caractacus; but the Romans crossed the Thames quite easily (*sine ulla jactura sine ullo prœlio aut sanguine*), and, although Colchester was the capital of the province, the road system centred on London.

It seems to be well established that British settlements preceded Roman towns, and equally probable that highways of a primitive character, eight in number, were constructed by the Britons. The Romans straightened and paved the streets and perhaps centred them on London. British trackways were too important commercially to be ignored, and the durability which Roman construction gave them enabled them to outlast the long period of neglect which followed the recall of the legions. The Roman engineers "literally paved the way for Angles and Saxons, Danes and Normans, priest, soldier and merchant and all that they brought of government, religion, culture and prosperity . . . and their contribution to the making of Britain is imperishable."

London, as the last bridgehead over the Thames, soon gained importance, especially as the roads were centred on the city. It was a prominent commercial centre to begin with, not a capital. Gibbon speaks of (A) the road from York to London and an extension to Rutupiæ or Richborough, but he does not mention (B) the north-westerly road that led through Sulloniacæ (Brockley Hill), Verulamium (St. Albans), Durocobruvæ (Dunstable), Venonæ (High Cross), Letocetum (Wall, near Lichfield), Pennocrucium (Penkrup) and either Viroconium (Wroxeter) or Deva (Chester), a road which the Britons had called Sarn Gwdellin, and which the Saxons were to call Watling Street (after one Vitellianus, according to Camden); nor does he give (C) the south-westerly road to Pontes (Staines), Calleva (Silchester), Spinæ (Speen), Aquæ Sulis (Bath), nor (D) a north-easterly way to Camulodunum (Colchester) and so to the Wash at Brancaster, or (E) Ermine Street, along the Kingsland Road to Tottenham, Edmonton and Enfield, and so to Eboracum (York), all five of which pass through the old Saxon area of Middlesex. When the highways had been constructed London's preeminence was only a question of time, and it must always be remembered that Winchester was only the capital of Wessex, not of England.

Middlesex shares with London the early miles of several all-important roads, and many folk have written with bated breath of the tremendous influence which has been exercised by the Highway. "One of the great institutions of mankind . . . it is the Road which determines the sites of many cities and the growth and nourishment of all . . . and moves and controls all history." Thus writes Belloc, echoing the comment of Richard Jefferies, who calls a good road "the groundwork of civilisation." Robert Louis Stevenson claims that the simplest roads, once built, may go on being useful "hundreds of years after we are mingled in the dust." John Buchan admires the bridge even more than the road as "a symbol of man's conquest of nature," because it overcomes the barrier provided by rivers and regulates the lines of traffic. "History, social, economic and military, is found more thickly about bridges than about towns and citadels."

How roads originated it is difficult to explain, but the need for communication was the prime factor, and either the cattle or their driver was responsible for early British trackways. The Romans preferred their roads to be straight, and so, in Kipling's lines,

> "The Romans came with a heavy hand,
> And bridged and roaded and ruled the land."

Geoffrey of Monmouth tells us of an early King Molmutius who furnished Britain with a beautiful structure of highways by magic, and the story is repeated in Michael Drayton's *Polyolbion* several centuries later.

It seems certain that, even if the Romans superimposed their well-built roads upon British trackways, some credit must be given to the original construction and to the drunken British sailor (not English, as Chesterton would have us believe) who made the drunken British road.

We can scarcely believe Dr. Stukeley when he claims in 1749 that there is a Roman camp surrounding old Kingsbury Church. He measured the dimensions of the churchyard with its ditches and ramparts, and decided that Cæsar's next camp on his way to Verulam was at Kingsbury. But the churchyard covers only three-quarters of an acre, while a single cohort required at least 3 acres; a legion may have occupied 50 acres, and Cæsar's troops probably numbered 14,000! Simon Potter, who discusses the problem with keen and scholarly interest, poses the question : "Did Julius Cæsar camp at Kingsbury?" And he replies : "A wonderful question to ask ourselves on a golden evening in autumn as we stand in the old churchyard and the leaves fall silently from the limes."

In the Antonine Itinerary there are only two places mentioned in what is now Middlesex, outside London : Ad Pontes (Staines) on the road to Aquæ Sulis (Bath) and Sulloniacæ (Brockley Hill), both places close to the boundaries of the county. The British Roman road, which we now call Watling Street, was almost dead straight from the Marble Arch, where there used to stand a monolith, perhaps a Roman *millarium* (milestone), to Brockley Hill, and there are clear indications of a Belgic settlement as well as Roman remains before the road changes its direction from twelve miles northwest and bears north-north-east for nearly a mile. After Elstree it diverges again and runs north-north-west to Verulamium, while the modern road runs from the King Harry, at a slight angle, to St. Albans.

The old road proved in parts so deep and miry in winter "that it was refused of wayfaring men and carriers, in regard whereof it was agreed betweene the Bishop of London and the Countrie that a new waie should be layde forth through the said Bishops parks, beginning at Highgate Hill to leade directly to Whetstone" (Norden).

BROCKLEY HILL

The proverb which Lysons quoted in 1795—

"No heart can think, no tongue can tell,
What lies between Brockley Hill and Pennywell,"

hints that Roman antiquities may well be discovered at Elstree, and during the six years of the second World War those of us who manned the Royal Observer Corps post C2, close to misnamed Fortune House (destroyed by a bomb) and Penniwell's Cottage, hoped to make some important discovery as we dug our allotments in our off-time, but nothing emerged on the Elstree side.

The earliest commentator on Sulloniacæ, or Brockley Hill, was perhaps John Norden, a Somerset man, who came to Hendon in Elizabeth's reign after a survey at Holt, on the River Dee, just opposite to Farndon, the birthplace of John Speed, his successor in the topographical world. He praises Camden for placing Sulloniacæ at Brockley Hill instead of at Chipping Barnet, and refers to decayed buildings and "sundry pieces of Romish coyne" discovered there. So it is to William Camden, Headmaster of Westminster School, author of *Britannia,* and a generous benefactor of John Stow, that this identification is due. But neither Norden nor Speed mark it on their maps, and we hear no more till 1658, when it is mentioned in William Burton's *Antoninus his Itinerary.* In the 1695 edition of Camden the place is marked in two maps, but with absurd misspellings—St. Slomaca and Stullemaca. But there is a record of coins, urns and Roman bricks recently dug up on the site, and rarities of the kind found by the plough for about seven or eight miles round. Dr. Stukeley very naturally waxes eloquent about the finds, and good discoveries were made on both sides of Watling Street all through the eighteenth century.

Lysons in 1795 writes of fifty gold coins, two gold rings and a gold bracelet of Roman origin dug up at Bentley Priory in Stanmore, at the other end of Wood Lane; and in 1806 Gough reports coins of Constantine, Valentinian, Valeus, Gratian, Magnus Maximus, Theodosius and of Honorius, who recalled the Roman legions from Britain in A.D. 410. From time to time further reports of Roman finds were reported at Brockley Hill, at Radlett, at a site near Aldenham School, and in 1904 there was a rather important find, in Elstree village opposite the church, of a Roman cinerary urn, containing a glass vessel and a small black glazed pot, chronicled by the Rector, Canon Eales. A bequest to the London and Middlesex Archæological Society in 1937 made a trial excavation on Brockley Hill possible, and it was clear that there had been a Roman kiln on the east side of Watling Street. Flagons, bowls, jars, mortaria were found there, and it seemed likely that a Belgic town might be found at the corner of Wood Lane and Watling Street. Plans for a further digging in 1938 had to be cancelled at the last minute, and the second World War stopped all further effort in 1939. Two years after VJ Day a well-advertised scheme was carried out and good results accrued. There is considerable hope of really valuable finds in the near future at Elstree, and plans for careful excavations have been made which seem likely to give important results. Some have already done so.

The town of Staines stands close to where the Colne runs into the Thames, and Camden reports a wooden bridge over the river, and writes : "As to its name, it had it from a boundary stone formerly set up here to mark out the extent of the City of London's jurisdiction in the River." Gibson in his additions to Camden agrees with the author's conjecture as to the origin of the town's name, but does mention that some would have it so named from a Roman milliarium there placed. His objection is that "Staines doth not lye up on the Roman way between London and Pontes or any other of that kind; upon which the *Milliaria* or Milestones were only set."

But more modern writers claim that Staines is the Roman station *Ad Pontes,* and that the road to Silchester crossed the Thames there, and that Egham can be identified with the Roman Bibracte. Many Roman remains have been unearthed in and near Staines—a bronze coin of the Emperor Trajan, Roman bricks, files, vases, swords, some of the latter dredged up from the Thames, and a number of instruments from a Roman bath—pins, tweezers and strigils. Many of these have been collected into a local museum by a keen resident, Ernest Ashby.

It is impossible to isolate Middlesex in early recorded times. We must regard it merely as a piece of sparsely inhabited country through which some important prehistoric trackways ran, and in or near to which the vital settlements of Verulamium and Londinium were to be found. As cross-Channel trade increased and a greater variety of goods was imported into Britain a trading centre grew up near a convenient crossing of the Thames, and London was beginning to be a place of importance.

But it seems probable that there had been a way across the Thames farther west where the road from the coast continued

41

its way northwards towards Wales. When the three roads were Romanised or even laid down for the first time, Watling Street to the north-west, and the north and westerly roads, all based on London, that town must have begun to threaten the supremacy of Colchester. The destruction by Boadicea when Suetonius had retreated up Watling Street, before turning to reek vengeance on the Britons, did not put off the progress of London by much. As Britain became a peaceful, organised Roman province there was immigration from the Continent and plenty of traffic between Londinium and Verulamium up and down Watling Street. When, under Hadrian, Verulam became a rival of some of the cities in continental Europe, traffic must have grown still more; but even in those days the population of Verulam was perhaps not much more than 5,000, that of London perhaps three times as big. Metal goods and a copper coinage were developed in London, and the red-glazed "Samian" ware, which has been dug up at Sulloniacæ, was probably shipped to London in bulk and distributed by road to other centres. When Constantius Chlorus defeated Allectus, who had murdered Carausius, the leader of a revolt against the Romans, he was greeted by the Londoners as *Redditor Lucis Æterni,* the restorer of eternal light. At the Council of Arles in A.D. 314 of the three British bishops, two had associations with London—Restitutus, its Bishop, and Adelphius, Bishop of a *colonia* of London's. Attacks and counter-attacks brought many legions up and down the roads that led through the wooded area north and west of London, and if the stones and mortar of those well-built roads could speak they would have many a vivid story to tell us. It is rather remarkable that the *Antonine Itinerary,* a semi-official road-book, *c.* A.D. 225, does not give direct routes for getting from one important place to another. For instance, the road from London to Chichester, instead of going by Stane Street, is indicated as starting along the Bath road to Silchester, and the road to Lincoln goes through Verulam, which is certainly not the direct way. A unique experience in the history of London was the change of its name to Augusta. Britain was attacked by Picts, Scots, Saxon and Irish, and the Roman Wall built by Hadrian was breached. Theodosius landed at Richborough, marched to

London, reorganised its defences and advanced through the heart of England northwards and restored the garrisons of the Roman Wall. It was this triumph of short duration that caused the change of London's name, but the new name was as short-lived as the Roman triumph. The attacks on Britain by Picts and Scots from the north, the disastrous summons of Anglo-Saxon and Jutish aid to repel them, and the advances made by them up the eastern estuaries brought calamity on the whole country, and perhaps especially to the lands near London.

CHAPTER IX

SAXON MIDDLESEX

THE name Middlesex seems so easy of explanation, as that of the centre-forward of a line of attack from the coast with Essex and Wessex as the right and left wings. But the facts that we know show that Middlesex was an afterthought, and the name does not occur until a century and a half after the Saxon invasion began.

The change-over from a Roman civilisation to the Germanic lack of culture brought over by Angles and Saxons must have been gradual. In the first place, the culture displaced was not purely Roman, and we have hardly sufficient evidence to be sure what happened. Some have thought that destruction of towns and massacre of their inhabitants followed the Anglo-Saxon invasion, and this may have sometimes been the case. London seems to have remained, at the best, very sparsely inhabited, but Verulam was left desolate and was probably never populated again. What happened to Sulloniacæ placed half-way between will probably remain a mystery.

While there is a great deal of evidence of Saxons and Jutes in Kent, Sussex and Hampshire, it is not easy to be so confident about the settlements in Surrey, while the Thames might act as a sort of barrier between lands on the north and south. But the name Surrey suggests that it may have formed the southern province of an early people settled to the north as well as to the south of the Thames, and "a territory comprising both Middlesex and Surrey would be large enough to support one of the smaller peoples of the sixth century."

The latest authorities on English settlement come to the conclusion that "of the origin of Middlesex practically nothing is known." Middlesex was always dependent on Essex, and there are no royal dynasties in the county as there were in Essex, Sussex and Wessex, other members of what seems to be the same series of tribal areas. Archæologists connect the methods adopted in a cemetery in Shepperton in Middlesex with those of Mitcham-Croydon folk in Surrey and North-

44

fleet Saxons in Kent. It seems probable that all the south-east of England was divided into *regiones* in early Teutonic times, and there is extant the copy of an eighth-century charter in which Ethelbert of Mercia speaks of a *regio* called Geddinges (Yeading) in the *provincia* of the Middlesex Saxons. The land of the Middle Saxons and the south folk of Surrey seem to suggest that in this formative period the Saxons who settled round the capital were in the same political company as the other distinct and powerful units. It has even been hinted that in this period London was "a completely negligible factor in the political geography of the Thames basin." We certainly know that London is not mentioned by name between 457 and 604.

The cemetery at Shepperton shows signs of cremation urns as well as inhumation burials, and these resemble those discovered at Mitcham in Surrey and at Northfleet in Kent. A similar settlement at Hanwell must be added, and these are almost the only evidence of Saxon occupation other than the place names. Most of the Saxon population was near to London, and what evidence there may have been in Middlesex will probably have been removed by "centuries of unrecorded building, and commercial exploitation," which have disturbed the natural ground levels.

Brigadier Mortimer Wheeler, in his *London and the Saxons* (1935), favours the notion that there may have been some continuity of London's life through the dark centuries of early Saxon times, basing his opinion on some linear earthworks in the Chilterns, in Middlesex and in Kent; and Sir Montague Sharp, on different premises, came to the same conclusion. But R. G. Collingwood felt confident that the fighting of these dark times made a prosperous London impossible, and that it was a complete restart that made her, in Bede's words, "the mart of many nations." He supports the argument that there was no real continuity between Roman Britain and Saxon England, and that "if London retained a civic consciousness through the period, it was indeed an astonishing triumph over economic fact." The Venerable Bede throws light on the unimportance of London between A.D. 457 and 604 when he attributes St. Augustine's failure to stabilise a bishopric in London to the obstinate heathenism

45

of the inhabitants. They must have been pagan Saxons, squalid and primitive squatters in the ruins inside the Roman walls, and not descendants of the Roman occupation. That there were numerous early Saxon settlements in what we now call Middlesex is indicated by the place names along the Thames Valley, and their inhabitants must have been farmers of the simplest type, ignorant of any "economic and architectural complexities of town life." It seems quite clear that this Saxon line of settlements was not in any way controlled by the civic authority of London. The settlers in London's ruins must have had something in common with the many displaced persons today, who with their sometimes dubious ancestry and uncertain origin manage to make do in the ruined cities of Central Europe.

Along the main roads towards old Verulam and the Chilterns Saxon communities were rarer; and surviving natives, partly British, partly Roman, were more numerous. But along the Thames there was possibly a continuous line of Saxon *regiones* from that of the Geddinges at Yeading to link up with the West Saxons.

It has been suggested that Middlesex was an uninhabited borderland in pre-Roman times, and a desolate region after the Romans had colonised London, and its geography rather supports this view.

Dr. Guest feels sure that Middlesex is the portion left over when the neighbouring counties had been colonised by the Anglo-Saxons. The area consisted of a marsh in the south-east, a barren heath in the south-west, and a dense forest to the north, no part actually inviting settlement. The swamps of the Lea and the Colne and the northern forests probably saved it from the invasion by the East Saxons of Essex, and London may have defended it from Kent and Sussex. When the East Saxons advanced up the river valleys of their western border they captured Verulamium, came slowly down Watling Street and possibly by the tracks we now call A.6 and A.1 and captured Middlesex from the north-west. London fell before 552 and was definitely occupied by the East Saxons in 604, and it is significant that Middlesex for long was part of the kingdom of Essex and of the East Saxon bishopric of London. The marshlands along three rivers—Thames, Lea and

Colne—the many square miles of forest, the bleak area at Hounslow Heath, gave little chance of cultivation. Guest in his book on *Celtic Origins* finds in the place names an important clue to history, and in Middlesex only the three chief rivers and the important tributary stream, the Brent, have a Celtic origin. Brent is derived from the old British Brigantia, and means either holy or high river, but, as the Brent flows mainly through low-lying areas, the former is the more likely. Still, its origin is in the hills of north-west Middlesex on the Hertfordshire border.

It seems possible that Surrey, the southern region, was originally part of Middlesex, in much the same way as Southwark has been for centuries attached to London. It has been suggested that the rights of the citizens of London to hunt not only in the Middlesex forests but as far as the Chilterns indicates that early Middlesex also extended much farther north as well.

The overriding influence in the county of Middlesex has obviously been the presence of the capital city of London within its area, though the Lord Mayor's "Square Mile" has never been technically in Middlesex. Middlesex has little independent county history until after 1888, and its population was small and its towns unimportant until recent times. Even today, when both have increased, Middlesex is largely a London dormitory.

The Middlesex woods and swamps probably protected the area from the men of Essex, much as the fortified London and the Thames shielded it from incursions from Kent and Sussex. We know nothing of what happened between A.D. 552, when London fell to invaders marching down Watling Street, and A.D. 604, when it was in East Saxon hands. After the latter date London was the Essex capital and Middlesex was part of the London bishopric. The first notice of Middlesex by name is in 704, when the King of the East Saxons, owing tribute to Mercia, granted a piece of land in Twickenham "in provincia quæ nuncupatur Middleseaxon."

It was Wulfhere, the Christian son of the pagan Mercian King Penda, who overran East Anglia and then Essex, owing to stupid disputes among the West Saxons. All this time the county was still very poorly populated, being confined to the

47

four river valleys. Comment has been made on the absence of any county nobility and gentry in Middlesex, and it is certain that in Saxon times there was no native ruling house to hold the people together.

Ini, King of the West Saxons, was successful in developing his country's administrative, financial and warlike resources, and he was able to control London and Canterbury, the commercial and Church capitals. He conquered Essex and London (including presumably Middlesex) about 688, and published an important code of laws in c. 693. By this he recognised the three-field system (wheat, oats, fallow) and the existence of landowning freemen, called ceorls. He protected forests, regulated the amount of weregild, money payable as compensation for murder, and recognised the division of Wessex into counties and hundreds.

There are three other documents dating before the time of Alfred the Great, and one of them, a charter of A.D. 767, is preserved in a contemporary text. During the hurly-burly of rivalry between Mercia, East Anglia and Wessex, Middlesex presumably followed London and was captured and recaptured from time to time. Offa of Mercia recovered Essex in 775, and for another half-century Middlesex was under Mercia. Then by the victory of Egbert, King of the West Saxons, at Ellandun, Essex and London passed for ever from the power of the Mercians. Egbert found friendly relations with the Church in the person of the Archbishop very important, the Witanagemote was established, and large grants of land were made to the thegns; but no sooner had Wessex made itself the most important kingdom in England when a fresh danger arose in the coming of the Northmen.

The plundering raids of these skilful sailors and metal-workers were followed by a winter spent in Sheppey in 855, and by permanent settlements in England, mainly in Yorkshire; but in 870 East Anglia, including Middlesex, in all probability was captured, and nine years later a body of Vikings advancing from Cirencester and Chippenham, where the main army was stationed, "sat down at Fulham on the Thames." The two towns from which they advanced have history in their names of Roman and Saxon origin. Another Danish army invaded Middlesex, and both spent the winter

48

Norman Font, Hendon Church

at Fulham and then sailed across the narrows to attack Flanders. It was left to Alfred, a king still imperfectly appreciated in this country, to prevent the Danes from over-running the whole of England, and his famous victories over Guthrum brought about a division of the land into two kingdoms, separated by Watling Street. This left the Hundreds of Elthorne and Hounslow (now Isleworth), Spelthorne and part of Gore in Alfred's hands and the rest as belonging to Danelagh. When Alfred re-enacted the laws of Ini, dated A.D. 693, he probably recognised the divisions which had then been made. But Guthrum did not keep to his bargain, though he obeyed the Treaty of Wedmore to the extent of becoming a Christian. Alfred was glad of the excuse to recapture London, and a new treaty brought all the land between the Brent and the Lea into the Anglo-Saxon kingdom. The two kings and the Witan confirmed for themselves and their descendants, "as well for born as for unborn, who reck of God's mercy on ours," that the boundaries were "upon the Thames and then upon the Lea unto its source, then right to Bedford and then up the Ouse unto Watling Street." So Middlesex was united once more and back in the Anglo-Saxon kingdom of Alfred.

The career of Dunstan, whose work for Church and State stamps him as the great helper of King Edgar to maintain a united England against the Danes, has this association with Middlesex, that he is reputed to have given the Manor of Hendon to the Abbot of Westminster. The renewal of Danish attacks when Ethelbert the Redeless was King brought to Middlesex what Carlyle calls "anarchic stupidity, murderous devastation, utter misery, platitude and sluggish contempti-bility," and the paying of Danegeld did little or nothing to "get rid of the Dane." The comparative peace under Edward the Confessor, who confirmed the Abbot's claim to Hendon, was only a prelude to a still more formidable invasion by Norsemen from Normandy.

A good deal of the story of Middlesex can be gleaned from the place names, of which there are a very large number of Saxon origin compared with the small size of the county. Ealing and Yeading conceal tribal names; Uxbridge, Waxlow and Uxendon recall the Wixan folk; and among pre-Conquest names are Feltham, Shepperton, Sunbury, Halliford, Isleworth, Twickenham, Brentford, Cowley, Drayton, Greenford, Harlington, Hayes, Colham, Norwood, Northolt, Edgware, Harrow, Kingsbury, Stanmore, Horsendon, Hendon, Ickenham, Wembley, Winchmore, Tottenham; though it must be remembered that hardly one of this long list of names retains its Anglo-Saxon spelling. The *Hendon Extents and Surveys,* which the present writer has edited and published, are full of similar place names.

The division of Middlesex into six hundreds is of old standing, and before the Conquest they contained fifty-nine parishes, not always identical with the manors. The villages were mainly situated along Roman roads for convenience of movement, or on the banks of the Thames for fresh water and for fishing, or in clearings in the great forests that stretched from London to Waltham and St. Albans and Harefield. Place names testify to the prevalent woodland— Acton for oaks, Ashford for the ash tree, and the thorn in Elthorne. The six hundreds vary much in size and consequently in the number of villages contained in each. At an early date the Hundred of Ossulton was sub-divided into four groups of manors or parishes—Tower Hamlets on the east, Kensington on the west, and Finsbury and Wenlax Barn (Holborn) to the north. A later historian divides it on a slightly different method and adds a comment on the types of soil. The Hundred of Ossulstone includes :

(*a*) Barnet, Highgate, Hornsey (including Finchley), Hampstead, Willesden; and its soil is clay, mixed with gravel and loam.
(*b*) Stoke Newington, Clapton, Hackney, Bethnal Green, Stepney; and its soil is rich and mellow, and at Hackney there is some strong loam-like clay, called brick-earth.
(*c*) Islington, Pancras, Paddington; and its soil is gravelly loam, with a little clay.
(*d*) Kensington, Brompton, Chelsea, Fulham, Chiswick; and its soil varies from strong to sandy loam, mixed with sand and gravel, some black and fertile, some sharp and white. Chiswick has some pure surface gravel.

It seems that Fulham included Acton, Brentford, Chiswick and Ealing.

Elthorne includes Colham, Cowley, Cranford, Dawley, West Drayton, Greenford, Hanwell, Harefield, Harlington,

50

Harmondsworth, Hayes, Hillingdon, Ickenham, Kingsbury, Northolt and Ruislip. Uxbridge was included in Hillingdon and Norwood in Hayes. The soil varies from strong loam, with gravel, to light loam.

In *Edmonton* Hundred the places named in Domesday Book are Edmonton, Enfield and Tottenham. South Mimms was probably part of the Manor of Enfield, and Southgate and Wood Green are later developments. Its soil is clay and strong loam with some gravel.

In *Gore* only Harrow, Hendon and Stanmore are mentioned, and it seems that Harrow included Edgware, Kingsbury, Pinner, Wealdstone and Wembley. The soil of Gore is given as stiff clay with a little gravelly loam.

The Hundred of *Isleworth* (then called Hounslow or Honeslau) included Isleworth, Twickenham, Hampton and Teddington on the Thames. Heston was included in Isleworth. Its soil is reported as including hazel loam, rich and mellow, also strong loam and a little light gravel.

Spelthorne included Ashford, Bedfont, Charlton, Feltham, Hanworth, Kempton, Laleham, Shepperton, Staines, Stanwell, Sunbury. Littleton was included in Laleham. The soil included light loam, lean gravel and strong loam.

In Robert Morden's map of Middlesex in the 1695 edition of Camden's *Britannia* the area from Whetstone to Fulham and from Twyford to Tottenham is called "Finnisbury or Wenlaxbarne." This fresh name is found in the parish of St. Giles's, Cripplegate, and there seems to be no justification for styling this a separate hundred.

The prebendal stalls of St. Paul's Cathedral are named after various manors belonging to the Church, and they mostly take their names from places in Middlesex, such as Brondesbury, Brownswood, Chamberlainewood, Harlesden, Mapesbury, Neasden, Oxgate, Twyford, Willesden—all of them probably in Willesden, though some authorities claim Brownswood as in Hornsey.

A rather interesting revival of an old name in Middlesex occurred towards the end of 1946.

The Spelthorne Divisional Labour party, in what the *Daily Herald* called a "warped and weird manifesto," called for a modification of Labour foreign policy, which it declared was

51

in favour of the U.S.A. rather than the U.S.S.R., and therefore provocative and dangerous. The revival of the old Saxon name in this connection is worthy of mention, whatever view may be taken of the opinions there expressed.

EARTHWORKS

Archæologists have divided earthworks into ten groups, four of which are not represented in Middlesex. There are no promontory fortresses or hill forts, no ancient village sites or castle mounts with attached courts. When the Victoria Counties' History volume on Middlesex was published in 1911 no castle mount was recognised in the county, but since that time South Mimms Castle has twice been chronicled and examined, once by A. Hadrian Allcroft just before the first World War, and again by members of the Mill Hill Historical Society in 1930.

There are only one or two tumuli, a few rectangular camps or defensive enclosures, one or two earthworks which do not admit of classification, and quite a number of homestead moats and manorial strongholds. It is not surprising that there were many attempts to fortify manor-houses and isolated farms by means of moats. There was frequent danger of isolated robbers and brigands or marauding bands. Rebellions of barons, the anarchy of Stephen's reign, troubles under John and Henry III, all threatened the peace of Middlesex, and the rebellion of Wat Tyler and Jack Straw certainly invaded London from the north-west and north-east. There were three battles of the Wars of the Roses either in Middlesex or close to its borders, and attacking or defending troops must have advanced and retired, with equal possible damage to the prosperous houses near which they passed.

There are a number of these protective works in the rather exposed north-eastern part of the county, roughly in Tottenham, Edmonton and Enfield. Bruce Castle in Tottenham had a moat until the present century, but town development has been responsible for its levelling up. Mockings was a sub-manor of Bruce Castle, and its moated manor-house stood formerly on the south of Marsh Lane. There are, or were till recently, three homestead moats in Edmonton : a small quadrangular moat west of Angel Road station, now filled up;

Moat House Farm, to the east of Lower Edmonton, demolished in 1906, but its moat reprieved for a few more years; and a 30-foot moat at Weir Hall in Upper Edmonton. There is a modern house surrounded by the water which flows in from Pymmes Brook.

Enfield, having such wide open spaces as the Chase and White Webbs Wood, retains, or did till very recently, six defended sites. Enfield Camp is a semicircular fragment round the back of a country house; its partial demolition is due to the laying out of a garden more than a century ago, and its preservation is probably due to the same cause. The vallum varies from 5 to 8 feet in height, and without is a fosse from 3 to 4 feet deep. It seems that the camp probably had a water supply in addition to being a water-girt stronghold. Durant's Arbour was a fourteenth-century manor-house half a mile north of Ponders End. Close to Enfield town station a large moat was in existence until about 1910, but it was then filled in and houses built thereon.

West of Old Park Farms, on the Golf Links, a small elevated area was surrounded by a diamond-shaped moat fed by a small stream from the Lea. North-east of the Enfield Lock station, on Plantation Farm, was a quadrangular moat crossed by two bridges. Perhaps the most famous of all the moats in Enfield is Camlet Moat, north of Trent Park and south of Enfield Chase. The house has gone long since, but the moat is distinguished because it figures in Scott's *Fortunes of Nigel*—"little more than a mound, partly surrounded by a ditch, from which it derived its name."

Finchley has been too much developed to retain much ancient work. There was a rectangular moat belonging to the ancient manor-house; Ducketts, or Dovecoats, an old manor-house north-east of St. Mary's Church, Hornsey, with a moat fed by water from the New River; and a fort with moat mentioned by John Norden in his *Speculum Britanniæ*, 1593—"a hill or fort in Hornesey Park, and so called Lodge Hill, for that thereon for some time stood a lodge, when the park was replenished with deare; but it seemeth by the foundation it was rather a castle than a lodge, for the hill is at this time trenched with two deep ditches, now olde and overgrown with bushes." This belonged to the See of London from the twelfth to the fourteenth centuries, near Manor Farm House, northeast of Bishop's Wood, between Highgate and Finchley. The lodge was pulled down in the fourteenth century, but there are some traces of a moat, 210 feet square.

CHAPTER X

MIDDLESEX UNDER NORMANS AND PLANTAGENETS

DOMESDAY BOOK AND VILLAGE LIFE—CIVIL
WAR AND RECONSTRUCTION—KING JOHN
AND MAGNA CARTA

As all men of importance, and many simpler folk, who approached London from north-west and south-west must have come through Middlesex, it is not difficult to find items of historic interest for every decade in the centuries, and a summary of their reactions on the county may be of value. Lanfranc, the Norman Archbishop, who was so wise an adviser to the Conqueror and to William Rufus, built Harrow Church, which was consecrated by his successor, Anselm. A dispute arose as to whose right it was to perform the act of consecration, seeing that Harrow was in the diocese of London. The problem was referred to Wulfstan of Worcester, the only surviving Saxon prelate, and he gave his verdict for Anselm. As a consequence of this decision all Archbishops of Canterbury have since then exercised special privileges in Harrow. Through the Norman era the archbishops often resided at Hayes or Harrow, much as the Abbot of Westminster spent some time each year in Hampstead and Hendon.

There is no mention of Middlesex troops at the Battle of Hastings, but the London contingent was commanded by the Staller Esegar, Sheriff of the county. Although Esegar was wounded, he was carried back to endeavour gallantly to defend London against William. When the Conqueror marched from Berkhampsted southward and entered Middlesex from the north-west, his march was peaceful, because London had already accepted William's terms. The Norman troops advanced by several routes and did some damage to Enfield, Edmonton and Tottenham. All the lands held by Esegar the Staller were given to Geoffrey de Mandeville, the first of an interesting family closely connected for several generations with the political life of London and Middlesex.

Most of Middlesex belonged to the Church, and the King did not hold a single manor in the county. The chief ecclesiastical landholders were the Bishop of London and the Abbot of Westminster. The Bishop held Finchley and Hornsey in Middlesex as we know it today, while the Manor of Fulham covered part of the present-day county and included Acton, Brentford, Chiswick and Ealing. Friern Barnet, which was in Middlesex, was part of the Manor of Whetstone and belonged to the Priory of St. John of Jerusalem at Clerkenwell. The other Barnets belonged to the Abbot of St. Albans and counted in Hertfordshire. The Abbot of Westminster held (Hampstead and) Hendon, Ashford, Cowley, Greenford, Hanwell, Staines, Shepperton, Sunbury, with certain rights in Laleham. The Archbishop of Canterbury (Lanfranc) held Hayes and Harrow, the second of which was to bring several very important figures into the history of Middlesex. The Dean and Chapter of St. Paul's held West Drayton, West Twyford and Willesden, while Harmondsworth (Hermodesworde) had been given by the King to the Abbot of Rouen.

Geoffrey de Mandeville was the most important lay tenant, and his manors were Northolt and Perivale (Greenford Parva) in the south-west; Hartley, Enfield and Edmonton in the north-east. Roger, Earl of Arundel, held Colham (near Uxbridge), Dawley in Harlington, Hanworth, Hillingdon and Ickenham (Ticheham). William Fitz Ansculf held Cranford; Richard FitzGilbert, Earl of Bronx, held Harefield; Ernulf de Hesding held Kingsbury and Ruislip (Riselepe); Walter FitzOtter held East Bedfont and the overlordship of West Bedfont and Stanwell; Roger de Rames held Charlton and Little Stanmore or Whitchurch; Earl Mortain held Great Stanmore, Feltham, Laleham and Kempton; Walter de St. Waleric held Hampton and Isleworth (Gisteleworde); and, finally, Tottenham was held by the Countess Judith, widow of Waltheof, who had been Earl of Northumberland, Huntingdon and Northampton.

The Charter of William to the Citizens of London is perhaps the most precious document that they possess, for it is the earliest of their charters, and was tactfully granted to them at a moment when their prized independence was in the melting-pot. It is addressed to William, Bishop Gosfreyd, the Portreeve, and all the citizens of London, whether French or English. The Portreeve must be Geoffrey de Mandeville, whom the Conqueror appointed to be Staller in place of the famous Ansgar.

Geoffrey held a soke which probably adjoined the Tower (of which his son William was custodian) and property besides in eleven different counties when Domesday Book was compiled. In a charter relating to Westminster the address is to the Justiciar and the Sheriff *omnibusque ministris et fidelibus suis Francis et Anglis in Middlesexan*. A charter of *c*. 1100-1 was addressed, among others, to William de Mandeville, and all faithful subjects, French and English, of Middlesex.

William de Mandeville, son and heir to the first Geoffrey, was made by William, Constable of the Tower, and this added to the importance of the family. Both Geoffrey de Mandeville and Roger, Earl of Arundel, held vastly greater estates in other counties, notably Geoffrey in Essex. It has been pointed out that Geoffrey the first could not establish his claim to be justiciar by right of his succession to Ansgar the Staller, but he did succeed, at the beginning of Rufus's reign, in obtaining the justiciarship and shrievaltry of the whole of London and Middlesex at farm. He seems to have kept the superior office of justiciar for himself, and to have appointed a certain Roger and Richard de Par at various times as Sheriff of Middlesex. Hugh de Buckland is another interesting Norman arrival, and he is recorded in the Abingdon Chronicle as Sheriff and Justiciar of Middlesex (d. 1115). In addition to similar tasks in seven other counties, he seems to have succeeded Geoffrey de Mandeville in his various Middlesex functions.

MIDDLESEX AND LONDON

The problem of London's suburbs has always presented itself for solution, and various schemes have been launched, but few have been successful until the planning of London's Green Belt. The growth of outlying districts has often eluded

the efforts of planners, and neither the prohibition of new
buildings nor efforts to extend London's suzerainty have really
been successful. Perhaps the earliest plan was the combined
effort of Henry I and the citizens with regard to the farm of
London, which was purchased for £300. This entitled them
to appoint a sheriff and to carry on their hunting as well and
as fully as their ancestors had done—that is to say, in
Chiltre and in Middlesex and Surrey.

W. J. Loftie, half a century ago, had a theory that Middlesex had been ravaged and harried to such an extent by the
Danes that the grant of the county to the City of London by
Cnut might have altered history completely. "London as the
county town of Middlesex, the Londoners as the chief landowners, their tenants as the colonists of a fallow but fertile
track might have wrought great things."

The delay of the grant by about a century came too late to
give London a greater control over the suburban but as yet
undeveloped areas. Loftie is convinced that it was a detri-
ment to Middlesex that so much of the land was under the
control of the Church, but it does not seem obvious that the
Norman landowners who held the smaller half of Middlesex
were any better in their relation to villeins, bordars and cottars
than, for instance, the Abbot of Westminster in his Manor of
Hendon or the Archbishop of Canterbury in Harrow.

He claims that, great as were the traditional privileges of
the City, the ancient assemblies, the husting and the folk-mote,
the election of magistrates by the burghers, the choosing of
two sheriffs, the grant of Middlesex was more than these.
"There was a certain income from the Courts which may
eventually have been greater than the rent; the military protection of the city was rendered more easy when its civil
jurisdiction extended so far beyond the walls, and the right
conceded to the citizens to hunt in their surrounding forests
formed the outward symbol of the completeness of their rule
—a symbol which signified more under a Norman King than
at any time since." The grant of Middlesex was a proclamation to all England that, under the King, London was a free
city. An important conclusion to which many may have come
is that "London is not in Middlesex; that it never was in
Middlesex, that ages before Middlesex was thought of as

the name of a people, a Kingdom, a county, a district, or what you will, London had looked out from its watch-towers upon the wild woods of the northern hills, is a fact of which we have to be constantly reminded."

George Norton, in his valuable *Commentaries on the History, Constitution and Chartered Franchises of the City of London,* suggests that "the franchise bestowed on the citizens of London, of farming the sheriffwick of the County of Middlesex at a stipulated rent must be considered as a very distinguished mark of the royal favour. It is probable that the many interests which the citizens possessed throughout the County of Middlesex, in the detection and arrest of malefactors, in lands, in goods, in the fairs and markets, in the privilege of hunting, and in their continual trading occupations, as well as in the dispensation of justice in the County Court, would render the shrieval authority over that district not only of intrinsic value to them in itself, but almost a necessary adjunct to the secure enjoyment of their more peculiar civic franchises."

DOMESDAY BOOK IN MIDDLESEX AND LIFE IN ITS VILLAGES

For very many folk in this country our history begins at 1066, when the successful Battle of Senlac, or Hastings, gave to Duke William the Norman this fertile land, which had been invaded in earlier eras by Roman, by Saxon and by Dane. No one could possibly have told that the Norman conquest was to be permanent, and that after another nine centuries England was to have weathered the threats of many invasions, all of them unavailing. Just about twenty years after his arrival in London, William decided to take stock of the acres which he and his "barons, brigands and landless adventurers" had succeeded in conquering; and the carefully compiled details which his commissioners collected formed the famous Domesday Book, the first great survey of England. We possess in facsimile copies of the Bayeux Tapestry, a graphic picture of the Conquest, and of the rival armies that won and lost the struggle; and in Domesday Book a detailed story of the extent of each manor, "how many hides, how many plough teams, how many villeins, how many cottars, how many serfs, how many freemen, how much wood, meadow, pasture; how many fisheries and mills; who held it in the time of King Edward (T.R.E.), who holds it now; its value T.R.E., its value when received, its value now."

Here are the owners of some of the Middlesex manors as recorded in Domesday Book. The Bishop of London held Ealing, Finchley and Hornsey. The Abbot of Westminster held Sunbury, Shepperton, Greenford, Hendon, Hanwell, Staines, Ashford, Cowley, and had some rights in Laleham; the Canons of St. Paul's held West Drayton, West Twyford and Willesden. The Earl of Mortain held Laleham and Feltham, Kempton and Great Stanmore; Walter de St. Waleric held Hampton and Gistelesworde or Isleworth. Walter Fitzother held Stanwell and one of the manors of Bedfont, the other being held by the Earl of Mortain. Roger de Montgomery, Earl of Arundel, held Hanworth, Colham, Hillingdon, Ickenham (let to three knights and one Englishman), Harlington (let out to Alured and Olaf) and Dawley. Charlton and Stanmore Parva, or Whitchurch, was held by Roger de Rames; Harmondsworth was held by an alien priory, the Abbey of the Holy Trinity at Rouen of the King; and Ruislip was held by Ernulf de Hesding, who bestowed it on the Abbey of Bec in Normandy. He also held Kingsbury. Geoffrey de Mandeville was well rewarded in Middlesex for his services, and he held himself or leased out to others the manors of Northolt, Greenford Parva or Perivale, Edmonton or Adelmetone, Enfield, Hadley and Ickenham. William Fitz Ansculf held Cranford; Richard FitzGilbert, Earl of Brioux, held Harefield. Tottenham was held of the King by the Countess Judith, widow of Waltheof, who had been beheaded for alleged conspiracy against the King; Harrow and Hayes by Archbishop Lanfranc.

A typical manor belonging to Westminster Abbey was Staines, which is thus described in Domesday Book as translated from the Latin : "The Abbot of St. Peter holds Staines for nineteen hides. There is land for twenty-four ploughs. Eleven hides belong to the demesne, and there are thirteen ploughs therein. The villanes have eleven ploughs. There are three villanes of half a hide each; and four villanes of one hide; and eight villanes of half a virgate each; and thirty-six bordars of three hides; and one villane of one virgate, and four bordars of forty acres; and ten bordars of five acres each; and five cottars of four acres each; and eight bordars of one virgate; and three cottars of nine acres; and twelve bordmen; and forty-six burgesses, who pay forty shillings a year. There are six mills of sixty-four shillings; one weir of six shillings and eightpence; and one weir which pays nothing. Pasture for the cattle of the village. Meadows for twenty-four ploughs, and twenty shillings over and above. Pannage for thirty hogs, and two arpents of vineyards. Four berewicks belong to this manor, and they belonged to it in King Edward's time. The whole value is thirty-five pounds; the same when received; in King Edward's time forty pounds. The manor lay and lies in the demesne of the Church of St. Peter."

Thorold Rogers, in his *History of Agriculture and Prices,* places Middlesex, exclusive of London, as the second richest county in England, second only to Norfolk. In 1341 a wool tax was levied and Middlesex was assessed at 236 sacks, one sack for 760 acres. Norfolk was one for 610 acres, Herts, Bucks and Surrey about one to 1,250 acres, but Essex one to 1,580.

In the Domesday survey there are 2,132 tenants mentioned for Middlesex, of whom 1,936 are unfree—villeins 1,133, bordars 342 and cottars 461—and in addition 104 slaves. Thirteen knights are mentioned in the survey, 1 francus, 12 priests, 10 foreigners (*francigenæ*) and 46 burgenses at Staines.

The majority of medieval villages were small, and from fifty to one hundred was the average population. All the villagers were engaged in agriculture or in ancillary trades, and they shared rights and privileges and discharged duties under the control and protection of the lord of their manor or his agent. Manor and village are not interchangeable terms, and in several parishes in Domesday there are more than one manor; and not more than half a century after the Conquest there were three or four manors in the same parish of Hendon, which explains why Hendon splits up so easily into wards. Professor Kosminsky has shown that in Danelagh manor and village are often different; out of 650 investigated,

61

336 are not identical. When Danelagh was first staked out the dividing line was Watling Street, which divided Middlesex almost exactly into equal parts, with the whole of Elthorne, Spelthorne and Hounslow (Isleworth) on the Anglo-Saxon side, Edmonton on the Danish side, and Gore and Ossulstone fairly evenly divided. However, in the second of Alfred's treaties the River Lea was the boundary, and this placed the whole of Middlesex under Alfred's wise, firm and tolerant rule.

The investigations of Vinogradoff, Seebohm and Maitland show that manors have not a common origin or similarity in design, but there was, as a rule, a collection of houses or cottages built close together, each with a plot of garden, with arable land close by, with meadows beyond, with commons on which all had grazing rights, and with waste, woods and forests where assarting was permitted. Individual farming was not easy in the common arable land, and uniformity was desirable, but in the private closes and in the assarted land from waste or wood there was more room for originality.

It is obvious that the condition and prosperity of a married couple living in a manor would depend largely on the size of their family and the sex of their children. If there were too many sons to be able to support themselves on the father's plot, some might work directly under the lord, or might try to reach a town and remain there the specified time for emancipation. Plague, pestilence and famine would work unequal havoc in the various manors and families, and while some names occur over and over again in the early extents and surveys, others died out completely. Privileges were altering from time to time, and the number of free tenants was increasing without people being very conscious of the progress.

CUSTUMALS, EXTENTS AND SURVEYS

Few people realise that Poets' Corner in Westminster Abbey is not so wide as Statesmen's Corner in the opposite transept, and the reason is that a piece of cloister reduces the size of the ground floor but leaves the next storey intact. There they had planned the old muniment room of the Abbey, and for several years I used to spend two afternoons most weeks, out of sight, working on extents with Laurence Tanner,

the Custodian of the Abbey Records, while the choir sang
Evensong below.

The earliest custumal of a Middlesex manor is not a Westminster one, but is of Harmondsworth, dated 1110-11, in the
reign of Henry I, and is the sworn verdict of twelve jurymen
on the customs and services owed the Abbot of St. Katherine's
of Rouen as lord of the manor. Every villein tenant had to
plough and harrow one acre of corn and one of oats, with
seed provided by the lord, fetched by the villein, who returned
any surplus to the lord's grange. All the villeins, but not the
cottars, had to mow at hay harvest time, helped by two
mowers supplied by the lord. Each tenant might take away
as much hay as he could lift on the heft of his scythe. If he
piled too much on the scythe and broke it he forfeited the hay
and was fined. When the mowing was finished the tenants
were given either a ram or 13d. All tenants, including the
cottars, had to load and stack hay, except those who had a
cart to carry it. Stacking had to be done while the cart did the
journey to and fro three times. If rain hindered the work, the
tenants had to make up the lost time, while if any hours of
work were not needed at hay harvest they must be made up
at corn harvest.

There were some rewards and compensations called *dies
precariæ*, boon-days, on which the lord had to provide food
and sometimes even drink. In Hendon, a Westminster manor,
each tenant "shall finde a man at the Lord's Great Reape,
and one man at the Second Reape of the Lord's Corne,
Reaping in Autumn at the Lord's Diet; also he shall find 2
men at the Reape called Drued bederip at the Lord's Diet
once in a Daye namely Bread and Pottage, and ffish and
cheese."

At Harmondsworth there were three boon-days : a water-
bedrippe, the great Precaria, and the ill-named love-bedrippe,
a source of constant friction. Each tenant had to attend when
summoned by the crier, coming with servants and tenants at
Prime and working till Vespers. The Harmondsworth Custumal gives an average estimate of villein life, but there may
have been considerable variations in other manors. The
typical meal included a broth of peas and beans, bread, cheese
and beer, and fish or meat worth 1½d. for every two men.

Any folk too tired (*gravati*) to wait could take their meal home. Stewards, who had to watch for bad work, had beer in the lord's hall twice a day. The distinction between a wet and a dry bedrip is obvious, and the meal was sometimes given in the lord's hall too. Carts and wagons had to carry three loads to the grange, and neither man nor beast was fed. To miss the two bedrips put a man at the lord's mercy. When the wheat had been carried the animals were allowed to "common" on the fields. Every three years villein tenants had to provide one man to weed and clear the ponds, and for this they each got a meal of bread, cheese, beer and meat or fish.

Every three years tenants had to fetch stakes from the manor and fence off one perch each, and there were some few tenants who were bound to do any tasks imposed by the reeve. The position and importance of this official varies from century to century, if not from decade to decade, and perhaps still more from manor to manor. In Harmondsworth, as probably elsewhere, each villein tenant had to serve as reeve or crier, and during their year of office they dined at the lord's table or received an allowance, and were quit of all services. It was the crier's duty to lodge in the meadow and watch the haycocks. Chaucer's reeve, depicted by us more than two centuries later, was more of a portrait than a type.

There was much woodland in Harmondsworth, Hendon and Enfield—in fact, in most Middlesex manors—and tenants bordering on the forests had rights of wood and pannage for pigs. Year-old pigs paid 1d. for the privilege and younger ones ½d., and were all inspected at Martinmas. The lord provided a goderer to act as herdsman, and Golders Green perhaps owes its name to John the Godere, who figures in Hendon's Black Survey of 1321.

Heriot of the best beast was payable in Harmondsworth and in most other manors when a tenant died, and merchet was a 5s. fine for marrying outside the manor. In a medieval village complete lack of sanitation, inadequate water supply, and the dangers of childbirth, coupled with normal wastage, increased to monstrous proportions during plague-time, meant that it took two years to add one soul to the manor's population. Canon-law rules as to consanguinity were strict but often

64

disobeyed and inbreeding and incontinence were common. Chaucer's summoner would allow a man to live in sin for a year in return for a draught of wine. The rules in Harmondsworth forbade marriage without the lord's consent, also required for a villein to leave the vill or enter holy orders. No sub-letting or moving of boundaries was allowed without sanction.

The dishonest fellow in William Langland's *Piers Plowman* mentions a somewhat common practice in which he used to indulge when he says : "If I went to the plough I pinched so narrowly that I would steal a foot of land or a furrow, or gnaw the half-acre of my neighbour; and, if I reaped, I would over reap, or give counsel to them that reaped to seize for me with their sickles that which I never sowed." There is no mention of such tricks in Harmondsworth or Hendon.

Tallage was a tiresome and arbitrary feudal tax imposed on every bondage tenant when the lord went overseas, and may be regarded as a defence tax paid by all exempt from military service. Rules for woods and water were strict, and no one in Ruislip might shake down mast or thresh in the woods. A fisherman might only fish for enough to feed himself and his wife, and any fish more than a foot long belonged to the lord. Tenants owing rent to the lord at Trinity had one day to pay up, or their house or their ox team could be seized for a day and a night or permanently in case of no payment.

A very useful member of the manor team was the smith, who in Harmondsworth was quit of all obligations save a rental of 2s. a year. In return he repaired and replaced the demesne ploughshares, the lord providing the iron and steel. The smith sharpened the villeins' scythes when employed for the lord, and he had to shoe the front feet of two beasts all the year round, keeping the old shoes as perquisites. At Isleworth the smith received 6s. 8d. for repairing the demesne ploughs, and at Paddington 18s. Such tasks were probably done by men with small holdings of five acres or less, not by a tenant with a virgate or half a virgate.

In Hendon's Black Survey we find Stephen the Carpenter, William the Woodward, Alane the Soper, Alexander the Smith, John the Shepherd, John and William, both carters, and John the Hayward. They would find such jobs a help to

Bruce Castle, Tottenham

their small earnings. The woodward had originally the same
duties as Harmondsworth's forester, but in Hendon he had
in 1321 a messuage and twelve acres of land, paid 11s. and
"shall do haulfe of customs and services that John Godere
doeth." Well, John is no longer in charge of the swine, but
he has to "plowe with as many as he can joyne if he half cattle
as aforesaid by haulfe a day, and shall thresh and fanne III
bushells of wheat heaped as aforesayd, and shall find a man
at the Great Reape, and a man at ye second Reape, and II
men at ye Reape called Druidbedrip, and shall bind the
Lord's corne by haulfe a day, and shall carry III bushells of
corne to Westminster."

At Paddington, a Westminster manor, the woodward had
two acres free of all services in return for his duties as
forester, and also pasture in the wood and loppings from
felled timber. The job was hereditary in Harmondsworth,
and a deceased forester's cousin and the second husband of
an incumbent's widow established their claim to succeed.

In Middlesex, as no doubt commonly elsewhere, there are
payments of part of the rent in kind. Probably all rent to
start with was paid by service, often commuted to the duty of
sending someone to do the lord's work, possibly a tenant's
younger son. Next came payment in kind, and later on an
ordinary money rental. In the Black Survey of Hendon there
is a summary given of payments not made by service, and
the list includes bushels and quarters of oats, geese, capon,
hens, 106 eggs, ploughshares, bowstrings and two gilt spurs.

The causes of big events have frequently to be found many
years before they occur, and simple incidents have sometimes
concealed within them the seeds of a catastrophe or even of
a revolution. Manor courts were full of disputes between lord
and villein, between bailiff and reeve, between landlord and
tenant. Society was not stagnant, and we see efforts of tenants
to secure more freedom, while the changing value of money
and the growth of foreign trade helped to bring about
gradual but vital changes. In the Middlesex manor rolls there
are fines for trespass, fines for putting too many beasts on the
common, for not attending manorial courts and for non-
payment of rents and heriots. In Harmondsworth a foreign
lord found his villein tenants sometimes ten, twenty or even

thirty years in arrears for their rent, and the royal courts had to be consulted. When in 1233 the tenants insisted that Harmondsworth was ancient demesne and that the Abbot was demanding services and tallage never paid to the King, the Chief Justice fined the tenants 5 marks. A reference to Domesday Book showed that the tenants' claims were unfounded. But the tenants, "with presumptuous and inveterate fatuity," refused services and tallage, recovered, *Vi et armis*, the oxen teams which the Abbot had distrained, and threatened to burn down his house. The Abbot appealed to King Edward I, "lest by their insolence and rebellion worse should befall his prior." Where the Constable of Windsor failed, the Sheriff of Middlesex did his best to deal with their "pristine malice and rebellion," and the King's threats secured order for a time. Ten years later further trouble broke out when the Abbot found it increasingly difficult in 1289 to get normal services performed by his tenants. They challenged the third bedrip, refused tallage and merchet, and declined to bring their cottars for hay carting; but the verdict was once more given against them and for nearly a century Harmondsworth was quiet. Probably the problems were made more difficult by foreign control, and in other Middlesex manors there were not so many disputes.

There is sometimes an element of luck in finds of old archives, and an intelligent gardener, after an exhaustive sale at a seventeenth-century Middlesex manor, was allowed to rescue a vellum book and sell it to me for half a sovereign. A brief account of this manuscript Extent of Hendon in 1754 contributed to a local paper enabled me to buy five other Extents of Hendon, earlier and later, covering the years from 1321 to 1821. But the earliest was only a copy made in 1604. Where was the original? An earlier researcher had published an extent of the adjoining Manor of Hampstead, also belonging to Westminster, and this was located at Cambridge. A search in the University Library discovered these two and twelve other abbey manorial surveys bound up together. They all date from the beginning of the fourteenth century, and it is clear that the effort of Edward I, the English Justinian, to bring order out of some chaos was being copied by landlords up and down the country. The loss of Normandy and the

67

consequent concentration of owners on their English estates, with the compilation of a systematic treatise on estate management, produced co-ordination and adjustment of estates and services in many manors.

The two surveys of adjacent Westminster manors have much in common : lists of demesne lands, arable, meadow and pasture, free tenants and customary tenants. But it is remarkable that whereas in Hampstead (1312) there are only five free tenants, three of them heads of hospitals or priories, and forty-five customary tenants, in Hendon (1321) there are fifty-one free and seventy-five customary tenants. The Hampstead customary tenants had an average of six and a half acres apiece and seventeen days' work to do each year on the demesne lands. On the adjacent Manor of Hendon, only nine years later, the average was fourteen acres apiece and only eight days' work. Was this all brought about in this brief span of years, or were there local conditions sufficient to explain the difference? It is not easy to hazard a guess.

There is not much evidence of the three-field system in Hendon or Hampstead, but a series of hamlets with concentrated farms rather than a single village. Sub-infeudation may account for this and also that both manors were for a short time within Danelagh. In Danish manors we find economic independence, a cash economy, easy redistribution or alienation of holdings, and in these Westminster manors we also find the complete disappearance of common tillage and the emergence of considerable holdings. The status of the customary tenant had vastly improved, seeing that in a Peterborough manor in 1125 every villein worked for his lord 165 days in a year, while in 1321 in Hendon the corresponding figure was 8.

Views have changed as to the organisation of the manor, and in the Westminster records of Hendon from 1316 to 1361 prepositus or reeve and serviens or bailiff are alternate and not in office together. It was generally held that the reeve was chosen for a year only, and viewed matters from the tenants' point of view, while the bailiff took good care that the plough teams were out in good time and not unyoked too soon. In addition to the alternate appointment of reeve or bailiff, either of them might hold office for far more than one year. Richard Rich was bailiff from 1335 to 1345, and John Bonde was reeve from 1349 to 1361. There were three successive officials in the year of the Black Death, and it would be easy for one who survived to add field to field and strip to strip until he became comparable with Chaucer's reeve from Baldeswell in Norfolk.

After Bonde's twelve years in Hendon as reeve, Hugh Stodlee was reeve for seven years and John Goodhywe for four. Then in 1372 an important change was made and Frater John Lakyngheth became bailiff, with William Thebaud or Theobald as reeve and John Goodyer or Goodzer as bedell. It is difficult to explain the reason for this change, which made one of the monks in charge of the demesne farm, apparently for the first time in Hendon, and which lasted only two years. In 1372 John Goodhywe delivered the dead stock to his successor, William Thebaud, the new reeve under Lakyngheth, and there are two accounts delivered by William, one for 1372-3, Michaelmas to Michaelmas, and one for 1375, Michaelmas to November 15. The experiment now came to an end, and, though Lakyngheth was still alive in 1380-1 and appears in the Westminster returns for the poll-tax, he does not again figure in the list of officials of the manor.

In 1373-4 John Swan was bailiff, with John Goodyer as bedell and rent-collector, and there are accounts rendered by Swan for the remainder of his year 1373-4, rather elaborate reckonings for 1374-5, dealing with repayments from William Thebold, debts due to Swan on his final account, and the accounts of the rent-collector. In 1375-6 John Swan was bailiff, with John at Hegge, a customary tenant and son or grandson of a tenant in the Black Survey, acting as bedell and farmer of the demesne. Clearly, experiments were being made, and this latest manorial scheme seems to have a success, for we find that in 1379 John at Hegge was again made farmer and collector of rents and farms and courts, and he succeeded in holding the post through the troublous times of the Peasants' Revolt, vacating his post, possibly by death, only in 1409, after more than thirty years' tenure.

In Harmondsworth trouble broke out in the first year of

the reign of Richard II, and six of the tenants were fined 1d. each for not coming to the haymaking; three were fined for reaping their own corn on the day of the great Precaria. Seven others were fined for not coming to superintend the reapers, "as they were by law and custom bound." Three more were fined 6d. each for failing to attend at a bedrip, and there were other examples of what looked like organised opposition. Tenants were letting land without permission, others were trespassing in the Abbot's woods and poaching in his private waters. In full court one Robert Baker, who had refused to do haymaking, accused the jury of finding a false verdict; while Walter Breuer got into serious trouble with the seneschal for disorderly behaviour in court.

In the next year a tenant's servant opened the lord's sluices and flooded the hayfields. Further difficulties occurred, and the elected reeve preferred to be fined 13s. 4d. rather than to serve. In 1380 nine tenants failed to superintend the reapers and seven refused to attend the great bedrip and two missed the love-bedrip. The reeve who had been elected paid £1 6s. 8d. to avoid service.

Three centuries from the date of Domesday Book had brought about slow but significant changes in manorial custom and administration, and it remained to be seen whether local conditions applicable to some Middlesex manors were typical of conditions farther away from London, and whether the steady progress made by villein tenants would continue to evolve or proceed by revolution.

CIVIL WAR AND RECONSTRUCTION

We have strayed some centuries along our road and must retrace our steps into Norman times once more.

Middlesex played quite an important part in the Civil War between Stephen and Matilda. Geoffrey de Mandeville, grandson of his namesake and son of William, was hereditary Constable of the Tower, which made him Master of London, while his Middlesex estates were considerable and fairly consolidated, Edmonton, Enfield and Hadley being among them. Such was his power that he was able to detain in the Tower Constance of France, who had just been married to Eustace, son of King Stephen. This was perhaps intended as a warning to the King of the power which Geoffrey could wield, and Stephen had to overlook this outrage on the part of Geoffrey, but he never forgave it.

In 1140 the King granted him the earldom of Essex. The Empress Matilda meantime had landed in England, and her brother Robert, Earl of Gloucester, defeated and captured Stephen after a gallant struggle at Lincoln, 1141. The King was brought to Matilda at Gloucester and she herself was acknowledged by a Council held at Winchester as "Lady of England and Normandy." Like William the Conqueror, she preferred to approach London from the north, received a deputation of Londoners at St. Albans, advanced down Watling Street through Edgware to London, presumably using the switchway from the Hyde, up Colindeep Lane, through Hendon and Hampstead into the City. Stephen's wife collected troops in Kent, and the King granted a commune to London. But Matilda gave to Mandeville hereditary wardenship of the Tower of London. The citizens refused to accept this outrage, which would have placed them for ever under Geoffrey the Oppressor, the man without scruples, morals or religion.

And so when Stephen's Queen arrived in Southwark she found the Londoners already thoroughly tired of the Empress Matilda's methods, confiscations and demands for money, and they rose in arms for Stephen and his Queen. Matilda fled* with a few of her followers through Middlesex and galloped towards Oxford. Geoffrey de Mandeville changed sides once more, and the Queen entered London. Geoffrey showed his allegiance to Stephen by riding from the Tower to the episcopal Manor of Fulham to seize Sijillo, recently installed by Matilda as Bishop of London. Geoffrey is said to have insisted on a huge ransom from the Bishop, but whether it was paid or not Sijillo had reached the Empress before a month was up. The support given by Geoffrey enabled Stephen to escape from custody in exchange for Robert of Gloucester and regain the throne. He was crowned for the second time at Canterbury, and rewarded Geoffrey by granting him the shrievalty of London and Middlesex and Hertfordshire, as well as that of Essex. But loyalty meant nothing to him and, hearing a rumour of Stephen's death, he deserted once more

71

to Matilda. Stephen marched against his rival and besieged her in Oxford Castle, from which she managed to escape in white across the snow.

She had no hope of any further success, so she retired to the Continent and Geoffrey was arrested by the King. He was deprived of the Tower of London and other castles and his power seemed broken. But he was determined to make one more effort, raising, like Hereward the Wake, a new rebellion in the Fens. He fortified Ramsey Abbey and lived on plunder and cruelty. "He spared neither men, women or children, clerics or laymen. In the groans of the sufferers, in the shrieks of the tortured, men beheld the fulfilment of the words of St. John the Apostle : 'In those days men shall desire to die, and death shall flee from them.'" Stephen advanced against him at Burwell, near Fordham, in Cambridgeshire, and in the battle Geoffrey was mortally wounded by an arrow from one of the King's men in 1144.

The reign of Stephen was notoriously a bad reign, and greedy, treacherous tyrants like Geoffrey de Mandeville were largely responsible for it. We see feudalism and foreign domination at their very worst. William of Newburgh says there were "as many Kings—or rather tyrants—as there were lords of castles. And as each was anxious to excel, and could not bear, some a superior, others even an equal, they fought against each other with savage hatred. The fairest regions were devastated with rapine and fire, and in what had been once the most fertile of fatherlands, almost all the food was destroyed." The Saxon Chronicle sums up the character of such men as Geoffrey de Mandeville, who changed sides so often, when it records that these traitors "had done homage to the King, and sworn oaths, but had held no faith; they were all forsworn and forfeited their troth."

The *Victoria Counties History* suggests that as no feudal castles were built in Middlesex, owing to the unimportance of the lay tenures, the inhabitants were spared the worst evils, which is no doubt partly true. But Geoffrey held the Tower of London and had some castles in Essex, and the motte and bailey at South Mimms may well have been constructed at his order.

We must hope that the following extracts from the Saxon

Chronicle hardly apply to the inhabitants of Middlesex: "When the castles were made, they filled them with devils and evil men. Then took they those men that they imagined had any property, both by night and by day, peasant men and women, and put them in prison for their gold and silver, and tortured them with unutterable torture; for never were martyrs so tortured as they were. They hanged them up by the feet and smoked them with foul smoke; they hanged them by the thumbs or by the head, and hung fires on their feet; they put knotted strings about their heads, and writhed them so that it went to the brain. They put them in dungeons, where there were adders and snakes and toads, and killed them so. Many thousands they killed with hunger . . . and that lasted the nineteen winters which Stephen was King. . . . Thou shouldst never find a man sitting in a town or the land tilled. Then was corn dear, and flesh and cheese and butter; for there was none in the land; wretched men starved with hunger . . . never was more misery, and never heathens acted worse than them. . . . The earth bare no corn; you might as well have tilled the sea, for the land was all ruined by such deeds, and it was said openly that Christ and his saints were asleep."

When Geoffrey died he left by will the churches of Enfield, Edmonton, South Mimms and Northolt, with the hermitage of Hadley, to endow Walden Abbey, which he had founded in 1136. One imagines that he thought he could wipe out a lifetime of cruelty, treachery and crime by posthumous gifts to the Church, but his belated generosity could not restore life and happiness and prosperity to the many whom he and his like had brought down to ruin and to death.

The effect on Middlesex of his depredations and of the marching and counter-marching which his constant treachery made necessary is seen in the Danegeld returns recorded in the Pipe Rolls of Henry II. "Of the £85 0s. 6d. due from the County in Henry's second year, £10, or nearly one-eighth of the whole, comes under the heading *in wasto*." No wonder that the well-known chronicler from St. Albans Monastery tells us that the coming of Prince Henry, Matilda's son, seemed almost like that of a Messiah. ". . . The Knights will turn their swords into sickles, their lances into pruning-hooks; and from the camp to the ploughfield, from the tent to the workshop, the men, fatigued with long service, but breathing the common gladness, will return." And the historian adds his comment: "In these high hopes the people were scarcely disappointed."

The grant of the right of farming the County of Middlesex at a fixed sum of £300, which Henry I confirmed to the citizens of London, had already been given to Geoffrey de Mandeville. It seems probable that the practices of electing a sheriff and of farming the county were of old usage and may date from the reign of Edward the Confessor, a time which the citizens referred to as the time of their greatest freedom.

Gervase, an illegitimate son of Stephen, became Abbot of Westminster, and, besides his sub-infeudation in the Manor of Hendon, he also seized the Manor of Shepperton from the Abbey for his personal possession. When Henry, Matilda's son, was recognised as Stephen's heir, he rewarded Gilbert Basset, who had taken his side in the Civil War, by giving him the Manor of Uxbridge.

The woodland that still fortunately remains in part at least all along the border from Uxbridge to Enfield was of far greater extent in those far-off days. FitzStephen, in his early survey of London, which John Stow so effectively quotes, says that "beyond the suburbs of the City, which afford cornfields, pastures and delightful meadows, an immense forest extends itself, beautiful with woods and groves, and full of the layers and coverts of beasts and game—stags, bucks, boars and wild bulls."

R. S. R. Fitter suggests that these *tauri silvestres* were similar to those still preserved at Chillingham in Northumberland. Besides the wild life there were also brigands, and travellers used to gather into groups, especially when they had to leave the broad trunk roads and to advance along the lanes through the forests, shouting and blowing horns as a safeguard. Even before the Conquest Leofstan, Abbot of St. Albans, had cut through the woodland that separated him from the capital, smoothing the rough places, building bridges and levelling out the roads, especially Watling Street and the one we call A6.

Domesday estimates the extent of woodland by the number

of pigs that could be supported during autumn feeding or pannage. The woods also provided for fuel and building materials as well as for developing fresh land, called "assarting." It is significant that the present "Green Belt" area figures largely in Domesday for its pannage woods : Enfield (2,000 pigs), Harrow (2,000), Stanmore (1,600), Ruislip (1,500), Harefield (1,200), Kingsbury (1,200), Hendon (1,000), Hillingdon (1,000) and Harmondsworth (500). These account for more than half the total of swine recorded—12,000 out of 22,000. Two Middlesex manors have enough wood for hedging (*nemus ad sepes faciendas*); four have vineyards—Staines, Kempton, Colham and Harmondsworth; and FitzStephen reports "on the north side, pastures and a pleasant meadowland, through which flow river streams, where the turning wheels of mills are put in motion with a cheerful sound . . . and fat plains, that make crops luxuriant and fill their tillers' barns with Ceres' sheaves." He gives further praise to rustic Middlesex when he speaks of "goods proper to rustics, implements of husbandry, swine with long flanks, cows with full udders, oxen of bulk immense and woolly flocks. There stand the mares fit for plough, drag and cart; some big with foal, and others with their young colts closely following."

The same story of wild animals and brigands in the Middlesex woods is told by Matthew Paris for a rather different reason in his *Life of the Twelfth Abbot of St. Albans*. "The woods were of an almost impenetrable character, and so much infested by outlaws and beasts of prey that the numerous pilgrims who travelled along the Roman road for the purpose of devotion at the shrine of Albanus were exposed to very imminent danger."

In Norman and Plantagenet days Middlesex was a source of foodstuffs for London, and, as the walled city became more built over, it provided pleasure gardens, places for practising with the bow and arrow, and hunting grounds for the citizens. Quite early in London's history two great market-places were established in West Cheap for the King and Court and the monastery of St. Paul's, and in East Cheap for the burgesses. The East Cheap was largely built over by the close of the twelfth century, but West Cheap was divided

into precincts for the buying and selling of different articles—
Wood Street, Milk Street, Ironmonger Lane, Poultry,
Sopers Lane. To start with, some of the food and other stuffs
sold in these markets was brought from lands immediately
outside the city walls, but as building took place and population increased the supply of produce from these nearby areas
became inadequate, and corn was brought from Middlesex,
and through Middlesex on its way to London. The chief
roads by which food supplies came from the northern suburbs
were the one which runs through Edmonton and Tottenham,
and that from Barnet through Highgate. The corn that was
brought to London was ground by horse mills, and there
were supplies of bread from Middlesex and beyond to satisfy
the increasing population.

FitzStephen speaks of cornfields and pasture land, and
farther north there were in Middlesex the woods and forest
lands of St. John's Wood, Highgate and Hornsey, of
Hendon, whence came oak trees for finishing Westminster
Abbey, and, farther out, of Enfield Chase. In all of these
there were birds and beasts of the chase, which gave scope
for the sporting instincts of the Londoners. It is difficult to
be sure whether rules made for Londoners in these early
days applied equally to those who lived in Middlesex. In
1212 there was a proclamation made that everyone who
should build a house was to take care, "as he loved himself
and his," that he did not cover it with reeds, rushes, stubble
or straw, but only with tiles, shingles, board or lead.

Henry II was prepared to be friendly towards the Church,
and amongst other gifts he entrusted the Manor of Heston
to the monks of St. Valéry in Normandy, and granted to the
Abbot of St. Albans the privilege of holding a weekly market
at Chipping Barnet, which, though partly in Hertfordshire,
was sufficiently near to draw many Middlesex folk to its
markets and its fairs. Henry's friend and subsequent rival,
Thomas à Becket, stayed several times in Harrow, before
and after his exile. On his return from abroad Nigel de Sack-
ville, Rector of Harrow, and Robert de Broc, its Vicar,
maimed all of the horses carrying Becket's provisions to
Harrow. Excommunication followed, and this irritation to
the King's furious temper was one of the causes of Henry's

hasty words and Becket's consequent murder in the cathedral, so dramatically portrayed by T. S. Eliot. In the early years of Henry's reign we record the name of Nicholas Brakespear, whose name comes from a hamlet near Harefield, though he was born at King's Langley. Under the name of Hadrian IV he was the only Englishman in all the long history of the Papacy to become Pope.

KING JOHN AND MAGNA CARTA, AND MORE PLANTAGENETS

Staines is certainly one of the oldest towns in Middlesex, and tradition and constant discoveries of Roman remains seem to confirm its claim to be the Roman station *Ad Pontes*. It is sixteen and a half miles from Hyde Park Corner, and a Roman road runs from London through Staines to Silchester.

London stone was claimed by Stukeley as a Roman milestone, which is a possibility, but it was more probably the end of the City of London's jurisdiction over the River Thames, into which the Colne here flows in several branches. From Staines to the source is the Upper Thames; downstream to the mouth of the Medway at Yantlet Creek is the Lower Thames. In the forest which extended northwards to Hounslow Heath the citizens of London had free warren, and the Mayor of London was one of the river's Conservators. For about half a century now the Conservators have had control over the whole of the Thames from source to mouth, as well as over the whole watershed.

In Domesday the Abbot of Westminster is recorded as holding the Manor of Staines, and the Vicar of Staines was required to supply two large wax candles for the altar at Westminster on the eve of the Epiphany. Whether the Roman road from Londinium to Silchester crossed the Thames at Staines or not, the bridge certainly served to connect Porchester and Portsmouth, as well as Windsor, with the Metropolis. Several counties are close together here, and though Staines is in Middlesex, Runnymede is in Surrey, and Magna Carta Island is in the Thames between Berkshire and Buckinghamshire.

All kinds of legends have sprung up in the vicinity in connection with the great tradition of the granting of Magna

Carta. The actual sealing of the treaty between the Barons and King John has been described in prose by Hilaire Belloc in his *Eye Witness,* and in verse by Rudyard Kipling. An earlier poet, Akenside, invited all strangers to contemplate the scene with care :

> "This is the place
> Where England's ancient Barons, clad in arms
> And strong with conquest, from their tyrant King
> (Then rendered tame) did challenge and secure
> The charta of thy freedom."

The Barons had marched from the north to London and came as far towards Windsor as Staines. In spite of a legend which claims Duncroft House in Staines as King John's sleeping quarters the night before Magna Carta, it seems clear that the King rode from Windsor, and the Barons from Staines, and met somewhere just outside Middlesex. In the Great Charter of June 15, 1215, so admired and perhaps exaggerated in Stuart times by Lord Chief Justice Coke, the document is said to be given by the hand of the King "in the meadow which is called Runnymede, between Windsor and Staines."

The promise made by the King and contained in Section 40 of the Charter is vital : "To no man will we sell, to no man will we deny or delay right and justice." "The Great Charter was not an abstract statement of the principle of freedom; it was a businesslike loyal document, carefully prepared from a study of preceding charters by hard, resolute men," writes Dr. Kathleen Freeman in *Voices of Freedom*; and Professor Adams emphasises the "one principle that underlies and gives validity to all the Clauses—the principle that the King must keep the law."

The Knights of the Temple and of the Hospital, who came into being because of the age-long Crusades, which were so vital an element in the life of two centuries and more, and which accomplished so little, have links with Middlesex, but in a far smaller way than in London itself. To the Templars were given the Manor of Cranford, but it passed to the Hospitallers after the cruel and entirely unjustified persecution of the Knights of the Temple. Moor Hall, the old manor-house of Harefield, also belonged to the Hospital, and there is still preserved the Early English chapel, now used as a barn, with narrow lancet windows, the whole being built of flint and very thin bricks.

In the long reign of Henry III a good many churches were rebuilt or enlarged, and several in Middlesex have features dating from this period. The Manor of Acton was given by the King to St. Paul's Cathedral, and later in the reign Simon de Montfort is in arms at Isleworth, where the citizens of London destroyed the manor-house of Richard, Earl of Cornwall, the King's brother and the prospective Emperor of the West. He never attained that high dignity and he had to wait until 1947 before he was honoured with a full-length biography.

The fifth charter of Henry III, 1227, confirmed to the usual folk, with "the Knights and freeholders and to all the free tenants of the county of Middlesex, that all the Warren of Staines, with the appurtenances, be unwarrened and dis-forested for ever, so that all they aforesaid, and their heirs and successors may have all liberties and benefit of warren and forest, in the aforesaid warren, wherein they may till or plough all their lands, and cut all their woods, and dispose of the same at their will, without the view or contradiction of our warreners or foresters, and all their ministers, and within the which no warrener or forester, or justice of our forest shall or may in any wise meddle with their lands or woods; neither with their herbage or hunting or corn. Nor shall they, by any summons or distress, cause such free tenants to come before such justices of the forest in respect of their tenements situate within the warren; but they shall be free and quit of all exactions whatever in regard to forests."

Here is another grant by King Henry III : "Henry, by the grace of God, King of England, to the Archbishop of Canterbury, and to the bishops and abbots, earls and barons, justices and sheriffs, and to all his faithful subjects of England, French and English, greeting.

"Know ye that I have granted to my citizens of London, whole Middlesex to farm for three hundred pounds, upon accompt to them and their heirs; so that the said citizens shall place as sheriff whom they will of themselves. . . . And the citizens of London may have their chaces to hunt, as well and truly as their ancestors have done, that is to say, in Chiltre, and in Middlesex, and Surrey."

King John in 1199 had granted and confirmed to the citizens of London the Sheriffwicks of London and Middlesex, with all the customs and things to the sheriffwick belonging, within the city and without, by land and by water, and this important privilege was confirmed by Henry III in 1227. The city's privileges in Middlesex were confirmed in the next century, when by the fourth charter of Edward III, 1354, the Mayor's serjeants of London were entitled to carry maces of gold or silver everywhere in the said city, and in the suburbs of the same, and in the County of Middlesex and other places to the liberties of the said city appertaining.

Two years after Montfort's tragic end at Evesham the Earl of Gloucester rebelled and marched as far as Hounslow Heath, but the rising came to nothing. For some years Henry III had a small palace at Acton, and it was one of his favourite retreats. Edmund, Earl of Cornwall, King Edward's younger brother, had been given the empty title of King of Sicily by the Pope, in order to gain his support in the struggle that was beginning between Guelf and Ghibelline, the Papal party *versus* the friends of the Emperor. It was an empty honour, and of more real value was the Manor of Heston, which he received in 1300.

King Edward was called the Lion of Justice, and in certain respects he deserved the title; but he came up against privileges of nobles, clergy and Commons during his reign. Archbishop Winchelsey, who persuaded his suffragans to refuse taxes to the King without the Pope's consent, was living at Headstone Manor, near Harrow, at the time. He failed to win this victory, as the King promptly outlawed the clergy and compelled their surrender; but Winchelsey succeeded in uniting clergy and barons and extracting from King Edward the Confirmation of the Charters. This bound the King to keep the Great Charter and to take no general revenue without Parliamentary grant.

During the reigns of the first two Edwards the King's wardrobe became one of the chief financial and organising offices in the kingdom, and two men in succession, with important associations with Middlesex, had interesting connec-

tion therewith. These were Hugh de Cressingham and John de Drokensford, one from Norfolk, the other from Hampshire, who both held land either personally or as trustees in the Manor of Hendon. Cressingham was steward to Edward I's Queen, Eleanor of Castile, whose death in 1290 was such a sad loss to the King, who brought the body from the Midlands to Charing Cross, erecting a fair cross, a miracle of sculptor's and mason's work, on every spot where her beloved corpse had rested on its journey. Hodford, one of the submanors of Hendon, was given to the monks of Westminster to provide masses for the Queen's soul.

Cressingham now became a Justice in Eyre in the north of England, and he strained the King's legal rights to the utmost and incurred great unpopularity wherever he administered the law. His methods of administration both in England and on the Welsh border were high-handed and ruthless and were a warning of what was to follow in Scotland, where he was appointed Treasurer after Edward's victory at Dunbar and the removal of the Stone of Destiny to Westminster Abbey. Cressingham and his colleagues quickly exasperated the country beyond endurance and raised the antagonism of Robert Bruce and William Wallace. The country was soon in a blaze, and Wallace captured castle after castle, putting the garrisons to the sword. Cressingham had a great deal on his conscience, having infuriated the Scots by severity and rapacity, and having kept back money intended to repair the fortifications of Berwick. At Cambuskenneth he foolishly ordered the Percys to dismiss their troops so as to save money, but in the battle which followed he showed great courage. Wallace destroyed a bridge behind the English advance guard, and Cressingham, after grim fighting, was among the fallen. Such was the fury he had aroused that his dead body was flayed and his skin used for sword belts, saddles, girths and other trophies. The battle was on September 10, 1297, and the bad news of defeat travelled quickly, for on September 18 a writ was issued dealing with Cressingham's Hendon property. He held land of Richard le Rous by service of 21s. a year, and there was besides a grant of 249 acres in Hendon and 29 in Finchley, and he seems to have left no lawful relatives at all. It has been

"There was hardly a cloud to darken the agricultural outlook, unless it were the growing luxury and ostentation which
became a feature in the life of nearly all classes in the reign
of Edward III; while even this seemed to be justified by the
constant growth of commerce and the still more extraordinary
successes which attended our armies in the Great French
War."

And then came the Black Death, which seems to have
started in China, swept across the Middle East and the
Mediterranean, attacked Florence and led to Boccaccio's
Decameron, and arrived at a small seaport town in Dorset
on August 1, 1348. It was in London by November, and
refugees from the City and Westminster soon carried the
foul disease all over Middlesex.

It is not easy to assess the exact effect of the Black Death
upon the inhabitants of Middlesex, but the decline in population raised all sorts of problems. How big that decline was is
difficult to estimate, but the figures recently provided by G. G.
Coulton and A. E. Levett are generally accepted. Previously
haphazard guesses of contemporary writers were adopted
even when they were given under stress of anxiety and emotion produced by the ravages of the plague, and with the
remarkable inaccuracy which characterises many, if not most,
medieval estimates. Severe analysis of several episcopal
registers by G. G. Coulton shows that 44 per cent. of the
parochial clergy in the dioceses thus examined died of the
plague, but it is difficult to feel sure that this proportion can
be accepted for the whole country and for all classes. In this
connection it should be mentioned that the registers of institutions to benefices, which in other parts of the country have
proved so useful in estimating plague mortality, are missing
for the diocese of London from 1337 to 1361.

The one surviving court roll of the Manor of Stepney and
some court rolls of Teddington for the years immediately
following 1349 are a help; and the records of Hampstead
and Hendon in the Westminster Abbey muniments give some
indication of the death-roll. We may perhaps assume that in
Hampstead and in Hendon between a third and a half of the
population died, though in the latter manor its streams and
natural drainage, its hills and valleys, and its population

scattered in half a dozen hamlets, may have given it better health conditions than in the average manor. Simon de Burcheston, Abbot of Westminster, in vain took refuge with twenty-six of his monks in the manor-house at Hampstead. They evidently took with them the infection and all of them succumbed to it. We may imagine that the new parsonage at Hendon, with its wealth of rooms (as we learn from an inventory of 1540), was filled with refugees from the Abbey, but we have no details as to their fate. There are no exact figures as to the ravages of the plague in Hendon, but the disappearance of certain families and the rapid changes of officials at the time are possible indications of the mortality caused by the plague.

The court rolls of Stepney (no longer in modern Middlesex) give a record of appalling mortality. Here is the grim story of one family which lost the mother, daughter and two sons in December, 1348; a third son in February, 1349; later in the year three more of the family; and so the holdings passed on to heirs bearing a different name. Evidently the whole family perished, and this example was probably not an isolated case. Three ale-testers died during the plague, which killed off in six months 121 folk and left 105 tenements vacant.

The manorial accounts of Teddington are actually missing for the plague year, but in 1350 there are some suggestive figures showing the annual profits of the manor to be roughly two guineas as compared with nearly £14 ten years before. It was only natural that heavy mortality should produce acute disorganisation, and a contemporary record declares that the tenants of the St. Albans Manor of Barnet in Middlesex (presumably Friern Barnet) tampered with the manor rolls "when hardly any reeves or cellarers survived, and certainly could not care for such transitory and mortal things."

Scarcity of labour naturally produced increases in wages, as is clearly seen from statistics existing for Teddington. In 1335-6 the yearly wages for ploughmen were 6s., for carters and herdsmen 4s. 6d., and these had remained the same for sixty years. The year after the Black Death these wages had risen to 11s. Threshing of wheat had risen from 2½d. to 4d. a quarter, and barley from 1½d. to 3d. Efforts were made to reduce wages where possible, but never to the pre-plague level, and in Middlesex many leases of land were granted to villein tenants at money rentals.

The episcopal registers of John de Drokensford, the Hendon landowner who was Bishop of Bath and Wells, suggest that in normal times the parochial clergy were often ineffective. In many parishes there was no one qualified "to celebrate Mass, to rehearse the Marriage service or to administer the last rites to a dying man." During the plague permission was sometimes given to confess to a layman or even to a woman, and the sacraments could be administered by a deacon. "The calamity," writes G. G. Coulton, "did as much to break down the old medieval parish as the medieval manor; the divine right of the priest and the divine right of the landlord were equally shaken."

It is impossible to say whether Hendon was a typical medieval manor, but there was no great apathy on the part of the clergy then. Records of rectors and vicars exist from the twelfth century; the parsonage was a country seat for the rector or abbot; while the priest, mentioned in Domesday, handed on his virgate adjoining the existing vicarage undiminished for about eight centuries and a half to his successors, who seem to have been regularly resident in the parish.

The Statutes of Labourers were a definite consequence of the Black Death and were the outcome of an ordinance published in June, 1349, by the Council, seeing that it was not politic or even possible to summon on Parliament. Villein tenants and others were resisting the reimposition of obsolete services and were taking toll of scarcity of labour to demand better conditions. The ordinance required all unemployed folk under sixty to accept jobs, an interesting early example of the direction of labour, and the wages for them and for all others were to be what had been usual from 1343-47. Black marketing on the part of employers in offering higher wages was forbidden, and food prices were not to be unduly increased by the retailers. It seems to have taken two years before Parliament could meet and pass the Statute of Labourers, whose administration must have been at least a contributory cause of the Peasants' Revolt. In February, 1351, the statute declared that unoccupied folk of the employed classes must work, that their rate of pay must be regulated and so also the price of food, and that refusal to work for the scheduled wage was an offence. The punishment was a fine, but ten years later it was increased to imprisonment and branding. Vagabondage and begging were regarded as crimes save for the impotent poor.

The plague, or Black Death, as Mrs. Markham first taught us to call it, was certainly one of the causes of the Peasants' Revolt, but by no means the only one. It was so new and therefore so baffling and deadly that its crashing into a world that was already changing produced a severe moral and economic crisis, and might possibly have brought about "that impulse of independent research which we call the Renaissance, and that religious revolution closely akin to it which we call the Reformation." Views on this very important topic will always tend to be controversial, and the late Professor A. E. Levett, who had studied the manorial system of the fourteenth century in very great detail, thought that "the Black Death did not in any strictly economic sense cause the Peasants' Revolt or the breakdown of villeinage, but it gave birth, in many cases, to a smouldering feeling of discontent, an articulate desire for change, which found its outlet in the rising of 1381."

The Black Death left a big legacy of despondency and discontent behind it, and the French wars of Edward III, waged with no real justification, left both countries impoverished. The Black Prince interfered in Spain and showed a criminally callous attitude towards the population of Limoges, but he might have made a good King of England had he survived. But his premature death left the crown to his young son, whose promise of courage and ability was ruined by his goading uncles. The genius of Wycliffe and Chaucer had little immediate fruit, and the Lancastrian kings had all the disadvantages of being usurpers.

THE PEASANTS' REVOLT

England was now hurrying towards a disaster which might have been overwhelming, instead of moving slowly but surely to an almost Utopian condition of adjusted prosperity. The two methods of farming the demesne had been either by customary and unpaid labour of villein tenants, who in return had holdings for little or nothing, or by practically free paid labourers, who gave the lord rent for any holdings they might farm. Sheep-farming, which required so many fewer labourers, was becoming profitable with the increasing Flemish demand for wool, and in some manors the demesnes were being persistently leased to semi-free tenants who developed into that class of sturdy yeomen farmers who for so long formed the backbone of the country. The introduction of Flemish weavers into this country founded a home manufacture of draperies, especially in the eastern counties and the Cotswolds, and soon used up all the fleeces that the English farmer could supply.

Manors in Middlesex belonging to the Chapter of St. Paul's were sometimes farmed out singly to the various canons, but the system of cultivating under-bailiffs was not thereby given up. The tenants had the lawyers, if not the law, against them, and it was easy for the landlord to produce documentary evidence to support his claims, while the tenant had nothing in writing to help him. No wonder that when the revolt broke out one of the first things that the peasants did was to destroy all the manorial records on which they could lay hands.

In the first year of Richard II Parliament passed an Act annulling all claims to freedom based on the evidence of Domesday Book. "If such a venerable record was not respected, it was not likely that any others that the villeins could produce would be." The Act concludes by promising to the lords of the manor that they "shall have letters Patent under the Great Seal, as many and such as they shall need, if they the same require." This was tampering with the scales with a vengeance, and it was not likely that the villeins would tamely submit. The followers of John Wycliffe, the wandering friars, and John Ball, the Socialist Kentish priest, all leaned towards a somewhat revolutionary outlook and showed signs of establishing "agricultural unions and other formidable combinations against their employers."

In the Act above mentioned they are said to "menace the Ministers of their Lords both of life and member, and, which more is, did gather themselves together in Great Routs and did agree by such Confederacy that everyone should aid other to resist their Lords with strong Hand."

It needed only a spark to set the whole country ablaze with something akin to revolution, and the aspirations of the workers had been fanned into flame by John Ball's famous distich :

"When Adam delved and Eve span,
Who was then the gentleman?"

The taxation needed to pay for the growing disaster of the French wars and, above all, the iniquitous ungraduated poll-tax supplied the match which was needed.

The poll-tax in 1377 had been a groat, or 4d., on all of both sexes over the age of fourteen, except beggars. Two years later a further poll-tax was imposed, varying from a groat for the ordinary labourer, who showed "great grudging and many a bitter curse," up to £6 13s. 4d. on royal dukes like John of Gaunt. But with crass folly and amazing thoughtlessness the Government in 1380 laid a new tax of three groats on all sorts and conditions over the age of fifteen. This was thought half a century ago to be the equivalent of 15s. per head. It would be safe to call it £2 today. The resentment of the poor was shown in the song of an anonymous victim of the tax :

"To seek silver to the King, I my seed sold :
Wherefore my land lieth fallow and learneth to sleep.
Since they fetched my fair cattle in my fold :
When I think of my old wealth, well nigh I weep.
Thus breedeth many beggars bold, and there wakeneth
in the world dismay and woe, for as good is death
Anon as so for to toil."

The poll-tax was perhaps the signal rather than the motive cause of the rising, whose chief features were its almost complete range throughout England, the remarkable concerted organisation of the poor, the panic of the well-to-do, and the precocious wisdom and courage of the young King.

The sum demanded was far beyond the resources of the average villager, and in a poor village where there were no moneyed residents who might be generous enough to pay more than their share every tenant had to pay the full 1s.

In the Manor of Hendon there had been for at least sixty years a large proportion of fairly well-to-do folk, as is proved by the record of forty-five freeholders of the Black Survey, several of whom were important City merchants and one or two Knights of the Shire. In such a community the assessment might be adjusted. An easy remedy for the most iniquitous poll-tax was provided by a system of false returns, which happened in almost every village in England. The numbers over fifteen years of age would naturally be less than those over fourteen, comparing the two years of taxation, but in most parts of the country they were down by a third. In Middlesex the drop was from 11,243 to 9,937, only 12 per cent. down. Perhaps Middlesex was unusually honest, or proximity to London made falsification more difficult. In most parts of the country the villagers "had suppressed the existence of their unmarried female dependents . . . in a wholesale fashion," and most villages showed an incredible predominance of males.

There is an incomplete poll-tax return for Middlesex which Dr. S. J. Madge has discovered in the Record Office and printed in volume iv, part iv (new series) of the *London and Middlesex Archæological Society's Transactions*.

The suddenness of the revolt surprised everyone, and showed that there had been much sympathetic discussion of grievances and possible planning of concerted action. Many groups of villagers headed by their parish priests marched to London after burning local manor rolls. Those of the Middlesex manors belonging to the Abbey would perhaps have been kept at Westminster, where they would be safe from destruction, but, apart from isolated years, the manor rolls do not start consecutively till far later, so perhaps there was some destruction during the "hurling time." But the extents and the annual farm accounts were, in their way, just as important and informative as to the duties of tenants, and would give the monks of Westminster details as to the amount of rent and service which they could claim.

The revolt was short and sharp, and in the single month of June it seemed as if the "old order of things was about to crash down in red ruin, and that complete anarchy would supervene." The poll-tax, which precipitated this terrific conflagration, was the occasion of the outburst, but only the smallest of its causes. Irritation at the gradual loss of French possessions, the growing arrogance and the incompetence and possible treachery of the King's Ministers, the deplorable ending of the reign of Edward III and the natural inability of his young grandson to control his uncles, all made life difficult and disappointing, but would not have been sufficient to produce the revolt.

The revolt began in Kent, where Wat Tyler, under great provocation, murdered a tax-collector, marched to Canterbury to release John Ball from prison, and then hastened up old Watling Street at the head of a rabble which had reached 100,000 men by the time he reached London, slaying lawyers and destroying archives on the way.

The peasants in many Middlesex manors rose in support, and there was serious trouble at Barnet on the edge of two counties, and at Harrow, where Simon of Sudbury, the lord of the manor, was Archbishop of Canterbury and the King's adviser. While young Richard was attempting to pacify the peasants at Mile End, with promises of the abolition of serfdom and feudal services and a general rental of 4d. per acre instead, Wat Tyler and some followers seized the Archbishop in the Tower and beheaded him on a log of wood outside with eight strokes of the axe. Simon had studied canon law in Paris and had been an ambassador and Bishop of London before becoming Archbishop. His unpopularity was partly due to his disapproval of pilgrimages, a medieval way of taking a summer holiday. It must have been a clumsy headsman who took so many strokes to sever the unhappy prelate's neck. The Treasurer, Sir Robert Hale, suffered the same fate, and both their heads were mounted on pikes and carried round the City, the Archbishop's mitre being fastened on to his skull.

The Abbot of St. Alban's Mill at Oxhey was burnt by the peasants, who broke open his prison, tore up the pavement of his parlour, rifled his preserves and extorted charters of freedom. Their behaviour may well have encouraged the men of the adjacent manors of Harrow and Pinner to do damage in Pinner Park, which belonged to the Archbishop. In Froissart's *Chronicles* we read: "They slewe in the cytie

91

a riche marchaunt called Richarde Lyon, to whom before that time Watte Tyler had done servyce in France; and one tyme this Richarde Lyon had beaten hym whyl he was his varlet, the which Watte Tyler then remembered." There is reason to think that this Richard was the ancestor of John Lyon, who founded Harrow School about two centuries later.

The men of Essex marched to Mile End, where they were joined by the men of Middlesex, led perhaps by "Jack Straw," a Hampstead man, perhaps, and by the men of Hertfordshire, who had marched through Middlesex to their rendezvous at Highbury.

The dislike of the Hospitallers, which led to the complete destruction of the Priory of St. John's at Clerkenwell, may well have extended to Hendon, where they had a considerable holding near Temple Fortune and a larger one in the adjacent manor of Hampstead. This would seem to be suggested in the Anominal Chronicle of St. Mary's, York, discovered by G. M. Trevelyan and translated by Sir Charles Oman, where it speaks of the mob damaging "all the rented houses and tenements of the Hospital of St. John."

William Morris puts into the mouth of John Ball in his famous *The Dream of John Ball* : "What shall ye lack when ye lack masters? Ye shall not lack for the fields ye have tilled, nor the houses ye have built, nor the cloth ye have woven. Then shall no man mow the grass for another while his own kine lack cow-meat, and he that soweth shall reap and the reaper shall eat in fellowship the harvest he has won. And he that buildeth a house shall dwell in it with those that he biddeth of his free will. And the tithe barn shall garner the wheat for all men to eat of when the seasons are untoward and the rain drift hideth the sheaves in August. Faithfully and merrily shall all men keep the holidays of the church in peace of body and joy of heart. And man shall help man, and the saints in heaven shall be glad, because men no more fear each other, and fellowship shall be established in heaven and on earth."

Middlesex can hardly be said to have taken an organised part in the Peasants' Revolt, but in several manors there were a number of villein tenants excluded from the general amnesty.

André Reville in *Le Soulevement des Travailleurs d'Angleterre en 1381* (1898) gives a list of 287 exempted from pardon in the whole country; not a very great number, perhaps, considering the seriousness of the outbreak. Most of them were set free after a time of imprisonment and a fine, and amongst the few who suffered death were Wat Tyler and John Ball. Of this total of 287, 23 came from Middlesex, hailing from 15 different parishes, but 2 only were convicted and outlawed, 11 were acquitted in 1386-7, and the other 10 seem to have been let off.

In the Middlesex escheator's account occur Thomas Bedford, of Holborn, whose small household utensils were seized to the value of 4s., and Peter Walshe, of Chiswick, who held a cottage and 1⅓ acres but had no goods or chattels. John Stackpole, "of Middlesex," was tried by the sheriffs in November, 1382, and was beheaded as one of the insurgents in the Corpus Christi rising, and was a colleague of Wat Tyler's at Blackheath. Stackpole's goods and chattels were valued at 18s., amongst them a red and green cloth gown worth 8s. and *"unius cithere et gyterne, precium* 16d." Others were accused of various misdemeanours : one was guilty of helping to burn St. John's, Clerkenwell, of stealing a cup and slaying seven Flemings there.

John Norman, of Hammersmith, John Smart and John Nene, of Lilleston, and John Brewer, of Hoxton, were guilty but were not caught. Richard Taylor, of Harrow, Robert Powys, of Hounslow, and John Carpenter, of Greenford, were excluded from the amnesty, but were afterwards pardoned. Two inhabitants of Hendon were exempted from the amnesty, John Knot de Childeshill and John in the Hale, also associated with Ruislip, an indication of the breaking up of the manorial system, with one tenant having holdings in two manors not adjacent. These topographical surnames, "in the Hale" and "Childeshill," both occur in the Black Survey, so that these two rebels were evidently members of families which had considerable freeholdings. The well-known Thomas Faringdon, a London leader of revolt, was "captus et prisonæ deliberatus quo tempore idem Thomas fuit circa prostationem tenementi Johannis Knott in Steyning Lane." If these two John Knotts are one and the same, it suggests a definite association between the business life of London and the rural economy of Hendon.

The disturbances already mentioned in Pinner and Harrow and perhaps Oxhey as well warranted a royal enquiry. Others excluded from the amnesty came from Hounslow, Greenford, Twickenham, Fulham, Chelsea and Heston. At the last-named place three tenants, William Weyland, John Walter and Richard Umfray, attacked Nicholas Est, an old enemy, with swords and staves, with which they wounded him, and then imprisoned him for a day and a night until he ransomed himself for 40s. This was on June 5, 1381, and two years later they got off on the plea that they had only acted under the orders of Jack Straw and Wat Tyler, a plea that was supported by four witnesses.

It was hardly to be expected that no trouble would occur at Harmondsworth, with its local priory, acting for the Abbot of St. Katherine at Rouen. There the manor rolls seem to have been burned, seeing that the early custumals which have come down to our time are copies later in the reign of Richard II. Walter Carne, Richard Gode, Robert Freke, junior, William Pompe and John Pellyng had their lands confiscated, but they seem to have been pardoned quite soon, as the Prior had good reason for wanting them back owing to the shortage of labour. In Harmondsworth the discontent still continued, and some failed to come and superintend the reapers, some came late to a bedrip, and William Boyland, like several of his predecessors, refused to be reeve and was fined 10 marks for his non-compliance. An interesting case there was that of Roger Cook in 1399, who was summoned to cart wheat. He first refused, and then flung down two cartloads outside the Grange, where they were damaged by other carts being drawn in. He was summoned before the Manor Court and his fellow-tenants found that he "had done all things well."

Thorold Rogers and Stubbs were not perhaps correct when they claimed that the Peasants' Revolt meant the extinction of villeinage and the substitution of money payments for labour. This had happened in some Middlesex manors already, and possibly the various intelligent attempts made to solve economic problems may account for the small number in Hendon implicated in the revolt. In most Middlesex manors there was a decline in, and in some a complete disappearance of, servile tenures, and by the time of the Wars of the Roses there were few manors in the county where copyholders and rent-paying yeomen were not in the majority. The "hurling time" in which many tenants in Middlesex took part, and for which so few were punished, must have done something to bring to an end the age-long custom of villeinage.

AN EARLY RENAISSANCE

The fourteenth century held out hopes of widespread progress, and it almost looked in England as if two or three big movements were on foot. Chaucer's *Canterbury Tales* and Wycliffe's translation of the Bible gave the country a written native language of its own. Wycliffe's preaching began to throw doubt on some of the cherished doctrines of the Church; his poor preachers spread ideas of Socialism and brotherhood, and John Ball in particular asked why the poor should be denied all the advantages enjoyed by the rich. The Black Death had upset much of medieval economy and threatened to be the end of feudalism, while the Peasants' Revolt almost succeeded in changing the face of history. But something happened deliberately or unconsciously, and the Renaissance and the Reformation and possible revolution were postponed. The French wars and the domestic Wars of the Roses made people forget the early reformers, and Wycliffe's Lollards almost disappeared, save in the remoter villages of the Chilterns. Nothing ever happens without previous warning, and the Turks had been hammering at the door of Europe since the Crusading times for centuries before, in 1453, they crashed in and captured Constantinople. Some scholars had seen the impending danger and had retired into Italy, but a wave of emigration now ensued and refugees with Greek and Latin classics crowded into Italy, bringing that knowledge which was to influence Western Europe so widely. The English Renaissance came slowly, but Humphrey, Duke of Gloucester, whom we associate with Sion House at Isleworth, and John Tiptoft, Earl of Worcester, a savage fighter in the Wars of the Roses, Lord of the Manor of Shepperton, were both of them book-lovers and collectors of manuscripts. Duke

Humphrey's library found its way to Oxford, where it was the basis on which Bodley's later collections were established. Sir Owen Edwards, one of the great historians at Oxford in the 1890s, used to sum up the Renaissance and the Reformation in a shrewd analysis. The growth of nationality and of national languages brought a demand that the Bible should be in the vernacular which all could understand, and not only in Latin, which many priests were unable to read. When Wycliffe translated the Bible into English, men began to discover that God was no respecter of persons, but that rich and poor were alike in His eyes. The printing press published this idea broadcast, and the improvements in cannon showed that knight and peasant fell equally easily before the force of gunpowder. To sum it up briefly, the Bible said that all men were equal; gunpowder proved it, and printing told the world so.

Besides the courage and wisdom displayed by Richard at Mile End, Smithfield and at Clerkenwell, there were other occasions when his character and patience were harshly tested. It is not easy to follow the claims for divine right of kings put forward at this time, seeing that Edward II had been murdered and soon Richard was to share his fate. Richard's uncles never showed any recognition of the theory, and their extraordinarily selfish behaviour did an immense amount of harm to the condition of England.

The worst of all was Thomas of Woodstock, Duke of Gloucester, the Black Prince's youngest brother. In the year 1388 Richard made a progress round the country, staying with his friends, and towards the end of the year he received from the five judges at Nottingham a decision declaring that the Regency was illegal. In November Richard marched through Middlesex into London to prevent any renewal of the Regency and to punish those who started it. The news reached Gloucester on November 12, and he and the Earl of Warwick at once marched to London with a force under arms. When they reached Hornsey Park, near Highgate, and established a camp there, they were joined by the Earl of Arundel. Richard hoped that the Londoners would support him against his uncle, but the Earl of Northumberland and the Londoners would not "get their heads broken for de

Knightsland Farm, Barnet.
Wall painting

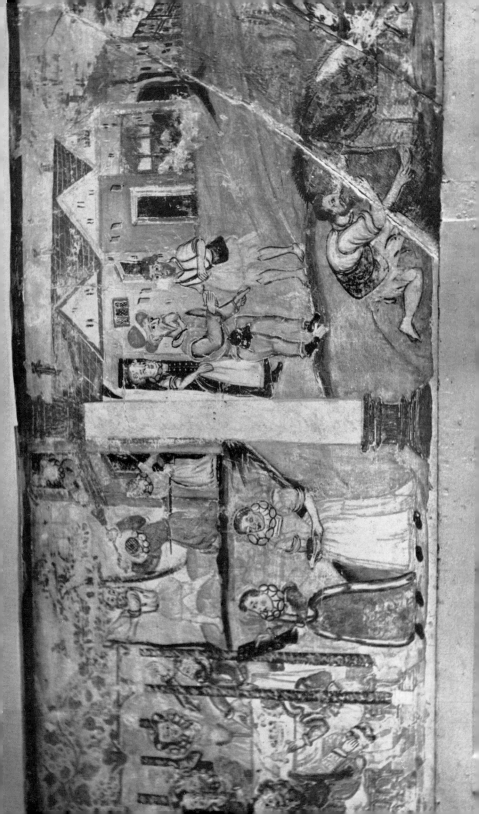

Veer's sake." Richard's own followers sympathised with Gloucester's hostility towards aliens. The King forbade the citizens to help Gloucester and his friends in any way, but the rebels marched with 4,000 men to Hackney, claimed that their sole idea was to rescue the King from traitors, and were joined by the Earls of Derby and Nottingham (the famous rivals in Shakespeare's play). On November 14, 1388, these five barons accused five of Richard's friends of treason.

In Richard's unfortunate reign a prominent supporter of the King against his uncles was Nicholas Brembre, citizen and grocer of London, who in 1371 had purchased from the Archbishop of Canterbury 166 acres of land at Roxeth, and had also acquired the Manor of Northolt. He was knighted for his support of the King at Smithfield, became Alderman and Mayor of the City, but fell a victim to the supporters of the Lords Appellant under Gaunt and Gloucester, the King's uncles, and was indicted ostensibly for beheading twenty-two prisoners in Newgate without a trial. Brembre's own trial was characteristic of the merciless or wonderful Parliament of 1388, which sentenced him and others of the King's friends to death. The acts of this Parliament "stamp with infamy the men who, whether their political crimes were or were not salutary to the constitution, disgraced their cause by excessive and vindictive cruelty."

When Richard resigned his throne and was deposed, Henry, son of old John of Gaunt, time-honoured Lancaster, succeeded him, and his Queen was Mary, heiress of the de Bohun family, who had succeeded the Mandevilles as owner of the Manor of Enfield. This was the beginning of Enfield Chase, the royal hunting ground, and it included all the land from Potters Bar almost to Waltham Cross and southwards to Barnet and Hadley Green and Southgate.

DISCONTENT AND CIVIL WARS

Two signs of unrest, religious and political, showed themselves in the reigns of the two later Lancastrians. Sir John Oldcastle was the focus of a good deal of disaffection at the condition of the Church and the usurpation by the Henrys. A plot was said to have been planned in 1414 for a mass gather-

Almshouses at Friern Barnet

ing of Lollards and of City prentices in St. Giles's Fields, where Oldcastle was expected to lead the rebellion and to depose the King and to destroy St. Paul's and the Abbey of Westminster. Whatever plot there may have been was betrayed to the King, and he returned from the Christmas festivities at Eltham to Westminster and proceeded to St. Giles's Fields with quite a small force. But it was large enough to produce a panic, and some of the rebels were killed, some captured, while the rest fled northwards into the open country of Middlesex.

The political unrest was shown in Henry VI's reign by the rebellion of Jack Cade, who claimed to be a Mortimer and therefore cousin of the Duke of York, who had a far better claim to the throne than Henry VI. Cade got most of his support from the counties south of the Thames, and it is doubtful if a single Middlesex man took part in the rebellion. Hostility to the Lancastrian usurpers, social distress among the peasantry, and a growing demand from many quarters that the lands of the bishops and greater abbots should be confiscated, as well as the disasters in France, were the causes of unrest and disaffection which eventually flared up in the Wars of the Roses.

The foundation of colleges on a large scale at both universities about this time is another sign of the times, and one at least of these was definitely intended for lay use and not to "provide livelihoods for a companie of bussing monks." On the contrary, Lincoln College, which was afterwards to be the home of John Wesley, was founded by Richard Fleming, Bishop of Lincoln, the prelate who ordered Wycliffe's body to be exhumed and burnt and the ashes thrown into the River Swift at Lutterworth.

ALL SOULS' COLLEGE AND SOME ALIEN PRIORIES

There is a memorial cross in the cemetery at Norwood, which was a precinct and chapelry of Hayes, recently erected to Archbishop Chichele, who died in 1443, with this inscription : "*Tenet tellus corpora sub cruce; Tenet Christus animas in luce.*" The manor belonged to Canterbury as far back as

830 and Chichele attached to it 4,000 acres from the parish of Hayes. Chichele certainly supported Henry V's unjustified war against France, perhaps in order to divert attention from the Church's great wealth. When he came near his end he regretted the loss of human life in the campaign at Agincourt, and in 1438 he founded a college at Oxford, whose inmates were to pray for all souls of those fallen in the French wars. He was a Wykehamist, both of Winchester and of New College, and some of the estates with which he endowed his new foundation were from suppressed alien priories, some situated in Middlesex.

Among the estates bequeathed to All Souls' College were the Manor of Edgware, on the east side of Watling Street and on the south side of the Elstree-Barnet Road, and several parcels of land in Hendon. These were to form the occasion of an interesting and amusing suit in 1587, in which Queen Elizabeth and several of her Court were to be closely concerned.

The Benedictine priory at Harmondsworth, which belonged to the Abbey of Holy Trinity at Rouen, was taken over by Edward III, and fifty years later the manor and advowson were given to William of Wykeham for Winchester College. The famous Gothic Barn, 151 feet long and 38 feet wide, is all that is left of the monastic buildings, and a projecting wing at the north end was long since removed to Heathrow, and blown down in a storm.

Bentley Priory, the nineteenth-century seat of Queen Adelaide, and the twentieth-century home of Fighter Command and the Royal Observer Corps, is said to have been founded in 1170 by Ranulf Glanvil, a well-known lawyer. Matthew Paris records in his *Chronicle* that a prior was suffocated in 1248 by a badly built hayrick falling on him. The priory was dedicated to St. Mary Magdalene, and the monks of Canterbury supplied a priest to say a weekly Mass. In 1512 it was learned that no priest had been sent for some years, and thirty years later Bentley Priory was given to Archbishop Cranmer and subsequently exchanged with the King for land at Wimbledon.

At Harefield there is a thirteenth-century flint chapel belonging to the Knights of St. John, and close by was the

Manor of Moorhall, a camera also belonging to the Hospitallers and only recently destroyed by fire. The Priory of the Holy Trinity at Tottenham was dissolved under the first Act dealing with smaller monasteries.

It has often been emphasised that Middlesex, unlike all other counties, had very few baronial castles or estates before the Dissolution of the Monasteries. For that reason the county, for its own part, had but little interest in the rival claims of Red and White Rose, though marching and counter-marching to and from London was bound to bring armed forces from both sides along the great Middlesex highways. The first of the fourteen battles of the Wars of the Roses took place at St. Albans on May 22, 1455, and, although only some six score were slain, Richard of York was victor and marched through Middlesex to London to act as Protector of the sick King. Five years later, after fleeing to the Continent, York and his friends came through London and Middlesex and marched with troops to defeat the Lancastrians at North-ampton. Then York returned through Middlesex to London, where he claimed the crown, but only a few weeks later the Yorkists were crushed at Wakefield and Richard was killed. With a devastating army of plunderers Queen Margaret advanced to St. Albans, won a decisive victory there, and pressed on through Middlesex once more. But her unruly troops and the open hostility of the Londoners deterred her from advancing towards the walls of the City.

While the situation was in the balance Warwick the King-maker and Edward, Earl of March, York's son, pushed on from the west, entered the county by the Bath Road, and reached London just in time, saving their cause by a few hours only.

After Edward had been acclaimed in 1461 at Clerkenwell and crowned at Westminster, Henry VI, who had been captured in Lancashire, was once more escorted through Middlesex to London. Warwick met him at Islington, struck off his gilt spurs, and took him in bonds to the Tower, where he was imprisoned for ten years.

Edward IV found the King-maker a difficult servant and refused to accept him as master. Warwick rebelled because he felt himself thwarted by the man he had befriended,

Edward escaped to the Continent, and Henry VI was restored in name alone. After a short exile the King returned and marched south to London, where he had always been popular, followed closely by Warwick. It was on Maunday Thursday that Edward marched through Middlesex into London, and he disappointed Warwick by observing only Good Friday and not the Easter festival. On the Saturday, having made every effort to equip his army well, he marched back all through Middlesex to meet Warwick. Hall describes his efforts in his *Chronicle* : "Harness, weapons, horses, all engines, instruments meet for the war, he neither forgot nor slackly furnished. What shall I say more? He determined clearly to spend all his riches, yea all that he could imagine upon the chance of the battle; firmly believing that this conflict should knit up all his labour and bring him to quietness." And to a great extent he was right, as the resulting battle fixed him firmly on the throne. While Edward was bringing his troops from London, Warwick left his headquarters at St. Albans and marched along through London Colney and South Mimms to take up a strong position on Gladesmore Heath, just north of Barnet. From there he might be able to defeat Edward's troops as they deployed north from the village, but the King was not an inexperienced soldier and he just sent his advance guard to drive back Warwick's outposts from the village while he kept his main body to the south. After darkness intervened Edward moved his troops on to the sloping ground running down from the Barnet-Hatfield Road, where Warwick's left was deployed. His manœuvre was noticed, and Warwick opened fire on the advancing troops, but they had already passed him and were protected by the slopes from the guns. Warwick's troops were drawn up along the main road under the slight protection of the hedge. Edward was careful not to reveal his exact position by any retaliatory gunfire, and so he was able before dawn on Easter Day to order his troops to advance in mist. Warwick's army was tired after its long marches, and it was unlucky for them Edward was able to get his troops quite near to them because of the fog. Edward "took not his ground so even in front as he should have done if he might better have seen his enemy," writes a contemporary chronicler. Warwick's artillery was firing all night, but the flash betrayed their position, and Edward, who was so close that the shots passed over the troops, kept them quiet.

The battle was singularly like some of the contests in the Civil War, because each side gained a strong advantage on one wing. When the Yorkists advanced in the thickish fog, without any sound of trumpet, Richard of Gloucester, on the right, though only eighteen, overlapped and held the Lancastrian left-wing Midlanders led by Warwick and Exeter. On Warwick's right wing, Montague and Oxford, with men from the north and east, drove back Hastings on the Yorkists' left through Barnet, where they spread the news that Edward had lost the day. But owing to the fog the rest of the Yorkists were quite unaware of the event, and "no man was in anything discouraged, because, saving a few that stood nearest to them, no man wist of the rout; also the other party, by the same flight and chase, were never the greatlier encouraged."

Gloucester was soon able on the Yorkist right to back the Duke of Exeter and his Lancastrian troops to such an extent that the whole two armies had now swivelled round and the Yorkists were facing south, while the Lancastrians defended Barnet. In the centre the King was fighting with coolness and courage, but the battle was still unsettled. Mist still hung thick on the ground and made co-operation extremely difficult. Montague on the Lancastrian right wing had kept some of his troops in hand and with them went to help Warwick, who was outflanked by Gloucester. However, Edward was beating Somerset in the centre; he "beat and bare down all that stood in his way, and then turned to ravage first on that hand, and then on the other hand, and in length so beat and bare them down that nothing might stand in the sight of him and of the well-assured fellowship that attended truly upon him."

Warwick was not aware that his left had driven the enemy off the field, and so when Oxford returned to the battle with his men wearing the radiant star of the de Veres, with streams, his troops, who had missed their way and came up behind Warwick, were thought to be those of the King, whose badge was a sun with streams. Warwick's men attacked them, and Oxford, amazed at this apparent treachery, raised a cry of "Treason" and left the field northwards precipitantly. Somerset also suspected treason, and so when the King realised the situation and charged home he won a complete and perhaps a rather unexpected victory. Exeter and Montague were killed, Oxford and Somerset had fled, and only Warwick was left. There are divergent stories as to his end. Some say that he was killed while trying to escape on horseback, others that he fought on foot much handicapped by his armour and eventually fell by a tree near Wrotham Wood.

Warwick's body and that of his brother Montague were carried along the Great North Road into London and exposed as a clear indication of Edward's victory. The King had serious losses on his side, including Lord Berners, Lord Say and Lord Cromwell, while few of the leaders of the Lancastrian side escaped wounds. Exeter was badly wounded and only Oxford got away unscathed. When the battle was won the King took some refreshment in Barnet and rode with his victorious troops through Middlesex into London.

Sir Charles Oman makes a comment on the Battle of Barnet, where "both Edward IV and Warwick were well provided with guns; a desultory cannonade was kept up during the night that preceded the battle, but in the mist of the next morning neither General found his artillery of any use." A. L. Smith sums up the situation when he says : "On Easter Day . . . the battle in the mist, with its strange incidents, decided for ever, by the fall of the King-maker and his brother Montague, the long strife of the two Roses, and closed the stormy history of the medieval baronage in a typical confusion of bloodshed, treachery and desperate courage."

Sir Jeremy Sambrook erected the obelisk close to Wrotham Park on Hadley Green, and the elm was still there in 1909 to mark the spot where Warwick fell. Considering the comparatively short life of the average elm tree, about 200 years, it seems highly improbable that it was the identical tree where Warwick fell 436 years before. An interesting relic of the battle is a desperate note from Warwick to Henry Vernon begging for reinforcements, now in the possession of the Duke of Rutland : "Henry, I pray you ffayle me not now, as ever I may do for you." Verney made no answer to Warwick's pathetic plea.

There is in the Library at Ghent a miniature in the manuscript report. Two armies in mail armour are engaged in fierce combat. Edward's banner has a gold rose on a red field, Warwick has no banner at all. Edward has a golden coronet round his helmet, a horse with red lined with blue and decorated with fleurs-de-lis. He has his lance in rest and has pierced his enemy, probably Warwick. The whole thing is purely fictitious but spirited.

CHAPTER XII

TUDORS AND MIDDLESEX

DISSOLUTION OF THE MONASTERIES—
HANWORTH—THE BELLAMYS OF UXENDON—
SIR WALTER RALEIGH—CAMDEN, GERARD
AND NORDEN

FEW centuries are more outstanding than the sixteenth, and few events have been more challenged than the final Dissolution of the Monasteries.

There were not a great many conventual institutions to dissolve in Middlesex, but large areas of land which had belonged to Westminster Abbey, St. Paul's Cathedral and St. Alban's Abbey changed hands at what has justly been called "the Great Pillage." Westminster, where so many documents dealing with Middlesex Manor are stored, had only recently been enlarged by the addition of Henry VII's chapel on the site of the Lady Chapel and the White Rose Tavern. To support this new shrine the King procured from the Pope permission to suppress two religious houses, and in the next reign Wolsey was permitted to suppress twenty-six smaller monasteries in 1523 and devote the proceeds to education, especially to Cardinal College at Oxford. These suppressions, coupled with the loss of alien priories under Henry V, were a dangerous precedent, of which full advantage was taken by Bluff King Hal and his adviser, Thomas Cromwell.

The land on which Hampton Court now stands belonged to the Knights of St. John until 1514, when Wolsey obtained from the Prior a lease for ninety-nine years. The palace which he built passed to the King in 1529, and two years later he took over the Manors of Hanworth, Kempton, Fulham and Teddington for his hunt.

As is only natural, all Henry VIII's six wives had some association with Middlesex. Catherine of Aragon, like Wolsey, stopped once at the Abbot of Westminster's lodgings in Hendon, and before and after her divorce she lived at Hampton and at Twickenham. In her happy days Anne

Boleyn lived at Hampton Court with Henry, and Jane Seymour's little son was born there, and the mother died there. Both Anne of Cleves and Catherine Howard spent some time at Hampton, and the heroine of Clifford Bax's play, *The Rose without a Thorn,* was imprisoned at Syon House before her removal to the Tower. Syon is still supposed to be haunted by her screaming ghost. The first few months of Katherine Parr's life as Queen were also spent at Hampton Court. As a widow and after her second marriage she lived at Hanworth.

One of the most distressing events in this country in the early fifteenth century was the passing of the statute *De Hæretico Comburendo,* which Henry IV caused to be enacted in repayment for clerical support and to destroy the influence of John Wycliffe and of the Lollards. Hardly anyone today justifies such brutal treatment for differences in religious beliefs, but in Middlesex at intervals for nearly a century and a half there were instances of the burning of so-called heretics. During the reign of Queen Mary Uxbridge saw three Protestants burned at the stake by order of Bishop Bonner. When John Denley was singing a hymn at the stake a certain John Story, a servant of Bonner's, threw a burning faggot in his face to stop his singing. When he was questioned in Parliament about his brutal act, he justified his action by saying : "I threw a faggot in the face of an earwig at the stake at Uxbridge, and set a bushel of thorns at his feet, and see nothing to be ashamed of or sorry for." When Elizabeth came to the throne, many plots were hatched in England against her, and the plotters suffered death at Tyburn for their treason. John Story was convicted of conspiring against the Queen, and paid the penalty for his plot to bring in a foreign monarch and depose Elizabeth.

SYON HOUSE

A singularly unspoiled piece of Middlesex today is just opposite Kew Gardens, where Syon Park and Osterley still preserve some of the medieval beauty of the Thames side. A footpath through Syon and a road through Osterley add much to the possibilities of enjoyment, coupled with the reminder that Simon de Montfort and other refractory barons pitched their tents near here against Henry III, and Fairfax had his headquarters here in the struggle against Charles I. Syon Monastery was founded by Henry V in 1415, and is referred to perhaps by Shakespeare, where the King says :

> "I have built
> Two chantries, where the sad and solemn priests
> Sing still for Richard's soul."

It was an unusual foundation, being one for nuns and monks, most of the latter being busied with at least nine services a day. It was a rich foundation, and only seven exceeded it in wealth at the Dissolution. The order of St. Bridget was founded in Sweden, and through royal intermarriage was introduced into England. Because of this fact the first nuns and monks at Syon Monastery were Swedes. After the Dissolution the nuns retired to Belgium, returned under Queen Mary, and then after many wanderings settled at Lisbon, where they remained for three centuries from 1594. When a Duke of Northumberland called on the order by the Tagus in Portugal they proudly showed him the keys which they had treasured for all that long period, in the hope of returning some day to their old home in England. But they were quietly told that the locks of Syon House had long since been altered!

Henry VIII had a special reason for attacking Syon, as it had been implicated in the treason of Elizabeth Barton, the "Holy Maid of Kent." But the inmates were generously pensioned, and £700 a year was found for seventy-seven displaced persons. Henry's swollen body rested at Syon for a night on its way to Windsor, and there is a legend that the corpse burst and bled and that dogs licked the blood of Henry as earlier dogs had licked the blood of Ahab.

Dukes of Somerset and Northumberland held Syon in Tudor times. A succession of disasters pursued the Seymours and the Dudleys and the Percys, one being executed for supporting Lady Jane Grey, and several getting into trouble for plotting against Queen Elizabeth and James I. Into a Syon House much restored by Inigo Jones came the children of Charles I, and from here they went to St. James's Palace to take a last farewell before his execution in Whitehall. Since then the property has belonged to the Dukes of Northumberland, and the famous "lion" was brought from Charing Cross when Northumberland House was pulled down.

In early days Syon was famous for embroidery and Church decoration, the Syon cope being world-famous. The school of religious needlework produced shields and devices, birds and figures in gold, silver and colours. The collection was taken to Lisbon, but is now to be seen in South Kensington Museum.

HANWORTH

Henry VIII found the area near Hanworth attractive and made his hunting-box there "his chief place for pleasure, having the Thames in prospect, and a delicious champaign about it, as well as two good parks on each side, the one called Kempton, the other Hanworth Park, where he had the diversion at all times of the buck or hare." Thus William Camden, as translated from the Latin; and the estate was left by Henry VIII to Katherine Parr, with whom he had spent happy months there before his death. She married, as her third or fourth husband, Sir Thomas Seymour, Lord High Admiral and brother to Protector Somerset. The Princess Elizabeth lived here for some months with her step-mother, and a good deal of scandal was talked about the relations between the Princess and Seymour. Gossip was free that the Admiral really wanted to marry Elizabeth, and the slander spread easily, and perhaps there was some justification for it. Professor J. E. Neale thinks that the games which they played were innocent fooling, but Hilaire Belloc puts the worst interpretation upon the story. Elizabeth's governess, Kate Ashley, was no help, and when Catherine was about to have a child the Princess prudently left Hanworth Park and resumed her own household at Cheshunt.

On leaving Hanworth, Elizabeth wrote most discreetly: "Although I could not be plentiful in giving thanks for the manifold kindnesses received at your Highness's hands at my departure, yet I am something to be borne withal, for truly I was replete with sorrow to depart from your Highness. . . . And albeit I answered little, I weighed it more deeper when you said you would warn me of all evils that you should hear of me. For if your Grace had not a good opinion of me, you would not have offered friendship to me that way, that all men judge the contrary. But what may I more say, than thank God for providing such friends to me." This was just after Whitsuntide when Elizabeth left Hanworth Park, where in the following September Catherine Parr died in childbed, and the way may have seemed open for Seymour to renew his suit with the Princess. When it seemed that Seymour was planning a *coup d'état* the Council was forced to take action, and Seymour was sent to the Tower.

Elizabeth was by now at Hatfield, and every effort was made to "wean her from her obstinate silence." In reply to a gentle letter from Protector Somerset trying to discover what had really happened at Hanworth the Princess wrote : "There goeth rumours abroad which be greatly both against my honour and honesty . . . that I am in the Tower and with child by the Lord Admiral. My Lord, these are shameful slanders. . . ." When the news of Seymour's execution reached Elizabeth and the Council perhaps hoped that she might give her secret away, if she had one, she made this cool, historic comment : "There has died a man with plenty of wit and little judgment." In spite of the experiences at Hanworth, which must have burned themselves into her memory, she revisited the place several times after she became Queen. After the execution of Protector Somerset the Manor of Hanworth was granted to his widow, who entertained Queen Elizabeth there in 1578 and again in 1600, when in spite of her age she hunted.

The two Killigrews leased the property, which in 1627 went to Sir Francis Cottington, later Baron Cottington of Hanworth. He was proud of his estate, where he entertained Queen Henrietta Maria, and thus describes it : "There begins to grow a brick wall about all the gardens at Hanworth, which, though it be a large extent, yet will it be too little for the multitude of pheasants, partridges, and wild fowl that are to be bred in it. There is a certain lay room made under the new building with a fountain in it, and other rare devices, and the open gallery is painted by the hand of a second Titian. Dainty walks are made abroad, insomuch that the old porter with the long beard is like to have a good revenue by admitting strangers that will come to see these rarities. It will be good entertainment to see the amazement of the barbarous northern folk, who have scarce arrived to see a well cut hedge, when the fame of these rarities shall draw them thither; . . . My wife is the principal contriver of all this machine, who, with her clothes tucked up, and a staff in her hand, marches from place to place like an Amazon commanding an army."

When Charles I was executed, Hanworth was given to Bradshaw, who presided over the court which sentenced the King. After many changes it came into possession of the Duke of St. Albans (Baron Vere of Hanworth), who, according to Horace Walpole, "cut down all the brave old trees at Hanworth, and consequently reduced his park to what it issued from—Hounslow Heath."

The house was burned down in 1797 and another one built on higher ground, where Henry Perkins collected a magnificent library. The stables of the old house survived and have today been turned into battlemented flats. Through the grounds still flows the King's River, leading from the Colne at Longford to provide water for the grounds at Hampton Court. It was cordially disliked by the villagers, who damaged the bridge and tried to fill up the canal. Cromwell had it cleaned out after he went to live at Hampton Court. The park, like so many other open areas in Middlesex these days, was conspicuously air-minded throughout the second World War.

THE BELLAMYS OF UXENDON

The problems which Romanists had to face in England after the Pope's action in 1570 in deposing Queen Elizabeth are grimly illustrated by the slight connection of the Bellamy family of Uxendon, near Harrow, with the last of the plots to put Mary, Queen of Scots, on the English throne by Father Ballard and Antony Babington. William Camden gives a graphic contemporary account of the plot, but two modern historians, Father Potter and Alan Gordon Smith, are inclined to dismiss it as a silly boyish trick. The destruction of the monasteries, the official banning of the Mass, and the heavy taxation of Catholic households had gradually aroused strong underground hostility to the régime of the Protestants under Burleigh; but it must be remembered, on the other hand, that Mary's reign of five years had been filled with ruthless and relentless persecution of the most brutal kind.

It was in 1586 that "Captain Foscue," alias Father Ballard, landed in England and gathered round him a group of friends, including Babington, who planned to seize Elizabeth and enforce toleration for Catholics. But these milder aims soon gave place to something more drastic—foreign invasion, the release of the Scottish queen, and "the dispatch of the usurping competitor." Opinions varied as to the lengths to which they might proceed, and some of the discussions took place "in a blue house on the right hand of the upper part of Holborne, nigh the stile going to the field there," an interesting comment on the small extent of Elizabethan London. Letters were passing to and fro, but all were examined and their contents reported to Walsingham. An enterprising brewer introduced some of them inside beer barrels and made a handsome rake-off from all concerned.

Babington was not a born leader, but he accepted the idea of killing the Queen, sent incriminating letters promising foreign invasion, and Mary wrote approving of the murder of Elizabeth. When Walsingham had all the facts in his possession he struck, but all the conspirators, save Ballard, fled, like Sir John Oldcastle a century and more earlier, to St. John's Wood, which then afforded good cover to robbers and outlaws. Camden tells us that Babington and his friends cut their hair short, and he even "besmeared and soiled the natural beauty of his face with green walnut shells." After a week of semi-starvation in the woods, "being constrained by famine," they fled to Uxendon, a farmhouse near Harrow, on the Kenton brook which joins the Brent at Wembley Park.

The Bellamys had remained Catholics, but like many other families they were married and buried in their local parish church. They had Babington and his friends for a week in a hay barn, but Walsingham knew of their whereabouts and brought them to trial in London. The plot caused great alarm, and all recusants were suspect, especially those living in the Middlesex areas. When Burleigh was driving up to London from Theobalds along the Tottenham-Edmonton road he noted in the villages groups of men standing about. At Enfield he enquired the reason, and was told that they were looking

111

for the conspirators, and that the only mark of identification was that one of the suspects had a hooked nose. Babington and his friends were executed in Lincoln's Inn Fields with the usual barbarities inflicted on all those convicted of treason, and the laws were stiffened up and more rigorously enforced. S. R. Gardener, fairest of all historians, calls the repression abominable, and so it undoubtedly was.

The Bellamys of Uxendon suffered severely for having supplied shelter and food to the fugitives. Mrs. Bellamy was committed to the Fleet Prison and thence to the Tower, where she died, "worn out with the rigours of her filthy prison." Her younger son, Jerome, was executed for having taken a basket of fruit to the fugitives after understanding that they had conspired the death of the Queen's majesty. Robert, who had no share in the story, fled to Holland, was captured and brought back to the Tower, where he "destroyed himself in prison." Bartholomew was imprisoned, and it is recorded that "Mr. Bellamy, Jun., hanged himself in the Tower." But W. W. Druitt, historian of Harrow, Pinner and Stanmore, gives good reason for thinking that they both died on the rack.

The surviving son, Richard Bellamy, sheltered several well-known Catholic priests—Fathers Campion, Parsons, Weston and Wingfield; and actually one of the most prominent of all was Dr. Richard Bristow, who lived at Uxendon as Cousin Springe, a poor relation of the family; died there and was buried by the Rev. Brian Crofts, Protestant Vicar of Harrow. Further trouble came on the family when Richard Bellamy's daughter Anne, only seventeen years old, was imprisoned for recusancy. She was persuaded by Richard Topcliffe, an important agent of the Queen's, to betray Father Southwell, and her father, who had sheltered him in one of his priests' holes, under the stairs, was imprisoned for ten years. His wife died in prison, and he died in poverty in Belgium. This seems to have been the last of the Bellamy family as far as Uxendon is concerned. Richard Page, an uncle of Richard Bellamy, acquired the land, and it was his family's fortunes some centuries later that gave rise to the well-known myth about the Page millions, only finally abandoned early this century. When Mrs. Brightwen, the well-known naturalist, author of *Wild Nature Won by Kindness*,

Wrotham Park, Barnet

died in 1906 and her property, The Grove, Stanmore, was sold to Sir Ernest Cassel, the customary claim to the Page estate, with its alleged millions lying in Chancery, was made, but was then and, we may hope, finally abandoned.

Uxendon Farm went on for a long time after the Babington Plot brought it into notoriety. Its land was gradually encroached upon, and the last vestiges were destroyed in 1933, when the new branch of the Metropolitan Line from Wembley Park to Stanmore cut through the site and the gardens.

HENDON WOODS

Queen Elizabeth knew Hendon well, as she had stayed three times with Sir Edward Herbert at Hendon Place, the old country house of the Abbots of Westminster. During her visits in 1566, 1571 and 1576 she can hardly have failed to notice some All Souls' College property just opposite Hendon Place, Holders Hill Woods, part of about 150 acres scattered about the manor, in addition to almost the whole of Edgware, on the east side of Watling Street. It may be stretching coincidence too far to suggest that it was her local observation that induced the Queen in 1587 to ask for a lease of the College's Middlesex woods to Lady Jane Stafford, widow.

This lease, to her dear and well-beloved friend, the Queen had no doubts "but ye will accomplish this our so reasonable request without any delay or other excuse or difficultie as we look for at your hands." Robert Hovenden, Warden of the College, made all kinds of excuse in Latin, pointed out how essential the woods were to them as a mainstay in case of disaster, and very politely but firmly declined to grant the lease. Archbishop Whitgift wrote advising tact; Lord Hunsdon, the Queen's first cousin, was peremptory; Lady Jane Stafford sent a letter, ill-written and ill-spelt and ill-composed.

The Warden and his friends rode up to London to see what could be done, spending a good deal of money on the way, including 7s. 10d. for three suppers and breakfasts at Colnbrook, and 6s. 6d. for horse meal there, on the way into London, and 22d. for one supper and breakfast at Uxbridge on the way back, the only items expended in Middlesex. Sir Walter Raughly (*sic*) wrote in a haughty, threatening manner

Gateway at Dyrham Park,
Barnet

to the Warden complaining of his "undutifull refusall of her highnes request."

It was unfortunate for the College that Hovenden had let the woods previously to his younger brother, and Lady Jane Stafford wrote a long and spirited letter which the Warden called "a cunning but untrue and slanderous answer." She accused the fellows of being "rather monkes in a rich Abbey than students in a poore College." Burghly now took a hand and advised the College to submit, but they found a wise friend in Sir Francis Walsingham. A further journey to London followed, and we read of "supper at Hounslow, 7d. Breakfast, bedding and horse meat at Hondslow [sic] 4s. 6d. and 6d. to six soldiers in the way out of London." There seem to have been three delegates on this journey. In March, 1588, the College wrote to complain of the "manie troblesome jornies," which had cost them in all £100. Walsingham continued to befriend them and advised Lady Jane Stafford to abandon her claim on this "poore house of learning."

We are now in March of the Armada year, and the Queen and her Ministers had more weighty plans to consider. When the Spanish threats had disappeared the All Souls' Woods in Edgware and Hendon seem to have been forgotten at Court. But Hovenden, the Warden (1571-1614), thought it wise to employ Thomas Langton to prepare five or six maps of the College property—another reason for his well-earned memorial, which states in Latin that he presided over this home of the Muses for forty-three years with great sagacity and prudence.

Land between the Town Hall and Tube Station at Hendon still belongs to the College, as does also the farm on Brockley Hill, where recent excavations of Roman pottery at Sulloniacæ have been made, and where one of the most superb views of woodland near London can still be enjoyed.

SIR WALTER RALEIGH

Each man is entitled to have his own heroes of history, and one of mine is definitely Sir Walter Raleigh, a man of Devon. He has several convenient associations with Middlesex, which allow him to figure in our long list of county celebrities. He is said, with reasonable authority, to have lived at Chase Side, Enfield, and Queen Elizabeth gave to him the Friary estate at Friern Barnet, now a public park. Raleigh sold it to Francis Bacon, who is associated with the county by his fatal experiment in preserving a chicken by cold storage near Highgate. Raleigh is mentioned elsewhere in his connection with the Hendon Wood part of the property of All Souls' College at Oxford, and his trial for alleged complicity in Lord Cobham's plot to put Arabella Stuart on the throne took place at Staines in 1603 in the old Market House, replaced in the nineteenth century by the present Town Hall. There was a particularly virulent outbreak of plague in London at the time, and so Coke's ferocious attack on Raleigh took place at Staines. It is not at all likely that Sir Walter was guilty of anything more than some indiscreet talk with Lord Cobham as to the relative claims of James Stuart and Arabella Stuart to the English crown. Queen Elizabeth herself had often spoken of Arabella as her successor, so that Raleigh's offence does not seem very serious. However, Coke's unfeeling harshness and arrogance secured Raleigh's condemnation to death. The sentence was not carried through, but Raleigh remained a prisoner in the Tower for twelve years with his wife as his constant companion, and while there he wrote the first part of his *History of the World*.

His story of an incident in the yard outside his prison so completely disagreed with the story as told by one of its participants that he threw the second volume, still in manuscript, into the fire and thus destroyed it. If he could not give an accurate account of what he had himself witnessed, what use to write history of times past?

His effort to discover a profitable gold-mine for King James in Guiana led to the death of his dearly loved son, a scuffle with the Spaniards and a sad return home. He was condemned on his old charge, and was executed in the Tower—butchered to make a Spanish holiday!

"Sixty-six years of danger, trouble and injustice had not shaken his poise, nor deprived him of his flamboyant sense of the dramatic." His courage and good humour on the scaffold rivalled that of Sir Thomas More. "What matter how the head lie, so the heart be right?" was his reply to the query as to which way he wished to face for his execution.

Bacon, soon to come to grief himself, drew up a pamphlet embodying *The King's Reasons for his Proceedings against Sir Walter Raleigh,* but the general public contrasted his heroic, dynamic courage and the romance of his voyages of discovery and his fighting against the Spaniards with the neurotic, vacillating monarch who was prepared to sacrifice the last of the old Elizabethans to please the Spanish monarch whose daughter he hoped that baby Charles would one day marry.

Raleigh's *History of the World* is a folio comparable in shape, size and interest with the first folio of Shakespeare, and nothing like so expensive. I bought a beautiful example in almost perfect condition in St. Martin's Lane before the first World War for 5s., and Oliver Cromwell's advice to his son to read the book for the many lessons it had to teach is equally sound today. It was a favourite study of my old Lincoln friend, Edward Thomas, Eastaway, the poet, who died so gallantly in France in the first World War. Here are two excerpts, almost too well known:

"Liberty is the proper inheritance of the subject, which is also a kingdom unto him, which makes him fight with an armed heart against the conqueror, who hath no other device painted on his ensign than the picture of slavery."

"If further reason be required of the continuance of this boundless ambition in mortal men than a desire of fame, we may say that the kings and princes of the world have always laid before them the actions, not the ends, of those great ones, they being transported with the glory of the one, and never minding the misery of the other, till it seized upon them. They request the advice of God while they hope to live, but when death cometh they believe what it tells them. Death without speaking a word persuades what God with his promises and threats cannot, though the one hateth and destroyeth man, whereas the other made and loveth him. . . . Death alone can make man know himself, show the proud and insolent that he is but abject, and can make him hate his forepassed happiness; the rich man he proves a naked beggar, which hath interest in nothing but the gravel that fills his mouth; and, when he holds his glass before the eyes of the most beautiful, they see and acknowledge their own deformity and rottenness. O eloquent, just and mighty death, whom none could advise, thou hast persuaded; what none hath presumed, thou hast done; and whom all the world hath flattered, thou hast cast out of the world and despised : thou hast drawn together all the extravagant greatness, all the pride, cruelty and ambition of man, and covered all over with two narrow words : *Hic jacet.*"

The famous story of the surrender of Sir Richard Grenville's *Revenge,* on which much of Tennyson's poem was based, we owe to Raleigh's *Report of the Truth of the fight about the Isles of Azores this last Summer betwixt the* Revenge, *one of her Majesty's ships, and an Armada of the King of Spain.*

He was executed on October 29, 1618, to King James's everlasting shame, and on the previous night he wrote his own memorable and matchless epitaph :

> "Even such is time, which takes in trust
> Our youth, our joys, and all we have
> And pays us nought but age and dust,
> Which in the dark and silent grave
> When we have wandered all our ways,
> Shuts up the story of our days !
> And from which grave, and earth, and dust,
> The Lord shall raise me up, I trust."

WILLIAM CAMDEN AND GERARD

Two Elizabethans who sing the praises of Middlesex are William Camden in his *Britannia* and John Gerard in his generous folio of 1,400 pages, the *Herball.* Camden commends the county because "the air is exceeding healthful, and the soil fertile and streets everywhere stately, and no part of it but affords a great many remarkables." And of the Thames he writes in verse :

> "Such fields, such woods, such stately piles appear,
> Such gardens grace the earth, such towers the air,
> That Thames with Roman Tiber may compare."

He describes a journey along the river bank from Staines and Runnymede, past Coway Stakes, where he places Cæsar's crossing; speaks of Harrow, the highest hill in this county, as he most inaccurately states; and Heston, where the wheat for the royal bread is obtained; Hampton Court, built by Wolsey "purely out of ostentation"; Thistleworth, where the palace of Richard, King of the Romans, was built by the Londoners; Syon House (so called from the holy mount of that name), built by Henry V after he had driven out the alien monks; and last to Brentford, where Edmund Ironside did force the Danes to a disorderly flight.

John Gerard, writing in 1597, culls news about plants in Lord Burleigh's garden in the Strand and his estate at Theobalds, just out of Middlesex; and also in Gerard's own house, with two acres of garden, just east of Somerset House abutting on the Thames, and northwards by Highgate and Hampstead Woods. Gerard was justly famous for his "singular and approved art, skill and industry in planting, nursing and preserving plants, herbs, flowers and fruit of all kinds." In the inner belt of suburban Middlesex he records wallflowers, campanulas, Canterbury and Coventry bells, golden rod, sweet william, mint, scabious, mullein, cowslips, marigold, periwinkle, saffron, musk roses—picked at random from his *Herball*. He found in various Middlesex gardens crane's-bill, bachelor's button, lupins, woodbine, dettany, honeysuckle, privet, syringa; but complains that neither he nor his friends find it easy to grow apricots, peaches or apples, because "the poore will breake down our hedge."

From the City Wall to Hampstead was only four miles, and most of the intervening ground was almost entirely open country. This provided ideal spots for Gerard's botanical rambles, in which he found wild cow wheat growing on the heath among juniper bushes, while orchids and cotton grass were to be seen "upon bogs and such-like moorish places . . . at the further end of Hampstead Heath in a valley upon the right hand neare a small cottage as ye go from London to Hendon." Golden rod is found in Hampstead Wood near a village called Kentish Town, as well as tutsan or parke leaves, yellow pimpernel, starwort, cotton weed, "in the dark woods of Hampstead." The Archangel nettle he found "under the hedge on the left hand as you go from the village of Hampstead," and butcher's broome, spleenwort and waterfun "at

the further end of Hampsteade Heath at the bottom of a
hill"—Golders Green, in fact. Kidney vetch grew on the
heath "right against the Beacon upon the right hand from
London neare upon a gravell-pit," and Gerard's comment on
furze and broom includes the remark that such plants grow
best "upon drie mountains which are hungrie and barren as
upon Hampstead Heath."

Gerard generally gives exact topographical details of his
botanical researches in Hampstead, cypress flourishing in the
Manor of Belsize, at that time belonging to "Master Warde,
one of the Clarkes of Her Majestie's Privy Council." Betonie
with white flowers flourished in the same garden, while
willow was discovered "neare to a bogge or grounds at the
further end of Hampstead Heath, upon the declining of the
hill, in the ditch that incloseth a small cottage there."

Whortle-berries, buckhorn plantain, foxstone orchid,
broad-leafed hyssop, a moss called Little Golde Locks
Sarnewort, white mountain crowfoot, tway blade or herbe
bisoile, satyrin royale, lily of the valley, wild mercurie and
devil's bit were also Hampstead plants, and some of them
Gerard mentions as likely to be found "upon the same Heath
towards London neare unto the head of springs that were
digged for water to be conveied to London, 1590, attempted
by that careful citizen, Sir John Hart, Knight, Lord Maior
of the Citie of London; at which time myselfe was in his
Lordship's Company and viewing for myself the same goodly
springs." He also has a record of "Adder's Toong . . . in
a near medowe the preaching Spittle . . . and in the
Mantles by London" (now Pentonville), while horse-radish
grows wild "at a small village neare London, named
Hogsden."

To vary the direction somewhat, we read that Gerard
found "Figgewoort . . . in greatest abundance in a woode
as you go from London to Hornsey," and sarnwort "in a
woode adjoining to Islington within the halfe a mile from
the farther end of the towne." Mullein he discovered "in the
hiewaies about Hiegate," while the "Wilde Clarie or Oculus
Christi groweth wild in divers barren places . . . especially
in the fields of Holburne near unto Gray's Inne."

Of earth or kipper nut he writes : "There is a field adjoin-

ing to Hiegate on the right side of the middle of the village
covered over with the same; and likewise in the next fielde
unto the conduit heade by Marebone, near the way that
leadeth to Pangridge." Whortle-berries are found on Hampstead Heath and in Finchley Wood near Highgate, service
tree and black-alder tree in Islington, and the woods beyond
leading to Hornsey village.

JOHN NORDEN

John Norden, a rival as a topographer to William Camden
in Elizabeth's reign, planned a geographical history of
the whole country in his *Speculum Britanniæ*. He succeeded
in writing a description, with a contemporary map, of Middlesex, the county in which he lived at Hendon House, but
he never succeeded in his bigger scheme. From his "pore
house in Hendone," where he notes that Sir John Fortescue
has leased Sir William Herbert's manor-house, he writes a
very convincing account of our county.

"Myddlesex is a small shire, in length not twentie myles,
in circuite (as it were by the ring) not about [*sic* above] 70
myles, yet for the fertilitie thereof, it may compare with any
other shire; for the soyle is excellent, fat and fertile and full
of profite : it yieldeth corne and graine, not onlie in aboundance, but most excellente good wheate, especiallie about
Heston, which place may be called *Granarium tritici regalis,*
for the singularitie of the corne. The vain of this especiall
corne seemeth to extend from *Heston* to *Harrow* on the Hill,
betweene which, as in the mid way, is Perivale, more truely
Purevale. In which vale is also *Northold, Southold, Norcote,
Greeneford, Hayes,* etc. And it seemeth to extend to Pynner,
though with some alteration of the soile. It may be noted also
how nature has exalted *Harrow* on the hill, which seemeth
to make ostentation of its situation in the *Purevale,* from
whence, towardes the time of harvest, a man may beholde
the fields round about, so sweetly to address themselves to
the siccle and sith, with such comfortable aboundance of all
kind of graine, that the husbandman, which waiteth for the
fruits of his labours, cannot but clap his hands for joy, to see
this vale, so to laugh and sing.

"Yet doth not this so fruitefull soyle yeeld comfort, to the
120

way-fairing man in the wintertime by reason of the claiesh nature of soyle; which after it hath tasted the Autumn showers, waxeth both dyrtie and deepe; But unto the countrie swaine it is as a sweete and pleasant garden, in regard to his hope of future profite, for :

> "The deepe, and dirtie loathsome soyle
> Yields golden gaine, to painfull toyle."

"The industrious and painefull husbandman will refuse a pallace, to droyle in these golden puddles.

"Towardes the time of Harvest, a man may behold the fields round about, so sweetle to address themselves to the siccle, and sith, with such comfortable aboundance of all kinds of grain, that the husbandman, which waiteth for the fruits of his labours, cannot but clap his hands for joy.

"This shire is plentifullie stored, and as it seemeth beautified with manie faire and comely buildinges, especiallie of the Merchants of LONDON, who have planted their houses of recreation not in the meanest places, which also they have cunningly contrived, curiously beautified . . . invironed with orchards of sundrie delicate fruites, gardens with delectable walks, arbers, allees, and great varietie of pleasing dainties."

CHAPTER XIII

MIDDLESEX UNDER THE STUARTS

CRIME IN JACOBEAN MIDDLESEX—
THE CIVIL WAR—LATER STUARTS

THE records of the ancient county of Middlesex were in 1890 handed over to the keeping of the *Custos Rotulorum,* and an important calendar in two volumes from them for the years 1612-16 has been edited by Colonel William le Hardy. They give a graphic picture from the Sessions Records of certain aspects of life in the county. The stocks were a very much used and a very painful method of punishment, as one who has experimented with them can testify. Offenders were often decorated with a paper cap indicating their offence. Richard Darry, of Hillingdon, and Nathaniel Ford, of Uxbridge, were put in the stocks on market day at Uxbridge for poaching fish at night. Ann Rowe was condemned to the stocks at Harefield for saying that her mistress had ordered her to steal a turkey. John Denchfield, of Little Stanmore, brewer, and William Cobbe, of Edgware, butcher, were ordered not to dress, utter or sell any kind of flesh meat during Lent. John Hyll, of Harrow, labourer, seems to have stolen four "hoggerell" sheep and three ewes, each worth 4s., from Rowland Hall at Staines, but he was not caught.

A rather more complicated case occurred in 1612, when John Tookey, of Cranford, mealman, was convicted of stealing sheep, each worth 3s. 4d., a calf worth 12s., and two bushels of wheat, each worth 4s. The prosecutors were Barnaby and John Courte, alias Chinkadager, of Bedfont and Cranford, and some of the wheat had been stolen from Twickenham. The accused was found guilty of petty larceny and, as he had no goods, he was sentenced to be whipped.

Thomas Oath, of Hendon, yeoman, for stealing eight ewe sheep, each worth 6d., belonging to Thomas Marsh, of a well-known Hendon family, is found guilty, seeks the Book, reads and is branded.

Some idea of the small extent of built-up area in 1613 is

shown by a list of badgers, kidders and drovers who were licensed at a sessions to exercise their functions in the various isolated parishes. Thirty places are specified, most with one or two persons on duty, but Enfield has 30, South Mimms 9, Harrow 8, Hadley 7, Harmondsworth 6, Edgware and Heston 5 each, Stanmore and Pinner 4 each, and Hendon 3. Sentences of branding were given against men from Burston-next-West Brentford for stealing four hogs worth 10s., and against others living at Willesden, but not natives, for stealing a ewe sheep worth 8s. and five wether sheep, each worth 10s. They admitted the crime, pleaded "benefit of clergy," were able to read the Book, and so had one thumb branded "T" to show that they had escaped Tyburn.

It is suggested that the Edward VI grammar schools must have spread the ability to read, for during a twelvemonth, though sixty-nine prisoners went to the gallows, sixty-one were able to plead "benefit of clergy" and so escaped hanging by being able to read.

There seems little doubt that the justices often reduced the value of stolen goods to a quite ridiculous figure so as to be able to avoid a death sentence. There is one instance of a prisoner being threatened with transportation to Greenland, but no further details are forthcoming. His subsequent experiences, if he ever went there, would make extraordinarily interesting reading, rivalling the adventures of Robinson Crusoe or Gulliver.

Thomas Johnson, of Willesden, yeoman, was accused of stealing cocks and hens and a pig, total value 11d., and, as he has no goods, he is to be whipped. George Brankes, of Edmonton, for stealing a brown bay gelding worth 40s. was sentenced to be hanged, but was afterward respited to prison.

Fair-day at Brentford sometimes led to crime, for Edward Sharp, of New Brentford, fellmonger, and some friends were ordered to keep the peace towards John Foxe, of Uxbridge. They had beaten and wounded him and committed other misdemeanours in the open fair, in disturbance of the King's Highness's peace by using "unreverent speaches."

To assistance in the maintenance of law and order, coroners, bailiffs, chief constables and sub-constables were appointed for the county and the various hundreds. In the

Hundred of Ossulstone, besides those areas now in the County of London, sub-constables were appointed for Chiswick, Ealing, Acton, Willesden, Kilburn, Hornsey, Finchley, Friern Barnet; in Edmonton Hundred, for Enfield, Edmonton, Tottenham, Mimms and Hadley; in Gore, for Harrow, Pinner, Hendon, Great and Little Stanmore, Edgware and Kingsbury; in Elthorne, for Uxbridge, Hillingdon, Hayes, Northwood, Cowley, Brentford, Cranford, Northolt, Harlington, Harefield, Ickenham, Ruislip, Drayton, Harmondsworth; in Spelthorne, for Staines, Laleham, Ashford, Stanwell, Sunbury, Shepperton, Littleton, Bedfont, Hampton, Hanworth and Teddington; and in Isleworth Hundred, for Twickenham, Heston and Isleworth.

In a Jury List noted at the same time most of the names come from Westminster or the inner suburbs of London, such as Whitechapel, but a few are summoned from Friern Barnet, Finchley, Hornsey and Willesden.

John Maddox, of Harrow Weald in Harrow-on-the-Hill, wheelwright, is indicted for keeping a tippling-house without licence, two labourers in Edmonton for house-breaking at about midnight and stealing eleven shirts worth 20s., a smock worth 12d., two dozen napkins worth 10s., six towels worth 2s., and two tablecloths worth 8d. One of them "seeks the book," but cannot read and is sentenced to be hanged. A yeoman of Finchley, for stealing shirt, smock and sheet, worth 1s. 2d. in all, and a yeoman of Harrow-on-the-Hill, for stealing a capon and a brood goose worth 3s. 10d. in all, were both sentenced to be whipped, as they had no goods. In July, 1615, three yeomen of Isleworth were charged with assaulting and robbing John Tayler, of Harmondsworth, and Isabel Davies, of Harmondsworth. Two were sentenced to death by hanging, but the third was respited to prison.

The repair of bridges and highways was a very important duty in earlier times, and in 1614 the inhabitants of Greenford were indicted for not repairing Greenford Bridge; Ealing for not repairing the highway at Hanger Wood Hill, leading from Alperton to Acton, being a mile in length; and the inhabitants of Staines for not repairing Longford Bridge. The Chief Constable of Staines appeared on their behalf and promised that all needful repairs should be done before the next general sessions. Sarah Draper was presented for not renewing Stone Bridge in Hornsey, and to show their impartiality the justices presented the Bishop of London for not repairing Stickleton Bridge in the parish of Greenford.

Difficulties about church attendance are exemplified in the indictment of folk from New Brentford, Hendon and Heston for refusing to come to church on Sundays. Sir Christopher Roper, of Ealing, was another offender, but most of the culprits seem to have been in the immediate vicinity of London. Most of those who defaulted were probably Romanists, but it is possible that there were some Brownists among them.

For not working on the highways according to a statute of Philip and Mary, twelve men from Ruislip and one from Pinner were presented, and later on fourteen from Tottenham, who should each have brought a cart, and Sir John Swinnerton, who should have sent labour.

There were clearly defined rules with regard to apprentices and servants. Francis Potter, of Finchley, is discharged by his master, a linen-weaver, who has to produce his indentures to be cancelled in court. Thomas Durant, of Enfield, yeoman, was brought in for detaining his servant's wages and was ordered to pay the arrears. A Harrow man was bound over for enticing away another man's apprentice. John Agalan, a labourer from Hounslow, was acquitted of stealing a mattock worth 6d. Bird-catchers at Teddington are indicted for taking pigeons without nets; several folk are presented for selling tobacco without a licence; a labourer and his wife, of Hampstead, are accused of practising evil and diabolic arts called witchcraft, enchantments, charms and sorceries upon human beings and upon a bay gelding worth £4, so that a lady wasted away, a man was slain and murdered, and the gelding died. A similar case occurred at Finchley, where Elizabeth Rutter was accused of exercising witchcrafts, enchantments, charms and sorceries upon William Lyon, so that his whole body is wasted away and he scarcely now can live; and upon three children of James Field, so that they languished and died. She was sentenced to be hanged for her diabolical arts.

A distressing case is recorded in 1614, when the parishes of Isleworth, Hillingdon and Ruislip all refuse to relieve

Joan Winchester, a distressed old blind woman. The justices are instructed to examine the case and arrange for the poor woman to be provided for according to the law.

Here are three striking cases of robbery in 1614. Two yeomen of Hendon are accused of breaking into a house and stealing brass vessels, pewter spoons, felt hats, a towel and bags, worth several pounds. John Baker was ordered to be hanged; Thomas Pryce was found not guilty. A barber at Uxbridge, Robert Fanninge, was accused of stealing a gold ring, a silver ring and a bodkin. He was found not guilty, but was respited for sureties for good behaviour. The third is more complicated. Two yeomen of Edgware were accused of assault in the highway at Bushey Heath in the parish of Little Stanmore, where they stole money, an inkhorn, a knife, 30 lb. of butter, three cheeses, a sorrell horse, a felt hat, a velvet girdle, etc., from three victims. The two culprits were sentenced to be hanged, but were respited for the Bermudas.

Half a dozen yeomen of Edmonton, who seemed to have formed a gang, broke into a house, alarmed the servants and got away with a long list of articles—sheets, tablecloths, napkins, riding breeches, frieze drawers, a birding piece, falling-bands, a ruff-band and three cross-clothes—mostly belonging to the indoor servants. They all pleaded not guilty and seem to have got off.

For stealing twelve wether sheep belonging to Thomas Tarvar, of Barnet, yeoman, which had been sent to Kentish Town for sale to a butcher, William Basse, not being able to read, was hanged.

All over Middlesex archery was ordered to be practised by young men, with a view to national defence in case of invasion; but in some instances football was preferred, and the authorities determined to put a stop to it. The justices gave orders that, "whereas great disorders & tumult doe often arise & happen within the streetes and lanes neere adioyninge to ye Cittye of London by playing at the footeball," the high and petty constables should "from tyme to tyme represse & restrayne all manner of footeball playe" in the streets and lanes, and bring offenders before the justices for punishment. Edward Wharton, of Edgware, draper, was taken at Uxbridge for abusing the constable of Little Stanmore and tell-

126

ing him that "he would not come to the Musters, and dis-
wadinge others, askinge them if they would goe see a
footeball playe." In spite of their previous orders, the justices
discharged him.

When it was proposed to impose a rate for making a
new house of correction, Michael Shorditche, of Ickenham,
gentleman, got into serious trouble for speaking divers unfit
and mutinous speeches on the subject, and threatening that
the county would withstand the rate. This is a really interesting entry, as it suggests that in the mind of a landowner out
at Ickenham there was sufficient county spirit about to justify
him in making such a threat.

In the *Domestic State Papers* we find references in the
reign of James I to keepers appointed to look after the game
in the borders of Middlesex and Hertfordshire, July 10,
1611; thus a "grant with survivorship to Alban Coxe and
John his son in reversion after John Pratt of the Office of
Keeper of pheasants and partridges in Barnet, Hadley, South
Mimms and Totteridge, in the counties of Hertford and
Middlesex." Eleven years later, in 1622, something seems to
have gone wrong, for Thomas Hall is appointed to be sole
keeper of game in the four parishes above named.

THE CIVIL WAR IN MIDDLESEX
Wiliam Noy at Brentford

The Stuart period will no doubt continue to arouse the
most contradictory views from historians, but Macaulay's
dictum still holds good that if Elizabeth's successors "had
inherited her wisdom with her crown, Charles the First might
have died of old age, and James the Second would never have
seen St. Germain's." To the efforts of King Charles to raise
money apart from votes granted by Parliament Middlesex
provided much opposition, and at the same time housed the
originator of ship-money. One of the Commissioners appointed in September, 1626, to raise a forced loan was
William Noy, a Cornishman living at Brentford, who had
been a strong supporter of national liberty and an opponent
of the King's doctrine of divine right until this new position
was offered to him. The Commissioners reported in October

that three Middlesex men—John Brooks, Edward Bastwick and William Webb—had contemptuously refused to contribute. To this refusal the King replied that those who would not serve with their purses should serve with their persons, and all three were conscripted into the Army. When thirteen more refused to contribute, warrants were issued against them. But worse was to come, for Noy, searching in old records for fresh means of taxation, came upon the precedent for ship-money among the records in the Tower, and drastic steps were taken destined to lead to Civil War and to the defeat and death of the King.

Noy was mainly responsible for revising and enforcing the medieval forest laws and for persuading the King to grant a soap monopoly, which irritated every liberty-loving household in the country. He had his share in the persecution of William Prynne, author of *Histriomastix*, a fierce attack on the stage, just when the Queen had been acting in amateur theatricals; and Noy is said to have watched the cutting off of Prynne's ears quite unmoved.

A very interesting connection with Hendon is provided by the fact that John Herne, of Lincoln's Inn, who defended Prynne, and subsequently Archbishop Laud, had a country house here. During the years of ship-money Middlesex was suffering from the plague, especially in 1636, and the loss of life and decline in tax rendered ship-money harder to collect. The assessment was therefore reduced for the country from £5,500 to £5,000, but the whole reduction was applied to the Hundred of Ossulstone, which included the cities of London and Westminster and other built-up areas.

At once the three more westerly hundreds of Elthorne, Spelthorne and Isleworth complained that they were receiving no abatement, though they had to bear the charges of watch and ward at Hampton Court as well as the carriage for the King's provisions. When in the same year Chelsea complained that they were taxed more highly than Acton, the sheriffs replied that this was due to the more fashionable character of Chelsea. Opposition to ship-money was spreading, and Clarendon admits that it was intended to serve not only for the Navy, but "for a spring or magazine that should have no bottom, and for an everlasting supply of all occasions."

Staines, High Street

The agitation in the next-door county of Bucks, under John Hampden, produced more objectors in the Hundred of Gore, when forty persons had to be prosecuted in Harrow. Two bishops' wars in Scotland were an expensive drain on the royal purse, and in Middlesex, as elsewhere, there were levies for the wars and demands for cost and conduct money. So widespread was the discontent that the trained bands throughout the county were exercised on all holidays so as to anticipate any riots.

During the friction between Charles and Parliament, which came to a head in the attempted arrest of the Five Members, some of the Middlesex trained bands were on duty at Whitehall in the new Guard House built by the King's orders. After Charles's misguided attack on Parliamentary privilege, which for once Clarendon and Macaulay, John Forster and Bulwer Lytton agree in condemning, he left London, where the populace had been hooting and shouting all day long at his palace gates, and retired to Hampton Court. The London and Middlesex trained bands marched to Westminster, the Commons returned by water, the four thousand freeholders from Buckinghamshire rode up through Colnbrook and Uxbridge to defend John Hampden. Early in January, 1642, John Hotham rode up through Tottenham and Edmonton to hold Hull for the Parliament, and soon the King saw his wife off from Dover and returned to Hampton before advancing to his unsuccessful effort to secure Hull. Directly the news reached London that the King had set up his standard at Nottingham, Essex began to prepare his troops for the encounter, and advanced through Middlesex to face the royal army, taking with him "his coffin, scutcheon and winding-sheet, as a sign that he would be faithful to the death." The war was beginning in earnest.

Middlesex was bound to play a big part in the crisis, seeing that it surrounded London on the northern and western sides, from which the royal attacks on the capital city were chiefly to be expected.

Troops were moving about the county almost all the time, and almost every market town and village must have been conscious of the imminence of war, especially when the trained bands were mobilised, fortifications were being dug

River Thames at Kingston

in the suburbs round London, and armies were being raised to defend the Parliamentary cause at Brentford and Turnham Green and to march to rescue Gloucester from Prince Rupert. It is obviously impossible and unnecessary to record every warlike movement in Middlesex, but there are a few outstanding events which demand investigation.

Edgehill was a drawn battle, but Charles was able to take up his headquarters at Oxford and to receive big reinforcements. Essex, fearing an attack on London, brought some troops southwards, and with the trained bands of London and Middlesex encamped near Acton. The King, with Prince Rupert in command of reinforced cavalry, reached Reading on November 2, an advance which struck the Londoners with the greatest horror. A false step might bring the capital and the popular cause down in ruin. Even before Edgehill some effort had been made to protect the suburbs and the city, and now, with peril at the door, Bulstrode Whitelocke tells us how wonderful it was to see how "women and children and vast numbers would come to work, digging and carrying of earth to make the new fortifications."

What was left of the two Houses ordered the city to be put "into a posture of defence . . . divers rebels, traitors and other ill-affected people being now marching against the Parliament." The Venetian Ambassador, Rushworth the Chronicler and Samuel Butler in *Hudibras* tell of heroic efforts of all classes and both sexes, especially the women, among them Lady Middlesex, Lady Foster and Lady Anne Waller, who—

> "marched rank and file with drum and ensign
> T'entrench the city for defence in.
> From ladies down to oyster-wenches,
> Laboured like pioneers in trenches."

Battle for Brentford

The Earl of Northumberland, who was living at Syon House, Isleworth, and had taken over the fleet to Parliament, headed a peace party, and its members arrived at Colnbrook to meet the King, whose advance to the Middlesex border "indeed exalted their appetite to peace" and made them anxious "for the removal of these bloody distempers."

130

Negotiations began on November 11, and Windsor and then Brentford were suggested by Charles for a meeting-place. Parliament told Essex to take the field but to refrain from hostilities, and Clarendon admits that the King's answer to Parliament suggested that he would not advance while negotiations were pending. Charles wrote that "after the departure of the Committee of both Houses with our gracious answer to their petition, we received certain information that the Earl of Essex had drawn his forces out of London towards us, which has necessitated our sudden resolution to march with our forces to Brentford."

Rupert realised the value of a quick victory, and came from Colnbrook undetected in a thick mist to Brentford and beat up the quarters of Colonel Hollis's regiment just west of the town. Hollis's "honest, religious soldiers" with Brooks's regiment had barricaded the narrow avenues of the town, casting up "little breastworks at the most convenient places." They fought with courage against a surprise attack delivered by superior forces, especially a Welsh regiment which had been "faulty" at Edgehill, but covered itself with some distinction in the drive through Brentford.

The battle began near Syon House, at Brentford End, and was stubbornly contested at Brentford Bridge. After a warm service the royal troops entered the town, killing many officers and men, driving many more into the river, where they were drowned, and capturing over 500 prisoners, including John Lilburne, 11 colours, 15 pieces of cannon and much ammunition. Charles watched the opening rounds of the contest from Boston House, Brentford. This was the situation which amazed Sir Peter Killigrew when he arrived to continue peaceful negotiations with the King. A battle at Brentford had been lost and won.

A contemporary tract gives us *A True and Perfect Relation of the barbarous and cruell passages of the King's Army at Old Brainceford*, near London, in which the merciless plundering and sacking of the town are described. Daniel Lysons, in his *Environs of London*, prints a reasonably unbiased and presumably accurate account of the battle from the Royalist standpoint. The officer was proud of the capture of the town after five assaults, but was heartbroken at the "miserable death of many goodly men," especially by drowning in the Thames. Next day fourteen barges laden with Parliamentary troops and ordnance attempted very indiscreetly to pass up the river, and cannon from the grounds of Syon House sank four or five of them. For his successes Ruthven was made Earl of Brentford, but the title died out in 1651.

Meantime Killigrew's alarming tidings had aroused the authorities in London. The Life Guards in Chelsea had heard the firing, the trained bands "with their brightest equipage" were mobilised, because it was rumoured that Rupert intended to pillage the city without check. On November 12 Essex led his troops all through the night to Turnham Green, where he mustered a force twice as large as the King's army. Sir John Ramsay, with 3,000 troops, held Kingston Bridge in the King's rear, and John Hampden occupied some high ground near Acton on the other flank. But Essex allowed the chance of surrounding the King to slide by withdrawing both these units, and he also failed to attack in spite of his decided superiority in numbers. His failure to hold Kingston Bridge allowed the King to retire through Isleworth, Twickenham, Teddington and Hampton Wick.

Essex's indecision allowed the King to hold Kingston Bridge, where the Royalists welcomed Charles on his return to his beloved Hampton Court. Essex now realised that he had been unwise in giving up the one bridge from Middlesex into Surrey without a struggle, and so he threw a bridge of boats across the Thames from Fulham to Putney, intending to transport his army across if Charles should march eastwards to join his supporters in Kent. But no such move followed, and after one night at Hampton Court the King moved to Oatlands, Reading and Oxford, which became his headquarters for the whole of the first Civil War. Charles was never so near again to a triumphal march into London, and perhaps Essex missed his one chance of ending the war at a single blow.

The ravages of the royal army had given the inhabitants of Middlesex an inkling of what the King's victory might mean, and the trained bands who relieved Brentford were surrounded by hungry citizens clamouring for food which the generosity of their wives and sisters enabled them to supply. The damage caused by battle and plunder was deplorable, and a desperate appeal was made to the "Honourable the Commons from the Inhabitants of the Town of Old Brentford." The ministers of Middlesex asked their flocks to have a compassionate consideration for the sufferers and contribute generously in their parish churches. "The action of the King, in the time of a Treaty, was ill resented by many men that they spoke very hardly of it." A generous response was made in Middlesex to the appeal for help, as it was felt that Rupert should not have been allowed to attack the town while negotiations were pending.

There were never so many landed gentry in Middlesex as in the adjacent counties, but most of the county magnates followed the King to Oxford after he retired from Brentford and Turnham Green. Among them were John Cary, of Marylebone Park; Sir Francis Rouse, of Headstone Manor, Harrow; Sir Henry Wroth, of Durrants; Sir John Kaye, Sir Robert Fenn and Sir Henry Spiller, of Laleham. A very keen supporter of the King from Middlesex was Sir Arthur Aston, of Fulham, who at Edgehill drove the Parliamentary right wing from the field. Aston was Governor of Reading and helped Rupert to storm Bristol. His cruelty and intolerance as Governor of Oxford earned him deserved hostility, and so, after the royal disaster at Naseby, he was sent to Ireland with the Marquis of Ormonde, and his task was to hold Drogheda with 3,000 men. He refused to surrender when Cromwell offered terms to the garrison, and suffered in the consequent slaughter. Before the Civil War Aston had served King James in Russia, had seen much war service with the Poles against the Turks, with Gustavus Adolphus in the Lützen campaign, and because of his wide experience he was appointed Sergeant-Major-General in Charles I's Bishops' wars against the Scots.

Middlesex paid heavily for its proximity to London. The fortifications, with the complete circumvallation and twenty-five forts, occupied a lot of farmland and required careful garrisoning. The Committee for the Advance of Money collected funds for defence from friend and foe alike within a radius of twenty miles, but later on taxation fell most heavily on "delinquents." Sir John Wolstenholme, of Stanmore, lost more than £100,000 in fines and confiscations, possibly because he had built a new church which Archbishop Laud had dedicated; and many others had to pay sums ranging from £200 to £2,000, including, amongst others, Sir Thomas Allen, of Finchley. Sir Nicholas Crisp, with a house in Hammersmith and Quex Park in Kent, had all his property confiscated.

It was an expensive business financing the trained bands, and the troops thus raised took away many labourers from the Middlesex farms. Hounslow Heath served as a training ground for the Parliamentary army, and much recruiting had to be done for the force with which Essex was to march to the relief of Gloucester. Commissioners were sent to inspect the troops, and found their leader very depressed because his recruits were "a very shattered and broken body." However, within three weeks Essex had three regiments partially trained and forming with the London trained bands an army of 5,000 men. On August 26, 1643, Essex marched from Uxbridge and Colnbrook "with an army so full of patience, as that with one fortnight's pay (being much incurred) they were content to march against all these difficulties." And the difficulties were, first, a long march to relieve Gloucester, and then on the return journey to fight a drawn battle at Newbury. When Charles withdrew to Oxford, Essex marched his now victorious troops back to London, and in September, 1643, he reviewed the trained bands in Finsbury Fields, just north of the city.

Next year the King took advantage of a separation of the Parliamentary forces under Essex and Waller to advance from Oxford through Buckinghamshire as though to march on London. Major-General Browne was put in charge of the defences, and Sir Gilbert Garrard was able to announce 4,000 men under arms in Middlesex by the end of June. Garrard's own regiment, also raised in the county, was sent to join Browne's troops and other law levies at Hertford; but Waller was able to stop the King at Cropredy Bridge, and it was perhaps as well that the very untrained Middlesex troops under Browne escaped action.

The lack of any real success under Essex and Manchester

at the second Battle of Newbury in 1644 alarmed the Londoners, and all available Middlesex troops were sent to guard the bridges of Staines and Uxbridge. We read of 60 horse being raised in Middlesex in March, 1644, of men from the county garrisoning Windsor Castle during the winter of 1644-5, while for Sir Thomas Fairfax's new model army 2,500 were raised in March, 1645, in London, Westminster, Southwark and Middlesex, and 800 more in the following June. Early in 1645 Major-General Browne marched from Hertford to Abingdon with his composite force in better trim after six months' training. They included forty men from Middlesex. Lack of pay, poor quarters and inadequate food led to lack of discipline and frequent desertions, so in June 200 more were sent from Middlesex to make up the deficiency.

When Cromwell was attacking Oxford, 400 infantry joined him from Middlesex, while Colonel Massey led a large county contingent, who "went forth with much cheerfulness" to the relief of Taunton. When Fairfax brought his army to Reading in 1645 he was joined by recruits from Middlesex. Whitelocke's story of Abingdon shows that the Parliamentary troops, which included Middlesex horse and foot, did yeoman service there. Prince Rupert, Prince Maurice and Sir Henry Gaye came from Oxford with 1,000 horse and 800 foot to attack Abingdon on the Culham side. To prevent them from destroying the bridge, Brown had to send troops into the flooded meadows. "With much cheerfulness they marched through the water, and after a hot dispute, which lasted over four hours, they beat the enemy from the bridge . . . from the hedges, and afterwards quite out of the field." Some Royalist cavalry attacked Browne's horsemen, but they were nearly all slain, wounded or captured; a cartload of dead men were carried away, and the Commons voted their thanks to Major-General Browne and £2,000 for his soldiers' pay. Here is a good piece of work which seldom figures in the usual records and reflects great credit on the Middlesex horse and foot.

In addition to digging and manning fortifications, providing taxes and troops, there was also the problem of billets—very urgent in Middlesex near Parliamentary Headquarters. The Petition of Right denounced billeting, but presumably war conditions overrode even such hard-won rights. Early in 1644 there was a *Petition of the Inhabitants of Middlesex* and other counties in the south and east of England, protesting against "the intolerable oppression and undoing grievance of free quarter" for their troops, which made the householders "no better than mere conquered slaves" at the hands of soldiers, who fed upon their hosts for so long and without payment, "like so many Egyptian locusts."

In November of the same year, in reply to a further petition from the gentlemen of Middlesex, the Earl of Essex was told to punish these "particular insolences" of which the gentlemen complained. The Lords agreed to this plan, but wished to exempt members of both Houses from billeting soldiers; but the Commons would not agree, "they desiring to be in no other condition than their fellow subjects were." In April, 1645, Fairfax was ordered to remove his troops from Middlesex, and only those officers and men who had warrants from their superiors could demand billeting within the county. About the same time mutinous troops marched with their inferior officers from Colnbrook through Middlesex into London, plundering as they went. The need for austerity is always felt in wartime, and "the custome of the Parish of Twitham (being that on Easter Day two great cakes should be broken in the Church and given to the Young People) was ordered to be forborn, and instead thereof Bread to be given to the Poor."

By the end of 1644 it was still doubtful which side would win, and efforts were made to bring the fighting to an amicable end. Uxbridge still retains the Old Treaty House (now the Crown Hotel) where the famous treaty was discussed in 1645 without any decision being reached. The house had been the home of Sir John Bennett, a prebendary and vicar-general and chancellor for the diocese of York, an M.P., and Chancellor to the Queen of Denmark. He was impeached for accepting bribes and was sentenced to fines and imprisonment. By pleading that he had a wife, ten children and forty grandchildren, he escaped imprisonment in 1644 and died three years later. His widow, Leonora, was a Belgian and had been married twice before. She died at the Treaty House in 1638 and is buried in Uxbridge Parish Church. It was at their house that the Royalist and Parliamentary Commissioners met on January 29, 1645, to discuss terms of peace.

In the Lords Commissioners there were four earls, and among the Commons representatives were Denzil Hollis (one of the Five Members and a holder of land in Hendon), Sir Harry Vane, Junior, Bulstrode Whitelocke, Mr. St. John and attendants, numbering eighty in all. Two ministers of the Gospel were appointed to attend the Commons, Mr. Marshall and Mr. Vines, and Sir Peter Killigrew was sent to the King to give in these lists, to ask for the King's Commissioners, and to arrange for a safe conduct. The King sent in a list of 108, including a number of peers, three parsons, some commoners and Sir Edward Hyde (afterwards Earl of Clarendon). We thus have the tale of Uxbridge told by Hyde and Whitelocke from opposite camps. Whitelocke's *Memorials* make an attractive contemporary volume, and my copy has a manuscript story telling of the fate of Prince Maurice in the West Indies.

The Commissioners on both parts reached Uxbridge on January 29, 1645, and had their several quarters, "those for the Parliament and all their retinue on the north side of the town, and those for the King on the south side, and no intermixing." Each party had the best available inn on their side of the street as their rendezvous. There were several visits paid before discussions began, Hyde visiting Hollis and Whitelocke, Culpepper calling on Vane, Whitelocke returning the visit to Hyde. Whitelocke tells us that they had "discourses about the Treaty, and to persuade one another to a compliance . . . tending to the furtherance of the business of the Treaty."

Clarendon maintains that the townspeople noticed that the Parliament's men did not look as much at home as did the Cavaliers, and that the former did not display that "alacrity and serenity of mind as men use to have who do not believe themselves to be at fault." But Whitelocke says that "this place being within the Parliament's quarters, their Commissioners were the more civil, and desirous to afford accommo-

137

dations to the King's Commissioners." It seems quite clear "the town was so exceeding full of company, that it was hard to get any quarter except for the Commissioners and their retinue; and some of the Commissioners were forced to lie two of them in a chamber together in field beds, only upon a sheet, in that cold weather not coming into a bed during all the Treaty."

The foreway into Sir John Bennett's house was for the King's party, the backway for the Parliament. "In the middle of the house was a fair great chamber, where they caused a large table to be made, like that heretofore in the Star Chamber, almost square, without any upper or lower end of it." There was too much crowding, with divines and secretaries as well as the Commissioners, but there were two withdrawing rooms for purposes of consultation.

On the first morning of the conference Christopher Love, a well-known Puritan divine, preached the market-day sermon. He had a large congregation and very tactlessly told them that the Royal Commissioners came "with hearts of blood," and there was as much gap between peace and the treaty as between hell and heaven. "The King's Commissioners complained of the Sermon . . . wherein they said were many expressions in derogation of His Majesty, and the present Treaty; the Parliament having notice thereof from their Commissioners, sent for Love, and referred the business to an examination." The Parliamentary Commissioners disowned Love, and he was afterwards reprimanded.

The meeting was to last twenty days, not counting the days of travel nor the days set apart for prayer, "there falling out three Sundays and one fast day in those first twenty days." There were long and learned discussions on episcopacy and presbytery, both sides claiming that their way was *jure divino*. The Marquess of Hertford and the Earl of Pembroke did not agree with either and proposed passing on to the next topic. They discussed the militia and Ireland, but nothing seemed forthcoming, and the Parliament affirmed in reply to the King's demand for more days for discussion "that there could be no expectation of a good issue of the Treaty, or inducement for the Parliament to grant longer time for the Treaty, when not one of the Parliament's propositions was

granted by the King, during the whole time of the Treaty."
"The Lord Mayor and Aldermen of London sent a letter to
the speaker, intimating the scarcity of flesh-meats by the
destruction of cattel in the time of these wars, and the good
by encouraging the fishing; and submitted the whole, not as
to the Keeping of Lent, but to prevent dearth, to the judgment of the Houses : who ordered an ordinance to be brought
in for this business."

There were complaints of the unruliness of the soldiers,
"stealing of horses, ravishing of women, and murdering of
them." A committee was appointed to investigate, but it was
realised that "these were the fruits of Civil War, Robberies,
Ravishings and innumerable wicked actions, committed by
the barbarous soldiers, to the unspeakable misery of the poor
country."

There was little chance of success in the negotiations, in
spite of the efforts of 108 Commissioners to represent the
King and the eighty to speak for Parliament, and so after
nearly a month's effort the conference broke up. On Sunday,
February 23, both sides exchanged the courtesies of farewell,
"parting with such dryness towards each other as if they
scarce hoped to meet again." Two days had been allowed for
the Royalists to get back to Oxford, but they were in their
coaches the first thing on Monday morning, and reached
Oxford and kissed the King's hand that same night, so
Clarendon tells us.

The "good house at the end of the town," as Clarendon
calls it, presumably passed down the Bennet family to Sir
John's grandson, Henry, who was one of the Cabal in
Charles II's reign, having been promoted to be Baron Harlington. An ignorant clerk seems to have been unaware of the
village in Middlesex from which the title was taken, and
omitted the "H." Two of the rooms in the Treaty House
still remain, but the panelling was sold some years ago for
export to the United States. "One end has a curved gable, on
one side are two original double-bay windows, and at the
back are the old gabled brick walls, and three old stacks of
six-sided and eight-sided chimneys." But it is time to correct
once and for all the erroneous notion that there "Charles
Stuart and Oliver Cromwell, with their commissioners, dis-

cussed the Treaty of Uxbridge." Neither of them was present.

During the Civil War one of the generals on the Parliamentary side seems to have enjoyed much the same kind of popularity with the soldiers from London and Middlesex as some of our commanders in the second World War, and we read in Whitelocke that "the trained Bands marched forth very cheerfully under the command of Major-General Skippon, who made short and encouraging speeches to his soldiers, which were to this purpose : 'Come, my boys, my brave boys, let us pray heartily and fight heartily. I will run the same fortunes and hazards with you; remember the cause is for God, and for the defence of your selves, your wives and your children. Come, my honest brave boys, pray heartily and fight heartily, and God will bless us.' Thus he went all along with the soldiers, talking to them, sometimes to one company, and sometimes to another; and the soldiers seemed to be more taken with it than with a set, formal oration."

When Essex resigned his commission in accordance with the Self-Denying Ordinance, Whitelocke is very contemptuous of the New Model Army, which he claims is called by many in scorn "new noddle." But they were to learn their mistake in June, 1647, when Fairfax, Skippon and Cromwell won their decisive victory over the King on June 14, and exactly a week later 4,500 prisoners and 55 of their colours were brought through Middlesex to London and thence to Westminster. The first Civil War was over.

The Second Civil War

The second Civil War was due to quarrels among the victors and to attempts made by the King and Royalists to profit thereby. In July, 1647, the Independents in the Army and the Presbyterians in Parliament were quarrelling about arrears of pay, problems of toleration and negotiations with the King. Sir Thomas Fairfax moved from Aylesbury to Bedford, and was anxious to take away all seeds of war and to secure a lasting peace. Crowds of young men thronged the House of Commons and the City, and protection was needed against them. The Independent members fled to Fairfax, the City ordered further mobilisation in London and Middlesex, and asked the Army to keep at a distance of fifty miles from the capital.

It was proposed to move the King's children from Syon House into London, and the City declared that Fairfax had no authority over the trained bands. The hostile attitude of the Londoners forced the General's hand, and by forced marches he brought his army to Uxbridge and thence to Colnbrook, where Fairfax lodged "at one Mr. Wilson's neere the bridge," where he came on Sunday night (August 1). To him for protection came Warwick, Manchester and divers other lords, and an urgent letter from the City, wondering what enemy Fairfax meant to fight, and asking for a reply to their previous notes.

Fairfax held a private meeting with those Lords and Commons who had asked for his help, and then told the City's Commissioners why he would advance to London. The Lord Mayor then ordered the trained bands to man the lines of communications, which had never been needed against the King. To alarm the city and so provide a peaceful solution, Fairfax ordered a "general rendezvous at Hunsloe Heath of twenty thousand horse and foot and a great train of artillery." When the City's Commissioners had seen the troops they were sent back to London, so as to persuade the citizens to take a reasonable view. Fairfax's army had been quartered at Brentford and Twickenham before the review, and to meet them on the Heath came the friendly speaker, fourteeen lords and a hundred M.P.s. The General with his visitors and the Prince Elector, whom he received with great respect, rode along the army drawn up in battalions with reserves, and the men shouted : "Lords and Commons, and a free Parliament." When Fairfax learned that Southwark was hostile to London and wanted his aid, he sent General Rainsborough with horse, foot and cannon to the south of the Thames, while he moved the rest of the Army to Brentford and Twickenham, with headquarters at Thisleworth. General Mason from London sent out some scouts to Brentford, but ten of the army beat off thirty of the trained bands and captured colours from the City troops.

Bulstrode Whitelocke, in his *Memorials*, gives a vivid picture of the City's panic. The militia and Common Council sat in the Guildhall waiting for news. When they heard that the Army had halted they cried, "One and all!" but news of advance brought the desperate shout, "Treat, treat!" After a night of anxiety they sent a humble letter to General Fairfax, which he received at Isleworth. With Southwark and London Bridge in his hands he could demand the surrender of the western forts, into which he marched three regiments of foot and two of horse. Fairfax advanced to Hammersmith, received a letter from the King disclaiming all responsibility for recent troubles, and then on August 6 the Independent Members were met at Lord Holland's house in Kensington, and the whole Army marched in triumph into the City, which received it without offence or prejudice. The soldiers confuted surprises by their civil and orderly behaviour under careful discipline. Thus ended an incident fraught with considerable possibility of disaster, avoided by moderation and sense and by a wise display of tact.

The King was now brought back to Hampton Court, where he enjoyed almost complete freedom and did his best to play off the rigid Presbyterians against the more tolerant Independents while he was intriguing with the Irish Catholics. The King was once more back with his loved pictures, and the Queen and Cardinal Berberini tried to influence him with old masters. They both hoped in this way to persuade Charles to become a Catholic. Barberini told Mazarin that he would rob Rome of its most treasured ornaments to write the King's name among those who submitted to the Catholic See.

Charles had many visitors while at Hampton Court : his children from Syon House, the Marquess of Ormonde from Ireland, Lord Capel from the Channel Islands, sometimes with encouraging tidings. Twice in one week after hunting in the Green Park he dined at Syon House with his children, and continued to accept the Parliament's demands for Presbyterianism and the control of the militia, while he toyed with the more generous proposals of Cromwell and his officers. But, as Whitelocke tells us, "his bishops persuaded him against his judgment and thereby ruined him and themselves."

During October, 1647, Cromwell often came over from his headquarters at Putney to Hampton Court for talks with

the King, but when the Heads of the Proposals proved un-
acceptable the feeling against Charles stiffened. Various plans
were hatched to get the King away, and in spite of Colonel
Whalley's precautions three Scottish peers brought horses
for the King's escape, worried as he was by a supposed plot
of the other side to kill him. Whalley sent the news to Cromwell, who came over to Hampton once again and reported
the King's escape to Lenthall, Speaker of the House of
Commons. Charles had left on his table a letter for Parliament, claiming that liberty was as necessary for kings as for
another, that he wanted to avoid bloodshed and was prepared
to be a *Pater Patriæ*.

Billeting of soldiers was becoming irksome, and Herts,
Bucks and Middlesex asked to be "eased of free quarters,"
to which the Commons sent a favourable reply, and in a few
months removed this grievance. Just after Christmas there
was great disorder in Ealing about the observation of the
general holiday which Parliament had forbidden, and, in
trying to enforce the rule, "officials were abused by the rude
multitude."

There were signs of a rising of opinion favourable to the
King in some quarters and of a firm resolve of Parliament
not to make or accept any more addresses. The prominent
Royalists in the Home Counties, including Middlesex, tried
to persuade the soldiers of Fairfax's army to help them in
bringing back prosperity by restoring the King, religion and
liberty, and in disbanding the troops after paying arrears of
pay. They complained that the freeborn people of England
were "in a greater servitude than at any time since the
Norman Conquest," and heartily and seriously invited the
soldiers to join them in revolt.

In April, 1648, while the three royal children were playing in Syon House after supper, the Duke of York, without
cloak or coat, slipped down the stairs and, abusing his
promise, escaped from Syon House, owing to some slackness
of the Earl of Northumberland. This was only another sign
of coming trouble, and Parliament in May ordered that all
malignants and Papists were to be put out of the lines of
communication and twenty miles distant from London. This
order, if obeyed, would empty Middlesex of all suspected

Royalists. In June, as the ordinance had not been fully obeyed, four days' limit was granted to leave the prohibited area, and a joint committee was named to control the militia of all the Home Counties.

Henry Rich, Baron Kensington and Earl of Holland, was prominent in Middlesex as the owner of Holland House in Kensington, and he showed as little stability and principle as a subsequent owner of Holland House more than a century later. He was one of those sent to France in 1644 to negotiate Prince Charles's marriage with Henrietta Maria, but although very popular with the Queen he was thwarted by Stafford and slipped into the ranks of the opposition. Clarendon writes of him that "he was visited and caressed with great application by all the factious party." He took part in the bishops' wars on the King's side, but served with Essex at Turnham Green, where his vacillation may have spoiled the Parliamentary chance of victory. Next he went to Oxford to join the King, who was naturally very suspicious and cold. After fighting on the King's side at Newbury, he once more changed over to the Parliament, and after a short imprisonment he was allowed to live in his own house, being able to do little good or harm. He tried, without much success, to justify his constant change of front, and discussed with his intimate friend, Bulstrode Whitelocke, a further change to serve the royal cause. "How honourable, just and pious a thing it would be to rescue our country from the misery and slavery they are now under, especially if it were done by those who in the beginning had perhaps too much hand in the bringing these straight upon us."

Holland took the field at Kingston on July 4, 1648, and succeeded in crossing the Thames, although the Deputy Lieutenant of Middlesex had been strictly ordered to guard the bridge and the ferries and to secure the boats on his side of the river. After four days' skirmishing with 500 horse, Holland just managed to push into Middlesex with a few soldiers, intent on avoiding any action. He got through the narrow lines round Harrow on his way to St. Albans. The final military incident in the second Civil War was Holland's capture on July 9 at St. Neots. He was first sentenced to banishment and then to death by just a casting vote given by

Kneller Hall, Twickenham

the Speaker of the House of Commons. He showed courage by refusing to worry his wife and children by seeing them before his execution, but avoided the ceremony required on such an occasion by dressing for the scaffold in a white satin waistcoat and wearing a cap trimmed with silver lace. Warburton, in a note to Clarendon's *History of the Great Rebellion,* says, unkindly, that Holland "lived like a knave and died like a fool."

In December of the same year General Cromwell wrote from St. Albans to the Lord Mayor to announce an immediate advance to London. There would be no plunder or damage, but £40,000 would be required to pay the troops, who would be quartered in the void and great houses in and about the City. In the advance from St. Albans to London Cromwell's troops must have advanced into Middlesex either through Edgware or Barnet, and his arrival in London was only a prelude to the great tragedy of the King's trial and execution.

LATER STUARTS

The Restoration of Charles II in 1660 seemed to have put the clock back to 1640, but a glance forward to 1690 shows that much of the planning of the Long Parliament and of the struggles of the Ironsides was to have its fruition in the Bloodless Revolution and the Toleration Act. It is interesting to wonder what might have happened if Cromwell's younger daughter Frances, who lies buried in the church of St. Nicholas at Chiswick, had been allowed by her father to accept Lord Broghill's suggestion that she should marry Charles II. Broghill tried to influence Cromwell and his wife, presumably at Hampton Court, but Cromwell thought that Charles was too debauched and would never really forgive the Cromwell family for his father's death.

When Monk had successfully brought the King back to his own again, he erected at Dyrham Park, north-west of High Barnet, but just in Middlesex, a triumphal arch built to celebrate the King's return. Charles married Catherine of Braganza and secured Bombay and Tangier as dowry. Cromwell had planned with Blake to seize Gibraltar, which would have given us both sides of the narrows, and Bombay was to

145   K

York House, Twickenham

prove of immense worth in the building up of our Empire in India, now handed back to its original owners.

Charles spent his honeymoon at Hampton Court, restored by Cromwell to much of its pristine beauty, and it was almost the only happy time that his unlucky Queen was to enjoy. Mistresses ousted her from her rightful place in Charles's affections, and Lauderdale House and Cromwell House at Highgate are associated with Nell Gwynn. The persistent story that she used to live at Littleberries, Mill Hill, has not the slightest foundation in fact.

Sir Matthew Hale, who was Chief Baron of the Exchequer, was very anxious that Richard Baxter and Edward Calamy, two distinguished Dissenters, should accept the bishoprics which Charles offered, but it was not possible. For Nonconformists to accept episcopacy we have had to wait until 1947, and then to see it come about in the co-operation of the South India Church.

The Clarendon Code brought considerable suffering to Dissenters in Middlesex; Philip Nye, who used to drive out in a coach and four to preach at Acton, lost his living there, and spent the rest of his life in extreme poverty; Dr. John Owen, Vice-Chancellor of Oxford University under Cromwell, lived in seclusion at Ealing. Richard Baxter lived quietly in Acton for eight years and wrote there his *Saints' Everlasting Rest*. He used to meet Sir Matthew Hale and discuss problems of philosophy and religion, and had keen arguments about the immortality of the soul. Baxter held services in his house between the usual services at the parish church, so as to cause no interference, but Dr. Bruno Ryves, the Rector, secured Baxter's imprisonment for six months.

Baxter left Acton during the Plague, but was back again in time to see the grim but magnificent spectacle of the Great Fire and to pick up burning pages of books blown as far as his house. Some time later he went to live at Totteridge, just a few yards from the Middlesex border, and there got to know Francis Wareham, ejected Vicar of Hendon, then living at the Hale, and Richard Swift, curate of Edgware, living at Mill Hill but busy preaching in London during the Plague.

Richard Swift spent a good deal of time in and out of gaol

for holding conventicles in his house, but the King's Declaration of Indulgence of 1672 eased things considerably, and the Nonconformist Grammar School which he founded in Mill Hill lasted, with varying success, for thirty or forty years until his death in 1701.

Clarendon's association with the intolerable code directed against Dissenters has been, I feel, exaggerated. For some time before his exile he lived at York House, Teddington, while "Dunkirk House" was being built for him in Piccadilly. After Clarendon's exile Lord (H)Arlington was prominent in the Cabal Ministry, and then the King's strong leanings towards Catholicism alarmed the general public. Lord William Russell, a son of the Duke of Bedford, accepted the Popish Plot invented by Titus Oates and endeavoured to force the King to moderate his home, religious and foreign policy. Unluckily, his scheme got confused with the Rye House Plot, a scheme to murder the King near the Rye House at Hoddesdon, on a journey back from Newmarket which would have brought the royal party down the Tottenham-Edmonton Road. Russell's arrest was ordered and King's Messengers were sent to Highwood House at Mill Hill, and Russell made an attempt to escape by taking a desperate leap from a second-storey window and by rushing along the famous avenue of trees into open country by Barnet Gate and Elstree. His amazing courage in the Tower and at his execution in Lincoln's Inn Fields, and the devotion showed by his wife both then and afterwards to his memory, brought back much credit to the Whig party and helped it to build up strength for resisting the still more drastic changes proposed by James II.

Charles had employed Hounslow Heath as a camping-ground for troops which he might use to disarm opposition. Evelyn relates a visit to the Heath, where, he says, "we saw the newly-raised army encamped, designed against France, in pretence at least, but which gave umbrage to the Parliament. His Majesty and a world of company were in the field, and the whole army in battalia, a very glorious sight. Now were brought into service a new sort of soldiers called *grenadiers,* who were dextrous in flinging hand grenades, everyone having a pouch full; they had furred caps with

147

coped crowns like janissaries, which made them look very fierce, and some had long hoods hanging down behind, as we picture fools. Their clothing likewise being piebald, yellow and red."

When James II ascended the throne all seemed well for him, and the abortive rebellion of Monmouth made his position even stronger. Pepys, one of his chief assistants in building up a strong fleet, was living at Brentford, and William Penn, founder of the Quaker colony of Pennsylvania, with its appropriately named capital, Philadelphia, was at Teddington. When James published his Declaration of Indulgence and proceeded to put Catholics into all sorts of places of trust, there was a rising feeling of antagonism, and among the seven bishops who refused to order their clergy to read the Declaration was Dr. Lloyd, Bishop of St. Asaph, who had a house at Acton, then obviously one of the most popular of semi-suburban resorts. James had taken over the camping-ground at Hounslow, where the grenadiers had been stationed a few years before, and intended to intimidate the City and the lawyers and Parliament. He collected "within a circumference of about two miles and a half fourteen battalions of foot and thirty-two squadrons of horse, amounting to thirteen thousand fighting men. Twenty-six pieces of artillery, and many wains laden with ammunition were dragged from the Tower through the City to Hounslow. There, Londoners saw this great force assembled in their neighbourhood with a terror which familiarity soon diminished. A visit to Hounslow became their favourite amusement on holidays. The camp presented all the appearance of a vast fair. Mingled with the musketeers and dragoons, a multitude of fine gentlemen and ladies from Soho Square. Sharpers and painted women from Whitefriars, invalids in sedans, monks in hoods and gowns, lacquies in rich liveries, pedlars, orange-girls, mischievous apprentices, and gaping clowns, were constantly passing and repassing through the long lanes of tents. From some pavilions were heard the noises of drunken revelry, from within the curses of gamblers. In truth, the place was merely a gay suburb of the capital." Thus Macaulay.

James himself had been staying in his Hounslow camp and

had brought there a movable chapel on wheels, in which daily Mass was celebrated for him. Nowhere was the news of the acquittal of the bishops received with more clamorous delight than in the camp. "The great force which the King had assembled for the purpose of overawing his mutinous capital had become more mutinous than the capital itself, and was more dreaded by the Court than by the citizens." When James heard the tumult he asked what it was at which the soldiers were cheering. "Oh, nothing," was the reply; "they are only glad the bishops are acquitted." "Do you call that nothing?" retorted the angry king. "So much the worse for them."

When the committee of all parties invited William of Orange to come over, the message was taken by the disguised Admiral Russell, a cousin of Lord William Russell of Highwood, Mill Hill, who had been executed after the Rye House Plot. James could not rely on his army or indeed on any number of his servants. One of the final reasons for the crisis had been the birth of an heir to James's Catholic Queen. When the mother and child had to be smuggled away to the Continent they were put into the care of one of the few families still loyal to King James, William Herbert, Marquess of Powis, and his wife, lord and lady of the Manor of Hendon.

In William's advance from Devonshire to London he halted at Salisbury, found some slight opposition at Hungerford, and from there some troops came along the Bath Road, crossing the Colne between Colnbrook and Longford, while others, after the conference at Windsor, came up the Staines Road and across Hounslow Heath. James had found his army at Hounslow so intractable that he had broken it up and sent the various detachments in different directions. And so the two sections of William's army linked up on the Heath and marched together through Brentford, Hammersmith and Knightsbridge to a London that was waiting to receive them.

William and Mary loved Hampton Court and employed Sir Christopher Wren to add several quadrangles to it, partly by pulling down some of the Tudor structure. Wren's demolitions were not popular, and it was said that Verrio disliked having to decorate the new wings so much that he did his painting badly on purpose. Sir Godfrey Kneller took the place

149

which had formerly been held by Sir Peter Lely, and his portraits are still to be seen there. In one of the small villages near Hampton there died in 1698 William Aldridge, who was 115 years old. He must have witnessed as a child the preparations to resist the Armada, and later on the excitement caused by Gunpowder Plot, the Civil War as it affected Middlesex and London, the Restoration, the Trial of the Seven Bishops, and the Revolution.

William III, like his two predecessors, found Hounslow Heath convenient for troops, employed for his various campaigns, but checked by the clauses of the Mutiny Act. On one occasion there was a spectacular review of troops, during William's absence abroad, by Queen Mary and John Churchill, afterwards the great Duke of Marlborough.

As usually happens after a war, there were thousands of people out of work, and near London many of them seem to have taken to the road as highwaymen. Carriages were attacked even in Hyde Park, and the mail coaches from North, South and West had travellers stripped, bound and flung into ditches. Macaulay reports that "on Hounslow Heath a company of horsemen, with masks on their faces, waited for the great people who had been to pay their court to the King at Windsor. Lord Ossulton escaped with the loss of two horses. The Duke of St. Albans, with the help of his servants, beat off the assailants. His brother, the Duke of Northumberland, less strongly guarded, fell into their hands. They succeeded in stopping thirty or forty coaches and rode off with a great booty in guineas, watches and jewellery."

William, as a Dutchman, was not generally popular, and some folk regretted their disloyalty to King James. A plot was made to assassinate William near Turnham Green at the corner of what is now Sutton Lane, and the chief conspirators were Sir John Fenwick and Sir George Barclay. Barclay met some of the lesser people in the plot at the old Wool Pack Inn. The failure of the scheme made William more popular, and there was increased support for his policy of resistance to the plans of Louis XIV to dominate Europe. When the plans were complete, William was riding through Hampton Court Park on February 20, 1702, mounted on his favourite steed, Sorrel. The horse stumbled over a molehill, throwing the

150

King and causing him to break a collar bone. After it had been set the King drove in his coach to Kensington Palace, but the jolting over the rough roads brought on inflammation and a fever from which he died. The Jacobites, in gratitude to the Mole, used to drink to the health of the little gentleman in brown velvet!

CHAPTER XIV

FAMOUS HOUSES AND WORTHIES

PART I

MIDDLESEX was never a county of big houses such as are still found in Kent or Somerset or the Dukeries, or indeed in almost any other shire of England. Furthermore, the development of suburbia, the construction of roads and railways, the spread of factories, have all tended to curtail the number of big estates; but for all that Middlesex still possesses about a dozen historic mansions that are almost world-famous.

Most accounts of Hampton Court begin by explaining that it belongs to the nation rather than to the county, which is true enough; yet its geographical position is unequivocally in Middlesex, and the county is justified in the pride which such a situation has produced. Apart from Windsor Castle and Westminster Abbey and St. Paul's, Hampton Court is among the very few buildings around which sufficient historical interest has gathered to enable the story of England during several centuries to be written from the events which occurred in just one place. The Manor of Hampton was bequeathed in 1211 by Lady Jane Grey to the Knights of St. John, and their last Prior, Sir Thomas Docwra, granted the lease to Cardinal Wolsey in 1514. Though twelve years were spent in erecting a superb palace of five quadrangles, enough was completed in two years for Wolsey to entertain the King there. By 1520 its magnificence began to excite the King's envy on his return from the historic and extravagant "Field of the Cloth of Gold." In one of the lavish entertainments provided by Wolsey for his guests, masques were performed, countless supper dishes were offered, "large bowls of ducats and dice were placed on the tables for such as liked to gamble," and dancing was enjoyed till far into the night.

It was this magnificence, far surpassing anything that the

King could do at Windsor or St. James's, which prompted Wolsey's enemy, the satirical versifier Skelton, to write :

> "The Kynge's court
> Should have the excellence,
> But Hampton Court
> Hath the pre-emynence."

Wolsey seems to have taken the hint, for in 1526 he offered the palace to Henry with all its contents. Never before or since has so magnificent a gift been bestowed by a subject on his sovereign. After the King had accepted this amazingly generous gift Wolsey still sometimes lived at Hampton. Indeed, in 1527, at Henry's request, the Cardinal entertained the Duke of Montmorency, Grand Master and Marshal of France, and some hundred of his retinue, and extraordinary magnificence was again displayed in evidence. In each bedroom there stood "a bason and ewer of silver, some gilt or parcel gilt and some two great pots of silver in like manner, and one pot at the least with wine and beer, a barole or goblet and a silver pot to drink beer in, a silver candlestick or two and a staff torch."

From 1529, in which year Wolsey was disgraced owing chiefly to the failure of Henry's divorce proceedings, the King occupied the palace with each of his six wives in succession, and he enlarged and improved it. Although for some 250 years Hampton Court was the chief royal residence apart from Windsor Castle and St. James's, George III never liked it, and from that time onward the greater part of the palace, about 1,000 rooms, has been occupied by members of important families in recognition of services to Crown and country.

About forty or fifty people or families enjoy the use of large suites of fifteen to twenty rooms apiece, and on the accession of Queen Victoria the rest of Hampton Court, including the big halls and picture galleries, as well as the superb gardens and two tennis courts, were thrown open to the public without fee or restriction. Full advantage has been taken of this gracious privilege renewed by each succeeding monarch, and the detailed story of the palace has been collected with the utmost diligence and exactitude by Ernest

Law. His summary of its story during a century and more is worth quoting :

"Truly during these years Hampton Court has been as an emblem and monument of English History, consecrated by antiquity and combining the picturesque and romantic elements of an ancient monarchy with the orderly development of popular freedom; linking together the honour and prosperity of the Royal House with the problems and happiness of the toiling multitude; standing, too, as a symbol, palpable and tangible, of that tender attachment of beloved sovereign and people which has distinguished the reigns of recent monarchs, and which inspired the gracious act of freely opening to all their subjects the beautiful home of their ancestors at Hampton Court."

The entrance to Hampton Court is at the south-east corner of the green, close to Hog Walk (then Island) and the bridge across the Thames from Middlesex into Surrey. Through the main gates a wide approach leads to the outer Green Court and the west front. On the left are the barracks, built under Charles II and enlarged by William III. Cardinal Wolsey built the central part of the west front, including the clumsily restored gatehouse, but Henry VIII added the wings in 1535-6. At the same time he built a stone bridge across the moat with a dozen or more "Kynges Beestes," traditional figures supporting armorial shields. These with the bridge and moat were covered up in 1690 by William and Mary, and the figures were not rediscovered until 1884 by Ernest Law, after methodical research.

Passing under the arch of the great gatehouse, one comes into the Green or Box Court, on the left of which is Anne Boleyn's Gateway, with a staircase leading up to the Great Hall, 100 feet long, 40 wide and 60 high. The hall, which may be compared with those of the Inns of Court and of Trinity College, Cambridge, and more especially with that at Christ Church, Oxford, was built by the King and not by Wolsey. It has a splendid roof, comparable with that of Westminster Hall; a minstrels' gallery, with restored balustrade, good modern glass, just about a century old; and magnificent tapestry, designed by Bernard van Orley, a Flemish painter from Brussels.

The Clock Court, with a fine Tudor tower, is part of Wolsey's original building, considerably altered and repaired. Just over the entrance are Wolsey's arms, with his Cardinal's hat and his motto, *Dominus mihi adjutor*. Perhaps he was haunted by this promise when he made his historic remark to Thomas Cromwell. A magnificent astronomical clock was made for Henry VIII in 1540, one of the most elaborate possible. For fifty years of last century it had been left uncared for in a shed, but in 1880 it was cleaned and put back into position, just under the canopy above the gatehouse.

The Fountain Court is all Wren's work, and it is certainly designed to resemble parts of the French royal palace at Versailles. William III was inordinately proud of the additions thus made to the work of Wolsey and King Henry, and he claimed that the "new apartments, for good proportions, state and convenience jointly, were not paralleled by any palace in Europe." Apparently Wren's additions, which involved much destruction of Tudor work, were severely criticised at the time, and Ernest Law seems to have thought that the additions were imposing rather than beautiful and that the red brick gave to Wren's work "an aspect of commonplace uniformity." He disliked the "ugly and incongruous forms of the brick chimneys," and contrasts Wren's style with the truthful old English Gothic.

A good opportunity of comparing styles occurs in the Clock Court, where the far sides of the quadrangle belong to different periods. The west side, with the Clock Gateway, is Wolsey's; on the north side can be seen the windows of Henry VIII's Great Hall; opposite is the colonnade built for William and Mary by Sir Christopher Wren; while the cast side is Georgian.

The Fountain Court, in spite of criticism, is a superb piece of work, 660 feet long and 60 feet high, with four storeys and a parapet and many windows. Those on the south side have been filled in, and instead of glass have frescoes in chiaroscuro of the Twelve Labours of Hercules, painted for King William by the French artist Laffcrerue.

From the Broad Walk one gets a fine view of Wren's east front, completed in 1692, and having a typical Renaissance entrance with three doorways surmounted by four

155

pillars and a pediment—as great a contrast as possible to the Tudor gateways of the earlier period. In the pediment is a carved "Triumph of Hercules over Enemy," by Gabriel Cibber.

The south front is also by Wren, and bears a later inscription to the effect that the whole was built at the cost of William and Mary. Just where the Wren block joins Henry's work there is a small piece of Tudor work still there. The two oriel windows were added by Elizabeth (1568), and behind is a turret from which Charles I is believed to have escaped on November 11, 1647, on his way to Carisbrooke Castle.

The gardens are nearly 50 acres in extent and are famous for Queen Mary's Bower, possibly mentioned in its earlier form by Evelyn; this was used by Mary when busy on the needlework which she and her Court industriously stitched, and altered by George II. The Great Vine came from a slip from Valentines at Ilford in Essex, and its annual crop, though 650 bunches a year, is only a third of its earlier record.

There is a Knott garden laid out by Ernest Law in imitation of the one at Shakespeare's house in Stratford-on-Avon; an orangery built for Queen Anne, and containing Montague's cartoons of the Triumph of Julius Cæsar. To Anne's reign belong the Lion Gates, possibly designed by Jean Tijou.

The other objects of great interest are Henry VIII's tennis court, the oldest in England, used about three centuries before lawn tennis was thought of; and the Maze, a triangular growth of yew, hornbeam, holly and privet. It is said that 10,000,000 people have been lost in two centuries. Perhaps the most famous victories occur in Jerome K. Jerome's *Three Men in a Boat*.

It would need a book to describe the pictures in Hampton Court, over one thousand in number and all the personal property of the King. The collection was begun by Wolsey and added to very considerably by Henry VIII, with his splendid examples of Holbein, Mabuse and Jean Clouet. A few portraits were added under Elizabeth and James I, but it was Charles I who formed one of the most famous collections ever accumulated of most of the great artists of Western

Europe. Many of these pictures were sold from 1648 to 1653, over 350 of them for less than £5,000. Some of them were recovered at the Restoration, but most are abroad. The late Stuarts were great patrons of art, but there is not much to remind us at Hampton Court of the Georges. William IV sent from Kensington Palace and from Windsor Castle Sir Peter Lely's famous pictures of Court favourites called "The Windsor Beauties," and the remarkable collection has from time to time been reconstituted and rearranged.

The thousand and more pictures, by about 300 artists, belonging to almost every country and almost every style are hung in forty rooms, and in their magnificent setting provide perhaps the most superlative art spectacle in the world.

Besides Hampton Court Gardens there is Bushey Park, 1,100 acres, with magnificent avenues of chestnut and lime, with the famous Diana Fountain, and with the Queen's or Cardinal's River flowing through its confines. In Bushey House lived Bradshaw, the regicide, who presided over Charles I's trial in Westminster Hall and refused to allow the King to "speak after sentence." When an earlier Lord Halifax was living in the existing house in Bushey Park he closed the drives to the public. A shoemaker in Hampton Wick, named Timothy Bennet, served Lord Halifax with a notice of action, told the Earl to his face that the people had always used the park, and that he had taken up the challenge because "he was unwilling to leave the world worse than he found it." Bennet's courage won the day and the public still have access to Bushey Park.

Another rediscovery that we really owe to Ernest Law is Henry VIII's Newe Wyne Seller, built between 1530 and 1535, but only cleared and revealed in 1927. Mr. Williams, priest, seems to have been the architect, and there is another cellar, almost identical, in Whitehall under the Board of Trade offices. The cellar was originally constructed perhaps by Wolsey and enlarged under King Henry, and it seems that the King had several other wine cellars in different parts of the palace. Wolsey himself had drawn up strict rules for the preparation and delivery of drink; the brewers were bidden "to brew good and seasonable stuff, without weevil or fustiness," and not to put "hoppes nor brimstone in their ale, so

157

that it may be found good, wholesome and perfect stuff, and worthy the Kynge's money." It was a matter of grave concern to Ernest Law that the reign of the Puritans, followed after a brief interval by Dutch William and then by dull Hanoverians, destroyed the tradition of "generous regal hospitality and the ancient glories of Henry VIII's greate kychen, sellers, boterie and drynkynge house passed away for ever."

EVELYN AND PEPYS AT HAMPTON COURT

It is only to be expected that both Evelyn and Pepys should have left us accounts of their visits to Hampton Court soon after the Restoration. Evelyn is enthusiastic about the building, "as noble and uniform a pile, and as capacious as any Gothic architecture can have made it," and admires its contents, "incomparable furniture in it, especially hangings designed by Raphael, very rich with gold; also many rare pictures especially the Cæsarian triumphs of Andrea Montegna, formerly the Duke of Mantua's; of the tapestries I believe the world can show nothing nobler of the kind than the stories of Abraham and Tobit. The gallery of horns is very particular for the vast beams of stags, elks, antelopes, etc. The Queen's bed was an embroidery of silver on crimson velvet, and cost £8,000, being a present made by the States of Holland when his Majesty returned. . . . The great looking-glass and toilet of beaten and massive gold was given by the Queen-mother. The Queen brought over with her from Portugal such Indian cabinets as has never before been seen here. The great hall is a most magnificent room. The chapel-roof excellently fretted and gilt. . . . The park planted with sweet rows of lime trees; and the canal for water now near perfected; also the hare park. In the garden is a rich and noble fountain, with screens, statues, etc., cast in copper by Fanelli, but not plenty of water. The cradle-work of horn beam in the garden is, for the perplexed twining of trees, very observable."

Pepys, of course, is more interested in the people, and under the date July 27, 1685, he records: "To Hampton

Court, where I saw the King and Queen set out for Salisbury, and after them the Duke and Duchess, whose hands I did kiss. And it was the first time I did ever, or did see anybody else kiss her hand, and it was a most fine white and fat hand. But it was pretty to see the young pretty ladies dressed like men, in velvet coats, caps with ribbands, and with loud bands, just like men. Only the Duchesse herself it did not become."

John Evelyn went again to Hampton Court after the Bloodless Revolution was over and Wren was beginning his replanning. "To Hampton about businesse, the Council being there. A greate apartment and spacious garden with fountains was beginning in the Park at the head of the Canal." This was, of course, the King's or Cardinal's River.

Nathaniel Hawthorne visited Hampton Court on March 24, 1856, "a clear day for England," and left a very vivid story of the place, complaining of the difficulty of seeing so many pictures in so many galleries, "like trying to read a hundred poems at once—a most absurd attempt." He says : "Vandyke's picture of Charles I, on a white horse beneath an arched gateway, made more impressions on me than any other, and it seems as if I could see the King's noble, melancholy face, and armed form, remembered not in picture, but in reality." He does not seem to have been impressed by "all Sir Peter Leley's lewd women, and Kneller's too." The picture which he remembered most clearly was one which he calls "a ridiculous old travesty of the Resurrection and Last Judgment where the dead folk are represented as coming to life at the sound of the trumpet . . . one man picking up his skull and putting it on his shoulders." But the final impression made on his mind was a lasting one.

"What a noble palace, nobly enriched is this Hampton Court! The English government does well to keep it up, and to admit the people freely into it, for it is impossible even for a Republican not to feel something like awe—at least, a profound respect—for all this state, and for the institutions which are here represented, the sovereigns whose moral magnificence demanded such a residence; and its permanence, too, enduring from age to age, and each royal generation adding new splendours to those accumulated by their predecessors. If one views the matter in another way, to be sure, we may feel indignant that such dolt-heads, rowdies, and every way mean people, as many of the English sovereigns have been, should inherit these stately halls, contrasting its splendour with their littleness; but, on the whole, I readily consented within myself to be impressed for a moment with the feeling that royalty has its glorious side."

In the late summer of 1947 the astronomical clock and the bells in the turret of Hampton Court were restored by the Ministry of Works, and in the process the bell founder's name was identified on two quarter bells as William Culverden (1510-23). The hour bell was cast by Thomas Harrys, 1478-80, and the clock as a whole was installed by King Henry VIII.

SOUTHALL MANOR-HOUSE

Southall is a district where a great deal of unregulated building has recently taken place, and the population has increased more than fortyfold in the last century. Some effort has been made to safeguard open spaces, but Martin Briggs has good reason to lament the loss in quite recent times of "the chalybeate springs which gave the name to Dorman's Wells Farm, the quaint wooden water-mill in Windmill Lane, the medieval bridge over the Brent, the stocks near the Co-operative Stores, and the blacksmith's forge at the corner of South Road and High Street, together with many old houses and cottages."

The outstanding feature in Southall is the old half-timbered manor-house, dating from about 1587, a year before the Armada, with mullioned windows and gabled windows. In the centre are two smaller gables, one containing the main entrance. One of the big gabled wings has a two-storeyed oriel, the other has two windows in brackets. The house belonged for some centuries to the Awsiter family, London merchants, lawyers and aldermen, who are mainly buried in Norwood Church.

The Manor of Southall (perhaps South Holt) was held during the Middle Ages by the Shoredykes, under the Archbishop of Canterbury, then by Cheesemans, and later by Fynes, Lord Dacre, who lived at Dormans Well Farm, north of the Uxbridge Road.

160

The manor-house has additions of the eighteenth century, and some of the original panelling is to be seen in the hall, with a handsome fireplace carved with the Awsiter arms and the initials R. A. The house belongs to Southall and Northwood and is a welfare centre for children. The grounds have been well laid out with clipped yews, ponds and an aviary, and quite close at hand the memorial to those who fell in the first World War.

SWAKELEYS

Ickenham is a small place with a village green, a pond and pump, a quaint inn and a charming church which claims to be of Saxon origin but has nothing earlier than the thirteenth century. Its small wooden belfry with tiny spire is reminiscent of Cowley, Greenford, Northolt and Perivale, and within the church are many memorials to the famous Newdigate family, to the Shorediches of Ickenham Hall and to the later Clarkes. There is also a bust of the Earl of Essex, the Parliamentary General, which was brought from Swakeleys. William Sage, Registrar to Queen Elizabeth, is buried there, and there is a fine brass commemorating him and his wife, their seven sons and nine daughters. Less than a mile south-west of Ickenham village stands the glorious Jacobean mansion of Swakeleys, which derives its name from Robert Swalclyve, who owned the manor under Edward III. The property passed in 1629 to Edmund Wright, who built the present house in 1638 and was Lord Mayor of London three years later. Some parts of an earlier mansion may be included in the square red-brick house, with large oriel windows in its slightly projecting wings. There are two main storeys with a parapet above and scrolled gables and well-designed chimney stacks to complete the design. The bay windows at each end of the wings give the house an H shape, and the principal entrance is through a two-storeyed porch in the centre of the west side, with a bust just above it.

During the Civil War Swakeleys was held by Sir James Harrington, one of King Charles's judges in 1649, who had married Edmund Wright's daughter. When Charles II regained the throne, Harrington escaped to the Continent, and

Mews at Hampton Court

the estate passed from his wife to Sir Robert Vyner, another Lord Mayor and friend of Pepys.

The diarist's tale of his visit to Swakeleys need not be quoted save to remark on the screen in the hall, which most intrigued him. "Pretty to see over the screene of the hall, put up by Sir J. Harrington, a Long Parliament man, the King's head and my Lord of Essex on one side, and Fairfax on the other; and upon the other side of the screene the parson of the parish and the Lord of the Manor and his sisters." There was also the dead Black Boy, dried in an oven and preserved "entire in a box."

Martin Briggs notes that Broome Park in East Kent, the home of Lord Kitchener, distinctly resembles Swakeleys, and was built at much the same time, while others see a strong likeness to Holland House and Knole.

In 1750 the house was bought by Thomas Clarke, and it remained in his family for two centuries and a half, having a narrow escape from fire in 1884. The Clarkes were very lucky with their domestic staff, and their gratitude is recorded on memorials in the church and in the graveyard: thirty years' service of a housekeeper, forty of a housemaid, and forty-two of a nurse. The housekeeper was "one of the most admirable and exemplary of women, and the best servant surely that ever came within the walls of the house."

The grounds are well wooded but are intersected by the River Pin, which has been dammed to form a lake, with several small islands therein.

There was a serious risk some years ago that Swakeleys might be pulled down by iconoclastic vandals and the estate split up for building, but the danger seems now to have gone, as between the wars it was bought with its fine stable court and its gardens of 28 acres as a country club for the Foreign Office Sports Association. As in the more recent case of Apsley House, "No. 1" London, the owner still lives in an upstairs suite. A splendidly illustrated book about Swakeleys was published in 1934 by the London Survey Committee, and it was written by W. H. Godfrey, one of the most competent writers on London. H. Avery Tipping had given it a short excellent survey in his *English Houses,* published in 1927.

162

HAREFIELD

Harefield is situated in one of the most beautiful corners of Middlesex, and it has more interesting historic and literary association than anywhere else in the county save Hampton Court. It is high and well wooded, it is on the border of Herts and Bucks, and the Grand Union Canal as well as the various branches of the Colne flow through its broad meadows. The manor is traced from the days of Edward the Confessor, through Bacheworths, Swanlands, Newdigates and Egertons. Sir Thomas Egerton, the famous Chancellor and adviser of Queen Elizabeth, owned Harefield, and was the friend and patron of Bacon, of Ben Jonson, William Camden and Samuel Daniel. He married as his second wife Alice, widow of Ferdinando Stanley, Earl of Derby, patron of Edmund Spenser. Spenser, Nash and Chapman wrote poems about Derby and his wife, with whom Spenser claimed some bonds of affinity. He hailed her as Amaryllis and her husband as Amyntas. Soon after her marriage to Egerton the widowed Dowager Countess entertained at Harefield Queen Elizabeth, who arrived on July 31, 1602, when she was about seventy years of age, and stayed for three days. The players and dancers hired to amuse her cost £64 18s. 10d., and there is an old tradition that the Lord Chamberlain's Company played *Othello* and that Shakespeare directed the play. The Queen still liked flattery, and she was greeted as—

> "Beauty's rose and, virtue's book,
> Angel's mind and Angel's look."

In 1635 John Milton, who was living only four miles away at Horton, wrote his *Arcades* to entertain the Dowager Countess of Derby at Harefield. Her daughter married the Earl of Bridgwater, for whom at Ludlow John Milton and Henry Lawes collaborated in the famous masque of *Comus*.

The Countess of Derby's Almshouses are still in Harefield, and there is a fine recumbent figure in the church representing her in red dress with ermine coat and five bead necklaces. Her daughters are commemorated there, and many of the Newdigates. The Breakspear Chantry takes its name from the old Tudor house, with Jacobean panelling, hard by.

There seems to be good reason for associating the place with the Breakspear family, which supplied the only Englishman who ever became Pope, Nicholas Breakspear, who was raised to the chair of St. Peter in 1154. His occupation of the Papal See lasted for only a few years, and was chiefly noteworthy for his share in the death of the wise reformer, Arnold of Brescia, whose tactful rule of Rome for ten years gave promise of an earlier and bloodless reformation. The estate of Breakspears, extending to over 572 acres, has been bought under the Green Belt scheme, and it continues the Ruislip reservation of 850 acres up to the Middlesex border of Harefield.

When Sir Charles Sedley, one of King Charles II's boon companions, was staying at Harefield he allowed his candle to start a fire while he was reading in bed, and the whole house was destroyed. It was rebuilt in 1675 and pulled down in 1800. Besides its church, Harefield has Moor Hall Chapel and perhaps the finest collection of sixteenth- and seventeenth-century farmhouses, inns and cottages to be seen near London, all recorded in the *Historical Monuments Inventory*.

OSTERLEY PARK

The West Middlesex Regional Town Planning Report of 1924 recommended the purchase of Osterley Park of 313 acres, of Syon Park (154 acres) and a riverside strip along the Crane of 128 acres. Osterley Manor at the Dissolution belonged to the Abbess and Convent of Syon, and was granted by Henry VIII to Henry Courtney, the Marquis of Exeter. Courtney was unluckily related to the Tudors; his father, John, died in the Tower, he himself was executed for alleged treason, and his son died in exile at Padua, after having figured as a possible husband for both Mary and Elizabeth.

Edward VI granted Osterley with its ancient manor-house to his uncle, Protector Somerset, but when Somerset was executed it again reverted to the Crown. In 1570 it was granted by Elizabeth to Sir Thomas Gresham, a pioneer in London finance, who built the first Royal Exchange. Gresham at once began to build a splendid palace, which was quite unnecessary, seeing that he already possessed five mansions in

Norfolk, one in Sussex and two or three more in different parts of England. Gresham was not content with the estate he had received, but enclosed much common land nearby, to the annoyance of his neighbours and the prejudice of the poor. When Elizabeth visited him in 1578 a play was specially written in her honour, and elaborate preparations were made to please her. She suggested that the courtyard would look better with a dividing wall, and so Gresham summoned workmen from London, who did the wall quickly and quietly during the night. When Elizabeth awoke she was delighted and her courtiers were amazed at the transformation. Someone wittily remarked that it was easy for a man who had built a change to change a building. During the Queen's visit, indignation at Gresham's enclosures goaded local peasants to burn his park palings. The Queen indignantly insisted on the offenders being locked up in the Marshalsea prison.

John Norden, writing some years later, described Osterley as a fair and stately building of brick standing "in a park impaled, well wooded and garnished with manie fish ponds, which affordeth not only fish and foode, as swans and other water fowle, but also a great rise for milles, as paper milles, oyle milles and corn milles, all of which are now decayed, a corn mille only excepted. In the same park was a fair for the increase and preservation whereof sundry alurements were devised and set up, fallen all to ruin."

Elizabeth had an unreasoning jealousy of the Greys, sisters of the hapless Lady Jane Grey, for ten days nominal Queen of England. Lady Katherine Grey had been married for a very brief time to the Earl of Pembroke's elder son, but divorced directly it was seen that Mary would get the throne. Katherine was imprisoned in the Tower and there got married, much to Elizabeth's indignation. A third sister, Lady Mary Grey, was foisted on Sir Thomas Gresham at Osterley, in spite of his protest, and he had to keep her a close prisoner there for three years. Gresham died at Osterley only a year after Elizabeth's visit. Evidently the stables date from Gresham's time, with octagonal towers at each end, and a clock and cupola above the roof—very reminiscent of Bruce Castle at Tottenham.

On Lady Gresham's death the property passed to her son

by a former marriage, Sir William Read. His great-great-daughter, the Countess of Desmond, who had a romantic marriage, lived here, and then in 1655 Osterley was bought by Sir William Waller, the Parliamentary General, whose early success in the West earned him the short-lived title of "William the Conqueror." His defeat at Bath and Devizes and Cropredy Bridge spoiled his fame, but he did better when serving in the West under Cromwell. Waller tried to oppose the advance of the Army to London in 1647, and was one of the Presbyterian Members excluded from Parliament by Pride's Purge. He wrote a *Vindication of Sir William Waller* to justify his conduct during the wars. For a short time it seems to have belonged to Dr. Nicholas Barbon, the speculative builder who developed the Strand and Holborn in post-Fire London.

Sir Francis Child, the famous banker, purchased Osterley in 1711, and it was extensively altered by Robert Adam then and largely reconstructed fifty years later. The four Elizabethan towers at the corners were refaced, the red-brick mansion 140 feet by 127 feet was replanned, and an Ionic portico was added in the centre of the principal front, approached by a flight of steps. A letter of Horace Walpole, then living at Strawberry Hill, to the Countess of Ossory in 1773 gives a graphic picture of his visit:

"On Friday we went to see—oh the palace of palaces!—and yet a palace *sans* crown, *sans* coronet, but such expense! such taste! such profusion! and yet half an acre produces all the rents that furnish such magnificence. It is a sapphire got without a crime. The old house I have often seen, which was built by Sir Thomas Gresham; but it is so improved and enriched that all the Percies and Seymours of Syon must die of envy. There is a double portico that fills the space between the towers of the front, and is as noble as the Propylæum at Athens. There is a hall, library, breakfast room, eating room, all *chefs d'œuvre* of Adam, a gallery one hundred and thirty feet long, and a drawing room worthy of Eve before the Fall."

Robert Child succeeded his brother, and the Earl of Westmorland asked him, as his banker, how to marry a rich man's daughter without the father's consent. Child, having no idea that the daughter in question was his own, advised an elopement, and the Earl took him at his word.

The portico at Osterley is of unusual dimensions, being double colonnaded, with a pediment each side, a decorated ceiling and twelve slender Ionic pillars.

Robert Child's grand-daughter and heiress conveyed Osterley Park in marriage to the Earl of Jersey, in whose family the house still remains. It is typically Georgian in style and has a magnificent collection of furniture and pictures, famous relics and wall-paintings. Holbein, Van Dyck, Rubens, Reynolds, Angelica Kauffmann and Lawrence among the portrait painters are well represented, and there are landscapes by Claude, Ruysdael and Gainsborough. Lord Jersey has co-operated with the National Trust and the Georgian Group in preserving the historic treasures of Osterley. He also began in 1939 a garden of historic trees, seedlings and of shoots from the Hatfield oak, where Elizabeth received the news of Queen Mary's death; from the Boscobel oak which sheltered Charles II; from a mulberry tree known to Milton at Christ's College, Cambridge; from Bacon's catalpa at Gray's Inn; from Hougoumont, St. Helena and Ypres; from Gilbert White's yew tree at Selborne; and many other historic specimens. The second World War naturally hampered the progress of this interesting and important enterprise.

BRUCE CASTLE, TOTTENHAM

Tottenham has grown in population with remarkable regularity throughout the last century and a half from 4,000 in 1801 to over 160,000 today. Of its 3,000 acres, reduced from 4,600 by the deduction of 1,600 to Wood Green in 1888, a fair proportion is scheduled for open spaces. It has a fine Central Library and unrivalled local collections, its historians have been generous and competent, there is a good deal of romance still to be discovered in its byways, and Tottenham Hill has its memories of Izaac Walton. In 1824 Pinnock writes that "Tottenham, usually called High Cross . . . is a long straggling village, not remarkable for its beauty nor pleasantness; yet it contains many handsome mansions." The finest group of these still surviving is con-

gregated round the old parish church of All Hallows, with
its stone tower repaired with brick in its upper storey. Local
tradition attributes the foundation of the church to David of
Scotland, who by his marriage with the daughter of Earl
Waltheof became lord of the Manor of Tottenham. Near to
the church is Bruce Castle, reputed to stand on the site of
Waltheof's palace, and owing its name to Robert Bruce,
who, like David, became King of Scotland. Oddly enough,
one of his rivals, John Balliol, one of the family associated
with the famous college at Oxford, also possessed a manor in
Tottenham.

Bruce Castle was rebuilt in 1514 by Sir William Compton,
who entertained King Henry VIII there and also Henry's
sister Margaret, Queen of Scots, from whom our unfortunate
line of Stuarts was descended. In 1578 Queen Elizabeth
visited Bruce Castle in one of her many country-house tours,
and the only part now left of Compton's building is an isolated
brick tower.

The Comptons lived at Bruce Castle till 1630, when it
passed to Hare, Lord Coleraine, who evidently rebuilt the
place in seventeenth-century style. A daughter, born in Italy,
of the last Lord Coleraine, inherited the property, but in
spite of her marriage to an Englishman the estate escheated
to the Crown. It was restored in 1792 and sold, and then in
1827 it became the property of the Hills. When their school
was given up in 1891 the Tottenham Council bought the
house for a museum and the park for a public recreation
ground.

Bruce Castle is of red brick with stone dressings, and at
either end of the main building are semi-octagonal wings,
with extensions beyond. Above the central porch there is a
square tower with balconies above and below, a clock, and
above a small turret and cupola.

West of Tottenham Church is the Priory, built about 1620
by Joseph Fenton, whose name is seen on ceilings and on
fireplace overmantels. There are two finely panelled rooms,
but considerable rebuilding occurred about a century later,
and there is another finely carved chimney-piece in the dining-
room. A magnificent iron gateway, brought from the old
vicarage, has been placed in the fine brick wall that stands

between the garden and the public road. The Priory has been used by the Vicar of Tottenham for about half a century, and, as Martin Briggs cogently remarks, "it is most essential that it be preserved from the hands of the land-shark; here is the one corner of Tottenham that still retains the charm of old days."

BOSTON HOUSE

Boston House at Brentford derives its name from the old Manor of Bordeston or Burston, belonging to the Convent of St. Helen's, Bishopsgate. King Edward VI granted it to his uncle, Duke of Somerset, but it returned to the Crown after Somerset's execution. Robert Dudley, Earl of Leicester, held it for a short time under Queen Elizabeth, but he sold it to Sir Thomas Gresham, whose family held it, like Osterley, till 1598. Sir William Reade, Lady Gresham's son by a former husband, lived there till 1621. His widow was responsible for much of the beauty of Boston House, and in the ceiling of the state drawing-room can be seen "M. R. 1623." Lady Spencer, as she became, died in 1658, and later the house was damaged by fire. Boston House was purchased in 1670 by James Clitherow, restored in 1671, and remained in the family's keeping until 1927, when it was bought with its park as a permanent open space.

The house, a three-storeyed building of brick and stone, with a handsome porch, magnificent reception-rooms and staircases, is surrounded by very fine gardens where grow three unusually tall cedars. The state drawing-room on the first floor has a remarkable carved plaster ceiling with many allegorical figures. A striking feature is the fireplace with an overmantel with carved figures surrounding a medallion depicting Abraham being prevented by the angel from sacrificing his son. There was, as is so usual, a desire to attribute the carving to Grinling Gibbons, but the date seems to make this quite impossible.

Fred Turner's exhaustive *History and Antiquities of Brentford*, which is so enthusiastic about Boston House and the good works of the Clitherows for 250 years, ends his volume with a gloomy story of the sale of the family heirlooms. These included portraits and landscape by Titian and

169

Zucchero, Van Dyck, Rubens and Lely, and three family portraits by George Romney. Considering the paltry prices paid, it seems a great pity that early steps were not taken to secure for the community the contents as well as the house and grounds.

GUNNERSBURY HOUSE

Gunnersbury means Gunnhill's Manor, or fortified dwelling, and, as King Canute is associated with the battle of Brentford in 1016, it is not unreasonable to wonder whether the place took its name from his sister, who lived in England until she was banished for some unspecified misdemeanour in 1044. Another woman of royal associations held the manor in the middle of the fourteenth century—Alice Perrers, the evil genius of Edward III's later life. She was a member of Queen Philippa's household, and after the Queen's death acquired such influence over the King that she could almost dictate his policy. The Good Parliament of 1376, under Peter Delamere and supported by the Black Prince, impeached some of the King's favourites for fraud, and forced Alice Perrers to promise "never to return to the King's presence." In spite of the collapse of reform after the Black Prince's death and the return of Alice Perrers and her friends, impeachment had been tried and the responsibility of ministers had been tentatively asserted—two reforms of far-reaching importance. Alice Perrers continued her baneful influence over the King, and when he died she stole his rings from his fingers. She was once again banished from the realm in 1378 and Gunnersbury Manor was confiscated to the Crown. An inventory tells us that there were a hall, chapel, kitchens, bakehouse, stables and barns; two gardens of small value, only 1s. 6d. a year because the wind had destroyed the apple trees; 4 acres of arable land at 26s. 8d. a year; 60 acres of pasture at 8d. an acre; and 17 acres of meadowland at 5s. a year. Two years later Alice Perrers was reprieved from banishment and married Lord Windsor, to whom in 1388 Richard II granted Gunnersbury Manor.

In the next century it belonged to the Hawicks, also associated with South Mimms. Under Charles II, John Maynard, a former pupil of Sir William Noy, was rewarded for his tactful behaviour during the previous crisis and became King's Sergeant. His success as a lawyer enabled him in 1663 to purchase Gunnersbury and rebuild the house from designs supplied by Webb, a successor to Inigo Jones. He lived at Gunnersbury for nearly thirty years and was appointed in 1689 one of the Lords Commissioners of the Great Seal by "their most excellent Majesties King William and Queen Mary." When Maynard met the King it was suggested that he must have survived all the lawyers of his day. He replied that if William had not come to the rescue he would have outlived all the law too! Maynard's third wife survived him by thirty years, married the Earl of Suffolk, and lived at Gunnersbury till her death in 1721. In 1761 the house was bought for £9,000 by H.R.H. Princess Amelia, aunt of George III, and she planted many trees in the gardens, improved the house in various ways, and lavishly entertained many people of distinction. Once again we turn to Horace Walpole as gossip :

"I was sent for again to dine at Gunnerbury on Friday, and was forced to send to town for a dress coat and sword. There were present the Prince of Wales, the Prince of Mecklenburg, the Duke of Portland, Lord Clanbrassie, Lord and Lady Clermont, Lord and Lady Southampton, the Princess, Lady Barrymore and Lord Pelham and Miss Hood . . . the rest of us played three pools at Commerce till ten. I am afraid I gaped. While we were at the dairy, the Princess insisted on my making some verses on Gunnersbury. I pleaded being superannuated; she would not excuse me. I promised she should have an ode on her next birthday, which diverted the Prince—but all would not do—so, as I came home I made the following stanzas and sent them to her breakfast next morning :

'In deathless odes for ever green
Augustus' laurels blow;
Nor e'er was grateful duty seen
In warmer strains to flow.

Oh! why is Flaccus not alive
Your fav'rite scene to sing?
To Gunnersbury's charms could give
His lyre immortal Spring.

171

As warm as is my zeal for you,
Great princess, could I but show it;
But though you have a Horace too—
Ah, Madam, he's no poet.'

"If these are poor verses, consider, I am old, was half asleep, and made them almost extempore—and by command. However, they succeeded, and I received this gracious answer from the Princess :

"'I wish I had a name that could answer your pretty verses. Your yawning yesterday opened your vein for pleasing me, and I return you my thanks, my good Mr. Walpole, and remain sincerely your friend Amelia.'

"I think this is very genteel at seventy-five."

When Bute was in disgrace after his dismissal by the King, the Princess Amelia tried to bring about a reconciliation by arranging a meeting in a narrow piece of the grounds. The King promptly turned on his heel and declined to meet his former Minister. A happier occasion was the entertaining of thirty poor housekeepers at Gunnersbury Park by the Princess, at the conclusion of which she presented them each with a guinea.

On the death of the Princess in 1786 the property was sold and changed hands several times, the house being demolished in 1801. Alexander Copland built a smaller house in the grounds, and Baron Lionel de Rothschild lived in the present house for many years, being succeeded by Leopold de Rothschild. Among many distinguished visitors during the Rothschilds' time at Gunnersbury was Benjamin Disraeli. In 1925 the houses and estate were bought by the joint Councils of Acton, Ealing and Brentford-Chiswick, and a fine collection of Middlesex antiquities is housed there. The temple, a small building in Greek design, is almost all that is left of the Princess Amelia's buildings, but the gardens, with their many cedars, laid out by Kent, are still as well kept as ever.

CHISWICK HOUSE

Chiswick today retains a good deal of village aspect, with several historic houses still standing, more spacious gardens than in many suburbs, Chiswick Mall and Strand on the Green almost unspoiled. Chiswick House was first built in the sixteenth century, and it was here that Robert Carr, Earl of Somerset, and his notorious wife retired after having been first convicted of the murder of Sir Thomas Overbury and then shamelessly pardoned by King James I. This fine Elizabethan mansion was acquired by the first Earl of Burlington with its 66 acres in 1702 for £4,600. To this house he added in 1704 the Grosvenor wing to the north-east, which still exists, and then from 1730-1736 William Kent added the central portion for Richard Boyle, third Earl of Burlington, adapting his design from a villa built at Vicenza by Palladio.

In 1788 the Elizabethan house was pulled down and wings were added on either side of the Palladian villa designed by James Wyatt. This work was done for the Duke of Devonshire, who had acquired the property, where the hospitality extended by him and his famous wife Georgiana was proverbial. One of the most famous of all their guests was Charles James Fox, Foreign Secretary in Grenville's Ministry of all the Talents formed after Pitt's death early in 1806. Fox was to all intents and purposes Premier; he and King George had made up their quarrel, and the Minister was endeavouring very tactfully to push through at one and the same time peace with France, Catholic Emancipation and the Abolition of the Slave Trade. But he was destined to control England's destinies for only a few months. In August, 1806, Fox was attacked with severe dropsy and begged to be taken to St. Anne's Hill. But the doctors advised shorter stages, and the Duke of Devonshire offered Chiswick House as a halfway house. On August 27 Fox left his London home, and he "had a brown loose mantle thrown over his shoulders, and wore very wide nankeen pantaloons, and a fur travelling cap. Its appearance excited great emotion among the spectators, many of whom shed tears on seeing the change in his countenance."

Several painful operations were performed, but the end was only being delayed, and his wife Elizabeth and friends and relatives took it in turn to read to him from Dryden, Vergil and Swift and Johnson's *Lives of the Poets*. He was able to go out from Chiswick House for one or two drives with his wife, holding her hand all the while, asking her to kiss him and begging her to repeat Denham's lines on the Thames from Cooper's Hill. George Jackson, home from Russia, came on official business and was taken up to Fox's bedroom. Elizabeth took refuge, barely half-dressed, in an adjoining room, and, when Jackson's stay was protracted, begged to come out, as she was "so very, very cold."

On September 12 Henry Petty, Chancellor of the Exchequer at the age of twenty-eight, could not restrain his emotion at the sight of the dying statesman; a young clergyman said prayers, which Charles knew would be a comfort to Elizabeth, his wife, and then after a night of horror, followed by a morning of calm, he said farewell to his "dearest, dearest Liz" and "at twenty minutes before six by a watch regulated by the sun," he, whom Lord Holland ventured to call the best and greatest man of his time, died, to be lamented by his family, by his devoted friends, and even by King George III, who said : "I never thought I should have regretted the death of Mr. Fox as much as I do." As John Drinkwater sagely remarks : "A strange conclusion to one of the most relentless feuds in English history."

Another statesman who spent many years in the political wilderness and only came into his own for a brief spell was George Canning, a loyal supporter of William Pitt, whom he styled "the pilot who weathered the storm," and perhaps, even more than Disraeli, the founder of the Conservative party. His work at the Foreign Office was cut by a duel with Castlereagh over the unsuccessful Walcheren expedition of 1809, and "twelve eventful years were destined to pass before Canning was again to direct the foreign policy of Great Britain." But he watched with concern the continental wars and the collapse of Napoleon, the Congress of Vienna and the Holy Alliance, until the sudden success of his former rival, Lord Londonderry (Castlereagh), restored him to the control of foreign affairs. For five years he tried to clarify the policy for a European system, combated the feared domination of Russia, was interested in the internal affairs of Spain and Portugal, determined that if France ruled the Peninsula it should be without the Indies, supported the Munro doctrine and based his foreign policy upon a tacit alliance with U.S.A., "called a new world into existence in order to redress the balance of the old," and intervened to rescue the Greeks. He reached the summit of his ambition only a few months before his death, which occurred on August 8, 1827, in the same room at Chiswick House where Charles James Fox had died just twenty-one years before. The Duke of Devonshire recognised the serious character of Canning's illness, caused by a cold contracted at the funeral of the Duke of York at Windsor, and, like his father, offered the hospitality of Chiswick to the leading statesman of his day, in the unfulfilled hope that rest might prolong so valuable a life.

At Chiswick House the Duke of Devonshire entertained Alexander I of Russia and the other allied sovereigns who visited England between Napoleon's two banishments to Elba and St. Helena; the Queen and Prince Consort stayed there in 1842, and the Emperor Nicholas I in 1844. For some years King Edward VII lived at Chiswick House, but later on it was used as a home for the mentally deficient.

In the churchyard are buried Whistler, whose Thames studies may have been the genesis of impressionism and post-impressionism; Sir William Richmond, who decorated the dome of St. Paul's; William Kent, the landscape gardener; Henry Joy, who sounded the Charge of the Light Brigade at Balaclava; while in the church itself rest Barbara Villiers, created by Charles II Duchess of Cleveland; and Mary and Frances, daughters of Oliver Cromwell. There was a plan for Charles II to marry Frances Cromwell, but Cromwell mistrusted Charles and thought that Charles I's execution could never be forgotten. She married Robert Rich, heir to the Earl of Warwick, who died nine weeks after their marriage, and later Sir John Russell, who also died prematurely. After half a century of widowhood she herself died in 1720.

Chiswick House has a portico with Corinthian columns on the second storey, with four elaborate staircases, later combined into two, leading up to it. Behind it is an octagonal dome, and at the foot of the stairways are appropriate statues of Inigo Jones and of Palladio, the architects chiefly responsible for its design. There is a fine avenue of early cedar trees brought from Lebanon as seedlings, according to the legend, but not as early as 1641, as local legend insists.

The Royal Commission on Historical Monuments has given an inventory of over forty houses in Chiswick and Strand on the Green worthy of notice, including Woodroffe House, Bedford House, Red Lion, Strawberry, Morton and Boston Houses, Hogarth House, Burlington Corner and the Duke of Devonshire's Almshouses, all built before 1700.

Alexander Pope, a satirist in verse, and William Hogarth, a satirist in pen, both of whom we shall meet elsewhere, lived in Chiswick, and one of the greatest of Italian patriots, Ugo Foscolo, lived in exile for years at Turnham Green, writing on the Italian poets and longing for his country to be free. He died in 1827 and was buried in Chiswick churchyard, where Garibaldi laid a wreath on his grave. In 1871, when Italy was once more united and free, the Italian Government removed his body to the Church of Santa Cruz in Florence and carved on his tombstone at Chiswick:

> "This spot, where for 44 years the relics of Ugo Foscolo reposed in honoured custody, will be forever held in grateful remembrance by the Italian nation."

DAWLEY COURT AND BOLINGBROKE

Of the buildings approached or threatened by London Airport, several are scheduled by the Royal Commission on Historical Monuments as "especially worthy of preservation." These are the parish churches of East Bedfont, Cranford, Harmondsworth and Hanwell, the medieval barn at Harmondsworth, and the School House at Stanwell. But the village of Harlington, which gave its name, minus the "H," to the second member of Charles II's important Cabal Ministry, has some very attractive and historic buildings which ought to be safeguarded. The Church of St. Peter and St. Paul possesses a fine Norman font, a Norman south doorway with zigzag mouldings, and an Easter sepulchre. The elaborate doorway, with its twenty-five cats' heads in the outer member of the arch, has some likeness to that at Harmondsworth, and has been considered the equal in design and execution of the better-known doorways at Barfrestone and Patrixbourne, near Canterbury, and Iffley, near Oxford. The Easter sepulchre, which was constructed only about

176

1535-40, incorporates the slab and brass of Gregory Lovell, who died in 1545.

In the churchyard is a magnificent yew tree nearly seven and a half centuries old, with a trunk 24 feet round; in the vicarage garden is a particularly fine cedar. A family of Harpendens, taking their name no doubt from the Hertfordshire village, was followed by Lovells as lords of one of the three manors into which Harlington was divided. Lovells passed it on to St. John, Lord Bolingbroke, one of the most interesting figures in the early eighteenth century.

Bolingbroke lived in his "farm" at Dawley Court during the years after his return from exile, and was glad to be "in a hermitage, where no man came but for the sake of the hermit; for here he found that the insects which used to hum and buzz about him in the sunshine fled to men of more prosperous fortune, and forsook him in the shade."

Dryden, Swift and Pope paid visits to him at Dawley, and Voltaire was a frequent visitor while he was preparing his *Letters from England* during his exile from France.

Over the door of the house he placed an Horatian inscription, "Satis beatus ruris honoribus," and he might have borrowed an equally apposite one from Virgil : "O fortunatos nimium, sua si bona norint."

Bolingbroke's writings in his *Craftsman,* his *Dissertation upon Parties* and his *Letters on the Study of History* influenced the Tories in the struggle against America, gave to Burke some of the ammunition with which to bombard the French revolutionaries, and helped to mould the policy of Disraeli, who welcomed and imitated his hostility to the Whigs. "It was his inspiring pen," Disraeli wrote in his *Vindication of the English Constitution,* "that made Walpole tremble in the recesses of the Treasury . . . in a series of writings, unequalled in our literature for their spirited patriotism, their just and profound views, and the golden eloquence in which they are expressed."

In the first volume of the *Gentleman's Magazine* for 1731 there were some verses on Dawley's Farm, in which the writer praises Bolingbroke's modesty because

"no gaudy colours deck the rural hall";

177   M

Hampton Court, entrance gateway

and

"what he built a palace calls a farm";

compliments the noble St. John because at Dawley

"Here the proud trophies and the spoils of war
Yield to the scythe, the harrow and the car";

and is deeply sorry that this wondrous man is lost to fame and unable to help England :

Here, splendidly obscure, delighted lives,
And only for his wretched country grieves."

Bolingbroke left Dawley in 1739, and by 1776 all that was standing was the steward's wing, still there today more than 200 years after St. John left it. Pope wrote of Canon's words, which apply more aptly to Dawley now that the grounds, where Bolingbroke read a letter from Pope as he reclined on a haycock, are traversed by the Grand Union Canal and the Great Western Railway :

"Another age shall see the golden ear
Imbrown the slope and nod on the parterre;
Deep harvests bury all his pride has plann'd,
And laughing Ceres re-assume the land."

Only, alas! Ceres herself has now had to give way to the modern gods of factories and suburbs and airports.

Gordon Maxwell, in *Highwayman's Heath,* refers to Dawley Farm, "where Swift read Gulliver aloud," and it seems probable that the legend is a correct one. For many years the property belonged to the family of de Salis, who provided one military hero, General Rudolph Leslie de Salis, who led the 8th Hussars in the Charge of the Light Brigade at Balaclava and almost immediately afterwards fought through the Indian Mutiny. When the de Salis family parted with Dawley it was purchased by the Gramophone Company of Hayes, who still use the old house. It seemed probable that enlargement would mean the destruction of Dawley Farm, but it was reprieved just before the second World War. "To pull down this fine old house, with its wonderful silent

178

memories, merely to add to the din of an already noise-racked world, would have been an unpardonable crime."

JACOBITES

A contact with the reign of Queen Anne is the building of the present poor brick tower of St. Nicholas' Church by the Rector, Lewis Atterbury, brother to the famous High Church bishop who was prior to the plot for putting the Young Pretender on the throne when his sister Anne should die. Not long before Anne's death, realising that Bolingbroke was scheming on the Pretender's behalf, the Whigs crowded into the Privy Council Chamber and persuaded the Queen to give the seals to the Duke of Shrewsbury, who had a house at Isleworth, nowadays a Romanist convent. Much of the story of these intrigues is well known from Thackeray's masterpiece, *Esmond*.

The Jacobites were not satisfied with their previous efforts, and risings were organised in Northern England and in Scotland. The Earl of Derwentwater, who perished on Tower Hill, had a house at Acton, where his countess was living at the time, and it is thought that Derwentwater went to the Tower from his Acton home and that the gates were never open after that hapless day. More fortunate was Lord Nithsdale, whose wife Winifred was a daughter of Lord Powis, lord of the Manor of Hendon. She figures in Clifford Bax's play *The Immortal Lady,* in which he tells of the clever ruse by which she succeeded in getting her husband in disguise out of the Tower. An account of the adventure in her own handwriting was sent to her sister, who was abbess of a nunnery in Bruges, and the original is a very valued possession of the author of this book. It is his legitimate purchase from a second-hand catalogue, seeing that on the distaff side he can claim kinship with the Herberts.

CANONS PARK

One of the most magnificent houses in Middlesex no longer exists, though the North London Collegiate School for Girls has its home in a fine Georgian house on the same site. This is Canons Park, which perhaps owes its name to its possession by the Prior of St. Bartholomew the Great in West Smithfield, and which passed in succession to the families of Losse and Franklyn. Early in the seventeenth century the property was sold to Sir Thomas Lake, secretary to Sir Francis Walsingham and a trusted servant of Elizabeth and James.

Thomas Fuller, in his *Worthies,* speaks of his incredible secrecy and dexterity of dispatch, but he became involved (through his wife) in a quarrel with that "beautiful, bewitching, immoral little flirt," Frances Howard, wife of the Earl of Essex, and soon to be the murderess of Sir Thomas Overbury in the Tower and the wife of the King's first favourite, Robert Carr. It was an unpleasant gang with which to get awry, and Lake was dismissed from his post of Principal Secretary of State to the King, sent a prisoner to the Tower and fined £15,000. King James callously advised him to give up his wife and daughter, but he gallantly replied that he could "bear ill-fortune with patience, but would not cease to be a husband and father." Lake died in 1630 at Canons, which he had built, and was succeeded by his son Lancelot, who endowed a boys' school and restored tithes to the Church. It was his grand-daughter Mary who married James Brydges, Paymaster-General of the Forces in Anne's reign, who excelled all his contemporaries in cynical dishonesty. Seventeen million pounds were missing from his Army account, and modern research has not done much to clear the character of Brydges, who was rewarded with a peerage and his son with a dukedom. Emollett, in his *History of England,* says that Brydges ultimately accounted for all save three million pounds, and that villainy was so complicated and vice so general that he eluded all enquiry. His estate was a parallelogram of 400 acres, bounded by roads, and his house was a square stone building with twenty-two windows on each face and a big portico on the south side. It cost a quarter of a million to build, and James, of Greenwich, Gibb and Shepherd designed it, while Dr. Alexander Blackwell laid out the grounds, and Strong, who had worked with Wren on St. Paul's, built the north front.

Everything was on a most luxurious scale : marble sculptures, lavish paintings, gilt hinges and finger-plates, an army of servants, eight old sergeants from Chelsea Hospital who attended him like a Swiss Guard of pikemen, endless cere- mony at meals and a series of trumpeters to herald with a fanfare the approach of each course at dinner.

Chandos was a great patron of art and music, but seems to have been somewhat neglectful of poetry. To the facts are due some intimate criticisms of the man. He patronised Hogarth, the founder of the truly English school of painting and the painter of the historic march of the Guards to Finchley Common during the Young Pretender's threatened advance on London. Handel was organist and choirmaster for three years in the rebuilt chapel at Whitchurch; he organised the Duke's orchestra and wrote a good many pieces of music for his patron. This included the oratorio of *Esther*, two Chandos *Te Deums*, the twelve Chandos anthems, and *Acis and Galatea*. Chandos's neglect of verse brought him satirical poems from both Swift and Pope. Here is Swift's epigram :

> "James Brydges was the Dean's familiar friend ;
> James grows a duke ; their friendship here must end.
> Surely the Dean deserves a sore rebuke,
> For knowing James, to say he knows a duke."

Pope would never admit that he satirised Chandos under the name of Timon, but it is perfectly obvious at whom Pope is poking spiteful fun in his "Epistle on False Taste" in *Moral Essays,* addressed to a more lavish patron in the Earl of Burlington. Hogarth painted the poet standing on a scaffold- ing whitewashing Burlington House and bespattering with mud the Chandos carriage as it passes along Piccadilly.

The whole of Pope's lines are worth quoting, but a few specimens must suffice :

> "At Timon's villa let us pass a day
> Where all cry out, 'What sums are thrown away,'
> So proud, so grand, of that stupendous air
> Soft and agreeable come never there;
> Greatness, with Timon, dwells in such a draught,
> As brings all Brobdingnag before your thought.
> To compass this, his building is a town,
> His pond an ocean, his parterre a down."

The church at Little Stanmore or Whitchurch was altered

by Chandos in 1715 and has not been vitally changed since then. Grinling Gibbons carved the cherubs on the organ case. His father-in-law was responsible for much of the ironwork. There is a fine copy of Raphael's "Transfiguration" on the ceiling over the Duke's pew, and there is a monument to the Duke and two of his wives. Sir Newman Flower has destroyed the whole legend of the Harmonious Blacksmith and many of the alleged associations of Handel with the church and organ. But he did have some association with Chandos and Whitchurch, and he may have been one of the objects of Pope's satire :

"And now the chapel's silver bell you hear,
    That summons you to all the pride of prayer;
    Light quirks of music, broken and uneven,
    Make the soul dance upon a jig to Heaven.
    On painted ceilings you devoutly stare,
    Where sprawl the saints of Verrio or Laguerre,
    Or gilded clouds in fair expansion lie,
    And bring all Paradise before your eye.
    To rest, the cushion and soft dean invite,
    Who never mentions Hell to ears polite!"

Chandos did not become a duke till the reign of George I when he was made Marquess of Carnarvon and Duke of Chandos. He married as his third wife a country girl whom he had rescued from her brutal husband by purchasing her for £20 in the market at Marlborough. He had his money-spending planned by an accountant, sold his fruit and vegetables at a profit, and never gave a tip of more than 6d. "More," he said, "may make you idle and drunk." He lost money heavily through the South Sea Bubble and investments in the Mississippi, but he managed to live at Canons till his death in 1744.

The second Duke hit upon the hare-brained scheme of buying up all the land between Canons and his house planned and partly built in Cavendish Square, so that he might drive along one unbroken avenue from one to the other. Even his fortune was unique to the task of purchasing much of Kingsbury, Hendon, Cricklewood, Kilburn, St. John's Wood and Marylebone.

When the second Duke died his property had to be sold

in several lots in 1747, but what had cost a quarter of a million pounds was sold for only £11,000. The marble staircase was bought by Lord Chesterfield for his Mayfair house, which was designed by the architect Ware. The portico supported by round brick columns with Corinthian capitals of stone was removed to Wanstead House and later on to Garrick's villa, Hendon Hall.

The equestrian statue of George I was moved from Canons to Leicester Square and has disappeared. One of George II is still in Golden Square. A Grinling Gibbons carving was transferred to Bush Hill Park, near Enfield. The iron gates at the southern entrance are to be seen at New College, Oxford. In the smaller house built on the original site out of some of the original material lived Captain Dennis O'Kelly, owner of the famous racehorse whose amazing speed enabled Macaulay to coin the adage "Eclipse first and the rest nowhere." The name Canons Park still remains; the church still treasures memories of Handel and of the first Duke; while there is a group of almshouses, built round three sides of a square, founded in 1640 by Lady Lake, whose husband built the first house of Canons more than three centuries ago.

CHAPTER XV

FAMOUS HOUSES AND WORTHIES

PART II

PETER COLLINSON

HENDON, which hardly began to expand till the Tube burrowed its way under Hampstead Heath, owes a lot to the Garden Suburb, misnamed "Hampstead," at one end, to the Watling Estate in the Burnt Oak area at the other, and to the singularly unspoiled mile-long village of Mill Hill, with its School, its Seminaries and its Barracks. Quite a deal of the beauty of this most delightful of northern semi-suburban areas is owing to careful planting of trees and bushes, and more tribute than is usually paid for this happy work is due to the eighteenth-century Quaker botanist, Peter Collinson, who made his gardens at Ridgeway House, Mill Hill, a breeding-ground for nearly two hundred fresh specimens from abroad.

Collinson came of a Westmorland family, and he and his brother built up a business in woollen goods, doing considerable trade with the American colonies. From Meeting House Lane in Peckham he moved his trees and plants to his father-in-law's garden at Mill Hill, and went on adding to his collection for about twenty years. He was a Fellow of the Royal Society and of the reconstituted Society of Antiquaries, and the Royal Societies of Sweden and Berlin honoured him with membership. He numbered among his friends most of the eminent Whigs and not a few Tories, prominent Roman Catholics and Dissenters, and most of the foremost figures in scientific research.

His business connections with America made an exchange of seeds possible, and he secured a collector in John Bartram, of Philadelphia, who for over thirty years sent him boxes of seeds in exchange for the seeds of English shrubs or for a money payment. These were distributed to the owners of many of the most beautiful parks in the country, and he is

184

FAMOUS HOUSES AND WORTHIES

responsible for much of their beauty today. To Collinson the Duke of Richmond owed the marvellous cedar avenues at Goodwood, and he called the Quaker botanist his "affectionate friend." Lord Rochford wrote, "Honest Peter and I eat ham and eggs together," and the letters that passed between Collinson and Lord Petre are of extraordinary interest, seeing that Petre was a devout Catholic and had relations (Earls of Derwentwater) who had taken part in the Jacobite rebellions. Collinson was on friendly terms with the great Swedish botanist Linnæus, who attached Collinson's name to a genus of perennial labiates with yellow leaves. Collinson tried to make popular the new method of nomenclature that the Swede had invented, and he also tried to persuade him, apparently without success, that swallows did not spend the winter under water, as Linnæus seemed to believe.

Benjamin Franklin was in England for a number of years as a representative of the colonists in America, and he spent some time with Collinson at Ridgeway House, having been a close correspondent of his for many years before. Franklin's experiments in electricity were made possible by Collinson, and it was he who introduced Franklin's researches to the Royal Society in London. It was a very great pity that Franklin's conclusions were not taken more seriously by its members. Collinson was honorary agent for the Public Library in Philadelphia, and in 1917 the hundred and fiftieth anniversary of Franklin's visit to Ridgeway House was suitably celebrated at Mill Hill School in Collinson's garden.

It is not easy to estimate the influence which thinkers in England and the American colonies had on one another in the eighteenth century. A very interesting place of contact was the Club of Honest Whigs, which used about 1760 to meet on alternate Thursday evenings at the Queen's Head Coffee House in London to discuss religion, politics and science. Among its members was Benjamin Franklin, then living in Craven Street, Strand, as agent for the American colonies; Peter Collinson, the Quaker botanist of Ridgeway House, Mill Hill; Dr. John Fothergill, with Lord Clive and a Prime Minister as his patients, and with his botanical garden at Upton in Essex; Dr. Priestley, pioneer in scientific research and a keen student of the early writings of Rousseau, Montesquieu and Hume; and Dr. Richard Price, like the others a Dissenter, and a prolific writer on morals, politics, finance and economics, and later on a supporter of the Americans and French in their struggle for freedom. The Club was centred on Franklin, and in their Thursday discussions they sometimes exchanged views on politics, but they had no Boswell to record their sayings. He came to their nine o'clock supper once only.

Among Collinson's friends was Sir Hans Sloane, who relied on him for many additions to his collection of plants, and Dr. Fothergill, already mentioned as a fellow-horticulturist, who was the doctor who treated Lord Clive for severe internal trouble, and an overdose of whose medicine was the cause of his death.

William Bartram, John Bartram's son, drew pictures of plants which were sent over to Collinson, and he frequently did unconnected sketches round the margins. These were catalogued when Collinson's Life was written, and from one such series of sketches were recovered the pictures of early Williamsburg in U.S.A., from which the complete reconstruction of the old town was made possible.

Collinson began in 1751 a careful register of all the plants which he cultivated, and he gave as a title to the list this heading: "A catalogue of the rarer plants in Peter Collinson's garden at Mill Hill, in Hendon, Middlesex, tenn miles from St. Giles's Pound, in Holbourn. See the milestone (the first sett up near London for measuring the roads), my house within a bow shot of the X milestone." It came into the possession of Lewis W. Dillwyn, who compiled a full catalogue with memoranda taken from Collinson's notebooks, and this he printed privately at Swansea in 1843, over seventy years after Collinson's death.

Besides his American correspondents, mainly Puritans, he had Catholic friends in China who sent him seeds and plants. Father Heberstein, Provincial of the Jesuits in China, and Father D'Incarville sent him acacia seeds, rhubarb, asters and larkspur, and others came from China by way of Russia. Collinson's Deciduous Cypress is matched by others in most London parks. A good specimen is also to be found near the

Broad Walk entrance to the Zoological Gardens, founded, it will be remembered, by Sir Stamford Raffles, the founder also of Singapore, whose latest years were spent at Highwood House, Mill Hill. Incidentally, the tomb of his widow in St. Paul's Churchyard in Mill Hill village has recently been restored by the Association of British Malaya. This cypress does best in damp soil near a pond or stream, but it can flourish in rather dry conditions. Collinson's own specimen was planted in the sloping field to the south-west of old Ridgeway House, and the date was probably 1736. When the field needed levelling to serve as a football ground for Mill Hill's first fifteen there was a risk that this tree might suffer or even perish. A timely letter from Oxford, from the great lexicographer Sir James Murray, who had been for fifteen years a master at Mill Hill, raised interest in the preservation of this historical specimen, and very careful banking up of the soil with a brick surround has left this tree as one of the chief features in the right foreground of the magnificent distant view of Harrow-on-the-Hill from the Ionic portico of the School House at Mill Hill. There are three fine cedars in the Mill Hill grounds, two a return present from Goodwood Park, to which Collinson had sent 1,000 small cedars from Hendon Place, and one a gift in 1761 from a Mr. Clark. This was badly damaged by a very heavy snowstorm in 1916 when I was housemaster at the School House. What is perhaps the oldest cedar in England is the one planted in the Palace Garden at Enfield by the schoolmaster, Dr. Uvedale, between 1662 and 1670. Other imports of Collinson's included rhododendrons from Cadiz, weeping willows from the Euphrates, laurels from Madeira, junipers from the Tagus. Collinson was not unaware of his contribution to the study and cultivation of plants, and he well sums up his achievements in this sentence :

"I often stand with wonder and amazement when I view the inconceivable variety of flowers, shrubs and trees, now in our gardens, and what there were forty years ago; in that time what quantities from all North America have annually been collected by my means and procuring, and for some years past a great variety of seeds are brought from China, and many fine plants raised; the China Mulberry I first raised, and from Siberia many curious shrubs and flowers; very few gardens, if any, excel mine at Mill Hill, for the rare exotics which are my delight."

TWICKENHAM

Twickenham reached its peak of fame in the eighteenth century, when amongst others the Earl of Radnor was living at Radnor House, Lady Suffolk was at Marble Hill, Horace Walpole at Strawberry Hill, whose smaller cottage was occupied by Kitty Clive, and the original Pope's villa was occupied by Alexander Pope himself. The manor-house was associated in an earlier period with Catharine of Aragon and Catharine of Braganza, two hardly used Queens of England; at "Twitnam" Park Francis Bacon entertained Queen Elizabeth in 1592; at Cambridge House lived Richard Cambridge, author of the *Scribleriad*, who figures in Horace Walpole's *Letters* and Fanny Burney's *Diary*.

Orleans House was built in Queen Anne's day or just before her accession for the health of her one surviving son out of seventeen children, the sickly Duke of Gloucester. A victim of Pope's satire, James Johnson, Secretary of State for Scotland, built the house and added to it a fine octagonal room in which to entertain Queen Caroline, the wife of George II. This is the only part of the house now left standing. In 1800 the Duke of Orleans, later King Louis Philippe, bought the house, and he and his brothers lived there on and off until he succeeded to the French Crown.

Defoe, writing his *Tour through England and Scotland* in 1722, comments on the abundance of curious seats of the nobility to be found in "Twittenham," and Horace Walpole repeats the tale in 1750, observing that "Nothing is equal to the fashion of this place : Mr. Muntz says we shall have more coaches here than there are in half France. . . . We shall be as celebrated as Baiæ or Tivoli." A Plan of Twickenham, as surveyed by Samuel Lewis in 1784, shows that among its inhabitants could be numbered Mr. Walpole, Sir F. Basset, Captain Carr, Earl Paulett, Lady Shelburne, Lord Fortescue and Sir George Pococke, all within a stone's throw of the "Ayot."

York House is now the home of municipal life in Twickenham, having been bought by the Council of 1924, where it houses a local museum and enjoys attractive gardens. It belonged to Edward Hyde, Earl of Clarendon, not quite fairly saddled with responsibility for the Clarendon Code and held to blame for the childless marriage of King Charles II. The excuse usually given was that he was well aware of the clandestine marriage of his daughter Anne Hyde to James, Duke of York, the King's younger brother, and hoped that his own grandchildren might thus succeed to the throne, as indeed they did. Clarendon used the house in the summer, and when on duty at Hampton Court he came back to Twickenham for the night. He gave York House to James and his wife, remarking on the appropriateness of the name. He is said to have written some of his work in the gardens, and his two grand-daughters who both became Queens were born there. Many distinguished people have since lived there—a Viennese ambassador, Mrs. Damer, the eminent sculptor, the Comte de Paris, and the later Duke of Orleans.

At The Grove, Twickenham, lived Secretary James Craggs and his father, who, like Aislabie, who lived in Hendon, were mixed up in the notorious South Sea Bubble, which burst in 1720. Lewis Melville, just two centuries after the scandal, wrote a very well-documented survey of the whole transaction, and the evidence seems to point to their guilt. James the younger died of smallpox, and James the elder committed suicide while the case was being investigated. Pope evidently felt quite sure of the Secretary's innocence, since he wrote :

"Statesman, yet friend to truth, of soul sincere,
In action faithful, and in honour clear,
Who broke no promise, served no private end,
Who gained no title, and who lost no friend."

POPE'S VILLA

Alexander Pope lived for a short time in Mahson Terrace, Chiswick, where he translated part of Homer's *Iliad*, but he is associated more especially with Twickenham, where he lived from 1715 until his death in 1744. His success with

Homer helped him to lease a house on the river with five acres of land, which he improved with wise planting and to which he added a grotto, to link up two portions of the garden without having to cross the road. He was intensely proud of his house and grotto :

> "That my retreat the best companions grace,
> Chiefs out of war, and statesmen out of place.
> There St. John mingles with my friendly bowl
> The feast of reason and the flow of soul.

But he was by nature lonely and sad :

> "In vain my structures rise, my gardens grow;
> In vain fair Thames reflects the double scenes
> Of hanging mountains and of sloping greens;
> Joy lives not here—to happier seats it flies."

His translation of the *Iliad* and *Odyssey* brought him £5,000, "enthusiastic admiration which justly rewarded his great achievement," according to Thackeray, and Richard Bentley's well-known criticism—"a very pretty poem, Mr. Pope, but you must not call it Homer." Pope had many friends and kept most of them. Voltaire came to see him at Twickenham and flaunted his atheism, to the great disgust of Pope's mother; Swift and Bolingbroke, Atterbury and Warburton, Gay and Savage were amongst his frequent guests there. And most of them were commemorated in verse, Pope liking to think that only disinterested patriots were welcome at his villa :

> "Let such, such only, tread this sacred floor,
> Who dare to love their country, and be poor."

Pope retained his religious outlook in spite of Bolingbroke and Voltaire, and showed his Christian beliefs in his last will and testament. One of the witnesses to his will was the Rev. Stephen Hales, Vicar of Teddington, a very distinguished scientist of the eighteenth century.

His villa was bought by Sir William Stanhope and considerably enlarged, to the annoyance of Horace Walpole. When Stanhope died, his son-in-law, Welbore Ellis, inherited the property and showed great veneration for Pope's memory.

190

In 1787 it was bought by Lady Howe, whose father won the "Glorious First of June," and completely destroyed. The house which succeeded it was styled "Pope's Villa," and about 1880 passed into the possession of Henry Labouchere, the famous editor of *Truth* and Radical Member of Parliament. Pope's chief monument in Twickenham today is the memorial which he erected to his parents, who are buried there, *et sibi,* as he gave instructions in his will.

Pope was an invalid from childhood and was dependent on such devoted help as he received for thirty-eight years from his faithful servant, Mary Beach. He was sensitive to cats, needed stays to hold him erect, had to wear three pairs of stockings, and required help to dress and to undress. His diminutive person was seldom noticed by his friends, but it was a standing jest with his detractors. He was only 4 feet 6 inches high, very hump-backed and deformed, so Sir Joshua Reynolds tells us, and he must have looked a trifle odd in black suit and wearing a small sword. Children were alarmed at his figure as he walked along the lanes of Twickenham wearing his old soiled suit of black stained with snuff, and his cocked hat. He attacked his critics under the disguise of a *nom de plume,* and when they penetrated the disguise he was lampooned in savage, cruel verse mocking his "crippled case" and "shrivelled skin."

Martha and Teresa Blount were loyal friends for many years until, for some unknown cause, a complete estrangement took place. He was for years a great friend of Lady Mary Wortley Montagu, and there was almost a partnership in some of their writing. But so bitter did the subsequent relationship between them become that she published a libellous story about Pope which he thought fit to repudiate, and also called him the "wicked asp" much as others of his enemies called him the "Wasp of Twickenham."

Stephen Hales was a friend to all the scientists of the middle eighteenth century and was a pioneer in botany, in animal physiology and in the preservation of food. One of his finest achievements was a much-needed improvement in the ventilation of ships. This was applied to warships and slave ships with equally good results, and when used in prisons it almost abolished gaol fever. There is little doubt

191

that his scientific experiments enabled Priestley to arrive at his epoch-making discoveries later in the century.

Pope was buried in Twickenham Church, and there is a grim legend that during some reconstruction his coffin was unearthed and his skull taken to some private museum. The vicar at the time admitted that measurements were made and a cast taken, so that it is possible that this entirely unnecessary piece of sacrilege may have been enacted.

That most charitable and discerning of essayists, Augustine Birrell, urges everyone who is inclined to quarrel with Pope to study Kneller's portrait, which shows "well-nigh intolerable bodily pain" and has the power of "exciting compassion for infirmity. To abuse Pope before studying this picture is to speak evil of a stranger; to do so afterwards would be to stab the wounded."

KNELLER

Sir Godfrey Kneller lived for thirteen years at Whitton House, which he himself had built, and his fame at Court is shown by his holding of the post of painter to the reigning sovereign during five reigns. His vanity was considerable but perhaps well founded, and Pope had no doubts about his skill when he wrote :

"Kneller, by heaven and not a master taught,
Whose art was nature, and whose pictures thought;
Now for two ages having snatched from fate
Whate'er was beauteous, or whate'er was great,
Lies crowned with princes' honours, poets' lays,
Due to his merit, and brave thirst of praise.
Living great nature feared he might out vie
Her works; and dying, fears herself may die."

A less well-known tribute to Kneller by Pope deals with drawings of the statues of Apollo, Venus and Hercules :

"What god, what genius, did the pencil move
When Kneller painted these?
'Twas friendship warm as Phœbus, kind as love,
And strong as Hercules."

Kneller Hall has been almost entirely rebuilt since its first

owner died and was for a time a training college for teachers, of which the first Dr. Temple, afterwards Archbishop of Canterbury, was head. It has been for many years a music school for military bands.

STRAWBERRY HILL

When Horace Walpole came to Twickenham a new era had opened for that home of the Muses. He at once fell in love with his newly purchased property Strawberry Hill, and wrote on June 8, 1747, to his cousin, Field-Marshal Conway : "I am got into a new camp, and have left my tub at Windsor. It is a little plaything that I got out of M. Chenevix's shop, and is the prettiest bauble you ever saw. It is set in enamelled meadows, with phillagree hedges."

Twickenham has a long list of worthies, and Horace Walpole summed them up in verses which he called "The Parish Register" :

> "Where Silver Thames round Twit'nam meads
> His winding current sweetly leads;
> Twit'nam, the Muses' fav'rite seat,
> Twit'nam, the graces' lov'd retreat;
> There polish'd Essex went to sport,
> The pride and victim of a court.
> There Bacon tuned the grateful lyre
> To soothe Eliza's haughty ire.
> Twit'nam, where Hyde, majestic sage,
> Retired from folly's frantic stage,
> While his vast soul was hung on tenters
> To mend the world and vex dissenters.
> Twit'nam, whose frolic Wharton revel'd,
> Where Montagu, with lock dishevel'd
> (Conflict of dirt and warmth divine)
> Invok'd and scandaliz'd the Nine;
> Where Pope in moral music spoke
> To th' anguish'd soul of Bolingbroke;
>
> Where Fielding met his bunter muse
> And, as they quaff'd the fiery juice,
> Droll nature stamp'd each lucky hit
> With unimaginable wit.

No wonder that Horace Walpole's verses and letters seem an inexhaustible fountain of Georgian gossip.

Twickenham, looking towards
Eel Pie Island

Horace Walpole's efforts to enlarge the cottage in Gothic style was on the whole successful, and his "Castle," as he liked to style it, took twenty years to complete. It was quite finished by 1770, and Walpole complained that he had nothing to do. He had nothing new to read and was tired of writing. So apparently he felt it necessary to enlarge his castle by collecting designs from medieval buildings and by accumulating bits and pieces from elaborate tombs in cathedrals and using them for doorways, windows and even fireplaces.

This is what Maurice has to say about it :

> "At every step we take fresh raptures move,
> Charm in the house, and lavish in the grove.
> Within, the richest silks of China glow,
> Without, the flowers of both the tropics blow."

> "With heaven's blue vault the beaming sapphire vies
> And emeralds glow with ocean's azure dyes."

And when it comes to the prospect from the windows of Strawberry Hill the poet becomes almost dithyrambic in his praise :

> "A brighter, richer landscape shines displayed,
> Than ever Poussin sketched, or Claude portrayed."

The collection of antiquities and curios that Walpole accumulated at Strawberry Hill was of great interest, and he made a very careful inventory of all the items : portraits of the Walpole family; conversation pieces of men and of women by Reynolds; relics from Gloucester Cathedral and Westminster Abbey; Fairfax's presentation watch from Parliament after the Battle of Naseby; Charles II's warming pan; Torrigiano's bust of Henry VII; an old oak chair from Glastonbury; Wolsey's red hat, which was preserved in the Great Wardrobe instead of being hung over his tomb; these are some of the treasures with which Walpole adorned his home. Walpole was very proud of his collections, and at his private printing press he produced *A Description of Strawberry Hill*, with over a hundred pages to describe his "rareties, from many a clime conveyed."

He preferred small parties to visit his mansion, but sometimes would allow more than the requisite four to examine his treasures, of which he wrote : "The chief boast of my collection is the portraits of eminent and remarkable persons, particularly the miniatures and enamels, which, so far as I can discover, are superior to any other collection whatever." An explosion at the powder-mills of Hounslow did some damage to Strawberry Hill in 1772, and it looked as if it had suffered a siege. "Two saints in the hall have suffered martyrdom. They have had their bodies cut off, and nothing remains but their heads."

Walpole had a poor opinion of professional authors, though he was glad to be an amateur himself. "In England," he wrote, "we read their works, but seldom or never take any notice of authors." Perhaps that was why he treated Chatterton so shabbily. The unfortunate boy sent his poems to a rich man who might well have taken the trouble to be his patron. Instead, Walpole took the verses to Paris, did not trouble to return them, and was indignant when Chatterton complained. No wonder that the ill-used boy wrote to the wealthy hardhearted amateur :

"Walpole ! I thought not I should ever see
So mean a heart as thine has proved to be;
Thou, nursed in luxury's lap, behold'st with scorn
The boy, who, friendless, fatherless, forlorn,
Asks the high favour. Thou mayst call me cheat—
Say, did'st thou never practise such deceit?
Who wrote Otranto? But I will not chide;
Scorn I'll repay with scorn, and pride with pride."

Chatterton challenges Walpole with daring to treat him with contempt because he was poor and unknown. "But I shall live, and stand by Rowley's side, when thou art dead and damned." It is difficult to be quite sure of posterity's verdict on the relative merits of Chatterton and Walpole—Walpole, whom Burke called an "elegant trifler."

Macaulay is somewhat contemptuous of Walpole's gossip and scandal, his collections of morsels of painted glass, and his memorials to dead dogs and cats. "While he was fetching and carrying the gossip of Kensington Palace and Carlton House he fancied that he was enjoyed in politics; and when he recorded that gossip he fancied that he was writing history." And yet we still read his letters and "characters" with marked interest, and Dr. G. P. Gooch thought it worth while to collect twelve of his "characters" to form part of his recent *Courts and Cabinets*.

Walpole had many lady friends, but never succumbed sufficiently to their charms to marry any of them. It is to his credit that he admired Hannah More, so justly famous for her successful efforts to improve the condition of the poor. When he was seventy-three in 1791 he became Earl of Oxford through a nephew's death, but he ignored the title almost completely :

"An estate and an earldom at seventy-four !
Had I sought them or wished them, 'twould have one fear more—
That of making a Countess when almost four-score."

He was very proud when in 1795 George III's Queen and some of her family came to visit him at Strawberry Hill, and he died at his town house in Berkeley Square in 1797, the last of Sir Robert Walpole's descendants.

WESTWARD, LOOK THE SKY IS LIGHT

Young of the *Night Thoughts* was not the only one to realise that the Star of Empire was moving westwards. Horace Walpole, writing in 1774 to Horace Mann, prophesied that "the next Augustan Age will dawn on the other side of the Atlantic. There will, perhaps, be a Thucydides at Boston, a Xenophon at New York, and, in time, a Virgil at Mexico, and a Newton at Peru. At last some curious traveller from Lima will visit England and give a description of the ruins of St. Paul's, like the editions of Balbec and Palmyra."

Consciously or without knowing it, Shelley and Macaulay repeat the prophecy of St. Paul's in ruins and the bridges broken down ; only Shelley mentions Waterloo Bridge, since removed by Herbert Morrison ; and Macaulay chooses a broken arch of London Bridge from which his New Zealander is to sketch the ruins.

After years of splendour mingled with neglect, Strawberry Hill is now St. Mary's College, and in the early summer of 1947 the bicentenary of its foundation by Horace Walpole was appropriately celebrated. One can be quite certain that during that historic afternoon someone must have recited at least the first verse, written by William Pulteney, Earl of Bath, praising the merits of Strawberry Hill :

> "Some cry up Gunnersbury,
> For Sion some declare,
> Some say, that with Chiswick House
> No villa can compare :
> But ask the beaux of Middlesex,
> Who know the country well,
> If Strawberry Hill, if Strawberry Hill
> Don't bear away the bell?"

Macaulay complains that "serious business was a trifle to him, and trifles were his serious business," and contrasts what he calls the "daubs of Walpole" with the masterly portraits of Clarendon. And yet Mrs. Paget Toynbee from 1903 to 1905 showed great pioneering skill in adding very many fresh letters of Horace Walpole to those already known, and her edition seemed definitive. But American collectors have a new, fuller edition under way, and twelve out of a total promised of fifty volumes have already been published.

And the end is not yet, for in his essay entitled "All Horrid" Michael Sadleir discusses Jane Austen's attitude towards that part of the Gothic Revival which was exemplified by the Gothic romances of Mrs. Roche, Mrs. Radcliffe, Mrs. Parsons and Monk Lewis. Had it not been for Jane Austen's mention of seven novels, which are guaranteed to be "all horrid," in *Northanger Abbey,* it is more than likely that they might all have faded into oblivion. But these neo-Gothic romances, coupled with Macpherson's *Ossian* and Percy's *Reliques of Ancient Poetry,* were perhaps caused by a reaction against the classicism of the eighteenth century, and themselves helped to produce the atmosphere for Sir Walter Scott's historical romances, which are always considered to have been in part responsible for the Oxford Movement. Now, one of the earliest examples of neo-Gothic, or Gothistic art as Michael Sadleir prefers to call it, was Horace Walpole's Strawberry Hill with its "multifarious crockets and pinnacles." How it would have amused and

197

intrigued Horace Walpole to know that, by very distant
ancestry, he might one day come to be regarded as one of the
causes of Newman and of the Oxford Movement.

CAMBRIDGE AND CAMBRIDGE HOUSE

In St. Mary's, Twickenham, is buried Richard Owen Cambridge, who bought from Sir Windham Ashe a house begun
by Humphrey Lynd in the seventeenth century, and enlarged
by two generations of the Ashe family. Cambridge House, as
it was renamed, was a centre of hospitality, and its owner, a
man of ample means, genial presence, wit and learning,
entertained Pope and Walpole, Lyttelton and North, Garrick
and Reynolds, Johnson and Admiral Boscawen. He wrote the
once famous *Scribleriad,* occasional poems, a history of wars
on the Coromandel coast, 1750-1760, and contributed to the
World. As he was going to service in Twickenham Church
one Sunday a note was handed to him from the editor demanding a contribution for its next issue at once. During the
service Mrs. Cambridge, noticing that he was not listening to
the sermon, whispered to him : "What are you thinking
about?" To this he suitably replied : "The next *World*, my
dear." Johnson, Reynolds, Gibbon and Boswell once met at
Cambridge House for dinner, and the conversation is
described by Boswell.

Reynolds admired the pictures and Johnson the books, but
Sir Joshua felt that he could see more than Johnson, who saw
only the backs. Cambridge asked Johnson why people enjoyed
the backs of books, as he himself did. Johnson quickly replied :
"Knowledge is of two kinds. We know a subject ourselves or
we know where we can find information about it. . . . This
leads us to look at . . . the backs of books." Hardly an
epoch-making remark, but Reynolds commented on Johnson's
extraordinary promptness, and Boswell felt that his sword
was through you in an instant.

Fanny Burney (Madame D'Arblay) also records details
of a visit which she paid to Cambridge House with her
parents. She discussed life and death with her host, and with
less seriously forward and flippant women, with whom she
got on so well, as she told him. Cambridge told her that he
only liked amiable women, and they all liked him. He had

been most fortunate in his wife, to whom he had been most happily married for forty years. He then traced for Fanny Burney "the greater part of his life and conduct in former times and told a thousand excellent anecdotes of himself and his associates." They next had a small boating excursion, which so delighted Fanny that she says : "Methinks I should like to sail from the very source to the mouth of the Thames." After dinner, Cambridge and Fanny walked to a seat with a good view of Petersham Wood, and there they discussed the affectation of Gibbon and his unfortunate fall into the river, which Cambridge styled "God's revenge against conceit." Fanny was nearly blown in herself, but Cambridge made no comment.

Cambridge was a rich amateur who was generous to those who had to make their living by the pen, comparable to Samuel Rogers but without Rogers's assurance that, whatever poets were forgotten, he was sure to survive. He enjoyed, as the *Gentleman's Magazine* remarked, what the poet Thomson regarded as essential in human happiness :

> "An elegant sufficiency, content,
> Retirement, rural quiet, friendship, books,
> Ease and alternate labour."

He was able to "follow the bent of his genius, and only obey the inspirations of the muse when she chose to be propitious." It is a pity that his verse account of Gibbon's autobiography, with which Cambridge amused his friends, was never committed to writing. His son, Archdeacon Cambridge, collected his works into a single quarto volume after his death in 1802 at the age of fifty-five, and summed up his father's character as quick rather than deep, kindly and generous, elegant rather than profound. He took a philosophic view of the world, loved books and men alike, and had no time for laborious research. He was an amateur in letters, but was entirely without that contempt for the professional which is so marked a characteristic of Horace Walpole. His "native benevolence would not allow him voluntarily to inflict the slightest pain. . . . His life and principles were alike free from corruption; his purity and independence equally untainted."

HOGARTH HOUSE

Hogarth House certainly deserved preservation, and the generous gift of the house and its contents by Colonel Shepway to the Middlesex County Council in 1909 ensures the safety of Hogarth's "little country box at Chiswick." No one has so completely mastered the social life of the eighteenth century in England as Austin Dobson, and one naturally turns to him for the story of Hogarth's mulberry tree :

"Its scarred and blackened trunk, which spring, even now, is dressing with bright leaves, must have known William Hogarth in the flesh! It must have watched him scratching with a nail that homely mural tablet of Dick the bullfinch, which has mysteriously disappeared; it must have watched him playing nine-pins in his filbert avenue, or strutting through the walks in the red rouguelaure he wore in Leicester Fields. It must have been acquainted, also, with those friendly guests, who filled up the three-cornered enclosure on sunny afternoons. Hither, no doubt, when the *Epistle to William Hogarth* was yet unwritten, Mr. Charles Churchill would stroll with his pointers from Acton, bringing as his companion, it may be, that squinting patriot 'the heaven-born Wilkes.' Or, to go back somewhat earlier in time, Dr. Benjamin Hoadby, of the *Suspicious Husband,* would ride up from Chelsea, or Dr. Ralph would look round to have a chat about the *Analysis,* or worthy Justice Welch would make the dusty pilgrimage from Holborn. He it was who wrote that capital description of the *March to Finchley* in Christopher Smart's *Student,* and he has just said good-bye to Fielding at Gravesend. He has little hope of seeing his old colleague again, has honest Welch; and Mr. Ranby, Hogarth's neighbour and the King's Sergeant-Surgeon, shakes his head in confirmation. . . . So, I fancy, they sat and chatted and puffed at their long pipes of Virginia under the mulberry tree in Hogarth's garden 'when George was King.'"

In Hogarth's house the wife with whom he had eloped, Jane, daughter of Sir James Thornhill, lived on till 1789, twenty-five years after her husband. Folks in Chiswick, says Phillips in *A Morning Walk from London to Kew,* "long remembered the once handsome dame, transformed by age into a stately old lady, dressed in a silk sacque, with high crooked cane, raised head-dress, and black calash, whom a faithful and equally ancient man-servant Samuel, wheeled regularly in her chair to the church, where he carried her books up the aisle and opened and shut her pew."

From 1814 to 1826 the house was occupied by the Rev. H. F. Cary, translator of Dante and biographer of Hogarth. Keen interest in Hogarth's pictures was maintained by books and pamphlets composed and compiled by Horace Walpole, George Stevens and John Nichols. Charles Lamb regarded Hogarth's graphic representations with their "teeming, fruitful, suggestive meaning" as books rather than pictures. "They have the teeming, fruitful suggestive meaning of words." "Other pictures we look at, his prints we read."

Garrick, who wrote his epitaph for Chiswick churchyard, loved him as a friend and revered him as an artist.

ZOFFANY

If Hogarth is one of the earliest painters in Middlesex, he is by no means the only one. Zoffany was born at Frankfort in 1735, and after studying in Italy and painting successfully in Coblenz he came to England and was an original member of the Royal Academy in 1768. He was friend to Reynolds and Garrick and drew several portraits of the actor and of the royal family. Fifteen years in India gave him a handsome fortune, and in 1796 he settled at Strand on the Green. In St. George's Church, Brentford, which replaces "the ugliest of all the churches built in the darkest period of architectural science," is the "Last Supper," painted by Zoffany, using the local fishermen as disciples. St. Peter is Zoffany, and Judas is said to be a portrait of one of the churchwardens of Kew. George III enjoyed portraits by Zoffany, whose conversation pieces prepared the way for the fuller art of Gainsborough. Though Zoffany lived until 1810 at Strand on the Green, he was buried across the river in Kew.

GOLDSMITH AT KINGSBURY

Few groups of literary men have ever earned such fame as the famous club that gathered round Samuel Johnson. More than one of them is to be found in Middlesex as well as in London, and Oliver Goldsmith and David Garrick in Kingsbury and in Hendon have left a fragrant memory. Goldsmith and his neighbour in the Temple, Mr. Bott, took a cottage eight miles down the Edgware Road, at the back of Canons, where they went into temporary retreat. This small "Shoemaker's Paradise" had been absurdly decorated by the shoemaker, who built it and "laid it out with flying mercuries, *jets d'eau,* and other preposterous ornaments, though the ground it stood upon, with its own two rooms on a floor, its garden and all, covered considerably less than half an acre."

Friends used to drive down to see them after dining in town, and Goldsmith felt deeply indebted to Bott for timely financial help rendered in his worst straits, which removed the terrors of arrest which had been hanging over him. In a letter written shortly before he died Goldsmith recalled "such whimsical scenes of past days as when they used to drive down the Edgware Road at night, and, both their necks being brought into imminent peril by the gig's descent into a ditch, the driver (Bott) would exhaust all his professional eloquence to prove that at that instant they were exactly in the centre of the road."

Goldsmith was able to carry on his writing more or less at leisure, and his work included a *History of Rome,* commissioned by Davies, and his new poem, at which he worked in the lanes and along the hedgerows of Kingsbury. (Enjoying an unexpected spell of liberty, he was able to tune "his exquisite song outside the bars of his London prison.") Meantime his *Abridgement of the History of England* had been published for him by Davies, and we hear of a blustering reception vouchsafed to his very innocent book. "I have been a good deal abused in the newspapers for betraying the liberties of the people. . . . They set me down as an arrant Tory, and consequently an honest man. When you come to look at any part of it, you'll say that I am a sour Whig. . . . I have been in the country at a farmer's house, quite alone, trying to write a comedy. It is now finished, but when or how it will be acted or whether it will be acted at all, are questions I cannot resolve. I have been trying these three months to be something to make people laugh. There have been strolling

about the hedges, studying jests with a most tragical countenance. The Natural History is about half finished, and I
will shortly finish the rest. God knows I am tired of this kind
of finishing, which is but bungling work; and that is not so
much my fault as the fault of my scurvy circumstances." This
in his letter to his old friend Bennett Langton and his wife, the
Dowager Countess of Rothes. Goldsmith was too busy with
the comedy for which Johnson chose that title of genius "She
stoops to Conquer" to be much disturbed by violent party
noises. Legends of his doings while at Kingsbury are recorded
by John Forster in his *Life and Times of Oliver Goldsmith,*
published more than a century ago. It was possible to say
before the advance of suburbia :

"The farm still stands on a gentle eminence in what is
called Hyde Lane, leading to Kenton, about three hundred
yards from the village of Hyde, and looking over a pretty
county in the direction of Hendon; and when a biographer of
the poet went in search of it a few years since, he found still
living in the neighbourhood the son of the farmer (a Mr.
Selby) with whom the poet lodged, and in whose family the
property of the house and farm remained. He found traditions of Goldsmith surviving too; how he used now and then
to wander into the kitchen from his own room, in fits of study
or abstraction, and the parlour had to be given up to him
when he had visitors to tea; how Reynolds and Johnson and
Sir William Chandos had been entertained there, and he had
once taken the young folks of the farm in a coach to see some
strolling players at Hendon; how he had come home one night
without his shoes, having left them stuck fast in a slough;
and how he had an evil habit of reading in bed, and of
putting out his candle by flinging his slipper at it. It is certain
he was fond of this humble place. He told Johnson and
Boswell that he believed the farmer's family thought him an
odd character, and that he was to them what the *Spectator*
appeared to his landlady and her children. He was 'The
Gentleman.' And so content was he for the present to continue
here, that he had given up a summer visit into Lincolnshire,
proposed in company with Reynolds, to see their friend
Langton, in his new character of Benedick."

There is a long-established tradition in Mill Hill that

Goldsmith used frequently to walk over from Kingsbury past the old Green Man at the Hale and along to Laurence Street, where he would rest in the shade of a particularly well-shaped tree, which is still called "Goldsmith's Oak." Goldsmith naturally figured in our very successful "Pageant of Hendon" produced soon after the first World War.

GARRICK

David Garrick came from Lichfield to London in company with his old tutor, Samuel Johnson, and enjoyed a career on the stage which has seldom been equalled and never surpassed. His successes at Drury Lane hardly need mention, though it may be remembered that the hostility of his rivals sometimes led to riots. He brought back the tragedies of Shakespeare into popularity again, and showed remarkable skill in the parts of Macbeth and Hamlet. Garrick's generous nature led him to write epitaphs for the memorials of those of his friends who predeceased him. In Chiswick graveyard on the south side of the church is a tall piece of masonry, crowned with a funeral urn, which commemorates William Hogarth, who died in 1764. The memorial has carvings in low relief of a mask, maul-stick, palette, brushes, a laurel wreath, an open book with the title "Analysis of Beauty." Several of the Hogarth family are commemorated there and the tombstone was restored by a descendant, William Hogarth, of Aberdeen, in 1856. Garrick wrote these verses to be inscribed on the north side :

> "Farewell, great painter of mankind !
> Who reach'd the noblest point of Art,
> Whose *pictur'd morals* charm the mind,
> And through the eye correct the heart.
>
> If *genius* fire thee, reader, stay ;
> If *nature* touch thee, drop a tear ;
> If neither move thee, turn away,
> For Hogarth's honour'd dust lies here."

Within the church at Chiswick is a memorial on the north wall of the tower to Charles Holland, the actor, with a good bust of him and an epitaph written by Garrick :

204

"If Talents—
To make entertainments instruction,
to support the credit of the stage,
by just and manly action,
If to adorn society
By virtue

which would honour both Rank and Profession

deserve remembrance,
Let him with whom these Talents were long exerted,
To whom these virtues were well known,
And by whom the loss of them will be long lament,
bear Testimony to the Worth and Abilities
of his departed friend
CHARLES HOLLAND
Who was born March 12, 1735
dy'd December 7, 1769
and was buried near this place.

D. GARRICK.

On one side of the altar-tomb where the actor actually rests there is a further reference to Holland's connection with Drury Lane Theatre and this association with Garrick. Holland played the parts of Iago, Hamlet, Macbeth and Romeo, and was satirised by Churchill, though praised by Chatterton because he imitated Garrick. Garrick was sufficiently interested in Hampton and its Grammar School to become in 1774, in conjunction with John Beard, the well-known Covent Garden singer, and Lord North, a trustee of the Jones bequests; and in 1787 properties belonging to the Hammond endowments were transferred to the Vicar of Hampton and fifteen other trustees, including David Garrick, who had all been appointed at a joint vestry of Hampton and Hampton Wick.

Close to Hampton, and with gardens running down to the Thames, is Hampton House, bought in 1754 by Garrick, who employed one of the Adam brothers to design additions to the house and the stone octagonal Greek temple with columned portico on the lawn by the river. There used to be a marble statue of Shakespeare by Roubiliac, for which Garrick served as the model. There still is a statue there, but it is a copy of the original, which Garrick bequeathed in 1779 to the British Museum. Garrick's widow went on living at his villa until

205

1822, where she died. The villa is still much as Garrick and his widow left it.

Garrick bought the lordship of the Manor of Hendon in 1750, a thing made possible by his great dramatic successes, which brought him a larger fortune than any actor save Shakespeare's contemporary, Alleyn, who founded Dulwich College. He built Hendon Hall and lived there from 1756 till 1779. It is still in existence very much as he left it, but the grounds that went with the house have been cut in two by one branch of the Barnet-Watford Bypass. The portico was originally at Canons Park, then at Wanstead, and now, one hopes, permanently at Hendon. Garrick made several memorials to his hero Shakespeare in his grounds. He built a summer-house from which he could look up a slight rise to the pillar with four statues round it—Comedy, Tragedy, History and Terpsichore, muse of the dance—and an appropriate inscription. The building of the bypass destroyed the "Gazebo" in spite of efforts to preserve it, and the neglect shown to the statue has resulted in such damage that restoration is out of the question. A letter to *The Times* in 1947 brought sympathy and subscriptions, but the sum needed to mend the memorial is too big to be justified in these days of restrictions.

A greater contrast could hardly be imagined than that between the "miserably ragged and defaced" volumes of Samuel Johnson's library, ill-chosen, ragged, lying in confusion and dust, with their leaves sometimes cut with a greasy knife, and the stupendously bound treasures of David Garrick, neatly arranged according to subject in his library at Hampton or his small collection in his manor home at Hendon Hall. Small wonder that Garrick, "a precise, natty man," as Austin Dobson styles him, "with the ambitions, if not the instincts, of a connoisseur, and a punctilious respect for externals, should hesitate to lend his priceless old plays" to Johnson, who seldom returned the books he borrowed, but who "usually enriched them liberally with unsolicited marginalia."

After Garrick's return from France in 1751 he writes to his brother Peter from Lord Burlington's house at Chiswick telling him that France is the best place in the world for a visit. On a later visit to Paris at the end of the Seven Years'

War he extended his tour to Italy and wrote on the journey from Lyons to Turin to his brother George, asking for news of the theatre, and warning him not to let the sun spoil Hogarth's election pictures (then hanging in the bow-room at Hampton House).

One of his friends in Paris was Jean Monnet, author, Trappist, a prisoner in the Bastille and actor-manager, whom Garrick helped to bring his troupe of French actors to London; and when popular feeling and the Lord Chamberlain's edict put a stop to the acting, it was Garrick who helped him financially. A lifelong friendship followed, and Garrick showed great generosity in buying Monnet's books, giving him many and placing Hampton House at his disposal. Another French admirer of Garrick—and there were many— was Chastellax, who "expatiates on the beauty of Hampton and its weeping willow."

When he travelled in France with his wife he met Diderot, Beaumarchais and Marivaux, and was made free of the Comédie Française. He wrote plays which had some success and was responsible for the Shakespeare memorial celebrations at Stratford-on-Avon. Garrick was painted by Hogarth, by Sir Joshua Reynolds and by Gainsborough, and is the last actor to be buried in Westminster Abbey. He also purchased the advowson of Hendon parish, and was able to see that his nephew, Carrington Garrick, was vicar of the parish.

WILLIAM COWPER

It must have been his early memories that enabled William Cowper to compose the ride of *John Gilpin* with reasonable topographical accuracy. Islington, Edmonton and on to Ware in Hertfordshire, following in the footsteps of Izaac Walton, suggest one piece of county through which he strolled as a boy. Other memories tell us of walks along the Thames rather than the sea, and two centuries have made his verses a picture of the past that can hardly be rediscovered today in Middlesex :

"I have loved the rural walk through lanes
Of grassy swarth close cropp'd by nibbling sheep

And skirted thick with intertexture firm
Of thorny boughs; have loved the rural walk
O'er hills through valleys, and by river's brink,
E'er since a truant boy I pass'd my bounds
To enjoy a ramble on the banks of Thames."

It would hardly be possible for him, if he were living today, to replenish his "slice of pocket store" as he then did by feeding in lanes near the river—

"On scarlet hips and stony haws,
Or blushing oats, or berries that emboss
The bramble, black as jet, or sloes austere.
Hard fare! but such as boyish appetite
Disdains not, nor the palate undepraved
By culinary arts unsavoury deems."

GOVERNOR HOLWELL AND THE "BLACK HOLE"

Pinner Place, an old Tudor house which retained till recently much of its old charm, was for many years the home of Governor John Zephaniah Holwell, one of the few survivors of the "Black Hole of Calcutta." He was born in Dublin in 1700, and, after training as lawyer and doctor, went to India, and after some years found himself in charge of the English in Calcutta when Suraj ed Dowlah marched against Fort William, and the Governor and Commandant fled in terror. After two days, surrender was unavoidable, and Holwell was promised the lives of the 146 prisoners. Macaulay's grim story, based no doubt on Holwell's own thrilling reminiscences, tells of the horrors of the prison, its small, airless condition at the summer solstice, and the callous behaviour of the gaolers. "Nothing could be done without the Nabob's orders. Then the prisoners went mad with despair. They trampled each other down, fought for the places at the windows, fought for the pittance of water with which the cruel mercy of the murderers mocked their agonies, raved, prayed, blasphemed, implored the guards to fire among them." In the morning, through piles of loathsome corpses, twenty-three ghastly figures staggered out of the house. One of them was Holwell, who owed his life to the self-sacrifice of the others, who had placed him near the one tiny window.

208

Teddington Lock

Unable to walk, he was carried before the brutal tyrant, who abused and threatened him, but was persuaded by his own grandmother to spare Holwell's life, because of his invariable justice and mercy in the law courts. Tremendous retribution followed in Clive's victory at Plassey, and Holwell sufficiently recovered his health to be Governor of Bengal. He put up a memorial to the 123 victims of the Black Hole before he sailed for England. In spite of the tragedy through which he passed, Governor Holwell managed to survive until the age of ninety-eight at Pinner Place, to which he retired.

LADY HAMILTON

Another historic family who lived in Pinner were the Nelson-Wards, lineal descendants of Horatio, Lord Nelson, and Lady Hamilton. In a recent debate in the House of Commons (December, 1946), in discussing the ending of the Nelson pension, the Chancellor of the Exchequer commented on the magnificent achievements of the famous admiral and on the complete ignoring of his dying wishes that Lady Hamilton should be regarded "as a legacy to my King and Country." The pension that should have gone to Lady Hamilton and her daughter Horatia was given to the Rev. William Nelson, D.D., and it was to his descendants that it had been paid for 140 years. The Chancellor then made the astounding statement, which no one in the House contradicted, that Horatia, when she died in 1881, did not leave, as far as was known, any issue. This amazing misstatement was corrected in *The Times* the next day, when it was pointed out that Horatia married on February 19, 1822, the Rev. Philip Ward, Vicar of Tenterden in Kent, and had eight children. When her husband died in 1859 she settled in Pinner, where she died in 1881 at the age of eighty-nine.

The Chancellor showed great sympathy with Lady Hamilton, who, as he said, "found a pauper's grave in a foreign land and a passing Englishman paid for her funeral," and cries of "Shame!" greeted his statement that she was allowed to starve and died in a garret in Calais. The National Maritime Museum at Greenwich has a number of relics of Nelson, especially those contained in a small gallery opened

Eel Pie Island, Twickenham

in 1939 by one of Horatia's grandsons. There is a plaque at the entrance to the gallery, which records that "The relics in this room are given to England in memory of Horatia Nelson Ward, daughter of Admiral Viscount Nelson, and afterwards the wife of the Rev. Philip Ward, M.A., of Trunch, Norfolk, by her grandsons, the Rev. H. E. Nelson-Ward, M.A., and Admiral Philip Nelson-Ward, C.V.O." The Admiral died before the gift was quite completed, but the elder brother was still alive when the debate on the Nelson pension took place in December, 1946.

On the occasion of the centenary of Trafalgar in 1905 a special exhibition took place at Greenwich, and among the exhibits loaned at the time were twelve original Nelson letters, and his dirk, his wineglass, buckles, cuff links—all these taken from the *Victory* after his death by the boatswain. These, and a framed medallion of Nelson in plaster belonging to his sister, were the property of Eliot Pye-Smith Reed, of Hampstead. The letters were sent to be bound, but were most unfortunately burned. The other Nelson relics are in the possession of the author of this book.

WILKES AND BRENTFORD

It is a remarkable fact that Charles James Fox, later to become the greatest supporter of liberty in Europe, was opposed to the election of John Wilkes as M.P. for Middlesex. Wilkes attacked the unpopular Peace of Paris in language "exceeding in audacity and rancour any that has been published for many years." In No. 45 of the *North Briton* he satirised the King's Speech, and in subsequent publications he compared by name the relations of King George's mother and Lord Bute with those of Edward III's mother and Roger Mortimer. "The libellers of the Princess Mother and of Lord Bute did not give quarter to a single vowel."

Wilkes had earned some notoriety as a profane, licentious and agreeable rake, but he earned still greater fame through his continuous attacks on the Government. Brentford as the county town has many interesting memories, and here are buried Noy, Clitherows of Boston House and Berkeleys. But it is the historic Middlesex Elections that have brought

Brentford its outstanding fame, and especially those associated with John Wilkes. In 1701 the place of meeting was moved from Hampstead Heath to Brentford, where behind the market and Sessions House was the Butts, where archery seems to have been practised from Edward IV to Charles II. There are still some picturesque old houses facing on this open space.

Wilkes had returned from France in 1768 after a four years' exile to stand first for London and then for Middlesex, and his second choice was probably due to his meeting abroad with John Horne (Tooke), curate of Brentford. During Wilkes's trial in Westminster Hall, Hogarth, then living in Chiswick, "skulked behind a screen" and sketched the famous caricature of Wilkes seated on a Chippendale chair, with copies of the *North Briton* on a stool beside him and a pole in his hand with a cap of liberty upon it. In this cartoon Wilkes's ill-favoured features were said to have been made "ten times more grotesque than the original." There seems to have been a stay in Wilkes's imprisonment while the election took place on March 28, and Wilkes was returned at the head of the poll, 600 votes ahead of his nearest rival.

George Cooke was the nearest in votes to Wilkes, and he therefore also became M.P. for Middlesex, but owing to his death in December, 1768, one of the seats became vacant. Sergeant Glynn, a friend of Wilkes, stood against Sir W. B. Proctor, and when Glynn was obviously winning the day a set of ruffians with staves and bludgeons fought their way into the hustings, which they destroyed, and tore to pieces some of the polling books. The narrow lanes leading to the Butts were lined with more roughs, crowds paraded the streets with "Proctor and Liberty" in their hats, prize-fighters were rewarded with one guinea a day for their services, butchers attacked with cleavers, houses favourable to Sergeant Glynn were raided, and chaos prevailed throughout the town. A recent writer complains of the inaccuracy of the slogan "Wilkes and Liberty," thinking that Wilkes was to blame for the riots; but it was Wilkes's opponents and not his supporters who enlisted the services of the mob.

When Wilkes's election was declared null and void a further poll was needed. His supporters declared that they

211

would rather lose their lives than their liberty, and backed him to the utmost of their power. Wilkes secured 1,143 votes and his rival, Colonel Luttrell, only 296. The House of Commons, with its gang of so-called "King's Friends," refused to receive Wilkes and welcomed Luttrell instead. A contemporary squib offered the hint that this result was obtained by adding up the figures in Wilkes's total, thus making only 9, whereas Luttrell's figures tot up to 17!

Grenville, Wedderburn and Burke all attacked Lord North and his friends in 1774, but neither then nor in the four successive years could North be persuaded into accepting the verdict of Brentford. When Parliament was dissolved in 1774 Wilkes came to Brentford once again and was again returned, and after another eight years of determined effort Wilkes succeeded, when Rockingham was in power, in expunging from the records all the adverse orders on the Middlesex elections. Wilkes had succeeded in establishing the right of every constituency to return the Member of its choice.

Paul Whitehead, a forgotten poet, comments on the election in his well-known lines :

> "Bridges they cross, through lanes they went,
> Leave Hounslow's dangerous heath behind;
> Through Brentford win a passage free
> By shouting 'Wilkes and Liberty.' "

In a famous cartoon of the time Parson Horne figures among the group of electors as a friend of Wilkes, which makes more inexplicable the last line of the chorus of Wilkes's famous ballad :

> "John Wilkes he was for Middlesex,
> They chose him Knight of the Shire;
> And he made a fool of Alderman Bull
> And called Parson Horne a liar."

A MIDDLESEX ELECTION

Although the Reform Bill had been passed in 1832, there were still important Parliamentary reforms for which some sections of the country at least were pressing. One of the most vital of these was the Ballot, passing the Commons in 1710, demanded by the Chartists in the 1840s, but not passed into law until 1872. Middlesex elections, which had earned undying fame or notoriety in the era of John Wilkes, still retained some picturesque features which were to be noted in Brentford market-place, even though in 1847 the election was uncontested. Here is what *The Times* of February 4, 1847, has to say about it :

"There was a goodly assemblage of electors and non-electors present on the occasion. The hustings were erected in the market-place, and the arrangements were carefully made by the authorities to secure order in the proceedings. Shortly before the hour appointed for the nomination Lord Robert Grosvenor [afterwards Lord Ebury], who, as our readers are aware, was the only candidate in the field for the vacant seat, escorted by a party of friends and supporters, arrived in Brentford, and driving up in a carriage and four took his place on the platform. He was surrounded by Lord Marcus Hill, Sir Walter Sterling, General Sir De Lacy Evans, Mr. Whitbread and other gentlemen of influence and distinction. (The sheriffs and under-sheriff appeared on the hustings in their robes of office, with other officers. Lord Robert Grosvenor was proposed, seconded and declared duly elected; he responded in a speech occupying a column and a half, declaring himself 'warmly attached to the working-classes of this country.')

"There was a good display of banners in front of the hustings, with the usual party mottoes emblazoned upon them; but there was no marching in procession through the town, and (the crowd at the hustings once dispersed) the only visible signs of so important an event as the election of a representative for Middlesex was a huge flag suspended from a window of the principal hotel, and occasionally the sight of a sturdy farmer with the party ribands in his button-hole."

SOME EIGHTEENTH-CENTURY VISITORS
TO MIDDLESEX

In the century from the beginning of the Hanoverian dynasty to the Battle of Waterloo, in addition to those who lived permanently in Middlesex, we may select a few of the distinguished men of action or letters who have a passing

213

contact with our county. The Duke of Shrewsbury, whose attendance at an important council when Anne was dying checkmated the plans of Bolingbroke of Dawley and brought George I to the throne instead of the Old Pretender, had a house in Isleworth which is now a Roman Catholic convent. The Duchess of Kendal, one of George I's singularly unattractive mistresses, retired after his death to Isleworth, and quite believed that her royal lover had fulfilled his promise and had returned to visit her in the guise of a black raven, which she tended with great care until at length it flew away from the garden at Kendal House.

The South Sea Bubble, one of the romances of eighteenth-century politics, gives us three important contacts with the county. The plan for getting a monopoly of trade with the Spanish colonies sent up the shares of the South Sea Company to a phenomenal height and led to frenzied speculation of all kinds. When some of the bubble companies collapsed, the South Sea Company followed them and produced widespread disaster. Modern research has somewhat modified the panic-stricken demands of the moment, which wanted all the directors drowned in the Thames. As has already been mentioned, Secretary James Craggs and his father were living at Grove House, Twickenham. Aislabie, the Chancellor of the Exchequer, who was living at Hendon, was expelled from the House of Commons and all his recently acquired property, including his Hendon House, was confiscated. Robert Walpole, who had been opposed to the scheme but had privately made considerable profits by judicious buying and selling, was living at Lacy House, Isleworth. Perhaps it was his father's sojourn in Middlesex that prompted Horace Walpole to buy Strawberry Hill.

George II lived for some years before his accession at Berrymead Priory, near Brentford, and his daughter, Princess Amelia, at Gunnersbury. The Guards marched to Finchley to take up a strong position of defence against Bonnie Prince Charlie, should he get so far. In Hogarth's famous picture, which annoyed the King so much, they had only got as far as Tottenham Court Road. On his way to the victory at Culloden the Duke of Cumberland reviewed his troops at Hounslow Heath and marched north through South Mimms.

Admiral Byng, shot, according to Voltaire, to encourage the other admirals, lived at Wrotham Park just north of High Barnet.

For the last three years of his life, from 1787 to 1790, there lived at Chiswick Sir George Eliott, the hero of Gibraltar. General Eliott, who had been wounded in the historic Battle of Dettingen, the last in which an English king took an active part, was appointed, after service at Cherbourg, to be Governor of Gibraltar in 1774. In 1779 the Spaniards, who had joined the Family Compact with France in order to regain this stronghold, took advantage of our embroilment with America to make a combined desperate attack. For four years the garrison held out, organised and inspired by Eliott. The final attack by 40,000 men, ten invulnerable battering-ships and the combined French and Spanish fleets—forty-seven ships of the line, accompanied by innumerable frigates, gunboats, mortar-boats, cutters—was watched by members of the French royal family, French and Spanish nobles, and distinguished foreigners. Just before the attack an eagle "hovered majestically over the British fortress . . . and took its stand on the signal post which crowned the height." Red-hot cannon balls were prepared for the defence and were heated in grates and furnaces. Several important ships of the enemy burst into flames, and the fires enabled the English to "continue their cannonade with a terrible precision." All the battering-ships were destroyed, 2,000 of the enemy were killed or wounded, and only ninety casualties were reported on the English side. The capture of Gibraltar had been exhibited on the French stage, but "the invincible fortress, almost uninjured by the cannonade, still looked down defiantly on the foe." Lord Howe evaded the enemy, relieved the place and left it well stocked for further resistance, and in February, 1783, the preliminaries of peace were signed, and Gibraltar under Eliott (later Lord Heathfield) had withstood a siege of three years, seven months and twelve days.

Lord North, perhaps as much responsible as any one man for the loss of the American colonies, lived at Bushey Park. Dumouriez, an early General of the French Revolution, who came over to England and outlined plans for resisting and invading France, spent some time at Ealing, and there were two interesting associations with Waterloo itself. In 1814 the Duke of Wellington was driving through Brentford and had an accident which might well have been fatal and have left us to face Waterloo without him. The Marquess of Anglesey, who lost a leg in that historic battle, in which he led the heavy brigade in an overwhelming attack on D'Erlon's division, was lord of the Manor of West Drayton.

CHARLES LAMB IN MIDDLESEX

Few writers have had a more intimate association with Middlesex than Charles Lamb. As county councils had not been established, he and Mary were living in Middlesex during their years at Colebrook Cottage, Islington, where Dyer walked in error into the New River, and from where Lamb wrote to Wordsworth and Bernard Barton and Miss Hutchinson to tell them of his freedom, his recent emancipation, his gaol delivery. "I came home *for ever* (after thirty-three years of slavery) on Tuesday in last week. The incomprehensibleness of my condition overwhelmed me. It was like passing from life into eternity. Every year is to be as long as three, *i.e.,* to have three times as much real time—time that is my own, in it. . . . I can sit at home in rain or shine, without a restless impulse for walkings. I am daily steadying, and shall soon find it as natural to me to be my own master as it has been irksome to have had a master. Mary wakes every morning with an obscure feeling that some good has happened to us." This is how he wrote to Wordsworth, and in his other correspondence he was even more emphatic. "B. B., I would not serve another seven years for seven hundred thousand pounds! I have got 441£ net for life, sanctioned by Act of Parliament, with a provision for Mary, if she survives me. If I live another forty years; or, if I live but ten, they will be thirty, reckoning the quantity of real time in them, *i.e.,* the time that is a man's own."

In the August of 1825 he and his sister paid a long visit to Enfield from Islington, and this persuaded them to remove there later on. He wrote to Sankey from Enfield, "to which place we came about a month since, and are having quiet holidays. . . . We are on a half visit to Coleridge's friend,

Allsop, at a Mrs. Leishman's, Enfield, but expect to be at
Colebrook Cottage in a week or so. . . . You'll know who
this letter comes from, by opening slap-dash into the text, as
in the good old times. I could never come into the custom of
envelopes; 'tis a modern foppery."

About a year later, in July, 1826, the Lambs went for
another long visit to Enfield and ultimately settled there,
chiefly as T. N. Talfourd tells us, to benefit Mary, who found
the "crowd of visitors who pressed on him at Islington, and
whom he could not help welcoming," too exacting. One of
his earliest visitors was Henry F. Cary, once librarian of the
British Museum, whom he invited to visit with other friends
what he called his "doleful hermitage." Lamb was sometimes
(but not for long) uncertain whether he preferred the town
or the country, his "poor quiet retreat, to which we fled from
society." But even in his wilderness he was persecuted from
village to village, bothered with a heavy importation of two
old ladies. He never was better, and took walks of fourteen
miles on an average with his sporting dog, Dash. When he
left the dog with Patmore for a while, he wrote to ask
whether he went muzzled or *aperto ore*, whether his tail
wagged horizontally or perpendicularly. If he bit any
children they were to be shot, and Dash kept to see if it really
was hydrophobia. His address was at Mrs. Leishman's, The
Chase, Enfield, and he could offer cold meat and a tankard.

While at Enfield he was asked to subscribe to a memorial
to Clarkson, still living, to place at the wayside spot between
London and Cambridge, where he determined to devote his
life to the abolition of the slave trade. Lamb does not
approve of this notion, and suggests that they might as well
erect a monument where he himself "sate down upon a hillock
at Forty Hill, yesternight—a fine contemplative evening—
with a thousand good speculations about mankind."

It was not until 1829 that Lamb decided to live entirely in
Enfield and to give up Colebrook Cottage. He took what he
describes in a notelet to Talfourd as "an odd looking, gam-
bogish coloured house at Chace-side." "The situation," writes
Talfourd, "was far from picturesque, for the opposite side
of the road only presented some middling tenements, two
dissenting chapels, and a public house decorated with a swing-

ing sign of a Rising Sun, but the neighbouring field walks were pleasant, and the county, as he liked to say, as good as Westmorland." Lamb gives tiny glimpses of their life at Enfield, punctuated as it must have been by grim anxiety about Mary's health. "Mary, who is handselling her new aerial perspectives upon a pair of old worsted stockings trod out in Cheshunt lanes, sends her love. . . . Jokes are not suspected in Bœotian Enfield. We are plain people, and our talk is of corn and cattle and Waltham markets." Lamb found, on the whole, that Enfield was dull after London, but a ten days' visit to a friend in town showed him that it was the old familiar faces more than the streets and shops for which he pined. He felt that it was "better to get home to my hole at Enfield, and hide like a sick cat in my corner." House-keeping was too much for Mary, so they sold their old Penates and became house-sharers next door on Chaseside, Gentleman's Row; and then The Poplars, with pillared portico, which then gave place to Westwood's cottage, 42 inches nearer London.

Thomas Westwood's first glimpse of the Lambs occurred when he peeped through the window and saw "a slim middle aged man, a rather shapeless bundle of an old lady, and a dog carrying in its jaws a board with 'This house to be let' on it." Lamb made great friends with young Westwood, giving or lending him books and letting him have the run of his library. He would give the youngster new books because they did not fit in with old ones. "He would sometimes send them skimming through the apple trees to land at the boy's feet, or tumbling after him down the stairs." Lamb's books often needed repairing, which does not seem surprising; and West-wood would see the artistic cobbler stitching them up for their owner. Lamb would allow the boy to come in and sit in a corner listening to the gossip when Hazlitt or Tom Hood or Leigh Hunt or even Wordsworth and Coleridge came to visit their old friend. Before the Lambs came to live with the Westwoods, Mary would tap at the window to let the youngster know that some famous visitor had arrived.

But Charles never really liked the country save for a holiday, and he unburdened his soul to Wordsworth in a long letter of January 22, 1830, just a year since Charles and

Mary had seen him off "at the steps of Edmonton stage." He tells Wordsworth that they have "taken a farewell of the pompous, troublesome trifle, called house-keeping, and are settled into poor boarders and lodgers next door, with an old couple, the Baucis and Baucida of dull Enfield." He was angry with the lying poets, who enticed men away from the cheerful haunts of streets; he lamented his separation from London, that old Jerusalem, longed for the lofty fruiterers of Oxford Street, the crowds of St. Giles, the fine indifferent pageants of Fleet Street. He evidently loved London as deeply as Johnson or Boswell. Nothing, he felt, could make the country anything better than altogether odious and detestable. Adam was lucky to have sinned himself out of Eden. London meant haberdashers, goldsmiths, taverns, playhouses, satires, epigrams, puns, and he would gladly live in London shirtless and bootless.

There is no need to quote Lamb's portrait of his host, Thomas Wedgwood, Senior, famous for his "forty pounds a year and one anecdote." Wedgwood had been a thriving haberdasher within Bow Bells, had ridden one sweltering day in August into Dunstable on a mad horse, or it might have been Devizes. Once Lamb did seem reconciled to Enfield when he speaks of having "flown from the Metropolis and its cursed annalists, reviewers, authors, and the whole muddy inkpress of that stagnant pool." It was in Enfield that Lamb fell after emerging from a public-house and, being discovered with a bleeding face, was arrested for murder. He managed to stammer his way out of the magistrate's court. He wrote to George Dyer about a fire which was lit by some ill-disposed half-witted incendiary and burned down the barns and hayricks of a farmer not half a mile away.

Much of Lamb's story comes from his *Life* by Thomas Noon Talfourd, author of *Ion* and a Judge of the High Court, who also had associations with Middlesex. He was the first boy ever to be entered for Mill Hill School, and while there started the first school magazine. After visits from more friends and frequent dinners with Cary at the British Museum, going and returning by the coach, Lamb decided to move to Church Street, Edmonton, where he was destined to die. He had hinted at ten years' emancipation, was to enjoy nine. The kindly Waldens looked after both at Bay Cottage, where there is still to be seen the cupboard that used to hold Mary when her melancholy breakdown occurred. Coleridge's death in July, 1834, removed a lifelong friend, and the loss was a severe one. Lamb still dined with Cary and enjoyed roast pig with Barron Field, Barry Procter, John Forster and his biographer. In December, 1834, when Lamb was walking to John Gilpin's inn, the Bell at Edmonton, he fell and never recovered consciousness. Talfourd was summoned at once and made all needed arrangements, and set to work to write his *Life* without mentioning Mary's tragedy. "So died," says Talfourd, "in the sixtieth year of his age, one of the most remarkable and amiable men who have ever lived." Such was his first biographer's verdict after twenty years of friendship, and the century that has elapsed has confirmed his view. E. V. Lucas's definitive biography and his editions of Lamb's *Letters* have increased our admiration of "Elia," and the Charles Lamb Society carries on the task of keeping his memory green.

A few weeks before his death he had pointed out to Mary the exact spot in the church where he wanted to be buried, and his friends carried out his wish. Thirteen years later Mary followed him to the grave. Henry Cary, his Museum friend and the translator of Dante, wrote twelve lines of verse which are carved on the simple memorial stone. Facing the church is the Lamb Institute, and the Passmore Edwards Library close at hand is a memorial to both Keats and Lamb. Bay Cottage, now honoured with Lamb's name, still stands where it did, "squeezed in between two bigger houses, set back from the street and reached by a path with shrubs on one side, all cared for and trim in its long narrow garden." Many pilgrims to his shrine testify to the enduring affection with which the folk of Middlesex and elsewhere regard the gentle Elia.

At the west end of the north wall of Edmonton Parish Church there is a memorial to Lamb and to Cowper, a "monument to commemorate the visit of the London and Middlesex Archæological to Edmonton church and Parish on the 26th July 1888, erected by the President of the meeting, Joshua W. Butterworth, F.S.A." It consists of two inscribed white marble panels, enshrined in a graceful freestone design, the arches of which are supported by veined marble pilasters. Above are the portraits in relief, with Cowper on the right and Lamb on the left. The memorial to Lamb runs thus :

> "In memory of Charles Lamb, the gentle Elia
> and author of Tales from Shakespeare, etc.
> Born in the Inner Temple, 1775, educated at
> Christ's Hospital, died at Bay Cottage,
> Edmonton, 1834, and buried beside his sister
> Mary in the adjoining churchyard.

> 'At the centre of his being lodged
> A soul by resignation sanctified,
> O, he was good if e'er a good man lived.' "
>
> WORDSWORTH.

DICKENS AND TENNYSON AT TWICKENHAM

For a short time Charles Dickens had a house at Twickenham and entertained there a number of his friends—Harrison Ainsworth, Cattermole, Douglas Jerrold, Landseer, Maclise, Thackeray and Thomas Noon Talfourd (friend to so many writers of distinction, the patron to whom Dickens dedicated *Pickwick Papers*), Lytton and Browning.

An almost forgotten piece of Tennyson's life was spent at Twickenham soon after his marriage in 1880 to Emily Sellwood, to whom he had really been engaged for fourteen years. The advances made by Moxon in *In Memoriam* made marriage possible, and after an unlucky start at Warnington in Sussex they settled on April 20, 1851, at Chapel House in Montpelier Row. In this house, with a carved figure of a bishop on the staircase as if to bless, a stillborn child arrived on Easter Day.

"Dead as he was, I felt proud of him. . . . I am glad that I have seen him. Dear little nameless one that hast lived though thou hast never breathed, I thy father love thee and weep over thee, though thou hast no place on the universe. Who knows?"

In the years at Twickenham came the Great Exhibition in Hyde Park with its promise of universal and lasting peace, Tennyson's poems against the threats of Louis Napoleon, and the death of the Duke of Wellington. Tennyson's ode, which he wrote as Poet Laureate, was not well received, though it moved Benjamin Jowett to tears, and Ruskin and Maurice recorded their admiration for his genius. About this time Watts, Millais and Woolner the sculptor all endeavoured, with success, to record Tennyson's features.

On August 11, 1852, the second son, Hallam, was born, and Tennyson wrote to John Forster, the historian and biographer : "I never saw anything more beautiful than the mother's face as she lay by the young child an hour or so after, or heard anything sweeter than the little lamb-like bleat of the young one. . . . On the third day of his life . . . I saw him looking above with such apparently earnest wide open eyes, I felt as awe-struck as if I had seen a spirit."

At the beginning of 1853 he was asked to consider being Rector of Edinburgh University, an honour which he felt obliged gratefully to decline. The proximity of London to Twickenham began to alarm him—"lots of callers; I expect I shall be inundated"—and so, in order to control his life more as he wanted it, and fearing the rapid encroachment of the builder, he decided to leave Twickenham where two sons had been born.

MATTHEW ARNOLD AND LALEHAM CHURCH

More than half a century ago, in 1890, William Winter, a contributor to the *New York Tribune,* revised some sketches which he had written for that paper and published them under the title *Gray Days and Gold,* with the idea of celebrating "the beauties of our ancestral home" and of helping his countrymen to refine "the material civilisation of America by a reproduction within its borders of whatever is valuable in the long experience and whatever is noble and beautiful in the domestic and religious spirit of the British Islands." In his earliest sketch he visits two classic shrines : Stoke Poges, to commune with Gray, and Laleham, "a place destined to become, after a few years, as famous and as dear to the heart of the reverent pilgrim in the footsteps of genius and pure renown." Here is his description of Laleham, which he visited on a chill, sombre day in June, with the sky more like November, but fitting well with the scene and the thoughts which it aroused. "It consists of a few devious lanes and a cluster of houses, shaded with large trees, and everywhere made beautiful with flowers, and it is one of those fortunate and happy places to which access cannot be obtained by railway. There is a great house in the centre of it, secluded in a walled garden, fronting the square immediately opposite to the village church. The rest of the houses are mostly cottages made of red brick and roofed with red tiles. Ivy flourishes, and many of the cottages are overrun with climbing roses. The church is of great antiquity. The large low tower is of brick, and this and the church walls are thickly covered with glistening ivy. A double-peaked roof of red tiles, sunken here and there, contributes to the picturesque beauty of the building, and its charm is further heightened by the continuity of large trees, in which the old church seems to nestle. Within are low, massive pillars and plain symmetrical arches —the remains of Norman architecture. Great rafters of dark oak augment in this quaint structure the air of solidity and of an age at once venerable and romantic, while a bold, spirited, beautiful painting of Christ and Peter upon the wall imparts to it an additional sentiment of sanctity and solemn pomp. . . . The explorer does not often come upon such a gem of a church even in England, so rich in remains of the old Catholic zeal and devotion.

"The churchyard is worthy of the church—a little enclosure, irregular in shape, surface, shrubbery and tombstones, bordered on two sides by the village square, and on one by a farm-yard, and shaded by many trees, some of them yews, and some of great size. The poet's grave is in a secluded spot by the side of the church, a little removed from the highway, and screened from immediate view by an ancient dusky yew-tree. A small square of turf, bordered with white marble, covers the tomb of the poet and of three of his children."

There is a headstone of white marble to the memory of Matthew Arnold, who died in 1888, aged sixty-five, and three crosses to Basil Francis Arnold, who died, aged not quite two, in 1868; to Thomas, eldest child, who died the same year, aged sixteen; and Trevor William, who died in 1872, aged eighteen.

William Watson, a poet who deserves more renown than

he enjoys, liked nothing better than to laud his predecessors or his contemporaries, and he has left us verses on the grave of Wordsworth and some that have brought many pilgrims to Matthew Arnold's grave at Laleham. Matthew's mother and sister are buried close by, but Arnold of Rugby is fittingly interred in the school chapel. Watson writes of the "singer who lies songless here" but who in his life and verse—

> "Preserved from chance control
> The fortress of his 'stablisht soul;
> In all things sought to see the Whole;
> Brooked no disguise;
> And set his heart upon the goal,
> Not on the prize;
>
> And with those few he shall survive
> Who seem not to compete or strive,
> Yet with the foremost still arrive,
> Prevailing still;
> The Elect with whom the stars connive
> To work their will."

How far does the present age go with Matthew Arnold? Like John Ruskin, he seems to many to be *vieux jeu*, a period piece; and Sir Walter Raleigh, writing in 1912, could say of him:

"He was adorably insolent; priding himself on his courtesy and humanity, walking delicately among the little people of the earth, like a kind of Olympian schoolmaster dandy. . . . Nothing can exceed the quiet impertinence of his use of proper names. . . . Some of his critical utterances on poetry have the same note of calm extravagance."

He was alarmed at the tendencies of English literature and he had a conviction that there was "an almost imminent danger of England losing immeasurably in all ways." He criticised the English as either Barbarians or Philistines; he compared their literature, to their disadvantage, with those of France and Germany; he deplored the absence of an English Academy; but whatever one thinks of his criticism, his poetry deals with great things and has its magnificent moments. One writer has tried to convince the world that Matthew Arnold was at heart a Romanist. Another suggests, with more justification, that "the man who heeds Matthew

224

Church Farm, Hendon

Arnold's teaching will put no trust in creeds and superstitions, will place no reliance upon the cobweb structures of theology, will take no guidance from the animal and unthinking multitude; but he will keep the whiteness of his soul; he will be simply mindful and sweet, he will live for the spirit and not for the flesh; and in that spirit, pure, tender, fearless, strong to bear and patient to suffer, he will find composure to meet the inevitable disasters of life and the awful mysteries of death."

William Watson wondered whether Matthew Arnold was not more at home at Laleham, where he was born and lived for five years with his parents and for several years later with his uncle, rather than in the Lake District, where he was—

> "Guarded by summits lone and high,
> That traffic with the eternal sky."

Watson thinks of him in Laleham :

> "And nigh to where his bones abide,
> The Thames with its unruffled tide
> Seems like his genius typified—
> Its strength, its grace,
> Its lucid gleam, its sober pride,
> Its tranquil pace."

The words of Scripture on the headstones are worthy of record.

> "Suffer little children to come unto Me"
> "Awake thou, Lute and Harps! I will awake right early"
> "In the morning it is green and groweth up"

are on the children's tombs, while the text which commemorates the father is, "There is sprung up a light for the righteous, and joyful gladness for such as are true-hearted." All of them are from the Prayer Book version of the Psalms.

Matthew Arnold died in Liverpool one Sunday afternoon after attending the ministrations of Dr. John Watson ("Ian Maclaren"), when they sang Isaac Watts' hymn, "When I survey the wondrous Cross." He was heard to repeat it and declare that it was the finest in the language only a few hours before he died.

The house where the Arnolds lived has been pulled down, but there is still a cedar tree in Ashford Road which marks

Twyford Abbey, Alperton

the place where Thomas Arnold, the father, and Matthew, the son, spent perhaps the happiest years of their lives.

"LORNA DOONE"

It is not an uncommon thing for a schoolmaster to turn author, and Richard Doddridge Blackmore was both, and a successful fruit-grower as well. The Police Orphanage at Twickenham Green used to be a Wellesley House School, and Blackmore was a classical master there nearly half a century ago. About 1860 he bought Gomer House in Teddington, made a success there of his fruit-growing, and there wrote his novels. Gordon S. Maxwell, the historian, of Hounslow Heath, met an old gardener who used to work for Blackmore, and recalled his scrupulous fair-dealing and his dislike of conversation. Whether he was planning his novels while he walked round his orchards or not, he confined his remarks to the foreman and merely said "Good morning" to the others. The village folk knew that he wrote novels in his spare time; fruit production seemed to them his chief employment. His immediate success when he published *Lorna Doone* in 1869 is said to have been due to its coincidence with the marriage of the Marquess of Lorne into the Royal Family. Blackmore called his book a romance, and did not claim for his story the dignity or accuracy of an historical novel. Indeed, a visit to the Doone Valley in North Devon gives one an idea of how exaggerated Blackmore's description of the rugged countryside can be. He admitted that the incident, characters and scenery were alike romantic, and we must not take them too literally, but it is a first-class yarn, none the less.

Blackmore was at Blundell's as a schoolboy, and afterwards at Exeter College, Oxford, and the Doone legend was very well known in Devon. One of the family had fought for Monmouth at Scogmoor, but had escaped from the rough injustice of Judge Jeffreys. The Doones lived in a small group of cottages at Bagworthy in Exmoor, where they established a reign of terror in the neighbourhood. The family came to an end in the persons of an old man and his grand-daughter, who died in the snow in 1800 while trying to earn an honest penny by singing carols at Christmas-time. Alfred Tressider Shepherd in his *Art and Practice of Historical Fiction* quotes the Devon comment that *Lorna Doone* was "as good as clotted cream, almost," and notes that "even in the structure of its sentences and paragraphs it may be as properly called a poem; the words over and again, without any alteration or addition, shape themselves into blank verse."

Blackmore with his brother-in-law drove round North Devon to get local colour for his book. The facts had been published years before in a local guide to Lynton, and had been made the subject of a tale called "The Doones of Exmoor" which appeared in the *Leisure Hour*. But Blackmore put some genius into his novel, and there is no need to suggest plagiarism. What book is there which does not owe an immense debt to its predecessors, even though it is not "a great unblushing mosaic" like *John Inglesant*?

Blackmore lived in Teddington for forty years and used to walk on Sundays with his wife to the old church, carrying a huge Bible under his arm. He is buried in the cemetery, with the simple inscription "R. D. Blackmore, died Jan. 20, 1900." An attractive bronze plaque showing him with side whiskers has been placed in the public library at Teddington. Blackmore frequented the small modest brick church of St. Mary's, opposite the big ambitious church of St. Alban's, still unfinished. He was happy in Teddington, for there, too, are commemorated Paul Whitehead, a forgotten poet of the eighteenth century; Peg Woffington, the heroine of one of Charles Reade's novels; Thomas Traherne, a mystical writer of verse and prose; and John Walter, the real founder in 1788 of *The Times* or *Daily Universal Register*. It still today lives up to its full ancient title. Tom Harrison in the *Countryman* (autumn, 1947) demolishes one of the Doone legends and emphasises the gross exaggeration of Blackmore's waterslide with its "deep black staircase . . . the perpendicular walls of crag shutting out the evening." I can corroborate his criticism, for we visited back in 1901 the Bagworthy River, "six inches deep—at flood time," and my sister, who was suffering from acute asthma at the time, climbed the waterslide with ease !

Tom Harrison goes to great trouble to unravel the evidence given in *The Original Doones of Exmoor*, published just after Blackmore's death by "Audrie Doon," really Ida

227

Browne, and mentions the important fact that by a quaint
mischance all the evidence to back up her story—family Bible,
a quaint old diary, and some relics carved with the name of
Doone—were destroyed by a fire at Hunstanton in 1902!
Other evidence is given to show how valuable to Lynton,
Lynmouth and the Oare Valley is the connection with Blackmore's romance. "All in all, the ever-expanding Doone
legend is now a major factor in the tourist attractions of the
proposed Exmoor National Park."

WESTMINSTER GUILDHALL

The setting up of county councils all over the country took
away the old area from Middlesex which had figured in the
Bills of Mortality and had subsequently been administered by
the Metropolitan Board of Works. But the Middlesex Guildhall in Westminster, where Quarter Sessions are held and
where various powers of the Middlesex County Council are
exercised, is still regarded as being "within the county." Very
large and increasing powers are given to county councils, and
the budget adopted by Middlesex for a single year amounts
to more than thirteen million pounds, and, with the totals
expended by borough and district councils within the county,
it exceeds the budget of several independent states.

From 1550 to 1630 the county justices met at Castle Inn,
St. James's Street, Clerkenwell, and when Sir Baptist Hicks
built a hall adjoining the inn it was called Hicks's Hall, and
from it some main roads out of London were measured. In
1782 the Sessions House was built on Clerkenwell Green and
was used for forty years. For some years justices used a
building in old King Street as a Guildhall, until a new court
was erected on the site of the old Abbey Belfry. Until 1892
there was a one-storeyed Guildhall with portico, and then a
good deal of reconstruction took place, revealing beneath the
old sanctuary crypt a rubble raft 5 feet thick, built on oak
piles driven into the sand of the almost forgotten Thorney
Island.

The present Guildhall had its foundation-stone laid in 1912
by the Duke of Bedford as Lord-Lieutenant, and it was
opened a year later by the Duke of Connaught. J. S. Gibson
has designed a simple dignified structure which does justice

to its site and is ornamented with a frieze depicting Magna Carta, Henry III's Charter to the Abbey, and Lady Jane Gray accepting the Crown. There are many statues depicting the various functions of a county council, and within the building court rooms, committee rooms, council chamber, waiting rooms and accommodation for documents and for an ever-growing staff.

Until 1888, when the county councils began, the justices of Middlesex were also placed on the Commission of the Peace for Westminster. A special badge was authorised by George III, and the last to wear it was the late Sir Montague Sharpe, Chairman of the Quarter Sessions 1908-1934, and President of the County Archæological Society, of whom there is a fine portrait in the Guildhall by J. Spencer Watson.

Other portraits of interest are of Middlesex worthies, including Sir Baptist Hicks (Paul van Somer), the Duke of Bedford (John Collier), Sir Ralph Littler (Herkomer), Sir John Fielding (Hone), the Duke of Northumberland, the Duke of Wellington, the Marquis of Salisbury, three Lords-Lieutenant, the Earl of Strafford, and, lastly, William Mainwaring, Chairman of Middlesex Sessions (Gainsborough).

A very interesting ceremony took place in the Middlesex Guildhall in June, 1947, when panels were unveiled to commemorate the fact that during the second World War, when the greater part of Western Europe was overrun by the Nazis, London became the home of the Governments in exile. Britain, herself threatened with invasion, was the last bastion of freedom in the West, and a number of these exiled Governments set up courts to deal with maritime and military offences, and these courts were staffed by foreign judges and were held at the Middlesex Guildhall. The courts were set up under the Allied Forces Maritime Courts Act, and one of the panels bears the arms of the Netherlands in the centre, with those of Poland, Norway, Belgium and Greece at the four corners. This panel also bears the signature, amongst others, of Queen Wilhelmina, the late King George of the Hellenes, and the Prime Minister of Belgium. At the ceremony of unveiling, Viscount Jowitt, the Lord Chancellor, was one of the speakers, and Mr. Ernest Bevin, as Foreign Secretary, also took part.

229

CHAPTER XVI

SOME CENTURIES OF ENCROACHMENT
AND ENCLOSURES

THE change of Middlesex from country to town can hardly be better emphasised than by a glance at the deterioration that we find as we compare the country lanes from the Armada to Waterloo, as described by John Stow, Izaac Walton, Daniel Defoe and William Cobbett. If only the statute of Elizabeth had been carried out, which ordered that all cottages near London should have four acres of garden! There are isolated instances of prosecutions for disobedience in Paddington and Edmonton, but the profits to be made by overcrowded development were too tempting for those who should have given a wise direction to land use and town planning.

John Stow gives a delightful personal touch in his picture of Goodman's Farm, near the Minories, only a stone's throw from Tower Hill. There, in his youth, he "fetched many a halfpenny worth of milk, and never had less than three ale pints for a halfpenny in the summer, nor less than one ale quart in the winter." And he talks of Houndsditch, whose fields have just been parcelled out for fair houses of pleasure, and Hog Lane, where on both sides there were "fair hedgerows of elm trees, with bridges and easy stiles to pass over into the pleasant fields," now "a continuous building throughout of garden-houses and cottages." The country is still close to the city wall, but there is a serious risk that it will soon be overrun.

Compare this picture with one described by Izaac Walton on the outskirts of London about 1653, perhaps a century after Stow's story of Goodman's Fields and Houndsditch. *Piscator, Venator* and *Auceps* meet six miles from Hicks's Hall, walking northwards towards Tottenham, Goff's Oak, Waltham, Theobalds and Ware. Walton himself is the fisherman, and he speaks of the 325 English rivers mentioned in Dr. Heylin's geography book, of which he finds only six piscatorially worth while, and the Thames above all. "This

230

glorious river feeleth the violence and benefit of the sea more than any river in Europe, ebbing and flowing twice a day, more than sixty miles." The huntsman is expecting to meet a pack of otter-dogs in Hertfordshire, while the falconer is keenly interested in other birds besides his hawks. He loves the lark, blackbird and throstle, "little nimble musicians of the air," and smaller birds too, "the leverock, the titlark, the little linnet and the honest robbin." But his favourite is, perhaps, the nightingale, which "breathes such sweet loud music out of his little instrumental throat, that it might make mankind to think miracles are not ceased."

And all these birds were to be found in plenty all along this northern road, farther out from London than Stow's haunts, but still inside the confines of a walk. Walton is near to Tottenham and is walking in the cool shade of a sweet honeysuckle hedge, and he improves the occasion by thanking God for happiness, health and safety, for cheap enjoyment, for "flowers and showers and stomachs and meat, and content and leisure to go fishing." They then arrive at Tottenham and shelter from sun and shower in a "contexture of woodbine, sweetbriar, jessamine and myrtle," and they drink a nectar composed of sack, milk, oranges and sugar. In Richard Le Gallienne's delightful edition of the *Compleat Angler*, illustrated by E. H. New, there are maps and drawings of the way from Tottenham to Bruce Castle, Edmonton Church and Almshouses, and so to Goff's Oak, just over the Hertford-shire border, and in Walton's day every yard of the way was truly rural.

Defoe, in his *Journey through England*, apologises for having taken up so much time on London that there is not much left for Middlesex. "I must be the more cautious as to needless excursions in the country lanes." The influence of London, he finds, is felt extremely in Middlesex; for instance, in Hackney twelve hamlets or separate villages are almost joined together, and the whole fashionable area is now part of London. He quotes a satirical author, who complains that there were more citizens' coaches than Christians in the area.

Hackney is today part of London County, but not so Tottenham, Edmonton and Enfield, of which Defoe remarks that increase of buildings has made them "one continued

street, especially Tottenham and Edmonton." He comments
on the custom of having two houses, one in London and
another in Highgate, Hampstead, Barnet or Enfield Chase,
and hints that Hampstead "grew suddenly populous, and the
concourse of people was incredible." He is intrigued by the
view from the Whitestone Pond, "a most beautiful prospect
indeed, for we see here Hanslop Steeple one way, which is
within eight miles of Northampton." This is denied today,
but Banstead, Shooter's Hill, Redhill and Windsor Castle,
which he mentions, are still visible. For Defoe the Heath is
too bleak and the air too rarefied, and the winter has nothing
to recommend it. But the good company and warm houses of
Hampstead "go a great way to make amends for storms and
severity of cold." The country which Defoe enjoyed in
Middlesex to the north-west of the Heath remained almost
untouched for another two centuries.

William Cobbett, writing a century after Defoe, tells the
same story of unchecked, unorganised growth; and, for him,
London has become "the great wen." He prefers the small
market towns, such as Huntingdon, with about 5,000 souls,
surrounded by the most beautiful meadows that he ever saw
in his life. He likes it because it is "one of those pretty, clean,
unstenched, unconfined places that tend to lengthen life and
make it happy."

Small wonder that he disliked London. He speaks at first
favourably of the country along Watling Street, when on
June 19, 1822, he proceeds through Edgware, Stanmore and
Watford to St. Albans. "The crop is almost entirely hay,
from fields of permanent grass, manured by dung and other
matter brought from the Wen. Near the Wen, where they
have had the first haul of the Irish and other perambulating
labourers, the hay is all in rick. Some miles farther down it is
nearly all in. Towards Stanmore and Watford, a third perhaps of the grass remains to be cut. It is curious to see how
the thing regulates itself." On his walks through Middlesex
Cobbett noted the squads of labourers leaving cleared fields
behind them and marching on to the next, mowers with their
scythes on ahead, and haymakers with rakes and pitchforks
behind. He ends : "The public-houses are pouring out the
beer pretty fast, and are getting a good share of the wages of

these thirsty souls." But the tax collectors get the biggest share of the 5d. per pot. "Of this the Jews and jobbers get about twopence-halfpenny." The mowers, he finds, are all English; the haymakers are Irish (as they were within living memory near Mill Hill), but the Scots prefer "tying up flowers, picking dead leaves off exotics, peeping into melon-frames, publishing the banns of marriage between the 'male' and the 'female' blossoms."

Cobbett has great sympathy for the underdog, who has to perform "the digging, mowing, the carrying of loads; all the break-back and sweat-extracting work," and he fears, as the production of hay in Middlesex is so great, it will lead to a drop in prices. Here are all the evils of over-production, and he will not be surprised if hay, butter and milk are all taken into pawn.

So, riding his hobby-horse, Cobbett comes into Stanmore, and all the land up to there is "a very dull and ugly country, flat, and all glass-fields and elms. Few birds of any kind, and few constant labourers wanted; scarcely any cottages and gardens, which form one of the great beauties of a country. Stanmore is on a hill, but it looks over a country of little variety, though rich. What a difference between the views here and those which carry the eye over the coppices, the cornfields, the hop-gardens and the orchards of Kent! It is miserable land from Stanmore to Watford, where we get into Hertfordshire."

"As I approached Uxbridge (from Beaconsfield) I got off the chalk upon a gravelly bottom, and then from Uxbridge to Shepherd's Bush on a bottom of clay. Grass-fields and elm trees, with here and there a wheat or bean-field, form the features of this most ugly country, which would have been perfectly unbearable after quitting the neighbourhoods of Hempstead, Chesham and High Wycombe, had it not been for the diversion I derived from meeting, in all the various modes of conveyance, the Cockneys going to *Ealing Fair,* which is one of those things which Nature herself would seem to have provided for drawing off the matter and giving occasional relief to the overcharged Wen."

Cobbett starts off on another of his rural rides on September 25 of the same year, intending to go by a roundabout

Uphusband, near Andover. He tries to avoid Mid-
~~~ much as possible, but has to get back into the county
~~~ crosses Richmond Bridge. "All Middlesex is *ugly,*
notwithstanding the millions upon millions which it is continually sucking up from the rest of the Kingdom; and though
the Thames and the meadows now-and-then are seen from
the road, the country is not less ugly from Richmond to
Chertsey Bridge, through Twickenham, Hampton, Sunbury
and Shepperton, than it is elsewhere. The soil is a gravel at
bottom with a black loam at top near the Thames; further
back, it is a sort of spewy gravel; and the buildings consist
chiefly of tax-eaters' showy tea-garden-like boxes, and of
shabby dwellings of labouring people, who, in this part of the
country, look to be about half *Saint Giles'*; dirty and have
every appearance of drinking gin." Cobbett's comments on
the county are very severe, but his warnings, though un-
heeded, were most salutary.

The encroachments are noted everywhere and the country
is being swamped by the spreading of the all-engulfing town.
William Hone's *Every Day Book* (1827) and *Table Book*
are full of bitter, resentful rhymes :

"Thy fields, fair Islington, begin to bear
Unwelcome buildings, and unseemly piles;
The streets are spreading, and the Lord knows where
Improvement's hand will spare the neighbouring stiles."

And, before long, there is another victim to lament :

"Already, Highgate ! to thy skirts they bear
Bricks, mortar, timber, in no small degree,
And thy once pure, exhilarating air
Is growing pregnant with impurity."

Peter Foot's *View of the Agriculture of Middlesex* in 1794
is of unusual importance, as it gave a picture of a county
which was fast becoming "a sort of demesne to the metropolis, being covered with its villas, intersected with innumerable roads leading to it, and laid out in gardens, pastures
and inclosures of all sorts for its convenience and support."
The county still retained great fertility of soil, but it was no
longer the corn-producing county described by John Norden,
of Hendon, two centuries before.

SOME CENTURIES OF ENCLOSURES

Side by side with encroachments of London on the country-side comes the enclosure of common lands by the landlords. The practice of enclosures, from Tudor times, with the Dissolution of the Monasteries, up to Waterloo and later, finds few supporters today, but it was warmly approved by the landlords, who profited so largely by the Acts of Parliament which worked a series of agricultural revolutions. Thorold Rogers was unsparing in his contention that "from 1563 to 1824 a conspiracy, concocted by the law, and carried out by parties interested in its success, was entered into, to cheat the English workman of his wages, to tie him to the soil, to deprive him of hope, and to degrade him into irremediable poverty." His views are not so popular today, but Arthur Young, who lived through an important period of land-grabbing, wrote in a similar vein : "By nineteen Enclosure Acts out of twenty, the poor are injured, in some grossly injured. The poor in these parishes may say, and with truth, 'Parliament may be tender of property; all I know is, I had a cow, and an Act of Parliament has taken it from me.' "

The story of enclosures is cumulative, and the 1,500 acres "stolen" under Queen Anne had mounted to nearly 4,000,000 in the 3,446 Acts of George III. In Middlesex there were thirty-eight Enclosure Acts from 1769 to 1825, and in that time of communal loss 34,000 acres were confiscated out of the 150,000 of modern Middlesex. It is a staggering list which we have to record, covering every part of the county; and only to mention those parishes which lost more than 500 acres is to reveal a distressing story. Enfield lost 3,540 acres; Teddington 883; Edmonton 1,231; Harmondsworth 3,000; Ashford 1,200; Hayes 2,000; Finchley 900; Harefield 700; Hillingdon 1,400; East Bedfont 1,300; Isleworth, Heston and Twickenham 7,870; Greenford 640; Willesden 560; Harlington 820.

Luke Pope's *History of Middlesex* (1795) gives a more detailed story, with long-forgotten names of greens lost for ever perhaps, such as Mason's Green in Acton, Backer Green in Harefield, Hooking Green at Pinner, Piper's Green at Edgware, Peel Heath and Gould's Green in Hillingdon.

Hounslow Heath, which extended into fourteen parishes and hamlets, still included 5,000 acres by 1814, and enough was left nearby to form, nearly a century and a half later, London Airport at Heath Row.

It was simple enough to get an Act to permit of enclosures, and a pamphlet explaining the method was quoted by the Board of Agriculture with approval. In order to enclose a common field "two witnesses are produced to swear that the lands thereof, in their present state, are not worth occupying, though at the same time they are land of the best soil in the kingdom, and produce corn in the greatest abundance and of the best quality." The landlord thus converts twenty small farms into four big ones, and, by forbidding ploughing in the lease granted to the tenants, several hundred villages were reduced from four or five hundred to eighty or forty, or sometimes by one poor decrepit man or woman, housed by the landlords to avoid poor rates. The reports admit that this new system does not benefit the farmer or cottager, only the landlord and the tithe owner. They suggest that the old system had much to recommend it, and admit that the new plan enriches one class by impoverishing another.

Harefield and Moor Hall Commons were dealt with in 1811 and are perhaps typical of the methods employed. The Act states that the seven hundred acres of commons, moors and waste lands are incapable of any considerable improvement. A Commission is appointed to value, divide, and allot the land; notices are to be published in *The Times* and *Morning Chronicle,* and on the church door, and all rights of common are to be extinguished. The Commissioner is also allowed to close any highways, bridle- and foot-ways which he may regard as unnecessary. To help the poor, between 15 and 20 acres were allotted to satisfy rights of cutting furze or bushes for fuel; between 2 and 4 acres were given to Harefield for recreation, and some gravel pits were to be saved for watering cattle or washing sheep. Similar Acts were passed for Hanwell and Greenford just before Waterloo, and in the first case 4 out of 350 acres of common were allotted to the poor; in Greenford, out of 640 acres, none at all.

The *Gentleman's Magazine* gave a graphic account of the browbeating, bullying, frightening methods adopted, by which the lord of the manor threatens to drive the poor off what is his property; an attorney offers them a lease, and when the short lease is expired it is renewed at a rack-rent. The acceptance of a lease in sheer desperation by ignorant and intimidated commoners gives the lord of the manor the title he wanted, and another cruel and dishonest deal has been brought off.

CHAPTER XVII

THE CHURCHES OF MIDDLESEX

MIDDLESEX HUNDREDS AND PARISHES

MIDDLESEX is divided into six hundreds and fifty original parishes.

In *Edmonton* Hundred there are Edmonton, Enfield, South Mimms, Southgate, Tottenham, Wood Green.

In *Elthorne* a far longer list: Cowley, Cranford, West Drayton, Greenford, Hanwell, Harefield, Harlington, Harmondsworth, Hayes, East Hillingdon, West Hillingdon, Ickenham, Old Brentford, New Brentford, Northolt, Perivale, Ruislip, Uxbridge, Yiewsley.

Gore has Edgware, Harrow on the Hill, Harrow Weald, Hendon, Kingsbury, Pinner, Great Stanmore, Little Stanmore, Wealdstone, Wembley.

Isleworth has three only—Heston, Isleworth, Twickenham.

Ossulstone: Acton, Chiswick, Ealing, Finchley, Friern Barnet, Hornsey, West Twyford, Willesden.

Spelthorne: Ashford, East Bedfont, Feltham, Hampton, Hampton Wick, Hanworth, Laleham, Littleton, Shepperton, Staines, Stanwell, Sunbury, Teddington.

Middlesex is not well off in big houses, though it has Hampton Court, Syon House, Swakeleys, Forty Hall Enfield, Cromwell House, Highgate, and Boston House, Brentford; and it has far fewer small manor-houses than such an adjacent county as Herts. Now that London has for more than half a century taken most monastic remains away from the county, all we have to record of ecclesiastical buildings is in the main a series of "homely little edifices, admirably suited to the small villages they served, and entirely in harmony with their surroundings." It is a trite remark to suggest that building is often, if not always, determined by available materials. There is no good building stone available for churches, and so brickwork and rubble are used more often than in differently situated counties. So rubble, pebbles, flints and pudding stone with quoins and dressings of clunch from adjacent counties are used. Early brickwork is found in South Mimms (north aisle) and in Tottenham (porch), while Jacobean brick was used at Stanmore. Hayes, Ruislip and Hillingdon have used a good deal of flint, which is more easily available in that district. Shepperton and Hanwell have flint and clunch arranged in chequer-work. All through the centuries stone was imported from Reigate.

It is more fashionable nowadays to treat the old divisions of architectural features rather slightingly and not to follow as closely as formerly the division into Norman, Early English, Decorated and Perpendicular. Opinion is divided as to pre-Conquest features, but one likes to recognise the long and short quoins at Kingsbury and at Cowley and Willesden. Kingsbury old church claims to possess a Saxon door and two corner-stones, and some think that the font is a legacy from pre-Norman times. The Saxon door was bricked up for almost half a century, and its uncovering has given it a modern appearance.

The Norman Conquest and the distribution of manors among his followers by the Conqueror probably stimulated church building in the county of Middlesex, but most of what we find is not in the main structural. There are a few doorways, one or two windows, and several fonts. The best examples of twelfth-century fonts are at Harlington, Harrow, Hendon, Ruislip and Willesden. Harlington has a Purbeck marble font with octagonal bowl, supported on a central and eight small shafts and champered plinth. Harrow's font has a round bowl with moulded rim, and underside face cut with a scalloped ornament, stem fluted spirally and with a moulded base, also of Purbeck marble. Both these fonts are late twelfth century, but Hendon is probably earlier. It has a heavy square bowl with enriched intersecting according of eight bays on each face, springing from attached shafts with cushion capitals, enriched band below, stem consisting of central dwarf shaft and four small shafts at the angles, three of them being the original ones. Ruislip's font is a square bowl of Purbeck marble with foliated spandrels on the top surface, moulded edges and rolls at the angles of the bowl, the lower edge shaped for central and four subsidiary shafts, the former

239

with moulded capping and the latter with simple leaf capitals, bases repaired in cement, the whole being of Purbeck marble. Hayes' font has a round bowl decorated with acanthus leaves, a round stem with eight restored shafts.

The nave of Harlington Church is middle twelfth century, and the walls are of flint rubble with some ironstone conglomerate, while the dressings are of Reigate stone. The south doorway is a good example of twelfth-century work, and the west window in the nave is a single round-headed light of the same century, enlarged in the sixteenth. The south doorway, which has been partly restored, is also Norman work, having "a round arch of four orders with a label enriched with linked roundels; the innermost order is plain and continued down the jambs; the second order has chevron ornament; and the third an enriched roll and beak-head ornament in the form of lions' heads; both these orders spring from restored shafts with old foliated or scalloped capitals and enriched abaci; the innermost order had embattled ornament continued on the jambs below the enriched impost and flanked by other enriched shafts below the label." In the north aisle there is a much-restored and enlarged twelfth-century window of one round-headed light in the north wall.

Harmondsworth has some twelfth-century work in the south part of the nave, especially the south arcade and south aisle. The reset south doorway, which bears some resemblance to that of Harlington, "has a round arch of three orders, the outer with chevron ornament, the middle with a roll-moulding and beakhead and the inner with diaper ornament; the middle order rests on enriched shafts with scalloped capitals, but the other orders are continued down the jambs." A church was consecrated at Harrow on the Hill in 1094, but the only Norman work still extant is the lower part of the west tower (c. 1130-40).

The parish church of St. Mary, East Bedfont, was built on ironstone conglomerate with dressings of Reigate stone, and chancel and nave were built about the middle of the twelfth century. In the north wall of the chancel is a twelfth-century window of one round-headed light; the chancel arch of the same date is "semicircular and of one order with

240

Stanwell Church

chevron ornament and a defaced label; the responds also have chevron ornament and grooved and chamfered imposts. Both the north and south walls of the chancel have some twelfth-century stones of conglomerate quoins." The south doorway is also attractive Norman work, and during the restoration of 1805 two mural paintings were discovered, and one believed to date from the reign of King Stephen. "One represents, within a quatrefoil, Christ seated on a throne, displaying the stigmata in hands, feet and side. Below are angels sounding trumpets and the dead rising from their graves. The second painting represents the Crucifixion."

In a restoration of Hendon Parish Church in 1929-31 remains of a twelfth-century chancel, 16 feet by 12 feet, were discovered under the present church, and this discovery fits in with the reconstruction of the magnificent Norman font.

There may be some very late twelfth-century work in Northolt Church, but the nave, mainly of flint and ironstone rubble, seems to have been rebuilt and widened about 1300.

Laleham parish church of All Saints has a late twelfth-century nave with north and south arcades, now of three bays only, formerly at least of four, "with two-centred arches of one chamfered order with labels; the cylindrical columns and semi-cylindrical west responds have scalloped capitals and restored moulded bases."

The east end of the nave in Harefield Church is possibly late twelfth century; some fragments reset in the north aisle of St. Mary's, Finchley, indicate a twelfth-century church on the site; the nave of Cowley Church is very late Norman; but, apart from the somewhat unimportant instances given, most ecclesiastical buildings in Middlesex date from after A.D. 1200.

Harmondsworth has three-ball sedilia with cinquefoiled arches in a square mainhead (fifteenth century). Hayes has three thirteenth-century sedilia with moulded outer jambs, two-centred heads, detached shafts. In the chancel at Stanwell are two bays of sedilia of the fourteenth century which carry on the wall arcading of the chancel.

Transitional arcades with round columns, cushion caps and pointed arches occur at Harmondsworth on the south side of the nave. The arcade on the north side is early thirteenth-

Harmondsworth Church

century work. All Saints' at Laleham is a patchwork church, but circular arches resting on round pillars with Norman capitals divide the nave from the aisles.

Of thirteenth-century Early English work there are important examples at Harrow, where the chancel and nave were rebuilt and the north and south aisles added or rebuilt in the first half of the period; at Hendon, where the chancel, nave and south arcade, and possibly the north aisle, were rebuilt about the middle of the century. The south arcade is of the same period, and has three bays "with two-centred arches of two chamfered orders; the octagonal piers and semi-octagonal responds have moulded capitals and bases"; other examples occur at Hayes, where the chancel was built late in the thirteenth century at the same period as the north arcade of the nave; at Littleton, where the walls are of ragstone, chalk and flint rubble, with dressing of Reigate stone, the south arcade of the nave was built *c.* 1200, but the rest of the nave and the south aisle were rebuilt, the north aisle added, and the chancel rebuilt and enlarged *c.* 1280; at Stanwell, with north and south aisles dating from *c.* 1260 and the tower arches rather later; and at Willesden, where the south arcade of the nave dates from about the middle of the thirteenth century.

In the church of St. Martin, Ruislip, the nave, with its arcades, is thirteenth-century work, with alternating round and octagonal columns. The south arcade, which is half a century older, has five bays, and the north has six, the dates being approximately 1240 and 1260. The nave of Northolt Church is possibly very late thirteenth-century work, with a western window, dating about 1300, with "two trefoiled lights with a sixfoiled circle in a two-centred head; the internal splays one mullion are shafted, and the shafts have foliated capitals and moulded bases."

Finchley and Harrow have thirteenth-century fonts. The former, on a modern stem, is an octagonal bowl of Purbeck marble with two painted panels on each face; the latter, which some experts now place in the twelfth century, is also of Purbeck marble, "a round bowl with moulded rim and underside, its face cut with a scalloped ornament, and the stem fluted spirally and with a moulded base."

In South Mimms Church there are a few traces of thirteenth-century work in the chancel and of fourteenth-century in the nave. One of the chancel windows is a "lowside" of early fourteenth century, of one trefoiled light; the recess is carried down to form a shelf; while the doorway, with chamfered jambs and a restored head, is also fourteenth century. In the nave is preserved a thirteenth- or fourteenth-century chest of hutch type, with foliage carvings at the foot of the front posts, plain but very strongly built. The font is also thirteenth and fourteenth century and is a square bowl with chamfered angles and moulded under-edge, resting on four angle shafts, with moulded capitals and bases, octagonal to square central pier with tracery-headed panels on alternate faces.

The fourteenth century is represented by the chancel at Stanwell, which was rebuilt about 1330; it has on the north side two fourteenth-century windows, each with two cinquefoiled lights in a two-centred head with a label, similar windows on the south side. The chancel walls have fourteenth-century wall arcading of trefoiled ogee heads with curved spandrels under a horizontal string course, the arches resting on detached Purbeck marble shafts. Some of the arcading forms the sedilia. The chancel arch is two-centred and of two-chamfered orders, the inner lying on to the chamfered responds. More fourteenth-century work is found at Harlington, where there are two three-light decorated windows on each side of the chancel, each of three trefoiled ogee lights with tracery in a two-centred head with a moulded label and headstone, and at Willesden, where there are traces of fourteenth-century work in the nave.

The south aisle at Harefield, faced with flint and stone chequer-work, is fourteenth-century work, with an east window of three lights with tracery in a two-centred head, moulded jambs, rear arch and labels with defaced stops. On the south side are four similar windows much restored.

In the nave at Northolt, which has two windows in the north wall, one is of early fourteenth century and the other later; there is also a blocked-up doorway with jambs and a two-centred arch of two moulded orders. The south doorway is also fourteenth-century work.

At Pinner the church walls are of flint and ironstone rubble with dressings of Reigate and other freestone and ironstone. We have an exact date for the chancel, nave, transepts and aisles, which were consecrated in 1321. The chancel arch is two-centred and of tree-chamfered orders; in the north transept there are two fourteenth-century windows and a two-centred arch. There are windows and doorways of the same period in the north and south aisles. The tower of Tottenham was built early in the fourteenth century, and later in the same century the old chancel and nave with their arcades were rebuilt. At Willesden the south-west tower was added about 1400, and at much the same time the ruined chancel was rebuilt. The old low-side window, shown in old prints, has disappeared.

In the fifteenth and early sixteenth centuries there was a wide diffusion of Perpendicular architecture throughout Middlesex, hardly any churches throughout the county failing to possess some features in this style. The change-over from Decorated to Perpendicular was, of course, gradual, and there is a lot to be said for thinking more in terms of lancet and traceried styles, the latter including both the styles usually accepted, and for dividing the traceried style into curvilinear and geometrical.

It is never easy to account for any change, even a gradual and apparently natural and normal one, but it does seem probable that the rise and progress of the new style of architecture, which made only a very slight demand on the skill and inventiveness of the craftsman, should have begun just about 1350, when the effects of the Black Death, "that most potent of all influences in the fourteenth century," were being felt in every department of national life. The Statute of Labourers, which fixed the wages of a "master freemason" at 4d. a day, would not attract men of high artistic skill, and must have driven many artificers out of the country.

The growth of the wool trade, especially in the eastern counties and the Cotswolds, led to the making of rapid fortunes, and money was lavishly spent on church architecture, in spite of French wars and internecine struggles in the Battles of the Roses. London, as the home of the Court and the metropolis of trade, naturally shared in the general pros-

perity, and many Middlesex villages had their churches enlarged or rebuilt in the period from 1380 to 1530.

For the first thirty years after the Black Death remodelling
was more likely than proper rebuilding, "in recasing the
surface, in forming new windows in the old walls, in inserting
new glass, and generally in clothing the twelfth-century body
with a fourteenth-century dress." During these years the
panel, which had previously been used but sparingly, became
immensely useful. "Instead of the panel being sparsely used
to decorate comparatively small and narrow spaces, the whole
surface inside and outside—wall and arch, screen parapet,
basement and buttress—are now covered with it. Even the
windows, when, later on, the style gets thoroughly logical,
became simply an arrangement of these panels pierced to let
in the light" (Reginald Hughes in *Social England*, vol. ii,
p. 264).

There are many who feel that the architectural changes
were a clear indication of the decadence of Gothic art, and
that the consistency and strength of upright stonework, with
the splendid opportunities for a wealth of stained glass, were
but "a poor substitute for the elegant grouped lancets of the
Early English, or for the flowing tracery of the Decorated
style."

During the century and a half which are covered by the
Perpendicular period we find that almost all that the early
Gothic builders regarded as beautiful had disappeared.
Windows are now "contrivances for the admission of light,
and the exhibition of glass." The problem of beautiful curves
in stone is solved by changing them into straight lines; the
style has changed from pointed to square-headed doors; but
the reigns of the Lancastrians and Yorkists are memorable
for a succession of magnificent towers, both for cathedrals
and for simple parish churches. As far as the old portions of
the churches are concerned, West Drayton, Edmonton,
Finchley and South Mimms are almost entirely Perpendicular;
Harmondsworth, Hayes, Hendon and Ruislip are largely
of that period; and most of the church towers in Middlesex
date from the same time.

In the church of St. Martin at West Drayton there may be
remains of thirteenth-century lancet windows and of the

lower portions of the western tower, but the bulk of the church is fifteenth century. The chancel, vestry, nave, north aisle and the west tower of All Saints', Edmonton, were rebuilt in the fifteenth century, and there are somewhat restored windows, a doorway to the vestry, and a much-restored chancel arch. The west tower is of the same period and is of three stages, with a moulded plinth and a modern embattled parapet. The vestry roof is of the same period and has a double-chamfered tie-beam and wallplates and a chamfered edge.

Finchley parish church of St. Mary has a few fragments of twelfth-century material built into its walls of ragstone rubble with freestone dressings and some ragstone ashlar, but the chancel, nave, north aisle and west tower were rebuilt in the fifteenth century. Ability to spend so much money on the church was probably due to prosperity attained in the City of London by a group of wealthy families—Frowyck, Bidyk, Basing, Hadestoke, Drokensford and le Waleys.

South Mimms has been singularly fortunate in its historian, F. Brittain, and its story is unusually definite. Some remains of earlier work are found in the chancel (thirteenth century) and part of the nave (late fourteenth century), but a good deal of the nave is fifteenth century, the west tower is early sixteenth, and Thomas Frowick, who died in 1448, after having been the father of nineteen children, left a bequest for its upkeep.

Harmondsworth is unusual in having some barnacle stone in addition to stone from Reigate to serve as dressing to flint-rubble walls. To a twelfth-century nave and south aisle and a thirteenth-century north aisle and chancel were made considerable additions and alterations in the fourteenth and fifteenth centuries. The chancel was extended, remodelled and widened and the tower was added. The date of the tower is probably 1500, and the lowest stop is of flint, while the two upper ones are of brick finished off with an embattled parapet with pinnacles at the angles.

At Hayes to a late thirteenth-century chancel and north nave arcade were added in the fifteenth and early sixteenth centuries the north and south aisles, the south porch, and the west tower, of three stages, with a modern embattled parapet.

246

The windows and doorway in the tower have been much restored.

In St. Mary's, Hendon, the east window was rebuilt under the will of John Ware in 1408, and later in the century were added a rebuilt north arcade and the west tower. The north chapel dates from the early sixteenth century and is either an addition or rebuilding.

In St. Martin's, Ruislip, to a thirteenth-century nave and arcades were added in the fifteenth century a rebuilt chancel and north and south aisles and the west tower. This latter is of three stages with an embattled parapet, and has a bell chamber with four windows, one in each wall, of two-pointed lights in a square head with label.

The roof of the chancel is of the fifteenth century and is of three bays, with chamfered main timbers and moulded wall-plates; the cellar-beam trusses have curved wine-braces. Both north and south aisles have roofs (c. 1506) with spandrels carved with foliage and a grotesque face, with carved bosses at the main intersections.

Towers in the Norman period were possibly mainly used for purposes of defence, but in later times there was more idea of decoration. The tower of St. Nicholas, Chiswick, was built with a bequest from a vicar who died in 1435; St. Dunstan's, Cranford, has a fifteenth-century tower as to its lower stages, with a brick seventeenth-century bell chamber; West Drayton tower is mainly fifteenth century and has a good tower arch and west doorway; the west tower (fifteenth century) is almost all that remains of the old St. Margaret's, Edgware; Edmonton and Enfield have fifteenth-century towers; Harefield's tower is mid-fifteenth century, Harlington late fifteenth century, Harmondsworth c. 1500; Harrow tower is twelfth century as to its two lower stages, to which was added a top storey with an embattled parapet in the fifteenth century; Isleworth late fifteenth century; Littleton early fifteenth-century brick tower of three storeys, with one added in the eighteenth century.

Pinner, Ruislip, Twickenham and Willesden all have fifteenth-century towers; Stanmore has a seventeenth-century tower (1632), part of the church built by Sir John Wolstenholme and consecrated by Archbishop Laud; while the west

MIDDLESEX

tower of Staines Parish Church is of the same date and is
attributed to Inigo Jones.

The Middlesex church towers are said to have strong local
features, being in the main low, with bold angle turrets. In
many cases the towers have survived where almost or quite
the whole of the rest of the church has been rebuilt. Such are
Brentford, Chiswick, Edgware, Heston, Isleworth, Twickenham and Little Stanmore or Whitchurch.

Several small churches have timber bell turrets in place of
towers, supported on a framework, within the west end of
the church, as at Cowley, Ickenham, Kingsbury, Northolt and
Bedfont. There are only two examples of old spires in the
county, those at Harrow on the Hill and at Stanwell. They
are fifteenth-century erections of timber.

There are quite a number of fifteenth-century fonts in the
county, the best being at Brentford, West Drayton, Harefield, Norwood and Uxbridge. That at Brentford has an
octagonal bowl with moulded edges, quatrefoiled sides, two
adorned with roses, the whole mounted on an octagonal base,
each face with pointed panels. Some regard the font at West
Drayton as the most unusual in Middlesex. It has an octagonal
bowl, on whose sides are a pieta, the Crucifixion with the
Virgin and St. John, with half angels, human figures, beasts
and foliage. Norwood has a font with octagonal bowl, decorated with quatrefoils, a slender stem with cinquefoiled panels,
and a moulded base. Uxbridge's font is octagonal, with
quatrefoil patterns with rose and leopard alternately; base,
stem and bowl are of almost the same dimensions.

An interesting feature in churches is the arcade, several
examples of which have already been mentioned, including
the two twelfth-century ones at Harmondsworth and Laleham, with circular piers, cushion caps and pointed arches.
Thirteenth-century arcades occur at Harrow, where the
columns are alternately circular and octagonal; at Hillingdon,
where the columns are octagonal; at Littleton, where the
beautiful church of St. Mary Magdalene has a nave with
narrow penthouse aisles on either side. At Stanwell there is
a medley of architectural styles and some very interesting
tombs, as well as an arcade of light seats, used in medieval
times by the monks.

248

Fourteenth-century arcades are found at Hayes, where they are octagonal; at Harefield, clustered, with two centred arches of two moulded orders, with quatrefoiled columns and intermediate shafts and moulded capitals; at Hendon, Enfield, Pinner and Tottenham. The best Perpendicular examples are at West Drayton, Hardmondsworth (with octagonal columns and four centred arches) and at South Mimms.

There are not many churches in Middlesex with fine medieval roofs, but there are some good examples of the fifteenth and sixteenth centuries. Most usual are the braced rafter and the king-post type. Harmondsworth nave and chancel roofs and Harlington chancel are probably of the fourteenth century, but that in the north chapel at Harmondsworth is later in period, of the hammer-beam type, a simple variety of that employed in Hampton Court Great Hall, and the only one still in existence in a Middlesex church. Ruislip has a panelled roof in the nave, with ribs and bosses, and a collar-braced roof in the chancel. Hayes has a similar nave roof to Ruislip. Hendon and Harrow both have cambered-beam roofs in the nave, Harrow with figures on the wall-posts.

There is not a great deal of medieval wall-painting still extant in Middlesex churches, but what there is seems well preserved. At Bedfont there are paintings of the thirteenth century depicting the Crucifixion and Doom; the painting at Hayes of St. Christopher is fifteenth-century work, an exceptionally good example, well preserved; Ruislip, also fifteenth century, has a Weeping of Souls. There are some slight remains at Hendon (thirteenth century), Harlington and Ickenham. A far later example of wall-painting is to be seen at Whitchurch, rebuilt, save the tower, by the Duke of Chandos in 1715. A great deal of fresco work was employed and was duly satirised by Pope, as previously mentioned,

"And others upon painted ceiling stare,
Where sprawl the Saints of Verrio and Laguerre."

There are also some later fonts of the seventeenth and eighteenth centuries, of which Greenford and Great Stanmore (Nicholas Stone) are good examples.

Medieval clearstoreys occur in some half a dozen churches, all of fifteenth or sixteenth century. These are to be seen at

West Drayton, where there are three windows on each side of the nave, with fifteenth-century splays and rear-arches, otherwise modern; in St. Andrew's Church at Enfield, where, in the nave, the early sixteenth-century clearstorey has, on each side, five restored windows, each of three lights, with three-centred heads on the north side and four-centred heads on the south. There is considerable evidence of an earlier clearstorey here. At Finchley there is a clearstorey on the south side of the nave, with four windows, each of three cinquefoiled lights in a regimental head. At Harrow the nave has a fifteenth-century clearstorey with four windows on the north and five on the south.

Littleton's St. Mary Magdalene has in the nave an early sixteenth-century brick clearstorey with two windows on each side, each with two four-centred lights in a square head. Stanwell has a fifteenth-century clearstorey in the nave with three partly restored windows on each side, with two cinquefoiled lights in a square head.

Very little woodwork survives in the county, though Middlesex was for centuries famous for its woods. There is a fifteenth-century screen at Hayes, where the roof of chancel, nave and aisles are worthy of attention; there are some remains at Cowley, where poppy-heads from old pews have been used in the screen and in the chancel; while at Harefield some of the pews have fleur-de-lys poppy-heads and then box pews leading into the north chapels. There is seating with buttressed ends at Harmondsworth, where the sedilia and piscina date from the fifteenth century. At Hayes there is some good timber-work in the sixteenth-century porch and an old studded door with strap hinges, while the waggon roof of the chancel is supported on interesting corbels.

Littleton is famous today for the Queen Mary Reservoir, which has flooded fields and woods and part of the old village; but its church survives with old oak benches with buttressed ends, and the chancel screen has linenfold panels. The altar rails are probably seventeenth-century Flemish work, while the stalls were brought from Winchester Cathedral. Ruislip Church has several old wooden doors and benches, a carved pulpit, a Jacobean bread cupboard, with a carved armorial shield and ears of wheat.

The finest example of a screen is at South Mimms, where the north chapel is enclosed by five parcloses of the early sixteenth century. It has many traceried bays, with buttresses in between, and two doorways in it with leopards carved on the panels. The chancel screen has been designed in the same style.

There has been a great deal of quite ruthless destruction of Middlesex churches in the last two centuries, and the only record is often old prints and drawings. Sunbury was very largely pulled down and rebuilt in 1751; Brentford and Edgware lost all save their towers in 1764; Hanworth was twice rebuilt in the nineteenth century—by James Wyatt in 1810, when the medieval church was entirely replaced, and again in 1865, when tower and porches were added and the chancel and nave restored.

Chiswick is modern Perpendicular in place of original medieval work. The church was entirely rebuilt in 1882, except the west tower of ragstone rubble with Reigate dressings, built by William Bordall, who was Vicar from 1416 to 1435.

The tower at Hillingdon was rebuilt in 1629; Isleworth Church (1705-6), Twickenham (1712-15), and Handel's church at Little Stanmore (Whitechurch) are purely Classical, except their medieval towers. Feltham Church, rebuilt in 1802, is a particularly good design.

Very little glass is left, and a great deal has been destroyed since Sperling published his *Church Walks* about a century ago (1849). South Mimms has some very good glass in the north aisle dated 1526, and there are fragments remaining at Greenford and Hanworth. Tottenham has a three-light west window in the north aisle, of the late sixteenth or early seventeenth century. It represents David, Isaiah and Jeremiah. Hanworth is fairly well off in glass, figure and heraldic and miscellaneous glass of the fifteenth century, heraldic of the seventeenth; Enfield, both figure and heraldic of the sixteenth century; Harefield, sixteenth century of both kinds; Norwood, sixteenth and seventeenth centuries; Twickenham, sixteenth- and seventeenth-century figure and heraldic, both native and foreign; with other examples at Perivale, Ickenham, Tottenham, Greenford, Edmonton, Acton, Ruislip, Chiswick and East Bedfont.

251

There is an authentic altar at Laleham and possible examples at Acton and Willesden, and good Communion tables at Willesden (sixteenth century), Harefield, Hayes, Ickenham, Northolt and Tottenham (seventeenth century), Pinner (eighteenth century), Hampton and Isleworth.

St. Paul's Church at Mill Hill was built by Wilberforce the Liberator, and the first service held there was a memorial for the founder, who is buried in Westminster Abbey. There is an unusually fine east window which is of eighteenth-century Italian design and was given by Wilberforce.

The rapid growth of population in Middlesex during the last half-century or so has demanded more churches, and these have sometimes been built "free from old conventions, modern in every sense, and with a new kind of beauty and simplicity, a key-note of true reverence at the heart of it." Some of the fairly recent churches are lacking in charm; some of them have been constructed from material salvaged from discarded churches in the City of London; but there has been, on the whole, among Anglicans, Romans and Free Churchmen alike, an attempt to raise the standard of church building throughout the country.

St. Paul's Church at Brentford has some fine memorials in its nineteenth-century building, one by Sir George Hampton to the artist J. M. Ewan, R.A., and a mosaic to Walter Walker, who sang in the church choir for more than half a century. St. Nicholas at Chiswick was rebuilt in 1882, except its fifteenth-century tower, but its treasure of historic memorials both within and without the church still remain.

Near the village green at Ealing is the old parish church of St. Mary, rebuilt in the eighteenth and again in the nineteenth century. Several other recent churches are to be recorded in Ealing : Christ Church on the Broadway, designed by Sir Gilbert Scott for the daughter of the actor, W. T. Lewis, as her tribute to her father's memory; St. Saviour's, a cross-shaped church with green copper spire and very fine reredos, paintings, pulpit and font; the Church of the Ascension on Hanger Hill, the last of ninety-five dedicated by Bishop A. F. Winnington-Ingram; and the very beautiful Roman Catholic church in Charlbury Grove, St. Benedict's, designed by the same architect as Buckfast Abbey.

John Keble Church is just between Mill Hill and Edgware in a hamlet called the Hale, and it is built in severe Spanish style, with flat roof, a tower with belfry with a pillar above it surmounted by a golden ball and cross. The simplicity and dignity of the interior are remarkable, and the dedication commemorates the centenary of the famous assize sermon on "National Apostasy" which began the Oxford Movement.

Feltham has three recent churches : St. Dunstan's, rebuilt on an ancient site; St. Catherine's, dating from 1880, with a lofty tower and spire and some fine memorial stained glass; and a Roman Catholic church in Norman style, with some singularly beautiful stations of the Cross.

St. Thomas's Church in Hanwell was designed by Edward Maufe, architect of Guildford Cathedral, and it has a north tower with a cap of green copper surmounted by a golden cross. It has some sculpture by Eric Gill and an interesting reredos from the dismantled church of St. Thomas's, Portman Square.

Hendon has a garden city to south and north, the former due to the foresight of Dame Henrietta Barnett. In the central square there is an institute and two churches, all three designed by Sir Edwin Lutyens. St. Jude's on the Hill has a big central tower with an open belfry and spire, supported by large interior arches. There is some remarkably fine painting in the roofs of the nave and chancel, while the dome of the lady chapel is decorated with pictures of nearly two dozen good women, including Catherine Booth, Florence Nightingale, Harriet Beecher Stowe, Elizabeth Browning, Queen Victoria and Queen Alexandra. Basil Bourchier was the first vicar of this church, and he had a big say in its design. He is commemorated by a bronze plaque and the glass of the west window.

Hornsey, which now includes within its borough boundaries Highgate and Harringay, Crouch End and Stroud Green, Finsbury Park and Muswell Hill, has had to build new churches to keep pace with growing population. Only the tower remains of old St. Mary's, which was pulled down in 1927, but most of the old monuments have been incorporated in the new church. The old font has been used in the slightly earlier church of St. George in Priory Road.

There is a very fine Methodist church where Alexandra Park Road meets Colney Hatch Lane, with unusually fine coloured glass illustrating Christianity in action. The west window has Christ in the centre with Pasteur, Raphael, Beethoven and Shakespeare, standing for science, art, music and literature, and also representing France, Italy, Germany and England. The smaller windows combine biblical scenes with their modern counterparts, and are indicative of Christian virtues. Christian witness is illustrated by St. Stephen, St. Paul, Bunyan, Wesley and Lincoln; Christian stewardship by Albert Schweitzer, the Widow with her mite, and the Rich Young Ruler; Childhood has Christ blessing the children, with Pope Gregory and Robert Raikes; Youth depicts Christ with the doctors in the Temple, Baden Powell, and the scouts, guides, cubs and brownies. There are various ancient and modern scenes of mission work, culminating in Sir Wilfred Grenfell.

St. James's Church in Muswell Hill is a big modern church with tower and spire and effective design.

Kingsbury has two churches, one dedicated to St. Andrew, built perhaps in Saxon days of flint and Roman bricks, with a restored wooden turret and no difference in level between the roofs of nave and chancel. The other is a big, newly built church, carefully brought from Wells Street in London and re-erected at Kingsbury.

Potters Bar has grown from a tiny hamlet into a biggish suburb which has a church built about a century ago, now almost neglected, and another more recently, with some fine glass, including windows to the memory of John Keble and of Archbishop Davidson. Two Zeppelin airships were brought down in or near Potters Bar in September, 1916, and the thirty-five members of the two crews are buried in the church-yard and their names are commemorated on stone tablets let into the wall.

Another church in Middlesex that owes its origin to a dismantled London church is St. George's at Southall, built out of the proceeds of the sale of the site of St. George's, Billingsgate. Nothing of the parent church has been used except the organ case, with carvings by Grinling Gibbons.

Several modern churches are to be found in the growing

suburbs of Southgate, home of Leigh Hunt, Tom Hood and Gerald Massey, which has developed rapidly since the Tube was extended to this part of Middlesex. Sir Gilbert Scott built a fine modern church to take the place of a chapel built in 1615 by Sir John Wild. Christ Church has a carved pulpit to commemorate the end of the first World War; stained glass by Rossetti and Burne Jones; carved pulpit and reredos and recent wall-paintings.

Teddington's two churches are opposite to one another : St. Mary's, a sixteenth-century church, enlarged under its famous Vicar, Stephen Hales, and partly rebuilt in the nineteenth century; and St. Alban's, a modern unfinished church, with flying buttresses outside the chancel and seven silver altar lamps sent by the bounty of the Patriarch Nicodemus from the church of the Holy Sepulchre in Jerusalem. There is an unusually fine Roman church dedicated to St. Ignatius, with two towers, fine exterior carvings, good glass and a number of biblical scenes in mosaic.

Twickenham's old parish church of St. Mary's may have been built by William of Wykeham. It was certainly enlarged in Anne's reign, and Alexander Pope is buried in it. St. Stephen's was built in the fifteenth century, and further growth resulted in Wren's church of All Hallows, Lombard Street, being transported to Twickenham. Much of the stonework, pews and panelling by Grinling Gibbons and a peal of ten bells are among the material rescued when the City Church was bombarded.

Wembley's growth has demanded more churches to add to St. John's, designed by Albert Scott. St. Michael's is a modern Anglican church, and there is a distinguished Roman church just in Sudbury.

Perhaps the most remarkable growth in the whole of Middlesex is that of Willesden from a village within living memory into a large industrial district of nearly a quarter of a million inhabitants. It has several fine open spaces, but it needs them, seeing that it includes Brondesbury, Cricklewood, Dollis Hill, Dudding Hill, Harlesden, Kensal Green and Rise, Kilburn, Neasden and Stonebridge. Old St. Mary's has a fine Norman font, an old sundial, an Elizabethan altar table and some good brasses.

Amongst modern churches are St. Martin's at Kensal Rise, a memorial to a famous Harrow headmaster, Dr. G. Vaughan, with fine glass depicting, amongst others, Alfred the Great, George Herbert, Florence Nightingale and General Gordon.

The diocese of London extends, as its Bishop recently remarked in an appeal for new churches, "from Staines to Stepney and from Putney Bridge to Potters Bar." From that area we must cut out, for purposes of Middlesex, the portion transferred to London in 1888. In the twenty years before 1939 the population of the diocese increased by more than three-quarters of a million, all in the dormitory districts in north and west Middlesex. In 1930 the need for additional churches in these unplanned and haphazard townships was obvious, and plans were made for forty-five churches, of which more than half were finished before the second World War.

It is not easy to separate the war losses sustained in the whole diocese and in the area of present-day Middlesex. Ninety-one churches out of 701 were completely destroyed, mostly in London County; another 533 were damaged, and it is proposed to restore or repair all but about 50. Among Middlesex churches which were badly damaged were Finchley Parish Church, St. James's, Muswell Hill, and St. Mary's, Twickenham, and these will be restored. A good many churches in London north of the Thames have no longer the population to run them, and the Reorganisation Areas Measure of 1944 gives power of parochial reorganisation to the Ecclesiastical Commissioner. It is quite possible that three churches in Bethnal Green, four in Finsbury, two in Holborn, two in Hackney, two in Islington, four in Poplar, five in Shoreditch, eleven in Stepney, one in Chelsea, one in Fulham, one in Paddington, three in Westminster, two in St. Marylebone, and three in St. Pancras—forty-four in all—will not be rebuilt.

This decision may help to make possible the provision of thirty-four churches in newly built-up areas in Middlesex where they are needed. These include Kingsbury, Northolt Park, Staines, Cranford, Ruislip Manor, Hanwell, Hounslow, Harlington, Mill Hill, Whitchurch, East Hounslow,

Harefield Church

Harrow Weald (two), Whitton, Hanworth, Perivale Park, Southall, Edmonton, Hayes, Northolt, South Harrow, Colindale, Perivale, Sudbury, Edgwarebury, Northwood Hill, Heston, Preston, Wembley.

It is not possible to give more than a passing reference to the Free Churches in Middlesex, though mention has been made of some outstanding examples. There is far more co-operation between Anglicans and Nonconformists than ever before, and the admirable halls attached to most churches in the county are available for a great many meetings of a civic, philanthropic, social character. The mutual aid given in two world wars has created a feeling of brotherly kindness which is unlikely ever to be forgotten.

Almshouses at Harefield

Chapter XVIII

ROADS IN MIDDLESEX

BEFORE the Romans came to Rye, or out of Sussex strode, there were British trackways in various parts of the country of the Trinobantes, who lived in what is now called Middlesex. There is one such road that leads northward from Brentford to Kingsbury; Edgwarebury Lane from Edgware up to the hills of Elstree, and probably Watling Street itself, then called Sarn Gwdellyn, are also to be regarded as pre-Roman. But the Romans came with an iron hand and planned a nexus of fine roads built mainly with a military object, to allow the quick movement of troops from one station to another, with the idea of maintaining order as cheaply and efficiently as possible. For nearly four centuries the county was well administered, and the roads which concentrated on Londinium and not on Camolodunum (Colchester) helped to make this possible. The most important of these was the old British trackway from Dover to the Dee or to Holyhead, the London part of which is called today the Edgware Road. It is not at all certain where the Thames was crossed, but a recent suggestion is from Lambeth to Westminster and then up Horseferry Road, Park Lane to the Tyburn, the site now occupied by the Marble Arch. That small, narrow lane east of St. Paul's, which is called Watling Street, is found in the earliest records as Atheling Street, and there seems no justification for its more recent name.

From Tyburn along the Edgware Road to Brockley Hill, Sulloniacæ, where excavations took place in recent years, is rather more than ten miles and is almost dead straight. The efficiency of Roman building is shown by the fact that all building contractors in London specify for extra payment if Roman substructures have to be removed, and by the remarkable permanence of Roman work. Early in the twentieth century the Roman paving along Watling Street was cut through and it was "found to consist of large black nodular flints, weighing from four to seven pounds each, on a bed of rammed reddish-brown gravel of varying thickness. The gravel was supported by dwarf walls of gravel concrete, and on the levelled surface of the gravel lime grouting appears to have been laid, in which the flints were firmly set."

The second Roman road in Middlesex was from London along Bayswater Road, Brentford and Hounslow to Staines, the Roman *Ad Pontes,* where there is a bridge over the Thames. The third is Ermine Street, running up Bishopsgate, Shoreditch, Kingsland Road, Stoke Newington to Tottenham, Edmonton and Forty Hill. By Shoreditch Church Ermine Street is crossed by Old Street, from Tyburn to Old Ford, into Essex, and so perhaps to Colchester. This road, which passes just to the north of London, and the early crossing of the Thames at Westminster and not at London Bridge, are two items which suggest, perhaps not very forcibly, that London was not at first a really important place. Camulodunum and Verulamium possibly, or even probably, surpassed it in prestige. The last Roman road is from Cripplegate to Stoke Newington, Hornsey, Southgate and to Potters Bar, one of the gates of Enfield Chase. On this basis most of the roads running north and west were built up, and in Saxon times they still went on in spite of frequent neglect and possibly spasmodic improvements.

The Normans stiffened things up and, with the need for the conquering nobles to get about the country, roads were improved. William's policy of spreading the manors with which he rewarded his friends meant that people had to travel about far more regularly than ever before since Roman days. It was the duty of the parish to repair such of the main roads as passed through its midst, and the *trimoda necessitas* demanded attention to roads and bridges.

It would seem that the decision for the King's Law Courts to be stabilised at Westminster may have restored its preeminence to London. As Professor Tout pointed out, it is Westminster, with the King's palace, the Law Courts and the Houses of Parliament, that is the real capital. London is the commercial centre, but as it expanded along Fleet Street and the Strand the line of demarcation between it and Westminster ceased to function, and so London was styled the capital city.

Roads in England which were regarded as of royal importance had a certain standard of width : two waggons must be able to pass, sixteen armed knights must be able to ride side by side along them, and two oxherds should just be able to make their goads touch across them. In two centuries after Hastings some of the roads had gone from bad to worse. They compared very unfavourably with the worst cart-track of half a century ago. Wild beasts, wild men or wild weather made travel a real peril. Perhaps the roads near London were not so difficult or so dangerous. But it was an immense reform when in 1285 Edward I ordered that hue and cry was to be carried from parish to parish to catch highwaymen, and for some hundreds of feet on either side of the road all bushes, trees and brushwood were to be cut down, so as to give no hiding-place where robbers and outlaws could lurk for unsuspecting travellers.

It seems clear that, though the well-built Roman roads continued to have reasonably good surfaces, other roads were often mere rights of way, along which one travelled at some risk. Efforts were made from time to time to legislate in favour of regular upkeep, and landowners through whose territory roads passed were expected to be responsible for repairs.

There is an indictment against the Abbot of Westminster early in the fifteenth century for neglecting his duties by "not scouring and cleansing ditches between Kensyngton and Knyghtbridge, and in Hendon and at Tyburn on the south-syde in the parish of St. Martin's in the Feld between the Condytt and an alley called Portyblanc, and for not keeping a pair of stokkes in the vill of Stanes, and for not repairing a bridge in Ey, Co. Middlesex, and for not scouring and repairing the Highway leading from le Temple Barr up to Charing Crosse in Westminster adjoining the Abbot's garden called le Frerepyes opposite the House of the Bishop of Karlile, also the highway at Tyburn galwes . . . also the Highway called Cowhous Lane in Hendon leading from Hampsted to London, also the Highway called Kilburn brigge in Padyington leading from the bridge of Kilburn towards London." Evidently the Abbot or his servants had been remiss in their care for the repair of roads in the neighbourhood of the three monastic manors of Eye, Stanes and Hendon.

As the roads were poor, a great deal of use was made of rivers with barges, and heavy goods were often carried by sea, notably coal from Newcastle. Carriage in the early fourteenth century was cheap enough—1d. per mile per ton for heavy goods, including insurance, but 3½d. per mile for wine. When Hendon Church was being enlarged it was necessary to send to Reigate to fetch the stones, and probably an interchange of goods was effected. No doubt this sort of thing happened all over the country and helped to keep the chief roads tolerably serviceable.

Thorold Rogers's *Six Centuries of Work and Wages* and Jusserand's *Wayfaring Life in the Middle Ages* give a series of interesting pictures of regular or accidental traffic from one part of the county to another. The tenants of the Abbot of Westminster, who had their holdings in Hendon and Hampstead, two adjoining manors in Middlesex, undoubtedly joined forces to minimise danger when they carried the produce due to the lord of the manor through Golders Green over Hampstead Heath, through Belsize and St. John's Wood to Westminster.

Even before the Conquest efforts were made to improve travelling along Watling Street, where Leofotan, twelfth Abbot of St. Albans, cut down thick woods which were sheltering wild beasts such as boars, bulls, stags and wolves, and wild men—brigands, outlaws and fugitives from justice. Highwaymen were not an invention of Stuart and Georgian times.

Chaucer's pilgrims travelled through Kent, but other pilgrimages were made through suburbs north of London. Journeys to Walsingham, to Chertsey, to St. Albans, Abingdon and St. Edmundsbury might all pass through Middlesex, and the presence of companions would tend to make the journey safe even if it was uncomfortable.

The Wars of the Roses reveal the importance of the roads into London, and in Tudor times many privileges were granted to those who were prepared to bring corn and other requisites into the Metropolis, thus making the decent upkeep of roads essential.

The revolution in the sixteenth century which we call the Reformation and the Renaissance produced the first map-makers, whose work in delineating roads undoubtedly led to their improvement. It is obvious that roads depended a great deal on bridges, and it has always been a matter of great surprise that until the eighteenth century there was no bridge over the Thames between Kingston and London. The Brent needed to be bridged at various spots, and an important one was at Hanwell, where the two banks in Hayes and Hanwell belonged to the Archbishop of Canterbury and the Abbot of Westminster respectively.

This bridge was built in 1280, and tolls were levied on persons and goods passing over it. It needed repair in 1332 and again in 1450, and then in 1530 it had to be rebuilt, and there is a document with the bill for wages and materials paid during a period of five months preserved in the muniment room at Westminster Abbey. There is no room here to compare the rates of wages then and now, or the prices of materials, but it is of great interest to note that the labourers tried to get their wages paid even for holidays when they did no work. It must have been a bother to remember the weeks according to the saints' names instead of according to the normal calendar. A typical labourer on the job received 6d. or 7d. per day. In 1652 the bridge was moved nearer to Greenford, and then in 1922 the Middlesex County Council changed the wooden bridge into a stone one, charging the two lords of the manor for part of the cost, but extinguishing any future liability for repair or rebuilding.

It seems to be generally agreed that the Dissolution of the Monasteries had its effect on the state of the roads. There was not the same amount of wayfaring life, so well described by Jusserand, and pilgrimages diminished, and it was not possible for the Abbot on his ambling pad to visit the monasteries' manors, for they had all passed into lay hands. Henry VIII realised the change and, as the highways near London were "very noxious and foul and in many places very jeopardous as well on horseback as on foot, in winter and summer, by night and by day," he got Parliament to enact in 1543 that the streets in the suburbs "should be paved with stone, and channels made in the midst thereof, like those in

the streets of London, at the charge of the ground-landlords."
Later Tudors carried on the practice of improving the highways, and there were six Road Acts under Mary and nineteen under Elizabeth. That of 2 and 3, Philip and Mary, in
1555, placed the maintenance of existing highways on the
parish highway surveyors and on the justices of the peace.
Labour, tools, horses and carts had to be provided by the
parishioners; the surveyor was bound to keep accounts and
to view all highways and bridges three times a year, while it
was left to the discretion of the justices to see that all concerned performed their duties. At first four days' work each
year on the roads was demanded from everyone, but it was
advanced to six days in 1563, and the well-to-do usually paid
1s. 6d. a day for a substitute, 3s. for a man and horse, and
10s. for a horse, cart and two men. Surveyors were appointed,
and they had the thankless task of trying to keep the "King's
Loiterers" to the job. The pressed labourers lived up to their
name, and they spent most of their time demanding largesse.
It was possible to indict a whole parish if a "common and
ancient King's Highway became ruinous, miry, deep, broken
and in great decay so as to be a common nuisance to the
King's loyal subjects." In 1565 a true bill was presented
against the inhabitants of Highgate for the non-repair of
Highgate Hill, and it must have been a source of satisfaction
to road-users when so important a highway was put in fairly
decent order.

The condition of the roads into London in Elizabethan
times is graphically described by William Harrison in his
survey published a year before the Armada. He complains of
"cledgy" soil, loitering labour on the part of the road-
menders, neglect of landowners to ditch and scour their
drains and watercourses, and daily encroaching of the
covetous upon the highways. Shakespeare's plays give a
striking picture of inns, roads and highwaymen, and it will
be remembered that his approach to London from Stratford
must have passed through Middlesex. The road into London
from Cambridge by Edmonton and Tottenham was severely
criticised by the Duke of Würtemberg as villainous, boggy
and wild and impassable for a coach in rainy weather. The
remarkable increase in coaches during the later years of

Elizabeth demanded better roads, and there does seem to have been some improvement, as we gather from Fynes Moryson. But all roads in the hours of darkness must have been dangerous, as Shakespeare suggests :

> "When the searching eye of heaven is hid
> Behind the globe, and lights the lower world
> Then thieves and robbers range abroad unseen
> In murder and in outrage bloody here."

The topographers and map-makers of Elizabethan times based their road charts on the Antonine Itinerary, somewhat modified. John Stow made the number of main roads based on London as nine; Richard Grafton, his rival, gives thirteen; Holinshed twelve; while Adams subdivides them into seventeen. Distances in early days were measured from Cornhill, and in the Elizabethan maps there are rough indications of roads. After a while roads were measured from several different places in London, notably Hick's Hall or its site in St. John Street, the starting-place for roads to Hatfield and St. Albans through Barnet. Those to Rickmansworth, Watford and St. Albans through Edgware, and the roads to Harrow and Uxbridge, seem to be measured from Tyburn Turnpike, while the road to Hendon is measured from the St. Giles's End of Tottenham Court Road (St. Giles's Pound).

It was no easy task in Tudor times for large bodies of people to get about, and in her progresses Elizabeth would use the fields instead of the road, as she did on more than one occasion in getting from the Tower to Westminster. On another occasion, when she was moving from Enfield to St. James's Palace, the hedges and ditches of the roads through Middlesex were levelled to make her way easy. When James I arrived outside London for his coronation, a road was improvised for him across the fields from Stamford Hill to the Charterhouse, as the City was full of plague. Henrietta Maria, King Charles's Queen, was going in 1627 to take the waters at Wellingborough, and, as the roads were in poor condition, the county justices were ordered to see that "the most commodious ways and passages were made through the fields throughout the whole journey," and not merely in Middlesex.

264

The real trouble was with the new-fangled coaches, which became popular in spite of natural objection to new methods of locomotion. The watermen on the Thames were afraid that their livelihood would disappear, and John Tayler, the Water Poet, writing in 1622, sums up complaints that had been accumulating for half a century when he says :

> "Caroaches, coaches, jades and Flanders mares
> Do rob us of our shares, our wares, our fares;
> Against the ground we stand and knock our heels,
> Whilst all our profit runs away on wheels."

The Elizabethan age produced books of almost every kind, and among them Camden's description of the Queen's dominions, which he published in 1586 in Latin under the very elaborate title of *Britannia, sive Florentissimorum Regnorum Angliæ, Scotiæ, Hiberniæ et Insularum Adjacentium, ex Intima Antiquitate Chorographica Descriptio.* It proved a best seller and had run into a fourth edition by 1594. A new and enlarged edition appeared in 1607, with maps by John Norden, who naïvely marked his own dwelling-place of Hendon House on his map of Middlesex. *Britannia* was translated into English by P. Halland in 1610, and this version held good until 1695, when it was again translated by Edmund Gibson, afterwards Bishop of Lincoln and London, a distinguished divine who refused the primacy.

A problem which needs some explanation is connected with Watling Street, that famous old Roman road which runs from Marble Arch through Kilburn and Edgware, Brockley Hill and Elstree to St. Albans and thence to Wroxeter. In Camden's *Britannia* he writes thus about the roads of Middlesex (as translated from the original Latin) : "Towards the north bounds of Middlesex, a military way of the Romans commonly called Watling Street enters the County, coming straight along from the old Verulam through Hampstead Heath (from which one has a curious prospect of a most beautiful City, and a most pleasant County). Then, not where the road lies now through Highgate . . . but that more ancient one (as appears by the old charters of Edward the Confessor) passed along near Edgworth, a place of no great antiquity; so on to Hendon, which Archbishop Dunstan (a man born for promoting the interest of monkery) purchased for a few bizantine pieces of gold, and gave to the monks of St. Peter's in Westminster." This comment suggests that the swampy ground north of Cricklewood, where the Welsh Harp has since been created, made progress difficult, and so it was decided to use the other old road over the Heath instead, especially as it led to the City of London and not, as Watling Street seems to have done, to Westminster. It is worth noting that Morden, in a later map giving the main roads out of London, like Ogilby, ignores the road from London through Edgware to St. Albans. The fact that in various editions of Camden Colindale Lane is called Ancient Street suggests that it was perhaps the road from Tyburn to Red Hill that was the switchway and not *vice versa*. There was yet another route to the north-west from Hendon down Parson Street, along the green track of Ashley Lane (traditionally used by Wolsey), up Mylespit Hill, along the Ridgeway at Mill Hill, and by a grass track over Highwood, Grimsgate and Shenley to St. Albans, so frequently used by the Hertfordshire monks.

It was not until after the Great Fire of 1666 that effective surveys of the roads running out of London were made by Morden and Lea, Leybourne and Blome, Ogilby and Morgan. In Ogilby's *Britannia Depicta*, 1675, he gives the main seven or total of fourteen roads out of London, all starting, for purposes of measurement, from the Standard in Cornhill. He styles himself His Majesty's Cosmographer, states that the plans have been described and delineated by him and printed at his house in Whitefryers, and yet, in spite of his official position, he does not mention either of the two north-west exits referred to—neither the one through Kilburn to Edgware, nor that over Hampstead Heath, past the Burroughs and down Colindeep Lane.

The Edinburgh Road was measured from Shoreditch Church and went past two turnpike gates to Stoke Newington, Stamford Hill, Tottenham, Edmonton, Ponders End, Enfield Highway (Rose and Crown), Enfield Wash (The Bell), Waltham Cross, just in Hertfordshire, a distance of eleven miles two furlongs.

This road has memories of Cowper and his invention, John Gilpin, and of Izaac Walton and Charles Lamb. The dangerous state of its surface due to floods is well illustrated by an extract from Ralph Thoresby's *Diary* of May 17, 1695. He had come by Puckeridge to Ware and had seen passengers from London compelled to swim, and a poor higgler drowned, and he and his friend had to ride "to the saddle-skirts for a considerable way." The next day, in riding to Edmonton, his horse had to be "led about a mile over the deepest of the Wash." His final comment is illuminating : "I have the greatest cause of thankfulness for the goodness of my heavenly protector, that being exposed to great dangers by my horse's boggling at every coach and waggon we met, I received no damage, though the ways were very bad, the ruts deep, and the roads extremely full of water, which rendered my circumstances (often meeting the loaded waggons in very inconvenient places) not only melancholy, but very dangerous."

In most seventeenth-century plans for the replanning of London or the providing of a Green Belt it was the immediate environs which were chiefly concerned, but in 1670 there was a measure passed by Parliament for levying a rate to repair roads which had been neglected for several years in the whole County of Middlesex. Considering the enormous number of topics dealt with by Defoe, it is not surprising that, in his *Essay on Projects,* published in 1697, he should have suggested some solution of the road problem. He is writing of the road through Islington, so important for cattle destined for Smithfield, as being the greatest and most frequented road in England, but so handicapped by heavy clay and complete lack of gravel "that carts, horses and men have been almost buried in holes and sloughs." He suggests that if the parish of Islington "would part with all the waste-land upon their roads to be eased of the repair . . . a noble, magnificent causeway might be erected . . . 30 to 40 feet wide to reach from London to Barnet."

William King, in his *Journey to London,* published in the next year, 1698, speaks of the incredible ill-manners of the 'prentices, of the insolence of the carmen, the crowds of hackney coaches, the clouds of sea-coal, so that the roads through Middlesex into London on a foggy day afford "a resemblance of hell upon earth." The passengers complained that they were "jumbled about like so many peas in a child's rattle, running a great hazard of dislocation at every jolt," and that the roads and ditches near London were "full of nastiness and dirt."

The road to the North had for five centuries and more climbed over Highgate Hill to avoid the wetter, muddier way through Crouch End and Hornsey. It passed through the park of the Bishop of London, and he reaped the benefit of the tolls collected at the gate. Apparently only pack-horses were allowed to pass through, and not coaches. Previous to 1386 the Great North Road, according to John Norden, the famous Elizabethan cartographer, who lived at Hendon, started from Gray's Inn, past St. Pancras under the name of Longwich Lane, leaving Highgate to the west, along Tollington Lane, through Crouch Hill and Crouch End, Hornsey Park, Muswell Hill, Colney Hatch, Friern-Barnet, Whetstone and Chipping Barnet.

The new road, after surmounting Highgate Hill and coming down North Hill, went across Finchley Common to Whetstone. At the inn close to the Bishop's High Gate was performed the ceremony of the Horns. Travellers were made free of the Highgate's Liberties—whatever they were—and they made certain promises on the Horns. They would not eat brown bread or drink small beer, unless they preferred them; and they must not kiss the maid when they could kiss the mistress, unless they preferred the maid. To be on the safe side it would be better to kiss both. The landlord adopted the guest as his son, and plenty of drink was provided. Byron celebrated "the worship of the solemn horn" on the steps of Highgate in the first canto of *Childe Harold*, and Cruickshank and Crowquill drew pictures of it.

In 1810 the road from Highgate to Whetstone (eight miles) was controlled by a trust, which was allowed to charge tolls, but three years later the age-long complaint against the steepness of Highgate Hill led to a scheme for constructing a tunnel about 300 yards long. When nearly finished the whole thing fell in, fortunately without hurting anyone, and a cutting took the place of a tunnel, with an archway over the top carrying Hornsey Lane. It saved only 100 yards, but the reduction in hill-climbing was worth while for the ever-increasing coaching traffic. Considerable financial loss was sustained by the old inns on the top owing to the diversion of traffic. In 1813 Macadam eased off the steep gradient into High Barnet at a cost of £17,000, and eight years later the tolls on the Great North Road were let for £7,530 a year. The Holyhead mail did the fifteen miles from the Swan with Two Necks in Lud Lane to South Mimms on the northern boundary of Middlesex in one hour forty minutes. The rival coaches, Tally-ho and Independent Tally-ho, did considerable portions of the Holyhead route at about sixteen miles an hour. The coming of the railways seemed likely to drive coaches off the road for ever, but the Green Line and other motor vehicles have recovered much of the roads' former prosperity. The first Highgate Archway was built of stone, with a balustrade upon huge brick supports, but after three-quarters of a century of service it was superseded by an iron bridge.

The interval between the final disappearance of the stage-coach and the arrival of the Green Line can be covered, it would seem, by the span of a single lifetime. Towards the end of 1947 there died in Barnet Wellhouse Hospital, whose name recalls Samuel Pepys' visit to the physic well, an old local politician of exactly eighty-seven, who had devoted half a century of active endeavour to his native town and district. In the days when Barnet consisted of three main roads and but half a dozen bylanes he remembered seeing the landlord of the Red Lion wave a fond farewell to the very last London-to-York stage-coach, which had just changed horses at the posting stable next door.

Halfway from Whetstone to High Barnet the Great North Road went into Hertfordshire, but returned to Middlesex just north of the town. The road there forks and becomes the Great North and the Holyhead Roads (nowadays A1 and A6), and these both continue in the county to points just north of Potters Bar and north-west of South Mimms. Linking up with this group of roads there is the Regent's Park-Finchley Road, which cut across the road from Hampstead Heath to Hendon at Golders Green and went on to join the Great North Road at Tally-ho Corner.

Still more recent was the construction of the Barnet and Watford by-pass roads, which have certainly reduced the traffic on other main roads, but have presented problems of their own. From the Finchley Road by Childs Hill Hendon Way forks north-west, crosses one of Hendon's many "High Streets" at the Burroughs, using a piece of Queen's Road, which William Camden thought was Watling Street, and then forking right (under the name of Watford Way) to join another newish by-pass which forks left from Archway Road, comes along Lyttelton Way, Falloden Way, Great North Way, and runs into Watford Way just south of Mill Hill. The two run as one for a mile and a half through lower Mill Hill and then fork at Apex Corner, the Watford Road keeping on the level across the L.M.S. Railway across Watling Street just south of Elstree Hill and passing into Herts southwest of Aldenham Reservoir. Barnet By-pass climbs the hill between Highwood and Scratch Wood, enters Herts for two miles just south of Stirling Corner, re-enters Middlesex northwest of Dyrham Park, crosses the Holyhead Road south of South Mimms and leaves Middlesex close to Brookman's Park.

The *Gentleman's Magazine* for 1752 attributes the deterioration of turnpike roads to the selfish conduct of waggoners, who stated that "the roads had but one object, namely waggon-driving. That they required but five feet width in a line, and all the rest might go to the devil." Coaches had to travel in these waggon ruts, which were sometimes 8 inches deep in fluid sludge. Some of the waggons needed ten horses apiece, and Middleton, writing in 1797-8, says that horsemen and light carriages had the utmost difficulty in getting along, being driven by heavy traffic into a veritable quagmire on the edge of the road more than a foot deep with adhesive mire. Middleton's *View of Agriculture of Middlesex* mentions the Bath Road, through Brentford and Hounslow, and the Staines Road through East Bedfont, as being particularly filthy, though the King used the latter regularly, changing his horses at King's Arbour several times a week. Watling Street and the road from Tyburn to Uxbridge were equally used and just as filthy. It was no one's business to repair the main roads, and the branch ones, that joined the few Middlesex market towns together, were equally bad.

In the early nineteenth century the Middlesex roads

showed signs of improvement, and in 1837, the year before
the Great Western Railway was opened as far as Slough, the
Bristol Mail did 121 miles in ten hours with fourteen changes
of horses. Turnpike gates must have been a real nuisance to
all road-users, even though they indicated better roads, and
it is not surprising that Mr. Weller, Senior, says that turn-
pike-keepers were "all on 'em men as has met with some
disappointment in life. . . . Consequence of which, they
retire from the world, and shuts themselves up in pikes;
partly with a view of being solitary, and partly to revenge
themselves on mankind, by taking tolls. . . . If they was
gen'lm'n, you'd call 'em misanthropes, but, as it is, they only
takes to pike-keepin'." Well, there was plenty of room for
these disillusioned men, seeing that in what G. M. Trevelyan
calls "the brief interval of highway glory between Waterloo
and the Railways" there were 22,000 miles of good turnpike
roads in England with 8,000 toll-gates.

The 2,000 Road Acts of the eighteenth century and the
epoch-making efforts of Macadam with regard to road
surfaces were having their effect when there fell upon the
land the "calamity of railways," and the romance of the road
and the prosperity of the inn seemed gone for ever. It seemed
unthinkable that all the improvements in straightening and
widening of roads and the changes in surface and gradients
should be all for naught, but it was so, and the age of the
railway drove almost every traveller off the roads for nearly
a century. There is a very good essay by Sir Stenson Cooke
in which he describes the immense satisfaction with which a
typical innkeeper and his wife realise that the advent of the
motor-car, made possible by the internal combustion engine
and by the inflated rubber tyre, would restore a great deal of
the prosperity of which their parents and especially their
grandparents had told them.

One of the aims of the County of London plan is to
provide "parkways," which will add amenity value to the
normal seemliness of design and planting that every road
should possess. The various by-passes give scope for this kind
of development, and it is a pity that the Great West Avenue,
which forks off near to Kew Bridge, where the North Circular
Road comes down Gunnersbury Lane, should have already

been overloaded with factories, well designed though they are. But there is a splendid example of a parkway on the west side of the Barnet By-pass just before it reaches the London Caravan Club's headquarters at Stirling Corner. Here, close to Scratch Wood, associated perhaps with Grim's Dyke, is a widening of the grass verge and an accommodation road at right angles to the by-pass, where many cars are parked to allow the occupants to picnic in and around Scratch Wood. The whole area from Apex Corner to Stirling Corner gives a model of development which has been made by seizing chances when they have occurred, and by indulging in the right kind of wishful thinking accompanied by appropriate action.

Sixty years of urbanisation have done a vast amount of irretrievable damage to the rusticity of Middlesex, as a glance at H. J. Foley's *Our Lanes and Meadow Paths,* published in the middle 1880s, will show.

He writes of the rustic quiet of the Middlesex lanes and the shady recesses of its parks, of hilltops that command prospects of great breadth and beauty, with no factory chimneys to disturb the picturesque harmony of country life. He doubts whether, of its kind, the charm of the undulating wooded pastures between St. Albans and London, especially passing Mill Hill, can be surpassed elsewhere. Another pleasing feature of sixty years ago was the unchanged character of the villages and hamlets of Middlesex. Edgware had hardly changed since Handel walked its one long street; Twyford in 1251 had ten inhabited houses, and in 600 years these had diminished to eight; Perivale in 1816 had five dwellings; seventy years later these had increased by two. "The huge wave of modern brick had scarcely advanced, and the lover of the picturesque could yet discover as charming bits of rustic life close at hand as could be met with a hundred yards from the metropolis."

Here is his story of Hendon, with its fourteen scattered hamlets, reached from Child's Hill by a footpath crossing several meadows, golden with buttercups, then along a lane, across a stile into fields, along a grassy route with meadows prettily fringed with elms. He then reaches Hendon Church, passes out of the churchyard by a footpath over sunny hills,

272

Entrance gate at Highgate School

along a rustic lane, climbing beneath closely arching trees, across the road to a footpath leading up the hillside, with the village of Mill Hill at the top.

His description of the view from the Ridgeway does not sound very exaggerated today: "Beyond the wooded eminences of Harrow, Wembley and Pinner, the distant Chilterns are visible, and southwards we see the long purple line of the Surrey Hills. How luxuriant is the wood on every hand. Noble elms, groups of lime and ash trees, knots of rugged pines, with here and there a sombre yew. And yet could pasture be richer, or could any meadows be more full of beauty than these? The mossy roots of the elms form snug resting-place for choice wild flowers; here and there is a shady spot purple with hyacinths; while in the moister corners we shall not look in vain for the large golden crowns of the marsh-marigolds. The pale lilac petals of the cuckoo-flower, the bee and purple orchis, the meadowsweet and tall marguerite daisy, are here familiar friends; and the banks of the ditches which border the fields are studded with blossoms of all kinds. From the mile-long ridgeway the road climbed down and then up to Highwood Hill, by a leafy road past Hendon Wood, and then by one of the loveliest of Middlesex lanes to reach Barnet Gate, with its windmill."

C. E. Montague, in his adroitly labelled book of essays, *The Right Place*, discussed the importance of knowing at least one road really intimately, and one that he chooses is the road from Manchester to London, which traverses the various layers of rock from the granites and sandstones and coal measures down to the chalk and the clays and the gravel. But not only does it give you a clarified lesson in geography and geology, but it also shows man gradually conquering distance by planning and replanning trackways till they serve his utmost purpose; neglecting them when Trevethick and Stephenson bring the railway as a masterful rival; reverting to them and straightening and widening them when the internal combustion engine comes into use; and then, perhaps, in the not too distant future, almost discarding them for the speed and simplicity of the six-hundred-miles-an-hour aeroplane.

There is a very good spot to study man in his road-making

Church at Harrow-on-the-Hill

just where Hertfordshire and Middlesex join, close to London Colney and South Mimms. There, as Montague points out, you can see three roads running almost side by side. There is the Roman road, as straight as could be, almost as rigid as Watling Street from Brockley Hill to Hyde Park Corner. It was purely a military way, though civilians might use it. There is a curving, loitering way that twists and turns to oblige villages and farmsteads when hurry was of no great importance. And then there is Telford's well-graded straight road, reverting to the style of the Romans and anticipating the modern by-pass.

According to Montague, there seems to be only one spot in the southern portion of the journey where all three roads can be seen almost at one and the same time. Between London Colney and High or Chipping Barnet the trunk road crosses the county boundary twice, and three times it has been straightened out to speed up the journey for the coach-users : first, between Shenley Lodge and South Mimms, where the old road branches off in Herts and comes back in Middlesex; secondly, where it is seen over the edge of Telford's finely built-up road, a small byway, with half-disused ruts, running ingloriously beside the great highway, "a purposeless-looking track, deep in sand and arched over with hazels and oaks"; and again where the old road goes off at right angles "suddenly, as if remembering, just in time, that Wrotham Park (whose owner is perhaps Chairman of Quarter Sessions) is half a mile away on the left." It was along the by-lane that Swift, among others, journeyed to Dublin, following the loops and windings which Telford nearly a century later straightened out. And, as Montague reminds us, the Great Roman Road, really British in origin, and later on to be called Watling Street, was running straight as a ruler, with one odd bend at Brockley Hill by the old settlement of Sulloniacæ. And there is another road of which Montague hardly guessed in 1924, the Barnet By-pass, which cuts across Telford's road just east of South Mimms, and leaves that picturesque village still more isolated and still more get-at-able.

CHAPTER XIX

EDUCATION

EDUCATION in Middlesex has never perhaps been fully chronicled, partly because it is not easy to discuss it if entirely divorced from schools in London. The medieval monasteries, abbeys and cathedrals all had schools of some kind as part of their scheme of action. No monasteries or priories were established in Saxon time within the boundaries of Middlesex as defined in 1888, but St. Alban's Abbey, Westminster, and St. Paul's held large tracts of land in the county, and no doubt some Middlesex folk attended their schools. There were not many post-Conquest monasteries in Middlesex : Syon Abbey, founded by Henry V for Bridgettine nuns; a small Augustinian priory at Bentley; a house of Trinitarian friars at Hounslow; the Order of St. John of Jerusalem at Moor Hall, Harefield; and alien priories at Harmondsworth and Ruislip almost exhaust the list.

Post-Reformation schools opened up a new vista in education. The founding of *Mercers' School* and the refounding of *St. Paul's* and *Westminster,* the new schools of *Christ's Hospital* and of *Charterhouse,* will have helped some Middlesex pupils, but the main contributions were some half a dozen grammar schools founded in Elizabethan times in the county. Sir Roger Cholmeley's foundation at *Highgate* in 1562 was for forty scholars to be chosen from Highgate and Holloway, Hornsey, Finchley, and Kentish Town, "if there shall be so many in those places"; otherwise at the discretion of the governors. *Hampton* School was founded under the will of Robert Hamond, who died in 1557, and it was benefited further by John Jones, who bequeathed in 1692 the glebe and rectorial tithes for specific charities. The school was intended "for the gratuitous education of poor children of this parish." Other grammar schools that were founded in Tudor or Stuart times were *Enfield* Free Grammar School, founded by John Carew in 1507. Brayley, writing in 1814, speaks of the schoolhouse, rebuilt by the parishioners in the early seventeenth century. He says that the master enjoyed a liberal allowance and that the school was "eminently useful for the class of persons for whom it was solely appropriated by the founder." Others were *Latymer* School at *Hammersmith* (now in L.C.C. area) and *Latymer* School at *Edmonton,* founded in 1624 under the will of Edward Latymer, who bequeathed some property to clothe and educate eight boys. Later benefactors raised the number to fifty-one boys being educated and clothed. In 1811 a poor widow named Wyatt, by great economy, had managed to save £700, which, on the advice of the vicar, she left for the benefit of education. A new schoolroom was built with her generous bequest. In 1778 a girls' school was started, chiefly by George Hanbury, who later left £1,000 for the girls' school. This made possible the education and clothing of fifty girls in 1814.

Yet another free school was founded in 1624 at *Stanwell* by Thomas, Lord Knyvet, and Elizabeth, his wife, and the delightful Jacobean schoolhouse is still in good repair.

HIGHGATE SCHOOL

Highgate, with its "fantastical custom" of the Horns, its associations with Arabella Stuart, Lord Chancellor Bacon, and the Cromwell family, possesses a Grammar School older than that of Harrow. Norden and Newcourt tell us of an ancient hermitage or chapel on the top of Highgate Hill, dating back at least from 1386. About the middle of the eighteenth century this site and some adjacent land was granted to Sir Roger Cholmeley, Knight, Chief Justice of the Queen's Bench, who founded there a free grammar school in 1562. The rules of the school, issued in 1571, directed that the master shall be a graduate of sober and honest conversation, who shall "teach and instruct young children their A B C, and other English books, and to write, and also the grammar as they shall grow up thereto; and that without taking any money or other reward than as hereafter expressed,—i.e. 4d. at the admission of each boy into the school, and 4d. for books." A charter of Queen Elizabeth gave the affairs of the school into the charge of a body of governors; the salary of the master was to be £10 a year and a house; there were to be forty scholars, chosen from Highgate, Holloway, Hornsey, Finchley, and Kentish Town, "if there be so many in those places"; if not, the school was to be filled at the discretion of the governors.

The school chapel, which was for some centuries the only place of worship in the village, was probably built by Sir Roger Cholmeley, and there is a record in the possession of St. Paul's Cathedral of a conveyance from Bishop Grindall to Cholmeley in 1571. In the chapel itself Edwin Sandys, Grindall's predecessor, is credited with the gift of the chapel to Highgate School. It has from time to time been enlarged "by the pietie and bounty of divers honourable and worthy personages."

But the original idea of Cholmeley was not rigidly kept. True, some good religious and classical education must have been given for a century, if we may regard as typical Nicholas Rowe, classical scholar and Poet Laureate to George I.

It seems, however, that most of the money available from trusts and other sources went to the enlargement of the chapel, the building of almshouses, and not for education. About 1820 there was a lot of legal discussion on the subject, and after some years it was decided by law that the trustees had not been doing their duty by the school, to whom the chapel really belonged; and so another church was built for the villagers. In spite of this decision, the headmaster still devoted more time to his incumbency than to his teaching, and the school went down from its original forty to nineteen. In 1838 John Bradley Dyne, Fellow of Wadham College, Oxford, was appointed headmaster, and, by getting an able staff around him, starting two boarding-houses, buying an unrivalled cricket field, and securing high successes at the universities, he was able to give to Highgate School a great restart. The school outgrew its home and new buildings were erected in 1866. Dr. Dyne carried on until 1874, and since that time the school has more than maintained its high standard of work and games. The two World Wars have taken their toll of Old Cholmeleians; many honours have been won at the universities and in public life, and Highgate is one of the most efficient examples of a school both for day boys and boarders. Among recent Old Cholmeleians are two Lord Mayors, Sir Charles Baker and Sir Frank Alexander; Sir Charles Robertson and Professor V. H. Galbraith, distinguished historians; C. H. Andrewes, J. B. Buxton, and A. G. Tansley, distinguished scientists; Sir Geoffrey Shakespeare and F. G. Bowles, distinguished Parliamentarians; Lord Justice Mackinnon and his brother, Chairman of Lloyd's; recent Bishops of Lahore, Rangoon, Madras, and of the Upper Nile; and last, but not least, a bunch of famous athletes : G. R. O. Crole-Rees, captain of the English Davis Cup team; A. H. Fabian, star fives champion; D. G. A. Lowe, Olympic runner; and R. W. V. Robins, cricket captain of Middlesex and of England.

HARROW SCHOOL

Harrow was a famous place even before the days of John Lyon. It has an interesting manorial history : Archbishop Lanfranc founded its church, and Anselm consecrated it; a vicar retired to its hill in Tudor times to escape from a second flood; Cranmer surrendered the manor and church to King Henry VIII; the Bellamys, who helped Babington to try to escape the consequences of his plot against Elizabeth, lived near to it; and many distinguished folk are buried within Charles II's "visible church." Most famous of them all is really "Lyon of Preston, Yeoman John," as Edward Bowen, Harrow's school poet, likes to call him. He it was who founded, or possibly refounded, a free grammar school for poor boys, which has developed into perhaps the second best-known school in the world. Lyon left some landed property to the school and some to repair the roads of the district. Not long before his death the school offended him and he changed his will, giving the better farm for the upkeep of the roads. But the worse farm was nearer to London, and the school has distinctly scored by the change.

The Free Grammar School of Harrow, as E. W. Brayley calls it in 1814 in the Middlesex volume of the *Beauties of Britain,* was founded to supply education for a "meete and convenient number of scholars, as well of poor to be taught freely, and of others, to be received for the further proffit and commoditie of the Schoolmaster." Exhibitions were to be given to such as are "most meete for towardnesse, poverty and painfulness," with a preference for "his own poor kinsfolk, if any such there be; and to such as are borne in the said Parish of Harrow, being apte to learne, being poore, and meete to go to the University," with the proviso that the exhibition shall fall on "the most apt and most poore soule that shall be meete."

Harrow has its famous Fourth Form Room, which was the old classroom for nearly a century, and on its panelled walls are carved many famous names. Old Speech Room still stands, with its well-known inscription to the memory of Anthony Ashley Cooper, afterwards Earl of Shaftesbury. It was the wretchedness of a pauper funeral, with the coffin carried by drunken men, who dropped it and allowed the naked corpse to fall into the muddy road, that made the young Harrovian dedicate his life to the alleviation of suffering. Shaftesbury Avenue was driven through some of the worst of London's slums, and the famous statue of Eros, recently restored after six years' absence, is part of London's recognition of Shaftesbury's magnificent service.

There are also New Speech Room, where school functions are held, the School Chapel, the Vaughan Library, and the recent Memorial Building designed by Sir Herbert Baker in honour of the 650 Old Harrovians who fell in the first World War. Harrow can number on its roll of fame six Prime Ministers—Lord Palmerston, Sir Robert Peel, Lord Aberdeen, Spencer Percival, Earl Baldwin, Winston Churchill—and even among such a list, with two earlier highlights, the last named stands supreme.

The town is studded with school boarding-houses, and to be of service to residents who do not want the public-school type of education for their sons a Lower School of John Lyon has been established.

The lists of Harrow's V.C.s are grand records of achievement, and include eighteen up to the end of 1918 and several since.

Harrow has had famous headmasters : H. M. Butler, Canon Vaughan, Bishop Welldon, and Sir Cyril Norwood perhaps stand out; and, like all other great schools, she has her long list of equally devoted and equally famous assistant masters. Edward Bowen, who was educated at the old Blackheath School (now, alas! defunct), wrote the school songs, including the most famous of all, "Forty Years On," and John Farmer set them to music. Bosworth-Smith was an authority on Mohammedanism and bird life and wrote a *Life* of Lawrence of the Punjab. G. Townsend Warner was a scholarly writer of history books. John Smith was a real Christian saint. Robert Somerwell was an ideal bursar. Several of them have had their *Lives* written, and the fame which they achieved as assistant masters has been a constant inspiration to schoolmasters everywhere.

Perhaps the most picturesque figure in the Harrow story is that of Lord Byron, who had a chequered career both at school and in the world, and is commemorated on the Hill by the cage over John Peachey's tomb, where Byron used to laze and dream. His daughter is buried in Harrow Churchyard, and he at Missolonghi, where he died, to the consternation of Europe, while trying to free the Isles of Greece, where burning Sappho loved and sang.

Many famous soldiers come from Harrow, and in the second World War Field-Marshal Viscount Gort, V.C., and Field-Marshal Viscount Alexander perhaps stand out. Professor G. M. Trevelyan, O.M., is the greatest living historian, and the revival by the B.B.C. of the *Forsyte Saga* shows that Harrow's product, John Galsworthy, O.M., has few equals as a painter of the life of the late nineteenth century. In a life which attained such unparalleled political achievements as those reached by Winston Churchill there hardly seems time to have written the most effective story of the first World War, many studies of his contemporaries, and the final *Life* of his great ancestor, Marlborough, and to have attained real distinction as a painter.

The Eton and Harrow match at Lord's is one of the most famous of cricketing contests, and both schools have a long list of cricket Blues at both universities. The story of Harrow has been told more than once already, and it has recently been brought completely up to date, including the grim war years and the hospitality given at a time of crisis to Malvern School, in a book by Dr. E. D. Laborde.

Mill Hill School has an origin which differentiates it from almost all the other public schools in England, and that distinction gives it a special interest for Americans. The same spirit which was behind the sailing of the *Mayflower* in 1620 was in the mind of Richard Swift in 1660 when he founded the first Nonconformist or Free Church school in this country at Mill Hill, Middlesex, just ten miles from the centre of London. Swift had been ejected from his curacy in Edgware at the Restoration of King Charles II, and he was one of those ministers who were styled by the Earl of Peterborough as "sober, diligent and industrious."

There were 450 ministers ejected from their charges in the first two years of the reign, and nearly 2,000 on Black St. Bartholomew's Day in 1662, and in many cases education was the only profession to which they could turn their hands. The decisions made by Parliament in those momentous years divided the country into two distinct classes, and for two hundred years Nonconformists had to find their education outside the grammar schools and universities and in their own academies. The men trained in these surroundings had a different outlook on social, political and religious matters and developed what later generations called "the Nonconformist conscience." Swift kept his school going, with many ups and downs, for forty years, and, though there is no direct connection between the Mill Hill School of 1660 and that of 1807, the spirit that animated the two schools was the same.

In the century between the two schools there were quite a number of Quakers and other reforming types living in the village, but it does not seem probable that John Pye Smith and Samuel Favell and the other Dissenting parsons and London merchants who founded Mill Hill School were aware of Richard Swift.

The school's history has been eventful. It nearly closed down completely in 1868 and again in 1891, but since then the standard set by Sir John McClure has been maintained. With its Junior School it has over 150 acres of ground on both sides of the Ridgeway, and the view from the terrace in front of Sir William Tite's Ionic portico across the valley to Harrow is unspoilt. It was the view of Harrow and a pious hope that Eton was also visible that induced the founders to pick this spot for their school, where Peter Collinson, many years before, had enjoyed his wonderful gardens at Ridgeway House. All the usual school buildings are to be found near the early block : Chapel (designed by Basil Champneys), Big School, classrooms, Winterstoke Library, Murray Scriptorium, indoor and outdoor swimming pools, Science Block. Between the Schoolhouse and the Ridgeway stands the Memorial Gateway, on which are carved the names of 194 who fell in the first World War, and to which have now been added 121 names of those who made the supreme sacrifice in the second World War. It was opened by Lord Horne, and King Edward VIII, when Prince of Wales, passed through it. An interesting headmaster in the '70s was Dr. Richard Francis Weymouth, the first Litt.D. of London University, whose *Weymouth New Testament* is deservedly well known. Since his time the most distinguished headmaster was Sir John McClure, a doctor of law and of music, who occupied the position from 1891 to 1922, and died in harness, to the deep regret of pupils, parents, and old boys.

There are four boarding-houses in Wills Grove, with ample grounds round them, and behind Ridgeway and Burton Bank is the Park, a new cricket field with a playing area as big as Lord's. The two other boarding-houses (Collinson and Winterstoke) bear names honoured in the Mill Hill story, and to the Day Boys' was given by Maurice L. Jacks, headmaster between the two wars, the interesting name of "Murray." This commemorates the work of Sir James Murray, editor of the famous *Oxford Dictionary*, who was a master at the school for fifteen years. A delightful Elizabethan cottage, The Grove, is now the headmaster's house, and in the village close at hand is a very early Quaker meeting-house, dating from 1678, and now transformed into a dwelling-house. Dr. J. S. Whale was headmaster, 1944-51.

Mill Hill plays "rugger," and the school side and the Old Millhillians Fifteen have won considerable renown. An interesting experiment, made after the school's six years' evacuation to St. Bees in Cumberland, is the admission of between thirty and forty boys each year as boarders from the county schools of Middlesex. Among recent distinguished Old Millhillians are Sir Gordon Lethem, K.C.M.G., lately Governor

of Trinidad; Sir A. Dykes Spicer, Bart., for many years a
school governor; Sir Clifford Paterson, distinguished for
scientific research; Percival Gibbon and Coningsby Dawson,
who have won fame as novelists. Early records include Lord
Winterstoke, Lord Trevethin, and Lord Rochdale.

The *S.P.C.K.* (founded in 1698) had by the middle of the
eighteenth century started 1,600 charity schools, where boys
and girls were clothed, given religious instruction, and taught
the old medieval *trivia*, the "three Rs." Dr. Bray was the
prime mover and the inaugural meeting was held at the
London house of Mr. Justice Hook. Lord Guilford, Colonel
Colchester and Sir Humphrey Mackleworth were the other
famous members. Before these men of vision and generosity
began to provide general education for the poorer classes the
only schools were ancient foundations for aristocrats and
dames' schools. The establishment of *Sunday Schools* in
Gloucester by Robert Raikes was taken up all over England
and Wales, and all denominations adopted it with enthusiasm.
It gave a very important impetus to the education of the
poorer classes. But the most important step taken at this time
was the adoption of the *monitorial system,* which was put
forward almost simultaneously by Dr. Andrew Bell, who had
employed it while head of the military orphan school in
Madras, and by Joseph Lancaster, an enthusiastic young
Quaker. This method was economical in teaching staff, because one experienced master or mistress would impart the
lesson to twenty or thirty seniors, and they would each hand
it on to a classroom of youngsters. In this way one or two
teachers could be responsible for two or three hundred pupils.

Bell gave his support to the *National Society* for promoting
the education of the poor in the principles of the Established
Church, founded in 1821; while Lancaster joined with others,
mainly Nonconformists, in the *British and Foreign Schools
Society*, in whose schools the Bible was taught without note
or comment. The success of these two societies, which by 1833
were educating one out of eleven of the whole population, led
to a grant of £20,000, divided between them annually.

In 1839 a Committee of the Privy Council was formed to
administer the grant, and in 1856 an Education Department

was established. Robert Lowe was something of a pioneer in these years, but it was W. E. Forster who produced the Elementary Education Act of 1870, which made education available. In 1880 it was made compulsory, and in 1891 free. By the 1870 Act School Boards were established all over the country, so that in addition to borough councils there were two other bodies dealing with the Poor Law and with education.

Middlesex was probably as well equipped educationally in 1815 as any other county, and there were few towns or villages where no effort had been made to provide a school. In Chiswick there was a free school, founded in 1707, and providing education for 120 and clothing for 48. Lady Conway's benefaction at Acton in 1636 helped to educate 40 girls in the place, while at Ealing there were charity schools for both boys and girls. Mrs. Trimmer was a pioneer in Brentford in promoting "good morals on the basis of temperate religious principles," and her efforts, supported by local help, a generous contribution from George III's Queen, and subscriptions and charity sermons, enabled 200 boys to be trained on the Madras system and 90 girls to be taught such learning and plain work as were "calculated to render them useful domestic servants."

A Sunday school founded at Willesden in 1810 showed marked success in the improved manners of the children, but it aroused stern opposition from local farmers, who, we are told, were "so nearly allied to the clods which they cultivate as to suppose that even a moderate share of information . . . must render the children of the poor unsuitable for manual labour."

The schools of Uxbridge dated from 1695, and were enlarged in 1809 for 200 boys and 60 girls, taught on the Lancaster system. Thomas Clarke, of Swakeleys, founded a school at Hillingdon in 1814, and it came under some disapproval, owing to the passages from Luther and Calvin which were printed on a board outside the school. Clarke also started a school at Ickenham and one at Ruislip, with free clothing for such as needed it, and instruction on the Lancaster plan.

Hayes had a charity school for 52 children; Harefield gave

all the village children free information; Dr. Bell's plan was adopted for 35 boys and 30 girls in Finchley, with a free dinner every Sunday; while the school at Staines was run on the rival Lancaster system. The school at Isleworth dated from 1630, and by 1824 100 boys and 60 girls were being taught on Dr. Bell's plan, and many of them had free clothing. Twickenham had its old school reorganised on the Bell plan, and 100 boys and 20 girls were there trained, and about one-third of them clothed free of charge.

Greenford, Hanwell, Norwood, and Little Stanmore all had schools endowed in the eighteenth century; one of them was founded in 1706 to provide education for the poor "till the world's end." Sir Lancelot Lake, of Canons Park, had been responsible for building Little Stanmore School, for whose schoolmaster £15 was available as salary.

The free school in *Hendon* was built in 1766 by John Bennet on a piece of waste ground granted by David Garrick as lord of the manor. Bennet also bequeathed £100, to which several later sums have been added. With subscriptions and the collections at charity sermons sufficient money accrued to educate the greater part of the poor children of the parish. A clothing fund provided clothes for some of the children, and in 1814 it served for forty-two children best approved for good behaviour. Dr. Bell's system was in vogue.

One of the most successful private schools in the northern part of Middlesex was begun in 1827 by the Hill family of *Bruce Castle, Tottenham.* The school lasted until 1896 and was successful in both work and games, playing Rugby football against Mill Hill in the '70s. Sir Rowland Hill, most famous of all the family, earned undying fame as the inventor of penny postage, now for many years a thing of the past. In the upper storeys of Bruce Castle is a museum recording the history of the Post Office, with early maps, pictures of postboys and stage-coaches, surveyors' wheels (from which came the bicycle), and ending up with illustrations of telegraph, telephone, aeroplanes, and wireless.

The educational facilities at *Tottenham* in 1814 were considerable. Nicholas Reynardson, who founded almshouses in 1685, also directed that £20 a year was to be allowed to the chaplain, who was to act as schoolmaster and teach poor children reading and writing. The next year Sarah, Dowager Duchess of Somerset, left £250 to enlarge the school and £1,100 to be laid out in land to extend "the benefit of the school to all children of such inhabitants of Tottenham as were not possessed of real property to the amount of £20 per annum." Her interest in Tottenham was due to her marriage in 1675 to Lord Coleraine of Bruce Castle. A distinguished headmaster of the school was William Baxter, nephew of Richard Baxter, the Nonconformist divine, who later became headmaster of the Mercers' School. William Baxter was well known in his day as the author of a *Grammar*, a *Glossary of British Antiquities,* and editions of *Horace* and of *Anacreon.* But the establishment of new free schools on the Madras lines had, by 1814, "caused the free school to sink into comparative insignificance."

In 1735 a free Blue School for girls was started at Tottenham, at which thirty-six girls were clothed and educated partly by bequests and partly by subscriptions and church collections. There was also an industrial school (1792) for forty girls, who wore a green uniform and were chiefly trained for domestic service. Long years of continuous employment entitled the girls to "a pecuniary token of approbation from the managers." Two schools were started about 1814 on the Lancaster system for 150 boys and another for girls, mainly promoted by "the people termed Quakers," but open to children of all denominations.

In *Enfield,* in addition to the Free Grammar School (1507), two schools for girls had been established by 1814, in which eighty children were instructed and clothing was provided for seventy of them.

At *Hadley* a charity school for girls was established in 1773, enlarged in 1800, and converted into a school of industry. Twenty girls each year received £1 towards the purchase of clothes; thirty more were educated at a charge of 2d. a week, and they succeeded to vacancies among the free scholars. The Rev. Dr. Garrow built a gallery in the church for the girls. The boys' school educated seventy day scholars, twenty being admitted free with £1 towards clothing, and the rest paying 2d. a week. Adults to the number of twenty-four attended for evening school at the same price.

In Hadley there were big Sunday schools, run, as were the day schools, on the Bell system. Dr. Garrow was also a benefactor to these schools.

Nearby, at *South Mimms,* twenty children were educated at a school founded and endowed by the Byngs of Wrotham Park. There was also a Sunday school of seventy, and at both the Bell system had been adopted.

On Chiswick Mall William Makepeace Thackeray was at Dr. Turner's school in preparation for Charterhouse, and he used the school and its situation on which to build his famous Academy of Miss Pinkerton, which figures in *Vanity Fair.*

The Rev. Stephen Freeman had a school at Enfield, where Babbage, the mathematician, and Marryat, the novelist, were educated; while Mr. Clarke's school, also at Enfield, had the honour of educating John Keats. Brentford provided education for his contemporary, Shelley, before he went on to Eton.

The Welsh Charity School for Girls at Acton was founded in 1714, and a new building was opened in 1857 by the Prince Consort.

Ealing, the queen of suburbs, as it still likes to be called, with its many open spaces and big houses and estates, was an excellent educational centre a century or more ago. It still can boast that there is no street without a tree, and the commons will always preserve its rural amenities. At Great Ealing School, the Old Rectory, Dr. Nicholas had as pupils John Henry Newman, Thackeray, Marryat, Frederick Thesiger (afterwards Lord Chelmsford), Professor Rawlinson, Hicks Pasha, Sir Robert Sele, Charles Knight (the London historian), W. S. Gilbert, Bishop Selwyn, Sir Henry Lawrence, and Lord Lawrence.

At Ealing House, once the home of Melmoth, the translator of Pliny's *Letters,* Bulwer Lytton was at school in 1817, when Dr. Wallington was headmaster. Lytton afterwards lived for some years at Copt Hall, Totteridge, where his grounds adjoined Mill Hill and were on the edge of Middlesex. The notorious Dr. Dodd had a school at Manor House, Ealing, for some years, and in West Ealing there was founded Princess Helena College for the orphan daughters of officers, clergymen, and civil servants.

At *Laleham,* Thomas Arnold, one of the famous group

that included Newman and Keble, was Vicar from 1819 to 1828, and took pupils here before going as headmaster at Rugby. His successes at Laleham prompted his old tutor to prophesy that if appointed to Rugby he would change English education in a generation. For some unexplained reason his house was pulled down in 1867, and the bricks were used by the Church authorities to build a national school. Some cedars still mark the site of his home and school.

At Spring Grove, between Isleworth and Osterley Park, there used to be the London International College, a very good example of the pioneer work of Richard Cobden, who wished in 1867 to provide education on a cosmopolitan basis. But it was a scheme far in advance of its time and proved a failure.

In 1890 the Borough Road Training College, founded in Southwark by John Lancaster and his friends of the British Schools, was transferred to Cobden's well-built college. The work carried on in this well-built place, 260 ft. long, with high-pitched roof and dormer windows, has been a great success in training elementary-school teachers.

At Southgate was the well-known preparatory school kept by the Walker family, several members of which played cricket with distinction for Middlesex.

In Stanmore we hear of Hill House School, to which Dr. Samuel Parr brought a number of Harrow boys when he was not appointed headmaster, and in Stanmore Park for nearly half a century there was a very flourishing preparatory school, which sent most of its boys on to Harrow. The school at Elstree, since the Axis War one of the Oliver Borthwick memorial institutions, was for many years another preparatory for Harrow.

A recent chronicler of Middlesex has included within the Middlesex boundary the new Merchant Taylors' School at Sandy Lodge. Topographical accuracy makes this claim untenable, though the school's postal address is Northwood, Middlesex, and a great number of the boys attending the school come from the county and some of the masters live in it. In the nineties of the last century and for some years later the school's playing-fields were at Willesden Green, before building development drove the boys to Bellingham in Kent.

High Street at Harrow-on-the-Hill

There is also this excuse, that, after the ditch was dug that was to serve as London's last or last-but-one line of defence, the M.T.S. Home Guard was transferred from Rickmansworth in Hertfordshire to Northwood in Middlesex.

A school with such a long and honoured history would be welcomed by any county historian, but the undisputed fact remains that the very attractive habitat to which the school moved in 1933 from Charterhouse Square is really in Hertfordshire.

Robert Lowe's historic remark that "We must educate our masters" was inspired by the Reform Bill of 1867-8, which gave a wide extension of the franchise. A direct consequence was W. E. Forster's Education Act of 1870, which established school boards all over the country entitled to build schools, where they were needed, at the public's cost.

The establishment of the County Council in 1888-9 did not give to Middlesex any power over education, but the Education Act of 1902 abolished the school boards and transferred many of their powers to the various county councils. Local authorities still had rights of control if their population justified such a plan, and schools were now designated "provided" and "non-provided" schools. The former were those under council control, the latter were in the main administered by religious denominations.

The County Council was given new and wide powers with regard to higher education, and in consequence first-rate secondary and technical schools began to be built.

The first Middlesex County Council secondary school was opened at Tottenham for boys and girls in 1901, and before the second World War the number of secondary schools provided or aided by the Middlesex County Council had risen to fifty-one, with a school attendance of over twenty-five thousand. In the same period thirteen art and technical schools had been built, with a total attendance of nearly forty thousand.

In Middlesex the County Council has been the education authority for higher education throughout the county, and for elementary education in just over half the local government districts into which Middlesex is divided. In each area there has been an education committee, appointed by the appropriate council, with representatives of religious bodies and with educational experts co-opted.

Although Middlesex is still to a considerable extent a "dormitory" area, there are now a number of industries established in various parts of the county which call for improved technical instruction. It has not been easy to keep pace with the rapid growth of housing, but well-equipped technical colleges are either in action or nearing completion in Acton, Chiswick, Ealing, Enfield, Greenford, Harrow, Hendon, Kingsbury, Southgate, Southall, Staines, Tottenham, Twickenham, Uxbridge, Wembley, and Willesden. The standards of accommodation and equipment in the schools of Middlesex naturally vary considerably, but the recent "provided" schools and some of the "non-provided" ones are built and equipped up to the most modern requirements.

Such schools as Christ's College, Finchley; Hendon County School; Hendon Technical College; The Green School, Isleworth; Spring Grove House, Isleworth; Copthall Girls' School, Mill Hill; Pinner County School; Stanburn School, Little Stanmore; Shepperton School; Lady Margaret School, Southall; Tottenham Polytechnic; Twickenham Technical Institute; Evelyn's School, Yiewsley—these are all buildings of which anyone might be proud. They all date before the famous Butler Education Act of 1944, which has done what neither the Fisher, Hadow, or Spens Acts were allowed to accomplish, and has actually raised the school-leaving age to fifteen.

The Butler Act has also given supreme control over education inside each county, wherever provided by the rates, to the county council, save in the case of county boroughs. With large boroughs or urban districts considerable powers are delegated to the education committees, but financial control is vested in the county council. These excepted districts in Middlesex include : Acton, Brentford and Chiswick, Ealing, Edmonton, Enfield, Finchley, Harrow, Hayes and Harlington, Hendon, Heston and Isleworth, Hornsey, Southgate, Tottenham, Twickenham, Wembley, Willesden. The non-excepted districts comprise North-west Middlesex (including Ruislip, Northwood, Uxbridge, West Drayton, and Yiewsley), South-west Middlesex (including Staines, Feltham, and Sunbury), Southall, and Wood Green.

These county committees of divisional executives have sub-committees to tackle the varied activities for education in the area. A typical committee will have sub-committees dealing with primary schools, secondary schools, works and buildings, child welfare, finance, and general purposes, and, in the case of an area where there is still some room for expansion, a development sub-committee. Some executives appoint special sub-committees to deal with appointments, meals, physical training, lettings, safety first, and other kindred topics.

291

CHAPTER XX

AVIATION IN MIDDLESEX

HENDON AERODROME

HENDON has become world-famous through its aerodrome, and through the many successful civilian flights that have been made from there, the annual displays and contests that have taken place there, and the extraordinarily vital missions made from Hendon Aerodrome during the war by V.I.P.s. Today the size of planes and speed of landing and other kindred developments have made it into what has been called a taxicab rank.

The story of the aeroplane really begins in 1903 at Killdevil Hill, near Kittyhawk in North Carolina, where Wilbur and Orville Wright, employing a plane constructed by M. Chanute and driven by a 16-h.p. motor, succeeded on December 17 in flying 260 metres. There were also the days of Count Zeppelin's experiments on Lake Constance. In Jules Verne's well-known story, *The Clipper of the Clouds,* he predicts with remarkable accuracy the future in the air, when a plane supported by propellers proves a complete match for a dirigible balloon. Hiram Maxim was quoted in an article in the *Observer* in 1909 as saying : "I cannot see any future for the dirigible, which from its very nature will always be powerless against the wind. The dirigible, like the spherical balloon, can do little more than drift with the wind." History has proved the remarkable accuracy of these prophecies.

In November, 1906, the *Daily Mail,* which three years before had announced a three-mile flight by the Wright Brothers at Kittyhawk, offered a prize of £10,000 for a flight in one day from London to Manchester. The offer was not taken seriously, though it was prompted by the recent success of Santos Dumont in his "box-kite." A rival newspaper jocularly offered ten million for a round flight of five miles. For several years the *Daily Mail* challenge remained unanswered, but on July 25, 1909, Louis Bleriot won a

292

smaller prize which the paper offered of £1,000 for a cross-Channel flight. The paper hailed this striking event as one "which stuns the imagination by its far-reaching possibilities, and marks the dawn of a new age for man." H. G. Wells wrote a historic summary of some of its implications, which he himself had prophesied years before.

Hendon, like other early aerodromes, had an atmosphere of its own, being chiefly associated with experimental flights and with the development of flying sport. Hendon figured in the next great advance when the *Daily Mail* prize for the flight from London to Manchester was won. Claude Grahame-White was one of Bleriot's first pupils, and he made two attempts from Hendon, one on April 21, 1910, which failed through a small mishap after he had covered 113 miles. It was a dramatic moment when, at 5.15 a.m., H. Perrin, the Aero Club official, astride one of the girders of the gasholder at Kensal Rise, with a 160-foot drop below him, dipped his flag to acknowledge Grahame-White's start. He was cheered by crowds all the way along, the garrison turning out at Weedon, and a crowd collecting at Rugby, which he reached at 7.20 a.m. After an hour's rest he resumed his flight, but the breaking of a small screw brought his flight to an end. His second attempt was six days later, when he made a tremendous effort in the dark to overtake his French rival, the small and vivacious Louis Paulhan. I well remember getting up very early in the morning on both those occasions in the hope of seeing one or other of those pioneers from the splendid vantage-ground of the Schoolhouse at Mill Hill. On Wednesday, April 27, Paulhan arrived at Hendon with his assistant and began assembling his plane in a field between the Midland Railway and the Edgware Road. Grahame-White was back at Wormwood Scrubs seeing to repairs on his plane, and big crowds assembled at both places to watch the rival aeronauts.

The Englishman's plane was finished the sooner, but the wind was too violent and gusty to start. So Harry Farman, who had first flown a Voisin biplane in October, 1907, went across to Hendon to see Paulhan, who took off at 5.20 p.m. This news did not reach Grahame-White till just before six o'clock, and he was off at once, flying with great skill and reaching Roade before nightfall. Hearing that Paulhan was sixty miles ahead, he determined to start in the dark in a desperate but unsuccessful effort to overtake his rival. Grahame-White won great renown by his daring night flight, and when he was obliged to descend at Grendon and there heard of his rival's success he called for three cheers for Paulhan, "the finest aviator the world has ever seen, compared with whom I am only a novice."

For his successful flight from the embryo aerodrome at Hendon to Manchester Paulhan was entertained at a lunch at the Savoy by Lord Northcliffe and presented with £10,000 in a golden casket. Grahame-White fully earned a 100-guinea cup in recognition of his splendid effort. This dramatic flight had covered the 183 miles in 242 minutes, including a few hours' delay at Lichfield. The issue of the *Mail* on April 29, 1910, made this comment :

"What new horizons open before us, and what dangers ! Man, the all-conquering, who shall overcome all things, save only death, has achieved his greatest triumph. . . . For ourselves, we believe that our purpose in offering this prize has now been attained. We trust that our countrymen will recognise the lesson of this portent."

In spite of this severe setback, Grahame-White refused to be discouraged, and, after giving exhibitions at seven aeronautical meetings in this country and later winning the Gordon-Bennett Cup in America, he returned to England at the end of 1910 and inaugurated a flying school at Hendon. His name will always be associated with Hendon, and the opportunities for training were of up-to-date character, ahead in some ways of those of the Royal Aero Club. G. C. Turner, in *The Old Flying Days,* speaks of the courage, almost to foolhardiness, of early fliers. There were "machines which today would be refused a certificate. They were unstable, uncontrollable and structurally unsound; but the risk was not realised." There were many machines which the crack fliers of today would simply refuse to go up in, and if they went up would find extremely difficult to manage. A typical sentence from reports of those days runs : "Ofttime the aeroplane was estimated to be flying at a height of 25 feet."

In his introduction Turner recalls the names of some of

the early pioneers : Geoffrey de Havilland, Frederick Handley-Page, Colonel Moore-Brabazon, A. V. Roe, T. O. M. Sopwith, and the rest.

Hendon Aerodrome thus dates from Paulhan's successful flight to Manchester. Directly afterwards Richard Gates started clearing away hedges and trees and draining the ground. Although married, with a family, Gates learned to fly, piloted a Farman 80-h.p. Gnome from Paris to Boulogne with one passenger, and became the father of the "ragtime flying" so popular at the Hendon R.A.F. Pageants. This marvellous organiser and shrewd judge of public taste was appointed a director of Grahame-White's company and general manager of the aerodrome at Hendon, with which he was associated until the outbreak of the first World War, when he was killed in a night-flying accident. Two Black-burns, Robert and Harold, ran a flying school there, and Horatio Barber, whose Valkyrie machine combined the good features of both biplane and monoplane, started an aero-nautical syndicate and trained a number of pupils who later became famous. Although at Hendon Aerodrome there were held weekly meetings which helped to popularise air travel, the Government lagged far behind in its interest in this vital progress. The Parliamentary Aerial Defence Committee put in useful work, but it was left for amateurs to show to the authorities the rapidly increasing possibilities of the flying machine.

In 1911, in a wind of nearly gale force, and before a crowd of 16,000 people, Grahame-White gave exhibitions in his Farman biplane and his 70-h.p. Newport, while M. Gustav Hamel showed superb control of his Bleriot monoplane; and on Easter Monday, a year later, a cross-country handicap took place from Hendon to St. Albans and back, a distance of twenty-two miles. That summer there was even a ladies' race at Hendon. Mrs. Hewlett was the first Englishwoman to take out her aviation certificate, in November, 1911, and a day or two later Mrs. de Beavoir Stocks added her name as the second.

Another early flying contest was the European Circuit in June-July of 1911, which was designed to go from Paris to Liége, Utrecht, Brussels, Roubaix, Calais, Dover, Hendon,

Dover, Calais, Paris. The distance was 1,025 miles, and sixty aviators gave in their names, of whom thirty-eight started and nine completed within the scheduled time. Since M. Bleriot first flew the Channel in 1909 only six others had crossed the Straits. Now eleven succeeded in doing the crossing and all arrived within an hour of one another. The first official aerial postal service in Europe began at Hendon on Saturday, September 9, 1911, when letters were despatched from the aerodrome to Windsor. Gustav Hamel carried the mails on the first day, covering the twenty-one miles to a spot near the Royal Mausoleum at Frogmore in ten minutes.

Harry Hawker was an early test pilot from Australia who earned well-deserved popularity at Hendon, where, in October, 1912, he won the altitude contest (7,400 feet) in a Sopwith, a record which he exceeded the following month by climbing to 12,900 feet. Hendon is associated with the death at sea of Gustav Hamel, probably on May 23, 1914. He was flying a new Morane-Saulnier monoplane with a 160-h.p. Gnomeplane, and he flew on the first stage early in the morning towards Hendon, with the intention of taking part in the Aerial Derby from Villa Comblay to Le Croton, 108 miles in fifty minutes. He landed on the sand at the estuary of the Somme, at the Caudron aeroplane works. He flew another short stage to Hardelot, near Boulogne, and from there he sent a telegram to Hendon saying that he would arrive by air. He resumed his journey at 12.15 p.m., and was seen flying over Boulogne and probably, by a steamer, over the mid-Channel. He had only enough fuel and oil for two hours' flying, but this was quite adequate to get him to Hendon. There was some mist in the Channel, but Hamel had fourteen crossings to his credit, and he was an extremely competent judge of the risks involved. He was not seen again, and, though warships patrolled the Channel and aeroplanes of the R.N.A.S. took great and almost fatal risks over rough seas, it was found necessary to accept the word of some fishermen that his body had been seen in the water. Hamel was only twenty-five years of age, having learned to fly quite soon after leaving Westminster School and Cambridge. Two of his early successes were a race from Hendon to Brooklands in 1910 and the first aerial post from Hendon to Windsor in 1911.

When Adolphe Pegoud, along with Louis Bleriot, did the looping the loop at Brooklands it was soon taken up by English fliers, and Gustav Hamel and Major J. C. Turner did three loops at the end of a Hendon flying meeting in April, 1914, at Hendon. An interesting picture illustrates the landing on the Thames of Sir Alan Cobham in his D.H.50, manufactured at Stag Lane, Edgware, on October 1, 1926, after his flight to and from Australia. His plane was fitted with Jaguar engine and short all-metal floats instead of wheels, and it made the 27,000-mile flight with one mechanic.

With the threat of war hanging over the whole country, the flying meeting held at Hendon on August Bank Holiday, 1914, was not well attended. Some French pilots had already been recalled, and the programme was carried out in a very half-hearted manner. Major G. C. Turner, who was present, recalls how rumours were bandied about during the meeting; the Government, it was said, had commandeered all the petrol, and all London omnibuses were leaving for France. M. Salmet came in his Bleriot machine, only to announce a prohibition of his flight by the Home Office; and when M. Pierre Verrier landed from his plane he was almost arrested by a police inspector. That same evening it became clear that war was imminent, and all the best-known fliers, whose prowess had built up the reputation of Hendon as an aerodrome, were on active service.

It is interesting to note the views of experts in 1911 and see what progress has been made in thirty-five years, and how far their prophecies have been fulfilled. G. Holt Thomas, an international authority, who deplored apathy in England, tried to convince our Government of the vast importance of aviation to us even with a sea barrier, and Sir A. Verdon Roe expected that before twenty years had passed we should be crossing the Atlantic in eighteen hours. The problem of getting the powers that be to adopt new ideas is shown in all its difficulties by the reply given in March, 1907, by Lord Tweedmouth, then First Lord of the Admiralty, to the Wright Brothers, who had ventured to approach him on the subject of aeroplanes :

"I have consulted my expert advisers with regard to your suggestion as to the employment of aeroplanes, and I regret to have to tell you, after the careful consideration of my Board, that the Admiralty, whilst thanking you for so kindly bringing the proposals to their notice, are of opinion that they would not be of any practical use to the Naval Services."

When H. G. Wells in 1909 was asked at a moment's notice to write his impressions of the cross-Channel flight of Bleriot, he viewed it first and foremost as a warning to Britain that she could no longer rely on the fleet alone for protection against invasion. And yet Wells himself never cared to fly until three years later when Claude Grahame-White took him up into the air for the first time.

A company that has done yeoman service for aviation is the Fairey organisation, with more than thirty years of splendid production behind it. Charles Richard Fairey, who even while at Merchant Taylors' School showed skill in building model aeroplanes, and who in 1913 became chief engineer to Short's at Rochester, formed in 1915 the Fairey Aviation Company at Hayes in Middlesex and produced important planes for the Government. Soon after the first World War the Fairey Aviation Company produced the IIID and IIIF, and, in the former, two R.A.F. pilots, Goble and McIntyre, won the Britannia Trophy in 1924 for flying round Australia in ninety flying hours.

Other early types were the Flycatcher, for use at sea; the Fox, famous in R.A.F. annual displays; and the Portal, an early monoplane, which made the first non-stop flight to Karachi in April, 1929. A Fleet Spotter reconnaissance plane was first flown in 1926 and was still in production at Hayes a decade later. The Gordon did valuable work as a day bomber, or for reconnaissance and photography, from 1932 to 1936, when it was succeeded by the Fairey Battle, which took part in many gallant but costly operations in France in 1940. The Seal proved almost unsuitable, while the Swordfish, affectionately known as "Stringbags," was the most famous of all aircraft in service with the Fleet Air Arm. This plane inflicted far heavier losses than it sustained, especially in the moonlight raid on the Italian fleet in Taranto, in the shadowing and destruction of the *Bismarck,* and in the naval battle of Cape Matapan. A Swordfish pilot, making an emergency landing on the island of Lampedusa, was surprised to receive the surrender of the much-tried garrison.

In the story of *Malta, G.C.,* the three earliest planes were Gladiators, but later on they were joined by some Swordfish that helped to protect the island till the Luftwaffe left Sicily for the Russian front. The Swordfish was succeeded by the Albacore, which gave way in turn to the Barracuda, an effective monoplane. In the battle of the River Plate a Seafox plotted for the *Ajax* and *Achilles* and was able to give them the news that the *Graf Spee* had blown itself up.

THE STORY OF HANDLEY-PAGE

The story of Handley-Page, Ltd., began in Kent and Essex, and today extends into Hertfordshire, but most of its history has been recorded in Middlesex. In 1906 Frederick Handley-Page was an electrical engineer of twenty, and his pioneer days date from a time when "the aeroplane was still running neck-and-neck with the helicopter and the ornithopter for general acceptance as the flying machine of the future." Three years later the firm was registered at Somerset House, with office at Woolwich and with works at Barking and a kind of aerodrome at Dagenham or Fairlop. The Blue Bird was built, and two years later came the Yellow Peril or Antiseptic, so called from its non-rusting chrome paint. There are pictures of this plane standing on the aerodrome at Hendon, with its 50-h.p. Gnome engine and swept-back wings. In 1912 a monoplane was built for the Salisbury Plain competition, and Wilfred Park and A. A. Hardwick started to fly it to Farnborough. Unfortunately, it crashed at Wembley and these two very promising aeronauts were killed. It was in this year that the firm moved their headquarters from Barking to 110, Cricklewood Lane.

The first Handley-Page machine built at Cricklewood was a biplane launched in 1913, bought by Rowland Ding and flown by him regularly at Hendon week-end meetings. Several large planes were now planned, but the coming of the first World War dictated the type of machine that Handley-Page was to produce, and they scored a distinct success with the

0/100, a night bomber with two Rolls-Royce Eagle engines, of which forty were built for the R.N.A.S. From it developed the 0/400 night bomber, one of the most famous machines of the war, and one which brought to Handley-Page a well-deserved reputation. Good work was done on the Western front, but still better against the retreating Turks in Palestine and in a bombing attack on Constantinople. The first World War was timed to last a year more than it did, and for the big bombing attack planned for Berlin Handley-Page designed and produced the V/1500, weighing 10 tons with 2 tons of bombs and shockingly slow. One of these planes served in a small frontier skirmish against Afghanistan in 1919.

A very big step in aeroplane design was the introduction of the Handley-Page slot, which was taken up by pioneers in the Air Ministry and the Ministry of Supply and resulted in the saving of very many lives. A distinguished German designer, Dr. Kackman, co-operated with Handley-Page, and slots combined with flaps helped to make the success of the Handley-Page Hampden and the Westland Lysander.

Hounslow Heath played an important part in the opening of regular air services between London and the Continent after the close of the first World War. Both Handley-Page and Instone Air Lines worked from Hounslow in 1919, and though in the long run they both closed down, they were in at the beginning and so make Middlesex contemporary with Surrey as the birthplace of British commercial air transport. An early plane produced by Handley-Page at Cricklewood was the W. 8, a passenger-carrying aircraft used for the London-Continent service. In three years, from 1923-26, Handley-Page produced, besides the "S" type (H.P. 21), a single-seater slotted fleet fighter with Bentley rotary engine, and the Hyderabad and Hinaidi, which were heavy service bomber aircraft. Both were military adaptations of the W. 8 and were used as standard night bombers about the year 1930.

The *Handley-Page Bulletin* of May, 1929 (Vol. 1, No. 7), printed in three languages, was able to announce that the British Government had agreed to pay £100,000 in respect of the British slotted wing patents. Evidence in progress is given in the *Bulletin* for May, 1930, with a picture entitled

"Our Pastures New," showing a horse and cart surrounded by sheep and lambs in the fields, which were soon to lose most of their hedges and forest trees to become the Radlett Aerodrome. An all-metal Handley-Page Clive is seen flying overhead. A year or so later, in June, 1932, the *Bulletin* was proud to announce that 200 aeroplanes would appear at the R.A.F. Display at Hendon on June 25, and that all the multi-seater aircraft would be fitted with the Handley-Page wing-slots as standardised in the R.A.F. By November forty-three countries were using the wing-slots. In 1930 Handley-Page Hannibal and Heracles first flew, and they quickly established a big reputation for efficiency and for popularity with the travelling public. They were the largest biplane air liners of Imperial Airways and they carried on until the outbreak of the second World War and for a few months longer. In nine years the Hannibal class with four Bristol Jupiter engines flew many millions of miles without a single casualty.

They had flown from Cricklewood to Turkey, Cairo, Bagdad, India, and Kabul. June, 1937, saw the first public appearance of the Handley-Page Harrow at Hendon, and in the next year came a new plane, prophetically named after "John Hampden, defender of civil liberties," and produced at Cricklewood and also in Canada. The "Flying Suitcase" attacked Heligoland in September, 1939, and dropped leaflets over Germany in 1940. To start with Hampdens ranked as heavy bombers and took part in raids on Western Germany, on German warships near the Skagerack, and in attacks on German advances in Northern France. They were responsible for the first attack on the German mainland at München-Gladbach and for big assaults on marshalling yards from the Rhineland to the Somme. A Hampden wireless operator-air gunner won the V.C. for beating out devastating flames in his cockpit over Antwerp. More successes followed in attacks on the Dortmund-Ems Canal.

The next stage in the long line of heavy bombers designed by G. R. Volkert was the Halifax, first flown in October, 1939, and reported in action over Bremen, Berlin, Cologne, Essen, Lubeck, Rostock, and Turin. It took a vigorous part in fighting in the Libyan Desert, and with its speed of 254 miles per hour it escorted British and American convoys to

North Africa. The Halifax made its presence felt on many
fronts, and the stand in July, 1942, at El Alamein was made
possible by heavy bombers, Liberators supplemented by
Halifaxes. The four-engined planes could control a wider
field, and Benghazi could be reached and effectively bombed
by Liberators in the daylight and by Halifaxes at night.
When the final battle at Alamein took place in October there
was complete co-operation between the various arms, and the
heavies from Palestine slammed and held fast the "distant
back door of the Axis" at Benghazi. And what was true of
the desert front was repeated in Italy, in France, and in
devastating bombing raids over Germany. The months of
planning and days of final effort produced an effect which, in
the words of Air-Marshal Sir Arthur Harris, caused the
Germans to look back to earlier attacks as "men lost in a
raging typhoon remember the gentle zephyrs of a past
summer." These 1,000-bomber attacks over Cologne were
shared by many a Halifax, and final victory was due in no
small measure to our final strength in the air. A study of war
books and personal reminiscences shows what a debt we owe
to Sir Frederick Handley-Page and the many thousands of
his fellow-workers, and it is pleasant to remember what a
large share of credit is due to activities in Middlesex.

THE STORY OF DE HAVILLAND'S

A real pioneer in aircraft manufacture was G. Holt
Thomas, who founded in 1911 the Aircraft Manufacturing
Company for building Farman aeroplanes at a factory on
the west side of the Edgware Road, roughly in Cricklewood.
He took an important step when early in 1914 he persuaded
Captain (now Sir) Geoffrey de Havilland to become the head
of his designing department.

Captain de Havilland had been flying ever since 1910,
having acquired his technical training in the Crystal Palace
School of Engineering and in his experience in the Wolseley
Company and other motor-car manufacturing firms. Many
highly successful aeroplanes were made by the Aircraft Manufacturing Company all through the first World War, and in
1919 Holt Thomas conceived the idea of giving scholarships

to boys in North Middlesex of engineering promise to learn their aeronautical manufacturing in his factory. He asked me to do my best to make his generous scheme work, but with the end of the war everyone seemed to think that aeroplanes were not very important, and I could not persuade the various schools which I approached to take the matter up. Some time after the war the Aircraft Manufacturing Company was closed and the De Havilland Aircraft Company was established, first at Stag Lane, Edgware, and then at Hatfield.

Captain de Havilland fortunately realised the importance of sound training in aeroplane designing and kindred notions, and his technical school at Hatfield has more than justified his foresight and has brought into existence just that scheme for which Holt Thomas was so enthusiastic. The first De Havilland plane had been designed by Geoffrey de Havilland in 1908, with help from a young engineer named Frank Hearle. It took five months to draw the aero engine; the money was provided by an enterprising grandfather and, while the Iris Victor Company built the engine at Willesden, the "twin-screw pusher biplane of 36 feet span" was constructed in a shed off the Fulham Road, and all the seams of the fabric coverings were sewn there on a hand-turned Singer machine by the inventor's young wife. It was thus quite definitely a Middlesex plane, but it was tried out in Hampshire in December, 1909, and crashed. Using the same engine, they built at Fulham a stronger, simpler aeroplane, and in the summer of 1910 it flew.

When Holt Thomas in May, 1914, moved his factory from Merton in Surrey to a bus garage at the Hyde, Hendon, he engaged Geoffrey de Havilland as chief designer, and in his six years of effort, mostly war years, he produced the D.H. 1-4, the latter of which became world-famous. One-third of the total Allied air strength and all but 5 per cent. of American production were of De Havilland design, and the 12,000 U.S.A. planes as well as ours were kept in service until 1928. The slump after the first World War was serious, but De Havilland machines took British officials to the Paris Peace Conference and started the first air service between Hounslow and the Continent on August 25, 1919. The D.H. 4 won the first post-war Aerial Derby, and the D.H. 17 started as a passenger air liner; but the slump increased and the Birmingham Small Arms Company gave up their financial interests in Airco. Holt Thomas helped De Havilland with a generous loan, the B.S.A. allowed him to take away all the aircraft and engine designs, and so one of the romances of the air began in October, 1920, when the De Havilland Aircraft Company, Ltd., erected a few sheds on Stag Lane Aerodrome off the Edgware Road. Holt Thomas sold them a few lorry-loads of material, which absorbed half their capital, and they had only an order for two D.H. 188s for the Admiralty. However, nearly forty staff moved into Stag Lane, to be joined by others from Airco of Hendon, and fourteen of these were still serving the firm when it celebrated its twenty-fifth anniversary.

It was a change from the well-built offices of Airco to the simple sheds of Stag Lane. It was so cold that "ten minutes off for football" was a frequent device of Captain de Havilland to restore circulation. A gipsy woman in a nearby caravan provided the meals, and "everything was on a hand-to-mouth basis." Sir Sefton Brancker, who had been associated with Holt Thomas, had by 1923 become Director of Civil Aviation, and he used the De Havilland Flying School for training R.A.F. recruits. Alan Cobham organised the aeroplane hire-service, which carried newspaper photographers, rich folk touring Europe, and advertised Booth's gin in lights under the wings. To train the R.A.F. recruits the first Moth was designed, and in 1921 an apprentice named Bishop was enrolled as a designer, and he has been responsible for the Flamingo, Mosquito, Vampire, Hornet, and Dove.

Meanwhile the firm was planning a passenger plane for eight or ten, and after trial the D.H. 34 emerged. But it suddenly became essential to find £20,000 to purchase Stag Lane, and Alan S. Butler came on the scene, provided the money, and in 1924 became chairman of the company, a position still held in 1948. The D.H. 34 was a success both here and in Russia, and Alan Cobham won the Swedish prize for efficiency in a D.H. 50, dropping only one mark in a possible 1,000. He also made sensational flights to Rangoon, to Cape Town, and to Australia, and one machine won the King's Cup.

St. Andrew's Church, Kingsbury.
Moved stone by stone from Wells
Street, W.1

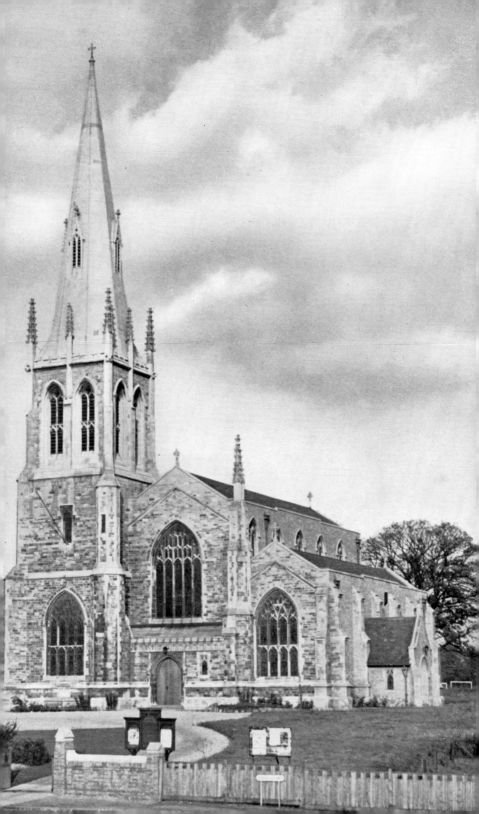

The refusal to take part in an Air Ministry competition in 1924 was a landmark in De Havilland history and led to the Moth, which was first flown on Sunday afternoon, February 22, 1925, with Major Halford's Cirrus engine. It revolutionised everything at Stag Lane. The factories there "hummed for the first time," and Moths poured out, yellow for the London club, red for Newcastle, blue for Lancashire, and green for the Midland club. In the same year Cobham flew to Zurich and back in a day, and in 1926 Hubert Broad won the King's Cup Race in a Moth. The factories at Stag Lane were enlarged; the Tiger Moth put up world records for light planes. Major Hereward de Havilland took a Moth by sea to Perth in Australia and flew it to Melbourne to start assembling other imported Moths. The De Havilland Company that was incorporated in Australia in March, 1927, less than seven years after the move into Stag Lane, was the beginning of a chain of overseas companies and a world-wide service that aviation had never known before. Moths were the basis of it all, and Canada was added in 1928, India in 1929, South Africa in 1930, and agents were appointed almost everywhere. In 1928 the idea that Holt Thomas had broached nine years previously was put into operation by Captain Geoffrey de Havilland, and the De Havilland Technical School, a notable pioneer, was formed to add theoretical training to practical apprenticeship.

Progress was tremendous, and in one year the pay-roll at Stag Lane went up from 400 to 1,500, and Moths won the King's Cup four years running. Amy Johnson flew one to Australia, and C. W. A. Scott and Jim Mollison established fresh records. Between the wars 1,800 Moths and 300 Puss Moths were produced at Stag Lane, but the new Tiger Moths came from the new aerodrome at Hatfield, with which the company went ahead in spite of the world trade slump of 1930. Careful husbanding of the company's resources made it possible to carry on, and the Moths became the most prolific aircraft family in the world. With Gipsy engines many trophies were won by various types of Moth, and in 1933 Captain de Havilland won the King's Cup, and in the next year the R.A.S. Gold Medal. Three more King's Cup victories, fresh designs for De Havilland Dominie (still flying

Wembley Stadium,
Olympic Games, 1948

today from Weston to Cardiff), Don, Albatross, Flamingo, and Comet, led up to still further triumphs.

The climax of De Havilland production was the Mosquito, which has justifiably won its place as the frontispiece to R. A. Saville-Sneath's *British Aircraft*. Its first brilliant raid was in September, 1942, when four Mosquitoes bombed the Gestapo headquarters at Oslo, just before Quisling was due to speak. In January, 1943, Mosquitoes staged the first daylight raids on Berlin, disorganising the anniversary broadcasts of Goering and Goebbels.

During the second World War it was obviously impossible for all the De Havilland accessories to be made either at Stag Lane or at Hatfield, and other factories, some of them in Middlesex, were mobilised for production. The number of employees on all De Havilland pay-rolls rose in seven years from 5,000 to 38,000, but tens of thousands of other concerns at Elstree, Colindale, Cricklewood, Welsh Harp, and Enfield all contributed their share. The war-time output is summarised as : 5,584 Mosquitoes, 3,744 Tiger Moths, 2,212 other aircraft (including Flamingos, Dominies, Hornets), 10,212 Gipsy engines, 140,046 propellers, 17,178 propeller blade forgings.

De Havillands have not entirely withdrawn from Middlesex, though the bulk of their post-war work is done at Hatfield; and Stonegrove and Stag Lane play their part today as they did during the second World War. Of engines 10,212 were produced during the war at the Engine Division at Stag Lane, and 23,210 propellers. 12,859 engines were repaired at Stag Lane, and in this group of factories on the west of Watling Street, comprising the original works and nine local dispersals, spread about in Kingsbury, Edgware, Colindale, and Mill Hill, work went on steadily for all the years of war, and in spite of hundreds of bombing "incidents" in the area around these busy hives of industry, not one of the factories suffered a direct hit. The official record of the growth of the De Havilland enterprise concludes with a determination to "exercise the assets of our hard schooling, our healthy growth, our stable direction, neglecting no lesson from our long experience as we face a horizon broad with opportunity and responsibility."

It will be remembered that two sons of Sir Geoffrey de Havilland gave their lives while acting as test pilots, one during the war and one soon after its conclusion. They had both done splendid service both in the peace years and during all the perils of the Axis war.

Other Middlesex firms which contributed to the struggle against the Luftwaffe include the General Aircraft Company, of London Air Park at Feltham, which made on their own the Cygnet, Owlet, Monospar, and Hotspur, and also built for other companies Spitfires and Oxfords during the second World War. Heston Aircraft Company, of Heston Airport, was financed by Lord Nuffield in an attempt to produce a plane faster than the Messerschmitt, while Tipsy Aircraft Company at Hanworth Air Park, Hafner Construction Company at Feltham, Airpin's at Longford, West Drayton, put in good work, and Napier's had a factory at Acton for producing aeroplane engines only.

An interesting comment on foreign notions of aircraft is given by Lord Templewood in his book *Ambassador on Special Mission*. He writes : "Only one Spaniard in authority seemed to appreciate what was happening in the air. This was the Infante Don Alfonso of Bourbon-Orleans, the holder of the Spanish pilot's licence, and now the Commander of the Air Force district of Andalusia. Year after year he came to the display at Hendon, and never ceased to follow in detail the training and technical developments of the Royal Air Force."

HEATHROW

Now that civil flying is recognised as a normal means of transport, it is essential to provide adequately for an area with as huge a population as that contained in Greater London. The road system which centres on London was developed very gradually over the centuries, whereas the railway system, now taken over by Government, came into existence quite quickly through a number of competitive companies. The problem of air transport can be considered *en bloc,* but the airport for London must be a good way from the centre. A business man during the early summer of 1947 seemed to have solved at least one problem when he landed by helicopter just outside his office in Fore Street, E.C.3.

The scheme for dealing with London's air transport involved the construction of a chief airport at Heathrow, with nine others which can be developed as occasion requires. Heathrow is twelve miles from Victoria, and Hounslow Station on the Tube is close to the aerodrome. One of the nine, Heston, is in Middlesex, the rest being in the other Home Counties. Heathrow is level ground with gravel subsoil and measures 3·72 miles by 3. It is agreed that a runway of three miles is essential, and land north of the Bath Road is ready for future development.

Heathrow, north-west from Hounslow Heath, was completely secluded until a dozen years ago. Writing in 1935, Geoffrey Maxwell describes the remote hamlets of Perry Oaks and Heathrow. "Turn down from the Bath Road by the Three Magpies, and you will come upon a road as rural as anywhere in England. It is not, perhaps, scenically wonderful, but for detachment from London, or any urban interests, it would be hard to find its equal; there is a calmness and serenity about it that is soothing in a mad rushing world." This *was* Heathrow, and Perry Oaks consisted of "a few scattered cottages, a delightful old farm, and some orchards and meadows. . . . Though certainly on the map, it is only just so, and there lies its charm." And now Perry Oaks is a sludge farm and Heathrow is London's airport.

Even as far back as 1937 it was clear that Heston, Hanworth, Northolt, and Hendon, all of them in Middlesex, would not be large enough, and a joint committee was set up under Mr. Willoughby Garner, which urged the adoption of Heathrow for its suitable size, the absence of smoke, and the good levels and accessibility. The Great West Road, two railways, the Piccadilly Tube, and other important features persuaded the Middlesex County Council and the Air Ministry to adopt the area as a standard all-weather commercial aerodrome only three years after Maxwell's comments on the rustic beauty of Heathrow.

The development of London Airport is threatening some historic villages and irreplaceable buildings, and the authorities are doing their best to preserve wherever possible. The land scheduled for the aerodrome is situated between main lines of the Great Western and Southern Railways; it adjoins the Staines and Great West Roads on the south; it engulfs part of the Bath Road to the north; it extends from Harlington, Sipson, and Harmondsworth to Hatton, the Bedfonts and Hanwell; while on east and west it is close to Hounslow Heath and the valley of the Colne. Harlington Church is a fine example of medieval Gothic, and Lord Nathan, then Minister of Civil Aviation, and the President of the London and Middlesex Archæological Society, promised to safeguard it.

The end of the war saw the establishment of commercial airlines from Heathrow and Northolt to almost every part of the world. It is true that some lines still use Croydon, and there are other stations farther away from London, such as Bassingbourn in Cambridgeshire, Hurn in Hampshire, and Poole in Dorset, but the bulk of the traffic is linked up with Middlesex. B.E.A. uses Northolt for journeys to Stockholm, Copenhagen, and Oslo; for Amsterdam and Brussels; for Paris, Bordeaux, and Marseilles; for Lisbon and Madrid; for Hamburg, Frankfort, Berlin, Vienna; for Prague and Rome; and for Athens, Ankara, Helsinki, and Istambul. A good deal of Swiss travel still takes off from Croydon, but Northolt is the starting-place for Geneva.

For world travel as opposed to European services the B.A.O.C. Speed Birds start from Heathrow for Cairo, Lydda, Beirut, in the Near and Middle East, but for India, Singapore, and the Far East, Poole is generally employed. K.L.M., the Royal Dutch airline, formerly used Croydon as well as Northolt and Heathrow, but from the autumn of 1947 they left Croydon for good. American Clippers used Heathrow, Air France uses Northolt, and few weeks pass without additional services provided by B.O.A.C. It has not been possible, for many reasons, to build up British Air Lines into a profitable concern in the early peace years, due partly to severe competition and also to essential neglect of passenger planes during the war. The year's loss for 1947 was somewhere in the neighbourhood of ten million pounds. However, the three British companies have built up a good reputation and in one year have flown over 250,000,000 passenger miles with regularity, good service, and safety. It will be seen that, in spite of London's spread, room has been found in Middlesex, both in war and peace, for aerodromes and aviation of a striking character. Hendon and Cricklewood, Stag Lane, Hayes and Northolt, and finally Heath Row, have all made a very important contribution to man's mastery of the air.

CHAPTER XXI

SPORT IN MIDDLESEX

HUNTING

I T becomes almost monotonous to have to apologise in every
chapter for the urbanisation of Middlesex, but the facts must
be faced, more especially when such sports as hunting have
to be chronicled. When Lysons collected material for his
Environs of London (1792) he could say with accuracy that
it was still largely an agricultural county. At the time of
Waterloo, Hadley, Enfield, Epping, and Hainault formed
one continuous stretch of turf or forest; Hounslow Heath
and Finchley Common were still unenclosed; there were nine
commons in the Harrow area, six in Uxbridge; and Ruislip,
Sunbury, Hanbury, and Wormwood Scrubs were still open.
But by 1837, when Grantley Berkeley's *Reminiscences of a
Huntsman* was published, cultivation had increased and
London was expanding quickly. By 1901 the population of
Middlesex had increased elevenfold during the century, and
urban districts occupied more than half the 150,000 acres
within the county. Not many years after the dawn of the
twentieth century hunting became obsolete throughout the
metropolitan county, and despite the preservation of the
Green Belt there is very little chance of its revival.

The earliest staghounds in the county were the Mayor's
hounds, a development of the ancient privileges confirmed in
Henry I's charter. In the *Liber Albus,* that compendium of
medieval London lore, John Courteney was common huntsman in the fifteenth century, and meets were held in Lincoln's
Inn Fields, St. James's, and Mayfair. It is vital to remember,
as evidence of the small size of London in Elizabethan days,
that "the Lord Mayor, Harpur, the Alderman and divers
worshipful persons, rid to the Conduit-Head before dinner.
They hunted the hare and killed her, and thence to dine at
the Conduit-Head. The Chamberlain gave them good cheer;
and after dinner they hunted the fox. There was a great cry
for a mile, then the hounds killed him at St. Giles; great

hallooing at his death and blowing of horns; and then the Lord Mayor and all his company rode through London to his place in Lombard Street."

Strype tells us of Londoners finding great pleasure in "riding on horseback and hunting with my Lord Mayor's hounds when the Common Hunt goes out." This was about 1723 when Mr. Cruttenden held the office; and Sir Francis Child and Alderman Humphrey Parsons were frequently hunting with the Lord Mayor. Unfortunately for the Lord Mayor's pack, they had a serious rival, the Royal Buckhounds, which about 1750 were very popular with "merchant princes of the City, the lawyers, the doctors, the clergy, and the rich though humble bagman, mounted on the now obsolete 'nag' on which he travelled, on business thoughts intent, throughout the land."

There is an interesting account of the Lord Mayor's hounds in the *Sporting Magazine* for 1795, and, in spite of Tom D'Urfey's ridicule in his *Pills to Purge Melancholy,* we read in 1822 that "the Cockney hunts are not to be laughed at and despised by clod-hopping squires who each thinks that he knows more about the thing than anyone else." But the development of London, and rival packs in Middlesex, tended to drive the Lord Mayor's hounds over the Essex border into Epping Forest.

A well-known pack of staghounds was formed in 1824, with kennels at Cranford, by the Hon. George Grantley Berkeley. Thirty couple of hounds were nearly all bred at Berkeley Castle in Gloucestershire, and so were the deer. All that survived of the latter were sent back to the castle for five months after the hunting season was over, and returned in excellent form for the next season. Grantley Berkeley claimed that they were superior to most used in the Royal Hunt.

After Cambridge and the Army, he was M.P. for West Gloucestershire for twenty years, and wrote in 1836 a romance called *Berkeley Castle.* This was savagely reviewed by Dr. Mcginn in *Fraser's Magazine,* owned by a well-known bookseller in Regent Street and edited by a writer of the same name. Berkeley assaulted and severely injured James Fraser, the publisher, and had to pay him heavy damages, and then had a duel with the real culprit, Dr. Mcginn. He it was who persuaded the House of Commons to allow women admission to the gallery in 1841.

Grantley Berkeley's staghounds hunted twice a week, mainly in the Harrow Weald area, with Guards officers and local landowners in attendance. One famous run, when the stag headed for Hounslow, Isleworth, Twickenham, and Brentford, was amusingly described by Lord Alvanley: "Devilish good run; but the asparagus beds went awfully heavy, and the grass all through was up to one's hocks; the only thing wanted was a landing net, for the deer got into the Thames, and Berkeley had not the means to get him ashore."

Grantley Berkeley, in his *Reminiscences,* tells of one stag that was hunted into Lady Mary Hussey's drawing-room at Hillingdon and of another that took refuge in a house in Montague Street, Russell Square, pursued by two hounds. Berkeley asked permission to "kill" in the front hall, and the indignant father came to the rescue of his two daughters and threatened to send for the beadle. A third stag took refuge in the kitchen of a private house and, in reply to Grantley Berkeley's apologies, the irate owner complained : "Your stag, sir, not content with walking through every office, has been here, sir, in my drawing-room, whence he proceeded upstairs to the nursery and, damn me, sir, he's now in my wife's boudoir."

The hunt went on from 1824 to 1836, with increasing support, but through diminishing country and with constant opposition from landowners and farmers. Hay suffered severely from the hunt, many enclosures took place, heath and common vanished; farmers refused to be mollified by offers of a dinner at Uxbridge; coursing was promised to the irate farmers, venison and game were distributed without effect, and Grantley complained that "babies' cries were heard on sites that in my remembrance were only waked by the prettier whistle of the plover."

A farmer called Barker brought an action against Berkeley, in which Scarlett succeeded in opposition to Brougham, and Berkeley had to pay £100. Just about the same time came the offer of the mastership of the Oakley Hunt, and so Grantley Berkeley's Middlesex Hunt came to an end. An earlier

Berkeley is believed to have kept thirty huntsmen in tawny coats and his pack of foxhounds near Charing Cross, then sufficiently rural for the purpose. The fifth Lord Berkeley revived the hunt in Middlesex and adopted the same orange-yellow kit. The country covered by Lord Berkeley far exceeded the limits of Middlesex, and in Nimrod's *Hunting Times* it was said to exceed eighty miles, from Scratch Wood to Cirencester. The kennels were at Stanmore in Middlesex, and also at Nettlebed, near Henley, and at Gerrard's Cross. When Berkeley died in 1810, Mr. Harvey Combe succeeded as Master and gave the hunt the name of the Old Berkeley. He and Mr. Marjoribanks made up any deficiency in the accounts, and Nimrod reports his hounds as "very steady . . . very true to their line, and with a scent pretty sure of their fox."

The pack was sold at Hyde Park Corner in 1842 and fetched the record price of 654 guineas for 127 hounds.

In spite of the sale, however, the Old Berkeley went on, and Brooksby, in his *Hunting Counties of England*, tells us that it became necessary not to advertise the meets "in order to avoid the pressure of a swarm of nondescripts, who, starting from every suburb of London, were glad to make a meet of foxhounds their excuse for a holiday on hackney or in wagonette, overwhelming the whole procedure by their presence, and irritating farmers and landowners, to the great injury of the hunt."

There was still "a small stretch of as good grass as is to be ridden over in England" near Harrow, but bricks and mortar and the spread of London made things impossible in most of Middlesex. And so, well before the close of the nineteenth century, the Old Berkeley was divided into Old Berkeley East, with kennels at Chorley Wood, Herts, and Old Berkeley West, at High Wycombe, Bucks.

There was nearly a fifty-year gap before staghounds got going again in Middlesex. In 1885 Sir Alfred Somerset started a pack of staghounds with kennels at Enfield Court to hunt in the Enfield country and to bear the historic name of the Enfield Chase Staghounds. As the area over which they hunted had been used for the same purpose in Elizabeth's reign, the dress adopted was Elizabethan—a red coat with blue lapels and gold buttons, yellow vest and cap. Colonel Sir Alfred Somerset continued as Master until 1899, when James Hills Hartridge, of Holmwood, Hendon, succeeded him and removed the kennels to Barnet. While J. H. Hartridge was Master of the hunt his sons were boys at Mill Hill School, and the Enfield Chase meet took place one day in Mill Hill village, between the Schoolhouse and the old King's Head Inn. When Mr. Hartridge retired in 1908 the pack was moved by the new Master, Mr. W. Walker, to High Canons, near Shenley, just in Hertfordshire. In 1910 Mr. D. D. Bulger kennelled the hounds at Pursley, and, although for a few years more that part of Middlesex round Potters Bar and Enfield Chase was hunted, the double move into Hertfordshire made the staghounds no longer a Middlesex proposition, and since that date the only connection with Middlesex is the name of the hunt.

Houses on the south side of Barnet Lane, especially those by Deacon's Hill and Woodcock Hill, have the great advantage of backing on to Scratch Wood, which gives a sense of completely rural surroundings. It has one slight disadvantage for those of us who keep chickens, and even if the literal hen-roosts are not invaded by human robbers there is always the danger from the foxes that live and breed in the more secluded parts of the wood. So tiresome did their depredations become soon after the end of the second World War that the Old Berkeley brought their hounds once more to Scratch Wood and effectively checked the damage at least for the time being. A check on the human marauders is not quite so simple. It is rather amusing to glance back six centuries and to find that in 1321, the year of Hendon's "Black Survey," geese and capons were being carried off by foxes from Hendon Woods. Churchwardens in Elizabethan Hendon were charged with the task of destroying vermin, and in 1671 a reward of half a crown was offered for killing a bitch fox. By 1732 the price was unchanged, but a he fox fetched 3s. 4d.

FISHING

Angling in Middlesex has a long history behind it, and today much of the available water is still being used by

315

enthusiastic fishermen. In Domesday Book eleven Middlesex manors are returned as leasing fisheries, and various religious bodies had special privileges on the Thames. A deed of Richard I at the end of the twelfth century granted the fishing in the Thames from Staines as far as the mouth of the river to the City Corporation to hold "for the common weal of the City of London, and of all his realm." At Staines there is the famous London Stone, at the exact spot where Middlesex, Surrey, and Buckinghamshire join, with the inscription "God preserve ye City of London." It marks the limit of the authority of London over the river, and it is also the boundary between the Upper and Lower Thames. The date is 1280, but the City's jurisdiction is far older than that.

As an instance of special privileges, no one was allowed by a charter of 1225 to fish before the weir of the Canons of St. Mary Merton in Brainford, though the King's bailiff claimed the right to net once a year on all private fisheries, and he exercised that right as late as 1820. Magna Carta included an order that all weirs were to be put down on the Thames, and from time to time strict rules were issued as to the use of nets. The City of London's jurisdiction over fisheries as far as London Stone at Staines was later invested in the Thames Conservancy Board. The present laws apply to the Thames and the Isis and "all creeks, inlets and bends between Teddington in the County of Middlesex, and Cantlet Creek in the County of Kent." Regulations for the protection of fish apply to six places on the Middlesex side of the Thames : Twickenham, Hampton, Sunbury, Shepperton, Penton Hook, and Staines.

As far back as 1848 T. C. Hoffland was complaining that salmon had been driven from the river by the gasworks and steam navigation, though specially fine specimens had formerly been taken at Isleworth and Mortlake and Twickenham. He still could report trout, pike, jack, perch, roach, dace, gudgeon, and others, and he specially mentions Brentford, Isleworth, Twickenham, Teddington, Hampton, Sunbury, Shepperton, Laleham, and Staines as profitable spots for anglers. The Thames Angling Preservation Society, formed more than a hundred years ago, has been doing a fine thing in protecting fish from poaching and in restocking the river, thus providing twenty miles of free water with perhaps the finest coarse fishing in England.

The Lea in Hoffland's time above Limehouse lay through "a beautiful pastoral country adorned with villages, through parks and meadows, containing countless herds of cattle and flocks of sheep." In 1907 the *Field* praised the Lea for its fishing possibilities, and there are still many followers of Izaac Walton who take their sport along its banks. The Colne and Brent originally were fishing rivers like the Thames, and the Colne still today has some pretence to afford sport for the keen angler, but drainage has made fishing difficult in some areas, and this process seemed at one time likely to increase rather than diminish.

The Thames Conservancy has control of six locks on the Middlesex side : Teddington, Molesey, Sunbury, Chertsey, Penton Hook, and Bell Weir, the last named being west of Staines and technically outside Middlesex.

The Thames Angling Preservation Society was founded in 1838, nearly twenty years before the establishment of the Thames Conservancy Board in 1857, celebrating its centenary just before the Axis war, and the two have worked in close harmony. The improvements in the navigation channel of the Thames diminished cover for spawning fish, and so restocking has been absolutely essential in the interests of anglers. The fish are usually turned into the Thames on the Middlesex side at Staines, Laleham, Hampton, Sunbury, Penton Hook, Twickenham, Shepperton, and Halliford, and the number each year varies very considerably. For instance, in 1921 and 1922 over 325,000 were turned in each year, in 1924 only 9,000. The total for 1929 was 96,000, for 1930 only 6,000. The varieties of fish include roach, dace, perch, chub, bream, gudgeon, jack, breach-roach hybrid, and the size varies from $\frac{1}{2}$ lb. to as much as 8 lb. Heavy frosts prevent nettings during some winters, and no doubt the amazing snow and ice of 1946-7 presented many and perhaps insuperable problems.

In the twenty years before the second World War about two and a quarter million fish were turned into the Thames between Staines and the Boundary Stone at Teddington, which marks the line between the Thames Conservancy and the Port of London Authority. The Angling Society is justly proud of its 112 years of service, and it enjoys the loyal help of an efficient committee and officers; it has twenty-six river keepers, whose business it is to "police" the twenty-one miles of river, which is free for fishers near the Metropolis at a time when nearly every bit of angling in the country is bought up by individuals or clubs. The Society asks all who use the river to be most considerate in preserving all its amenities from destruction and disfigurement.

The Thames Conservancy and the Port of London Authority do their utmost "to maintain London's great waterway as a pure river and a powerful lung," and the Angling Society is also helped by the Pure Rivers Society, whose object it is "to protect our inland estuary and in-shore waters from pollution." It is satisfactory to know that the Mogden Sewage Scheme has helped the fishing round Isleworth very considerably, and splendid catches have recently been recorded near there.

In a recent issue of the *Countrygoer* (Far Afield) there was an important comment on what were legitimately called "stinking rivers." Eight principal rivers were classed in this category, in which fish cannot live, still less spawn. The loss to amenities, health, and food supplies is of course heavy, but it is important to note that the Thames was not in the list of rivers thus stigmatised. A short broadcast on the same day on which the magazine appeared dealt with the problem of pollution of rivers, which by reducing oxygen often makes fish life impossible. The 1876 prohibition of pollution has had only a limited success. Poisonous stuff washed up and down has made the tidal Thames impossible for salmon and sea trout. But the Thames higher up is under the Thames Conservancy, which is able to co-ordinate powers and make it possible for good coarse fish to be caught above Teddington Weir. The success which close co-operation has produced on the Thames is to be tried elsewhere by dividing the country into a small number of catchment areas with adequate powers to stop this harmful and unnecessary pollution.

Figures for war years and post-war years are not yet available, but those for 1938 are full of importance. From Isleworth to Teddington 3,000 fish were turned in; Teddington to Sunbury, 45,000; Sunbury to Shepperton, 61,000;

Shepperton to Penton Hook, 12,000; and only about 250 up to Bell Weir—a total of about 121,000. The Society justly claims that it is doing an invaluable piece of work for all anglers in the London and Middlesex area, belonging to over 300 clubs, and needs all the financial support which these clubs can give it. There are important Thames fishery bylaws and regulations, and these and other useful hints for beginners are published by the Society, and advice is given of a most helpful character, especially with regard to the keeping of an angler's diary and the identification of fish. The Society's Blue Book contains a wealth of information, but it may be some time before its annual publication can be resumed.

For the River Colne, on Middlesex's western boundary, there is the City of London Piscatorial Society, which has fishery rights over twenty-seven miles of the river between Colnbrook and Wraysbury. As the Thames is a boundary between Middlesex and Surrey from the obelisk at Isleworth to that at Staines, it is obvious that Surrey has just about an equal share in the fishing rights which the various societies and bodies supply. Like all other privileges, these impose responsibilities on all who enjoy them, and it is to be hoped that all who participate in the joys of fishing will accept also the responsibilities as laid down in the Blue Book of the Thames Angling Preservation Society, whose secretary is S. R. Porter, of Harlesden, N.W.10.

The Thames during 1947 certainly provided much variety with its ice and its flooding, its scarcity of water and other vagaries. On November 12 at 10.15 a.m. porpoises were spotted at Southwark swimming with the tide upstream. It took them only just over two hours to reach Putney, seven and a half miles above London Bridge; and at 4.30 p.m. they were reported within the Middlesex borders at Cubitts Dock, Chiswick, twelve miles above the Bridge. Apparently they spent the night of November 12 in the Middlesex waters and swam down-stream the next day, reaching London Bridge soon after ten o'clock on the morning of November 13.

WEMBLEY

Wembley, which today is a huge suburb and the centre of many athletic activities, belonged to the Priory of Kilburn, which continued in possession until the Dissolution of the Monasteries. It was then granted to Richard Page and remained in the family for several centuries, until the death of the last known male heir gave rise to costly litigation and produced the mystery of the Page Estates. In Wembley are several old sixteenth- and seventeenth-century farms— Hundred Elms, Sudbury Court, Hillside, and Lyon's Farms, the last being the reported birthplace of John Lyon, who founded Harrow School. A thousand yards to the north-east of Lyon's Farm is the moot-site of the Hundred of Gore, which has been identified by Hugh Braun by a court-roll of 1445. The North Circular Road runs through Wembley, which has risen in population in less than fifty years from 5,000 to 125,000 folk, with 450 acres of open space reserved for games.

The Manor of Wembley was sold in 1802 to Mr. Gray, who rebuilt the manor-house in 1810. The Rev. J. E. Gray's death allowed the estate to fall into chancery and Mrs. Kathleen Davey tried to get possession on the plea that it was escheated to the Crown. The house fell into ruin; the estate was bought by the Metropolitan Railway Company, who built the extension of their line through part of the grounds and sold the rest for a pleasure park. Two hundred and eighty acres were devoted to this end, and Sir William Watkin, who was responsible for the railway up Snowdon, planned a tower to be 175 feet higher than the Eiffel Tower. For years the tower remained there, but only built up to the first storey. It could be seen from many neighbouring or far distant hills, notably from the summit of Bittacy Hill in Mill Hill.

Wembley came into great prominence during the British Empire Exhibitions of 1924 and 1925, when such a gathering of the clans from home and overseas was successfully attempted and carried out as no other nation had ever contemplated. Coming so soon after the first World War and the passing of the Statute of Westminster, it may have provoked jealousy from other nations not so successful in colonisation as ourselves, but it should also have served as a warning to those who were preparing to challenge the Anglo-Saxon races. Many of the Exhibition buildings are still used

320

Cromwell House, Highgate

as factories, and the Stadium serves an immensely useful purpose as a place for national and international sport.

The Stadium at Wembley was ready for use by April, 1923, and Bolton Wanderers and West Ham United played there in the final cup tie. Room was provided for 120,000 spectators, but the fact that the King and Queen were to attend, just after the marriage of the Duke of York to Lady Elizabeth Bowes-Lyon had taken place, attracted about 200,000 spectators. Questions were asked in the House of Commons about the discomfort of those who watched Bolton win the Cup, and tributes were paid to the efficiency and courtesy of the police, who prevented what might well have proved a disastrous overcrowding.

The idea of an exhibition had been discussed in 1913, but the first World War caused its postponement. In 1922 the work was begun of covering with buildings a semicircular track of about two and a quarter miles round, to include a palace of industry, one of arts, and one of engineering. Every race and country included in the British Commonwealth of Nations was represented, and people and products from all the kindred states were on view. The total area occupied was 220 acres, and the costs ran up almost to £3,000,000. The labour amounted to 450,000 man weeks; £1,000,000 was taken for admission during 1924; the number of folk employed each day exceeded 24,000; and during six months 17,500,000 visited the Exhibition. It was opened on April 23, 1924, by the King and Queen, who drove round the Stadium, amid loyal cheering, to meet the Prince of Wales, who was President of the Exhibition Committee.

The planning was as near perfect as possible, and schools made use of its educational facilities. It was possible in an afternoon to take two forms of boys over to Wembley, inspect the Dominion and Colonial exhibits, watch Nigerians or Kaffirs at work, have refreshments in "British Guiana" or "Barbados," see a coloured reproduction of the famous Kaieteur Falls in British Guiana, the highest then known, and thus enjoy a lesson in practical geography. "Rodeo," or very clever horsemanship, and demonstrations of steer-roping came in for much criticism, and the latter was wisely discontinued, but the Amusement Park was by no means the only

Highgate Archway

popular feature of the Exhibition. Such was its success that it was continued for another year, with rather less success financially, and the Labour Cabinet had to come on the guarantors to redeem their pledges.

There is an interesting and permanent reminder of the Exhibition in Hendon Town Hall. Malaya, including Singapore, had a fine exhibit round a hollow three-sided square, with a statue of Sir Stamford Raffles in the centre, a replica in brown plaster of the bronze statue in Singapore. When the authorities found that Raffles was buried in Hendon Church they tried unsuccessfully to obtain permission to remove the body to the port for whose planning he was mainly responsible. When that could not be arranged, they generously gave the statue to Hendon, and the author of this book, as an historian of the parish and borough, was privileged to write the inscription which is placed on the plinth. Two recent *Lives* of Raffles have shown the remarkable achievements of a man who died at the age of forty-five.

The Wembley Stadium with its twin towers is one of the most important arenas in the world; designed by Sir Owen Williams, it serves for athletic contest, and has its pool for water polo and swimming in the summer and for skating and ice hockey in the winter. The pool measures 200 feet by 60, and a thousand can bathe at one time.

It is a great satisfaction to have taken even a small part in the preliminary planning for the Olympic Games in this county in 1908. There had been previous gatherings at Athens in 1896, at Paris in 1900, and at St. Louis in 1904. And so a small committee was called at the Houses of Parliament under the chairmanship of Lord Desborough. The Rev. R. S. de Courcy Laffan, formerly Headmaster of Stratford-on-Avon School and of Cheltenham College, was acting Honorary Secretary, and he invited a colleague of mine at Mill Hill, A. J. Williams, and myself to attend. Plans were then outlined for securing world-wide support for the movement. Sir Howard Vincent and F. J. Wall were also there, I remember. There were to be 100 events, various banquets, and, above all, a marathon race to start at Windsor Castle and to finish in the Stadium at Shepherd's Bush. I had tickets for the stand for this race, but preferred to take a number of boys from Mill Hill School to Pinner to watch the race in progress. It was the occasion on which Dorando came in first for Italy, but he had fallen and had been helped on his way by too eager spectators, and so the race was awarded to Hayes from the U.S.A. The banquets at the Holborn Restaurant were an outstanding feature, and we got many famous people to sign our menu cards.

When the Games were held in Berlin during the early days of the Hitler régime the only field event won by Great Britain was the walking race, which went to a former pupil of Hendon County School, Whittuck by name. He very generously presented his prize oak tree to the governors of the school, who have had it carefully planted at one corner of the playing-field, and have made the Oak Stand into a handsome trophy for the best athlete in the school each year.

The Olympic Games for 1948 took place at Wembley from July 29 to August 14, and included seventeen different sports. Five thousand officials and competitors were accommodated in specially planned buildings; many permanent or temporary changes were made; seven lanes were provided for running contests. Equestrian contests mostly occurred at Windsor or Aldershot, shooting at Bisley, cycling at Herne Hill, rowing and canoeing at Henley, yachting at Spithead and in the Solent. Preliminary rounds mostly took place elsewhere, but the finals of Association football, basket ball, field hockey, wrestling, weight-lifting, and athletics generally were planned for Wembley Stadium.

The modern Pentathlon is based on the original Olympic Games, and it includes shooting, cross-country running, horse-riding, fencing, and swimming. The historic marathon race, which was run from Windsor to the White City, this year started and finished at the Stadium. Sir Arnold Bax, Master of the King's Music, was chairman of the committee to organise competitions and to train a massed choir and band.

The Olympic Flame was started at Mount Olympus in Greece, where logs of wood were kindled by magnified sun-rays, and relays of runners brought the flame across Europe and the Narrow Seas to the Stadium, where the flame was lighted on the first day, kept alight all day and night, was visible in all weathers, and was extinguished on the last day.

323

There were art competitions, as in ancient Greece, covering literature, painting, sculpture, music, and architecture. It is significant that, in the final preparations at Wembley for widening and improving the various approaches to the arena, German prisoners of war and Polish displaced persons had been helping British workmen to finish the task.

The Olympic Games, on whose planning such infinite labour had been taken, fully occupied the seventeen days allotted to them. The Fourteenth Olympiad was officially opened by King George VI before a crowd of more than 80,000 spectators, with 5,000 athletes massed on the grass infield of Wembley Stadium. Stretching almost from one side of the arena to the other were the huge delegations from Great Britain and the United States. Amongst absentees from the Games were the Japanese, who were not allowed to compete; the Germans, who were not invited; and the Russians, "who snubbed the whole show."

The athletes from the U.S.A. swept the board and scored nearly twice as many points (662) as their nearest rival, Sweden (353). France (230½), Hungary (201½), and Italy (183) came next, with Great Britain (170) only sixth in the list. A vivid way of showing the winners of each event was the use of victory platforms, with places on either side for those holding second and third place, and a higher dais in the centre for the actual winner. Athletes from California alone scored more points than any country save Sweden, France, and Hungary.

The show was a superb one by athletic standards, but the sun shone on only three of the seventeen days. Events of all kinds were held, on the track and in the field, for men and for women competitors : swimming and diving; canoeing, rowing, and yachting (elsewhere than at Wembley); weight-lifting, boxing, wrestling; horsemanship, cycling, shooting, and fencing; and such miscellaneous events as Association football, hockey, basket ball, gymnastics, and the Pentathlon.

The greatest Olympic performer was a Dutchwoman, Fanny Blankers-Koen, a thirty-year-old mother with two children, who was the only competitor to win three events— the 80 metres, the 100 metres, and the 200 metres.

In some ways the most interesting race was the marathon,

which took place almost entirely in Middlesex. The route lay along the Barnet By-pass to Stirling Corner in Hertfordshire, went a mile or so farther north, cut across to Watling Street, and returned south to the Stadium. Round Stirling Corner had gathered an immense concourse of cars and people, admirably restrained. And the finish in the arena was perhaps the most thrilling part of the race; a Belgian arrived there almost dead beat and seemed incapable of running once more round the track. Then two more competitors came in and passed him. The Belgian just managed to finish in third place. It was just about as exciting as the effort of Dorando, the Italian, in the Olympic Games when last held in this country.

The first six countries in the contest have already been scheduled. Following them came Finland (158), Switzerland (151½), Denmark (143), Netherlands (119), Czechoslovakia (93), and Turkey (88), the last named scoring nearly all its points by wrestling.

An American journalist summed up the situation with the comment : "The Games were marked by many broken records, lots of rain, admirable decorum, and very few quarrels."

OTHER SPORT

It will be readily appreciated that the position of Middlesex in relation to London has meant that many amusements for workers in the Metropolis are supplied by the adjacent county. It is difficult to decide whether a Test Match at Lord's, the Derby at Epsom, the Cup Final at Wembley, an International at Twickenham, or the University Boat Race is the most popular sporting event of the year. A longer list of choices could no doubt be made, but it is significant that of the five mentioned above four are in the County of Middlesex, and three of them in the abridged area of 1888. The Boat Race is designated as Putney to Mortlake, both in Surrey, but almost all the landmarks on the way are in Middlesex, entirely or partly : Putney Bridge, Fulham Palace, Craven Steps, Fulham Football Ground, Crabtree, Hammersmith Bridge, The Doves, Chiswick Eyot, Thorneycrofts, Duke's Meadows, and Barnes Bridge.

Not much horse-racing survives in the overbuilt Middlesex

of today, but in earlier uncrowded days the case was different. FitzStephen, in his description of London under Henry II, hints that horses offered for sale in Smithfield were usually tested by racing. "Bell courses" in Elizabeth's reign, with a silver bell as the prize, were regarded with favour even by the strictest Puritans as "yielding goodly exercise." Race meetings took place in James I's reign at Theobalds in Enfield Chase, and in Hyde Park under Charles I. The Cromwell régime may have stopped this. Later the Royal Stud was kept at Hampton Court or in Bushey Park, from 1700 onwards, and both George IV and William IV continued to encourage royal horse-breeding, which went on into the twentieth century. There was an early race meeting in 1788 at Enfield, but the company was far too mixed, including many pick-pockets. Ealing had occasional races and so did Harrow, but only two meetings survive today, those at Kempton Park and Alexandra Park.

The first game of polo ever played in England, after its introduction from India, was played at Hounslow between the 9th Lancers and the 10th Hussars. This was in 1872, and the headquarters were later transferred to Lillie Bridge and to Hurlingham. Wembley Park formed a club in the early years of the century, but two world wars have not helped the game to become as popular in Middlesex as could have been wished.

Football

Originally most schools had local rules of their own, which made uniformity difficult, so in 1863 C. W. Alcock invited football players to meet and unite under one code. Dribbling and passing and scrimmaging were to make mutual concessions, but when the association was formed at the Freemasons' Tavern some Rugby players insisted on the retention of "hacking," and as their view was not accepted they declined to join the "passing" group. By 1868 the association numbered twenty clubs, most of them in Middlesex, mainly public-school men, including such old boys' clubs as those from Eton, Harrow, Charterhouse, Westminster, and Winchester. Later on Repton and Shrewsbury joined in. With the great increase in professional games an Amateur Football Association was formed in 1907, and there are a number of amateur clubs in existence up and down the country. Public authorities and educational bodies take considerable pains to make football grounds available for amateur sides.

The Rugby Union was formed in 1871, and about the first thing that was done was to forbid "hacking." Early Middlesex clubs that joined were Ravenscourt Park, Harlequins, Belsize, Hampstead, Black and Red Rovers, and such Middlesex schools as St. Paul's, Merchant Taylors, King's College School, Godolphin School, Kensington Grammar School, Mill Hill School, and Christ's College, Finchley.

When the first international match was played against Scotland, Middlesex had several players included in the side, and in 1879 they beat Yorkshire by an odd try, losing by the same margin to Surrey. Eight years later Middlesex were only defeated by the champions of the North, Lancashire, by one try, and the match was watched by the Prince of Wales (afterwards King Edward VII). In 1888 Middlesex were generally regarded as the best county side, but since the County Championship has been established they have not been at the head of the table. In 1904 they were beaten in the final by one point by Durham; in 1907-8 they were champions of the South-eastern Division. They had, up to the first World War, a number of distinguished players who represented the country as well as the county. E. T. Gurdon, Alan Rotherham, C. G. Wade, C. J. B. Marriott, A. E. Stoddart, W. E. Maclagan, A. J. Gould, were among some of the most famous of their early internationals. Middlesex has as many clubs affiliated to the Rugby Union as any other county, and the idea of a London Referees' Society was started in Middlesex.

Between the wars a famous pair of half-backs were Wilfred Sobey and Roger Spong, who played for the Old Millhillians and for the county and figured in many international sides both at home and abroad, and had their names used as uprights in an anagram in the *Observer*.

The headquarters of the Rugby Union has always been in Middlesex, and in 1908 the England ground was opened at Twickenham as the centre of the Rugby game, where all home international matches will, in future, be played. The schools of Middlesex have done a great work in training future internationals, and in the *Victoria Counties History* a list of those coming from the various schools was given. Harrow, Mill Hill, Christ's College, Finchley, St. Paul's, St. John's Wood (now no longer open), Christ's Hospital (now in Sussex), Merchant Taylors, Isleworth College (no longer open), and Godolphin School, all had produced one or more internationals up to that date.

The visit of the Australian Rugby team in the winter of 1947 brought a series of important matches to Twickenham. In November the visitors played and defeated a London Counties fifteen chosen from Kent, Middlesex, Surrey, and Eastern Counties, which should be called Home Counties more accurately. In December the London Counties again played Australia at Twickenham and won, only just before the international match against England on the same ground, when the visitors were successful.

A glance at the sporting papers shows that, among Rugby football club sides, the following hail mostly, if not entirely, from Middlesex : Barnet, De Havilland (Stag Lane), Finchley, Harrow Town, Hendon, Mill Hill Village, Old Askeans, Old Millhillians, Old Twickenhamians, Staines, and Twickenham. The Association football list is just about as long, and comprises Barnet, Crouch End, Finchley, Hayes, Hendon, Hounslow, Old Stationers, Southall, Uxbridge, Winchmore Hill. For hockey there are Ashford, Ealing, Ealing Dean, Enfield, Hendon, Hounslow, Southgate, Staines, and Teddington. The only lacrosse side seems to be Hampton Court, but there is racing at Hurst Park, where in October such obviously local events as the Teddington Selling Plate and the Strawberry Hill Handicaps are contested. Among the dog-racing tracks that are advertised in the evening papers, Harringay, Hendon, and Wembley are in Middlesex.

The first golf links to be established in Middlesex were Staines and West Middlesex in 1890, Northwood in 1891, Hillingdon and Finchley in 1892, Enfield, Stanmore, Hampstead, and Neasden in 1893. The proximity of London has in some cases been beneficial, as Londoners want links as near home as possible, but building encroachment has done damage, as, for instance, at Hanger Hill.

328

There are many golfing societies which use other clubs' links, but the total of links in Middlesex today is : Ashford Manor, Acton, Edgware, Enfield, Ealing, Finchley, Fulwell, Hampstead, Hendon, Hanger Hill, Highgate, Muswell Hill, Neasden, North Middlesex, Northwood, St. Quintin's, Strawberry Hill, Stanmore, Hillingdon, Wembley, West Drayton, West Middlesex, Hampton Court (Home Park).

The name Harringay is the original one of the area now called Hornsey, and Harringay Manor-house remained standing until 1870. Through its grounds ran a small nameless stream, now banished underground, and in 1906 a writer on Middlesex made the comment that "the district stands well on rising ground, but has no history, for the whole neighbourhood was parkland until a few years ago." A lot has happened since then, and Harringay Arena today is famous for its dog-racing and its ice rink. Trials for the British ice hockey Olympic teams took place there in October, 1947, and when the Swedish team flew over in early November they had matches against Harringay Racers and then two international struggles with England, both staged at Wembley. Roller skating and wrestling of a good quality are also staged at Harringay, and in 1947 there was a musical festival from June 7 to July 6 in the arena, which can seat ten thousand listeners or spectators. Famous orchestras were brought to Harringay to be conducted by Sir Thomas Beecham, André Kostelanetz, José Sturts, and Sir Malcolm Sargent. Among the soloists were Solomon, Silveri, Eileen Joyce, Nino Martini, Kirsten Flagstad, and Richard Tauber, a very versatile and popular tenor and conductor who has since died.

In discussing sports in Middlesex, the most distinguished has been left to the last, and the county's achievements at Lord's merit a chapter to themselves.

Chapter XXII

MIDDLESEX CRICKET

THE date is 1877, the fortieth year of Queen Victoria's reign, and the place is Lord's, now in its ninetieth year. The Middlesex Cricket Club, formed thirteen years before, has just migrated to the M.C.C., thereby exchanging Prince's ground in Chelsea for the more spacious green of St. John's Wood. This move was a belated fulfilment of the hopes of the M.C.C. secretary, R. A. Fitzgerald, whose energetic and influential tenure of this office almost coincided with the early seasons of the Middlesex County Cricket Club. Realising the need for enlivening the mediocre programme of matches at Lord's, matches which in the 'fifties and 'sixties tended to interest few people except the players themselves, and which attracted correspondingly small crowds, Fitzgerald invited Middlesex to add their county fixtures to his list. The offer was declined, for the newly formed club had by then settled upon Prince's ground, near Hans Place, where Lennox Gardens now stand. If the eventual move to Lord's caused the rapid decline of cricket at Prince's, which soon afterwards vanished in the spreading development, the change saw the birth of a friendly and expanding association between the clubs of Marylebone and Middlesex. The M.C.C. receive an annual rent of £1,100, while the county takes the gate money, but not the receipts from the stands, and pays all match expenses.

Who were some of the leading figures who played for the metropolitan county in the seasons when county cricket was rapidly growing in popularity? Who were the players whose mastery of the game built up the reputation of the club among the half-dozen county teams of the period? The veritable founders of Middlesex cricket were the Walker brothers from Southgate. I. D. Walker played for twenty years and captained the team during its first eleven years of development. This hard-hitting batsman who excelled in driving was seldom one to score slowly, and he smote the ball into the

330

billiard room at Lord's pavilion on one memorable occasion. It was he who, almost at the end of his cricketing career, partnered the Hon. Alfred Lyttelton in a second-wicket stand of 324 runs against Gloucestershire; 225 of these runs were scored in a mere 105 minutes.

V. E. Walker, who played for the Gentlemen when aged only nineteen, and who was to be President of the M.C.C. in 1891, was one of the finest slow under-arm bowlers, and during the club's second season he took all ten wickets in an innings; the victims were men of Lancashire. We read of a match at Lord's in 1871 in which the M.C.C. broke the ground record by compiling 430 runs, to which Middlesex, their visiting opponents, promptly retorted with 485 !

Public interest in county cricket grew strikingly during these years, and in 1873 the championship was inaugurated. Whereas at the beginning of the 'seventies no county, with the exception of Surrey, played more than six inter-county matches in one season, and Middlesex played but two, by the end of the decade every county which took part in the championship played home and away matches with each of the other seven counties.

In 1875 A. J. Webbe, like the three Walkers an Old Harrovian, played his first season for the Middlesex eleven. He had already partnered W. G. Grace for the Gentlemen against the Players, and for his county he scored 97 off the Nottinghamshire bowlers. In the following June, Webbe, who was still playing for Oxford University during the term, contributed for his side against the county team he was later to captain 98 runs out of the huge total of 612. To this Middlesex responded with 439 and 166 for four wickets.

The removal to Lord's was celebrated in the summer of 1878, when Middlesex won the county championship for the first time, the county team gaining the ascendancy during this one season over such frequent champions of the early years as Nottinghamshire, Gloucestershire, Lancashire, and later Surrey and Yorkshire. A quarter of a century passed and a new century dawned before Middlesex could repeat this triumph.

Already one of the marked characteristics of the county's cricket was apparent—a high proportion of great amateur players. In 1885, when A. J. Webbe succeeded I. D. Walker as captain, and when C. T. Studd left for the mission field in China, such amateurs as the Hon. Alfred Lyttelton, G. F. Vernon, and the Walkers formed the backbone of the county batting strength. The departure of Studd was compensated for by the coming of a brilliant all-rounder named A. E. Stoddart, then aged twenty-three, who played Rugby for England and who was to become his county's most prominent batsman, being a rapid and graceful scorer. Stoddart started for the Hampstead club, for whom he made in 1886 the immense score of 485 against the Stoics, and he was to play regularly for Middlesex until the close of the century. He scored a masterly 251 against Lancashire in 1891, and two years later he made a century in each innings of the match against Nottinghamshire at Lord's, hitting 195 runs not out and 124.

Middlesex players were strongly represented with the first English teams that played in Australia during this period. A. J. Webbe was a member of the fifth touring team in 1878, and in 1882 no fewer than four of the county's amateurs were selected to play : C. T. and G. B. Studd, C. F. H. Leslie, and G. F. Vernon. The last named played in Australia five years later; this time he was in company with the hard-hitting T. C. O'Brien and with Stoddart, who was twice to captain the England eleven during the 'nineties.

Though strong in batsmen, Middlesex as a county team had possessed no bowler in the very top rank, despite the steady successes of men like E. A. Nepean and George Burton. It was a great pleasure to engage Burton as cricket coach at Mill Hill School and to sit with him in the professionals' gallery at Lord's; I watched many matches thence, got to know many famous cricketers, and heard their pungent comments with relish. Thus the acquisition to the eleven in 1890 of so outstanding a bowler as J. T. Hearne was a powerful advantage. So great were his results that in the very next year, when Middlesex finished third in the championship order, Jack Hearne took 118 wickets at an average of 10·4 runs apiece, and his name headed the first-class bowling averages. Patient and confident, and bowling with a rhythmic grace of action, Hearne had a command of pace and length which drew near to perfection, and he was to take more wickets at Lord's than any other bowler, 1,719 for 16·43 runs each.

1898 was the county club's twenty-fifth season. The Victorian century was closing with a host of great cricketing names on the lips of lovers of the game. This was a year in which W. G. Grace captained a Gloucestershire team that included C. L. Townsend and G. L. Jessop, and Lord Hawke's Yorkshire eleven numbered F. S. Jackson and Rhodes. "Ranji" and C. B. Fry were playing for Sussex, Tom Hayward for Surrey, A. C. Maclaren and J. T. Tyldesley for Lancashire. Kent had Mason and Martin, while W. Gunn represented Nottinghamshire and S. M. J. Woods captained Somerset.

And Middlesex? Webbe's fifteen years of captaincy came to an end, though his active connection with the club continued almost until his death in 1940, for he succeeded R. D. Walker as President of the county club in 1922 and held this post for another fifteen years. The new captain was Stoddart, who during the previous winter had led to Australia a team of which Hearne was also a member. 1898 saw T. C. (now Sir Timothy) O'Brien, that spirited hitter, drop out of the side. G. McGregor, the former Cambridge blue, who also played full-back for Scotland, kept many times for Middlesex during the 'nineties and was probably the finest amateur wicket-keeper since Alfred Lyttelton's day. While still at Cambridge in 1890 he played for England in a Test Match against Australia; he accompanied Lord Sheffield's team there in the following year, and played again for England with Stoddart in 1893. J. T. Hearne, who headed the bowling averages with 222 wickets, had a fine season and was nobly partnered in attack by an Australian from Victoria who had qualified to represent Middlesex. His name was Albert Trott, and his brother played for Australia.

Trott and Hearne won their county a sensational match against Somerset that summer. A first day of steady rain and no play left the wicket treacherous. As a result the two opening overs of the game saw eight wickets fall for a paltry five runs. The match was finished in five minutes over three hours, during which time 30 wickets had fallen and only 195

333

runs been scored. The damage was caused by Trott, who bowled eleven wickets for 31 runs, and by Hearne, who took eight wickets for 44. Trott, nine years later, was again to be the downfall of Somerset, for he bowled four wickets with successive balls, and not content with this feat, he took the hat trick in the same innings. This valuable Australian was no mere bowler either. In 1899 Trott was to drive a ball from Noble over the pavilion at Lord's, the only occasion on which this has been achieved. He had already banged one ball against the pavilion balcony. The second ball dropped over the roof.

A photograph of the Middlesex team in 1898 shows Stoddart, Hearne, Haymann, and Trott wearing straw hats, Trott with his brim tilted forward over his eyes. Seated beside the new captain are Sir T. C. O'Brien and the huge left-hander F. G. J. Ford, who had played against Australia four years earlier. Standing behind Stoddart is a youthful-looking P. F. Warner, playing his fourth season for the county, and decidedly clean-shaven amid a preponderance of heavy moustaches.

The years have passed, the Edwardian decade and the Great War are in history; the date is 1920, Pelham Warner's last season as captain of the county team. When Surrey was defeated by 55 runs, Middlesex wrested the championship from Lancashire, and thus won for the third time. It was Warner's last match, and this great Middlesex and England cricketer and captain retired from first-class play, only to continue as one of the dominating cricketing figures of the age. This post-war period was a high point in the club's story, for under F. T. Mann's leadership Middlesex won the championship for the second year running in 1921. And during that very summer the team compiled 612 runs for eight wickets against Nottinghamshire.

The 'twenties were in many respects dominated by two very great players of the game, "Patsy" Hendren and J. W. Hearne, the one weaving persevering care and Irish aggression into his batting, the other scoring with a polished elegance and precision. Hendren, that most popular of cricketers, with his small rugged figure and his mimicking

334

wit, his great variety of stroke play, his bat tucked under his
arm as he walked to the wickets, was one of the most memorable and lovable personalities of cricket. Pugnacious, never
blasé with success, energetic, his feet twinkling down the
pitch, Hendren was until his retirement in 1937 at once a
corner-stone and a shining light in the Middlesex team. He
scored more runs and more centuries at Lord's than any other
cricketer—25,000 runs and 74 centuries.

His runner-up in run scoring was J. W. Hearne, who,
despite the handicaps of illness and injury, achieved the title
of having on the green turf of Lord's compiled more runs and
bowled more wickets than any other player. He headed the
first-class batting averages in the summer of 1914, and in two
seasons he made 2,000 runs and took 100 wickets. Patience
and restraint were his qualities; he scorned the loose and
clumsy stroke, and practised with rare artistry the glance and
the cut rather than Hendren's characteristic short-arm hook.
If he preferred back play, of which his command was exemplary, to the more aggressive forward strokes, this choice
did not lessen the runs scored from his bat, though Hearne's
style tended often towards the colourless, when in later years
too great an artificiality pervaded his play.

Though Hendren and Hearne were the two greatest
professionals who played for Middlesex during the 'twenties,
there were other stalwarts of the team, men like the mighty
Durston, who opened the county attack with his fast deliveries
and who was a hitter of some renown. There were, too,
Murrell, the wicket-keeper, who gave twenty years' service
and who was succeeded behind the stumps in 1927 by the
slow-footed and waddling W. F. Price, a player who missed
but four matches in a dozen years; and H. W. Lee, who in
1926 scored more runs than all his fellow-players save only
Hendren. There was Hart, thrice selected as twelfth man
for England, one of the safest and most careful fieldsmen of
his day, a player who, though lacking the sparkle and quirks
of a striking personality, yet contributed by his very reliability
to the strength of the county team, especially during the early
'thirties. But that is running ahead with the story.

As was customary since the early days, the Middlesex
eleven counted in the 'twenties a high proportion of amateurs

who played on and off when affairs permitted. Though this constant flow of talent brought freshness to the county cricket, it also lessened the consistency of the team, and indeed no less than nineteen different amateurs played during 1926. Almost at the end of his career was that aristocrat among cricketers, the Hon. C. N. Bruce, later to become Lord Aberdare. He was a player of upright and classical style, polished and yet seemingly negligent, a case in which the ease and grace of stroke play appeared effortless, but were not so. At the start of his career was R. W. V. Robins, just down from Cambridge. At the end of 1928 Frank Mann handed over the post of captain he had held so ably to Nigel Haig. Almost legendary was Mann's feat four years before when, playing against Yorkshire at Lord's, he scored off Rhodes four sixes into the pavilion, of which two consecutive balls struck the uppermost balcony.

In 1929, a year in which Hearne made the highest score of his great career—285 not out—against the bowlers of Essex, and in which Jim Sims played his first and unpromising season for Middlesex, and in which G. O. Allen took ten Lancashire wickets in one innings, Nigel Haig assumed the captaincy of the county team. With Durston and Allen, his successor as captain, Haig in these years was one of the county's most successful and fiery bowlers, fast-medium in pace, able to swing the ball both ways, and using the height of his tall, slim figure to advantage. During this season three of the county amateurs—Haig, Robins, and Peebles—each obtained 100 wickets; this had never been done before. 1929 saw the arrival in England with the South African touring side of the brilliant H. G. Owen-Smith, another in the tradition of Middlesex amateurs who has excelled at other sports, for not only did he play full-back for Oxford and England, but he was also a talented boxer. This aggressive and irrepressible player, whose sparkling debut of 120 not out in a Test Match at the age of nineteen was characteristic of his calibre and temperament, displayed in his all too brief career with Middlesex that touch of genius which, when linked to his nimble feet and agile mind, possessed little of the orthodox and much of fearless independence and full-blooded expression.

With the turn of the decade and the economic crisis came

336

Gentlemen's Row, Enfield

the unfruitful years for Middlesex, despite such amateurs as G. O. Allen, Killick, and Enthoven, and as I. A. R. Peebles, who, playing for Oxford in 1930, had taken thirteen Cambridge wickets. But Middlesex ended the season last but one in the championship. True it is that there was Sims with his short shuffling run up to the wickets and his steady and increasingly cunning leg-break bowling, also the lively and cheerful J. H. Human, hard-driving at the wicket, fast of pursuit and return in the outfield. Joe Hulme, who played football for the Arsenal, was an outstanding fieldsman whose speed in chase of the ball was only matched by his refreshing running between the wickets. His exuberant dash and almost jaunty manner contrasted strikingly with the massive and ponderous Jim Smith, who arrived from Wiltshire in 1934. There was no mistaking Smith's giant form on the cricket field, whether he was pounding up to bowl with all his sixteen stone weight behind his delivery—he took 172 wickets at 18 runs apiece during his first season—or whether he was making the crowd laugh by his ubiquitous and mighty hitting. His was batsmanship that, having forsaken orthodox footwork, produced rapid runs notwithstanding, smote the ball with a good heart, and not infrequently mishit altogether. Jim Smith was a tower of strength to his side and a character favoured by the crowd. Sir Pelham Warner relates in his book, *Cricket between Two Wars,* how, after the following season was over, Smith actually scored, in a club match at Harrow, 177 runs in fifty-three minutes; this prodigious rate of scoring produced nineteen sixes!

1935 was Robins's first season as captain, Haig having retired after a distinguished all-round career, during which he had taken more than 1,100 wickets and had scored over 15,000 runs. The two previous years Middlesex had ended up twelfth and tenth in the county championship, though the team had improved considerably. And it was a tremendous advance when they gained third place. Then for four successive seasons Middlesex were runners-up, first to Derbyshire and thrice to Yorkshire. Yet during those same three summers before the second World War three great new batsmen appeared in the county team. Denis Compton, aged only eighteen—a schoolboy from Bell Lane School, Hendon

Enfield, Marden's Bridge,
Forty Hill

—created an immediate impression in 1936 as being a cricketer of quite outstanding quality, while in the following season Edrich, who had come from Norwich to join the ground staff at Lord's, made a brilliant debut. This was Hendren's last summer for Middlesex; he retired to become cricket coach at Harrow School, and in his final match, against Surrey, he responded to the cheering spectators by scoring 103—a characteristic swansong. He started playing for Middlesex in 1907 and maintained an average of 50 all the way—a remarkable achievement that included 119 centuries for his county. The third newcomer was J. Robertson, who joined the team in 1938 and has amply fulfilled his early promise.

That same year Robins found himself obliged to relinquish the captaincy, which he had exercised with exceptional verve and skill, and in the summer when the war clouds were blowing up towards deluge point I. A. R. Peebles took over.

The final stage of this brief account should have ended with 1947, in which unusually sunlit summer Middlesex won the championship under the inspiring, shrewd, and adventurous captaincy of Robins, who resumed that post after the war. A quarter of a century had elapsed since the county's victory in 1921, though Middlesex had been, as already indicated, hard challengers at the close of many of the intervening seasons. Both Edrich and Compton reached 3,000 runs in the season—never before had two batsmen from the same team achieved this—and both of these outstanding cricketers beat Tom Hayward's record, established in 1906, of making 3,518 runs in one season. Denis Compton amassed this total in forty-nine innings, twelve less than the great Surrey batsman. By scoring seventeen centuries during the summer he surpassed the other Surrey record of sixteen three-figure innings set up by J. B. Hobbs in 1925.

Edrich, Compton, and Robertson each scored over 2,000 runs for the county, followed closely by Brown, who partnered Robertson as opening pair for Middlesex. Though Young, Sims, and Gray captured more wickets than any other bowlers in the team, Edrich and Compton bowled with great success for both Middlesex and England, and so did Robins, the captain. It was twelve years since Edrich had come from Norwich, where he belonged to a family that could run its own cricket eleven, and in his opening season he had scored over 2,000 runs at an average of almost 45. In the next year, 1948, having compiled 1,000 runs by the end of May, Edrich was an obvious selection for the England team. Yet after the highest praise from all sides he failed in two successive Test Matches, and a reaction set in. The press criticised his abilities and his achievements, and when the selectors persevered with their new batsmen the attacks became bitter. Edrich did not shine in the first four Test Matches in South Africa, but he redeemed himself by scoring 219 in the final match. His reputation and future appeared to be seriously prejudiced in many quarters, but the storms have blown away, and those who retained confidence in Edrich have been most richly rewarded, and he and Compton still flourish. The three seasons from 1948 to 1950 saw Middlesex first drop rather low, then rise to the top of the tree again, bracketed with Yorkshire, and then sink once more in a year of mishaps.

And so we leave the Middlesex team, having lost its time of supremacy, but believe that wherever cricket is played, be it at Lord's or on the green turf of the pleasant county grounds, those who represent Middlesex in the future will practise the art that is cricket and will display all the best qualities of the game, with its grace and elegance, its leisured hours and its thrilling moments, its periods of anguish and strain, its times of expectancy and triumph.

CHAPTER XXIII

LOCAL AFFAIRS

THE ORDNANCE SURVEY

ALL our British maps today are based on the Ordnance Survey, which had its origin in Middlesex.

Hounslow Heath was the scene of the measuring of a base on which the whole Ordnance Survey has been built up. The origin of the scheme was the Young Pretender's rebellion in Scotland in 1745, when the Government realised how very important it was to explore the Highlands, map them, and construct through roads. William Roy, as Assistant Quartermaster-General, organised a survey of both Highlands and Lowlands, but the result was rather "a magnificent military sketch than a very accurate map of a country." Roy's efforts in cartography definitely led to the foundation of the Ordnance Survey only a few years after his death.

The Seven Years' War and the American War of Independence obstructed Roy's efforts to secure the complete mapping of the British Isles, but as the wars finished and peace was re-established between Britain and France the Cassini family suggested that the "triangulation of France should be extended across the Straits of Dover so as to establish the exact relative positions of the great national observatories of Paris and Greenwich." George III undertook the cost of the "instruments for measuring a base and laying out the triangles involved in the operations contemplated," and the Royal Society borrowed the services of Major-General Roy to co-operate with the French. In his *Account of the Measurement of the Base Line upon Hounslow Heath* General Roy records that "on the 16th day of April, 1784, Mr. Henry Cavendish and Mr. Blagdon accompanying the President of the Royal Society (Sir Joseph Banks) we began our observations at a place called King's Arbour, at the north-west extremity of the Heath, between Cranford Bridge and Longford; and having proceeded from thence through the narrow gorge formed by Hanworth Park and Hanworth Farm, we finished at Hampton, near the east side of Bushey Park, at the south-east extremity, the total distance, from the Survey of Middle-sex, being upwards of five miles."

Roy decided to employ soldiers on the duty of clearing the ground and for furnishing the "necessary sentinels for guarding the apparatus," and so a party of the 12th Regiment of Foot marched from Windsor to Hounslow Heath and camped there. It was intended to measure the base by means of deal rods, then customary on the Continent, but these varied in length according to the humidity of the atmosphere—more noticeable perhaps in this country than abroad—and so the base was measured by the use of long glass tubes, about an inch in diameter, one being 26 feet in length.

The King, not content with financial support, "deigned to honour the operation by his presence, entered minutely into the work of conducting it, which met with his gracious approba-tion." Sir Joseph Banks, "the respectable and worthy President of the Royal Society, ever zealous in the cause of science, re-peatedly visited the Heath, and in the final stages ordered his tents to be continually pitched near at hand, where his imme-diate guests, and the numerous visitors whom curiosity drew to the spot, met with the most hospitable supply of every necessary and even elegant refreshment."

The French side of the story was apparently described in a contemporary pamphlet, *Description des Moyens employés pour mesurer le Base de Hounslow-Heath*. The work seems to have occupied three months, and the length of the base, after applying corrections for temperature and reduction to sea-level, was 27,404·01 feet. It was necessary to construct an accurate theodolite for taking the angles, and the new elaborate instrument was not delivered until July 31, 1787. At the same time Roy was measuring a second base in Romney Marsh. Cassini came over to consult General Roy and Dr. Blagden, and the plans were undertaken with complete and cordial understanding. Four coastal stations were chosen in France—Dunkirk, Calais, Blanc-Nez, and Mont Lambert—where lights were exhibited for observations from Dover and other coastal stations. Agreement between the distances as given by French and English triangulations was close, the difference in estimated distance between Dover Castle and

Notre Dame in Calais being only seven feet. It is interesting to note that the only base used on this side of the Channel was that on Hounslow Heath.

Sir Charles Close, in his book on *The Early Years of the Ordnance Survey* (1926), commends General Roy's work at Hounslow. "It was the first accurate triangulation carried out in this country and set a remarkably high standard; it amply fulfilled its original scientific purpose; it provided for the first time a thoroughly reliable framework for map-making, and it led directly to the formal founding of the Ordnance Survey."

In Roy's day the terminals of the Hounslow Heath base were wooden pipes one foot in diameter. Just after Roy's death it was found that these wooden terminals were decayed, and so they were replaced by guns fixed vertically, muzzle upwards. On Hounslow Heath there are to be seen these terminals with a circular iron fence all round them. The second of Roy's terminals was 27,404 feet away in Cannon Field, Hampton Hill.

Roy was awarded the Copley Medal for this important work, which took him quite two years, because many of the most important observations could be made only at night with special white lights which did not burn for long. On Roy's work was based the triangulation of England, from which came in 1801 the first of our 1-inch Ordnance Survey maps. It took another half-century to complete the survey, with 250 stations, using a line on Salisbury Plain as a base, the average length of the sides of the triangles being thirty-five miles.

As a memorial to General Roy's initiative a tablet was affixed to each of these two terminals on the occasion of the two hundredth anniversary of Roy's birthday. The Astronomer-Royal, Sir Frank Dyson, unveiled the memorial on the South-east Terminal on February 22, 1927. Here is a commemoration of a very important piece of work undertaken by General Roy on Hounslow Heath in Middlesex.

LOCAL GOVERNMENT

Before 1888 justices of the peace, working through overseers, carried on much of the country's administrative work.

A county council budget today shows the extent and ramifications of its activities, and the items of expenditure can be classified under six main headings : Education, Public Health, Poor Relief, Highways and Bridges, Administration of Justice, Mental Hospitals and Mental Deficiency; and the total annual cost for Middlesex is just about £8,000,000, half for Education and Public Health, one-third for Poor Relief, Roads and Bridges.

The problem of the poor in medieval times was tackled by the lords of the manor, parish clergy, monasteries, and by the trade and craft guilds. Changes of all kinds and the Tudor debasement and depreciation of the currency forced the Central Government to pass two Elizabethan Poor Laws. Lord Passfield emphasised the fact that "for more than 130 years nine-tenths of the entire population, who were manual working wage-earners, or independent handicraftsmen, remained subject to this intolerable law." The coming of the Agricultural and Industrial Revolutions brought fresh problems, and there followed unions of parishes and the building of workhouses. The Speenhamland Act really anticipated by more than a century our modern methods, but it was too generous to last.

The Poor Law Act of 1834 was based on the notion that there was no promise of comfort or happiness, and was cordially disliked by all who came under its rules. Groups of parishes elected boards of guardians, the workhouse test was restored, and central control was exercised first by the Poor Law Commissioners, then in 1847 by the Poor Law Board, and after 1871 by the Local Government Board. Unions of parishes were not formed within strict county boundaries, and Edmonton Union included parishes in Essex and Hertfordshire. Boards of guardians quite unnecessarily continued to function for forty years after the first county council met in 1889.

Education has become increasingly important, and the various Acts have enlarged its scope. The Act of 1870 made the three Rs available, that of 1881 made them compulsory, and 1890 made them free. The various Acts since then have increased chances of secondary education, and the Butler Act of 1944 has raised the leaving age, made secondary education

343

largely free, and has given the county additional powers. The story of education in Middlesex needs a chapter all to itself.

The biggest towns have admirable library services of their own, with fine buildings, an extremely competent staff, free lectures on all kinds of subjects, and often collections of antiquities, prints and drawings, manorial deeds, and other items of local interest; branch libraries in the most important wards, and travelling library vans to take books to outlying districts. Local libraries under local control are to be found at Acton, Brentford, Chiswick, Ealing, Edmonton, Enfield, Feltham, Finchley, Harrow, Heston, Hendon, Hornsey, Isleworth, Southall, Staines, Sunbury, Teddington, Tottenham, Twickenham, Wembley, Wood Green, and Willesden. Full-time branch libraries are provided by the county at Friern Barnet, Hayes, Hillingdon, Kenton, Ruislip, Southgate, Uxbridge, and Yiewsley. The County Library at Ruislip is a most attractively restored sixteenth-century barn. A recent American visitor to England declared that she has felt more at home in the well-equipped, well-staffed Public Library at Hendon than anywhere else in this country.

Public health is a very vital part of local administration, and it is shared by the county and the boroughs contained in it. The aim of all concerned is first to prevent disease, and then, if it occurs, to cure it. Maternity and child-welfare services are carried out, school medical services deal with simple aches and pains, defective eyesight, removal of adenoids and tonsils, and even more serious troubles. Blind and mentally defective children receive special attention, teeth are attended to, and milk and meals are provided either free of charge or at a very low figure.

There are magnificent hospitals in various parts of the county, notably Clare Hall Sanatorium at South Mimms; Harefield Sanatorium in the north-west of the county; Redhill County Hospital at Edgware; others at Willesden, in Acton Lane, at Hillingdon, near Uxbridge; at Silver Street in Edmonton; and at Isleworth.

The County Council has a special concern for the very old and for the very young. Orphans or those whose parents are too ill to cope with them are cared for by the county, and there is an old people's home at Chase Farm, Enfield, and another at White Webbs, not far away, having delightful accommodation for the aged. The Middlesex County Council proudly claims that there are today in Middlesex 12,000 households entirely maintained by the County Council. There are only two casual wards for tramps in the county today, one to the north at Edmonton, one to the west at Isleworth.

The Act of 1888 transferred to the county the duties of visiting asylums, up to then in the care of Quarter Sessions. There are three main mental hospitals for which Middlesex is responsible, but owing to the spread of London all three have had to be placed outside the county. Springfield Hospital at Wandsworth was begun in 1841 as a Surrey mental hospital, but it was transferred to Middlesex in 1888, and now has 2,000 patients in well-equipped buildings situated in 145 acres of ground. Napsbury is about two miles south of St. Albans, with nearly 2,000 patients and over 400 acres of ground; and Shenley, which was opened by King George V in 1934, is planned on the villa system, with small nursing units, a staff of 500, 2,000 patients, and magnificent grounds. The Middlesex Colony is an offshoot from Shenley Hospital, with 400 acres and opportunities for all sorts of trades, including boot and shoe repairs, tailoring, brush-making, rug-making, and carpentering.

The Metropolitan Water Board has control over an area of more than 350 square miles as compared with the one square mile of the City, and it provides water for 7,000,000 people, again compared with 12,503 voters within the City— a falling off from 38,000 just before the war. Water is a vital necessity today, not only for the few pints a man needs for drinking each day, but for the forty gallons he uses each day for all kinds of essential services. It is interesting to note that the reservoirs of a water company have to be assessed, but their rating is usually reduced, seeing that most of the services do not benefit them at all. The construction of open-air swimming pools has put a heavy demand on the water supplies, and in dry summers this presents many difficulties.

DRAINAGE, ETC.

In 1935 a detailed Report, based on years of investigation, was issued by the Ministry of Health, dealing with problems of drainage in the Greater London area. The recommendations which were made envisaged a co-ordination of sewage disposal for the whole district within a twenty-five mile radius from Charing Cross, with a maximum of ten centralised disposal works, with which all existing and future sewage disposal works were to be combined. The three schemes that concern Middlesex are the West Middlesex Scheme, which was completed before the second World War; the Colne Valley Scheme, partly constructed; and the East Middlesex Scheme, planned but delayed till the end of the war.

The need for these important decisions was the tremendous growth of towns and villages due to unregulated building after the first World War, but the problem had begun to make itself felt at the beginning of the century. Only a decade after the establishment of the Middlesex County Council it was clear that the urbanisation of the county area had outstripped the sewage disposal schemes. Rivers were becoming dangerously polluted, and so Middlesex, first of all the counties, obtained sanction in 1898 from Parliament to take over all watercourses in the county, to see to their cleansing, and to proceed against persons who were suspected of allowing or causing pollution. More recently powers were obtained by which the County Council could acquire land compulsorily required for river improvements.

The streams which exist in Middlesex flow either into the Thames or the Lea. The Thames is controlled from its source in Gloucestershire up to Teddington Lock by the Thames Conservancy Board; from thence to the sea is under the Port of London Authority.

The Lea is controlled by the Lea Conservancy Board, and the two boards have "formed drainage districts for the catchment areas of their respective rivers and the main streams entering them." The County Council is able to control the Brent and the Crane and their tributaries, and the artificial streams, the King's River and the Duke's River. The former, sometimes called the Cardinal's River, was constructed under Charles I to supply the ornamental waters at Hampton Court. It was taken out of the Colne at Harmondsworth and flows through Stanwell, Bedfont, Feltham, and Hampton. Henry VII built a stream for the Abbess of

346

Syon to drive mills at Twickenham and Isleworth. These are no longer in use, and it was tiresome for a private owner, the Duke of Northumberland, who owns Syon Park, to control all kinds of development over the land through which his river flowed. The County Council's Act of 1930 gave Middlesex the right to acquire the freehold of the Duke's River, so that they now can supervise the flow of water in time of flood and also control the placing of roads and bridges, gas and water mains and electrical cables when they need to cross the stream.

I remember discussing problems of drainage with Sir Montague Sharp when he was Chairman of the Middlesex County Council, and he emphasised the fact that in the various catchment areas rainfall percolated through the sub-soil and eventually reached the streams. Low-lying pasture-land became flooded in times of heavy rain, thus forming a relief to the built-up areas of higher ground. The lower areas have now been built up, and the obvious method of carrying away superfluous water no longer functions adequately, and inconvenient flooding occurs.

A careful estimate, built up on statistics derived from well-placed rain gauges, gave enough information to make it clear how much straightening, diverting, and strengthening of various river-banks was required. New bridges have been constructed with more ample waterways, and movable weirs have been provided to control the amount of water during flood periods. Weeds and debris are collected, and it would help the Council's plans very much if garden rubbish were carefully burnt or allowed to rot on compost heaps and not thrown into streams.

Problems of sewage disposal were comparatively simple in earlier days, but the very rapid growth of population brought fresh difficulties. Ten years after the establishment of county councils Middlesex got Parliamentary permission first to deal with rivers and sewers and later to acquire land compulsorily for the purpose of drainage. The passing of the Land Drainage Act of 1930 divided the country into catchment areas for dealing with drainage. By this the Thames Conservancy and the Lea Conservancy control the two main streams, while the Brent and Crane and their tributaries are

347

retained by Middlesex, a total of sixty-eight and a half miles of waterway.

LONDON AND MIDDLESEX ARCHÆOLOGICAL SOCIETY

In view of the very close association of Middlesex with London, it is perhaps inevitable that the two counties should share an Archæological Society which has passed its eightieth birthday and seems set fair for its centenary. The Thames has determined London's development to a remarkable degree, and the royal palaces, the Houses of Parliament, the Government offices, and the Law Courts—that is, the head-quarters of the Executive, the Legislature, and the Judiciary —are all on the north side of the river; and in the older Middlesex (before the great schism of 1888-9) the Court and the nobility and the civil servants mainly lived in the West End, while the seamen and the less well-to-do landsmen tended to settle farther down the river below London Bridge, leaving the twenty-six wards of the city for the city companies and business interests. Southwark was the only ward south of the Thames, on the Surrey side, and so it was more natural for London and Middlesex to be associated together in an Archæological Society than London and Surrey or Essex.

The old Society of Antiquaries was naturally started in London, and it interested itself in the affairs of the Metro-polis and to a limited degree in Middlesex. Early historians and cartographers, such as William Camden, John Norden (who lived in Hendon), John Stow, John Speed, Wenceslaus Hollar, Newcourt and Faithorne, Ogilby and Morgan, E. Hatton, John Strype, William Maitland, T. Pennant, devote most of their interest to London proper, though Middlesex comes in more than Surrey; and Maitland definitely claims to be depicting London "within the Bills of Mortality."

It was not until the nineteenth century was past the halfway line that there were serious proposals to undertake the study of the County of Middlesex, which was fast having its per-sonality submerged in that of the expanding Metropolis. In 1854 Surrey started their society, and at their next annual meeting G. B. Webb, F.R.I.B.A., proposed that the society's activities should be extended to include Middlesex, but his proposal was not accepted. So G. B. Webb proposed a society for Middlesex only, but this was changed to London and Middlesex : not intended to trench upon the province of any of the three national societies, but to deal with interests "entirely and exclusively local."

The Marquis of Salisbury was the first patron, and Lord Londesborough was president; a strong committee was elected, almost all Fellows of the Society of Antiquaries, and an important trustee in the person of the Rev. Thomas Hugo, who had been conducting for some years a small gathering of enthusiasts on London's history who met at 57, Bishopsgate Within, at regular intervals. The objects of the newly formed society, which by the end of two months had attracted a membership of almost 200, were extremely wide and have not changed in the course of nearly a century. They were :

"To collect, record and publish the best information on the ancient arts and monuments of the Cities of London and Westminster and of the County of Middlesex, including primæval antiquities; architecture—ecclesiastical, civil and military; sculpture; painting on walls, wood or glass; heraldry and genealogy; costume; numismatics; records; civil and ecclesiastical history and antiquities; manors, manorial rights, privileges and customs and all other matters usually comprised under the head of archæology. To procure careful observation and preservation of antiquities discovered in the progress of works, such as excavations for railways, foundations of buildings, etc. To make, and to encourage individuals and public bodies in making researches and excavations, and to afford to them suggestions and co-operation. To oppose and prevent, as far as may be practicable, any injuries with which monuments and ancient remains of every description may, from time to time, be threatened; and to collect accurate drawings, plans and descriptions thereof."

The Society changed its place of meeting several times in the first few years, and it took some time to settle down in permanent headquarters. To begin with, Middlesex shared offices with Surrey and Southampton Green, then the Society migrated to Fleet Street, Mildred's Court, Danes Inn, Elm Court, Hart Street. This lasted up till 1870, when highly suitable offices were found at University College in Gower

Street for three years. Eleven years followed in Martin's Place, followed by eight in Dane's Inn. For fifteen years the meetings were held at the London Institution, and then in 1910 the Society settled down in hospitable quarters at Bishopsgate Institute, with good accommodation for meetings and councils and for the housing of the Society's library. It will be seen that never has there been any suggestion of housing the Society in Middlesex, nor is such a move at all likely to be made.

Early in its history the Society began to issue regular *Transactions* and from time to time costly quarto volumes of archæological and topographical interest. Among distinguished early editors were the Rev. Thomas Hugo, John Gough Nichols, Arthur Bonner, and Dr. William Martin. There have been more than fifty issues of *Transactions* in the ninety-two years of the Society's existence, and among the important monographs published from time to time have been three volumes on parts of Middlesex or thereabouts—*East Barnet, South Mimms,* and *Monken Hadley*—all by the Rev. F. C. Cass.

The Society has concentrated attention on the recording of all evidence of Roman occupation both in the city and the county, and many historic buildings have been saved from destruction partly by the Society's efforts. The parish church of Heston owes its preservation very largely to the efforts of the London and Middlesex Council.

There have been quite 600 meetings held in the Society's history, and quite as many visits to places of historical and archæological interest in London and in Middlesex. Charles W. F. Goss, F.S.A., a devoted supporter of the Society, who was active in his efforts for local archæology up to the time of his death in 1941, wrote that the 600 papers read before the members and, more often than not, by members cover "nearly every phase of the history and topography of London and Middlesex from primæval times up to the present day, including Roman remains, monastic life, churches, parish life and customs, City guilds, early municipal history, ancient edifices, public buildings, genealogy, heraldry, palæography, city records, and other topics."

The patrons of the Society have included such distinguished

men as the Marquess of Salisbury, the Duke of Wellington, the successive Archbishops of Canterbury and Bishops of London, the Lord Mayors and the Lords-Lieutenant of the two counties. The presidents have included Lord Londes-borough, Lord Talbot de Malahide, General Pitt-Rivers, Dr. Edwin Freshfield, Sir Edward Brabrook, Sir Montague Sharp, the Earl of Strafford, and Lord Nathan of Churt.

Two world wars have hit the Society both in membership and finance, but it is making very big and apparently success-ful efforts to carry on with undiminished vigour and to reach its centenary in really good fettle.

TELEVISION

The success of the Crystal Palace, after its removal from Hyde Park to Sydenham, was so great that it was decided to build a similar block for North London, and after its con-struction in 1873 it was called, in compliment to the Princess of Wales, the Alexandra Palace. It was destroyed by fire a few months after its completion, and Martin Briggs much regrets that the burnt structure was "most unfortunately replaced by the present gigantic abortion in 1875," and suggests that its demolition would be an economy.

The view from it is interesting and diversified; there was always the huge concert hall with a splendid organ, a winter garden, a small theatre, and, down below, one of the few racecourses in Middlesex, which on occasions attracted huge crowds. For some years we held a very successful annual musical festival at the Palace, and choirs from all over North Middlesex and Hertfordshire competed for challenge cups presented by music-lovers from all over England and from some of the Dominions.

But by 1937, although it had been purchased by the Mid-dlesex County Council and local authorities, Alexandra Park was not a success, and its dilapidated gardens needed large sums expended to help to brighten up this "funereal mon-strosity by which Wood Green was overpowered and vulgar-ised." Its central hall, nearly 400 feet long, capable of seating 12,000, with room on the platform for 2,000 performers, was only occasionally used, and the fine Willis-built organ was too often silent.

And then came a remarkable change. The Alexandra Palace, with its 7 acres of buildings in the midst of its 173 acres of park, became the first home of television in this country. J. L. Baird, who discovered its principles in a back street in Soho, has never had justice done to him. His industry and devotion at last had their reward, and when the picture of a wooden doll emerged he found a cripple boy named William Taynton in his gloomy lodging in Soho and made him the first human being ever to be seen on a television screen.

When the B.B.C. began its work in television in 1935 the range of operation was estimated at twenty-five miles. A corner of the Alexandra Palace was chosen to be the first television station in England, and the water tower was soon pulled down to be replaced by a steel mast 220 feet high on the top of a 300-foot hill. There are "girders radiating like stars to make its invisible powers to reach out for picture and sound," and at the top of the aerial is the red lamp which acts as a guide and a warning to aviators. In the brick tower below, and its adjacent rooms, are all the scientific apparatus which collects sight and sound, transforms them into electric waves, and broadcasts them to all places which can pick them up.

Before the war, during the spring and summer of 1939, I spent two holidays at Latimer Lodge on the edge of the Forest of Dean, 800 feet above a remarkable horseshoe bend of the Severn. In those comparatively early days it was a moot point how far television could operate, and fifty miles was considered to be a good achievement. Well, every evening, owing to the enterprise of our host, we could see the television programme as despatched from Alexandra Palace, though the distance was 130 miles.

Arthur Mee was in television some years before that, and he writes of his experiences with just pride. He had been a pioneer in motoring, he had helped Wilbur Wright to fly for the first time in this country, and had been the first in a real passenger plane. He had listened to sounds from the Eiffel Tower and the Kremlin in the earliest days of wireless, but he thinks that television is the most wonderful discovery of them all, and he was rightly proud that, although television was

The Manor, Forty Hill, Enfield

born in the County of London, in Soho, "it was in the county of Middlesex that it was first harnessed to the service of man." The early days were hard and complex, and to the onlooker it seemed chaotic, with lights and cameras and cables and busy people; but success was being achieved and "stroke by stroke the tennis at Wimbledon was coming through."

John Hilton was an early experimenter in television, and he realised that "he would have to brush his hair and put his tie straight." In television there is not the same control over what is said, because the broadcaster must not keep his eyes glued to a typewritten script. John Hilton, in a series of six twenty-minute programmes, was the question-master who discussed with experts such topics as "London's Green Belt," with Herbert Morrison as speaker; "The Future of Trades Unionism," with Sir Walter (now Lord) Citrine; "London's Industrial Belt," with Sir Harold Bellman; "Unemployment," with Sir William (now Lord) Beveridge. This was in pre-war days, and unadvertised progress was made during the war. When places were being discussed for post-war work, a range of about forty miles was used as a basis for calculation. Today the distances are greater, and any mailbag received at Alexandra Palace may bring reports of good viewing at Littlehampton (58), Felixstowe (68) or Wimborne (103 miles away). Reception is reported from Devon, where Torquay registers 168 miles and Haytor 176; and a viewer in Guernsey notes that he has renewed his pre-war activities at 180 miles.

There is clearly a big future for television, and the extremely successful programmes sponsored by the B.B.C. on the occasion of the wedding of Princess Elizabeth and the Duke of Edinburgh hold out a promise of very important developments in the near future. But it seems clear that the curvature of the earth's surface is always likely to limit the distance at which television is possible.

Enfield Chase Gardens

CHAPTER XXIV

THE MIDDLESEX REGIMENT (DUKE OF CAMBRIDGE'S OWN)

THE story of each county regiment contains in its details many of the episodes in British history, for so great a part of that history is, in the more popular imagination, composed of many wars in most corners of the world and interspersed by periods of precarious peace. That such a conception should owe some of its force to the shaken and harassed proceedings during the past half-century is no doubt true. It is also true that the county regiments of the British Army, even though in their earlier years they had but the slenderest connections with any one part of this island, played their rôle in the fighting of our wars, in the expansion and maintenance of an Empire, and in the exchange of impressions of one nation to another. The soldiers left upon the countries they fought in or garrisoned an imprint which for better or for worse was taken to be the mark and character of the British; and our troops, in their own way, brought back their tales of far lands, peoples, and customs. Many of our regiments shared in the same campaigns, fought in the same battles, took part in the same siege or the same pursuit. To homes in every town and village of the British Isles these soldiers brought back their trophies, their medals, and their memories. Their story is one of gallantry and endurance; it is a narrative of many glorious incidents and a few less happy achievements. And if such a tale seems to be one of wars and battles, it should be remembered that long months and still more weary years were spent in the boredom of garrison duties, in the daily routine of barrack square and guardroom, of parade and walking out. The regiments served many years across the waters while relatives waited and worried and longed for a return.

In the messes and museums of these regiments are kept with due pride the records and the trophies, the uniforms and weapons of former days. Here, too, are to be seen the decorations of men who won them decades ago, the diaries and albums, the correspondence and photographs, the portraits and battle scenes hanging round the walls. Wax figures stand in the corners and wear the bright uniforms of the pre-khaki times; relics brought home by prisoners of war are laid upon the tables or in the glass-topped cases; while towards the ceilings hang the colours and flags, the battle honours, and the inscriptions. In veritable armouries against the walls can be found the swords and lances, the muskets and pistols and dirks, the bludgeons and clubs, the rifles and helmets, which belonged both to our own troops and to our enemies of the past.

For close on two centuries the 57th Foot, and for some thirty years' shorter time the 77th, have served their King and their country in the heart and on the outskirts of as many years of history. In achievement and in record, in gallantry and devotion, in action and in garrison, these two regiments, which were later to become the Middlesex Regiment, stand second to none. And in the Inglis Barracks at Mill Hill they will show you all and more of the visible and tangible heritage of the past. And in their achievements, their conversations, and their pride may be found that less tangible but no less inspiring heritage—tradition.

The 57th was raised by John Arabin two days after Christmas in 1755. From Gloucestershire and Somerset came the recruits, whose uniform at the start was red coats, waistcoats, and breeches, set off with lemon-yellow facings and lace. During the Seven Years' War the Regiment garrisoned Gibraltar, and took possession of Minorca when the peace was concluded in 1763. Ten years later the Colonel was John Campbell of Strachur, who had fought at Culloden and served thirty years with his regiment. It was in 1776 that the 57th sailed to America for its first war service, and the battles at Brooklyn, Brandywine Creek, and Charleston were sufficient contrast to the seven years spent previously in various parts of Southern Ireland. When peace was declared in 1783 the Regiment moved north to Halifax in Nova Scotia and stayed there for eight years. In the previous year the 57th's title was, for no special reason, added to by the words "West Middlesex," not that the soldiers were born and bred in that county. On the contrary, many of the officers and men were Scottish, due largely to the influence of Colonel Campbell, and one-quarter of the Regiment was Irish, a result of the 57th's long stay there. It appears, indeed, that until the end of the century nearly half the officers and one-third of the men were of Scottish birth.

After Canada the Regiment returned to Portsmouth, only to see fighting in Flanders two years later. This was a time of widespread war, and the 57th in 1796 sailed under Sir Ralph Abercromby to the West Indies to recapture St. Lucia from the French, and later to quell a native revolt in Grenada. Yellow fever so decimated the Regiment that for a further six years the 57th served as garrison troops in Trinidad and did not return to England until 1803. Once again the men had but short stay within their native shores and were soon in Gibraltar, this time under the command of Colonel William Inglis, who had joined the Regiment as far back as 1781 in America.

Meanwhile a second Regiment had been raised, the 77th Foot. This occurred in 1787, when new bodies of troops were required for service in India. The first colonel of the 77th was an Irishman named James Marsh, and its first commander a Scotsman, James Balfour. Many of the early officers, as in the case of the companion 57th, were Scottish, including the senior captain, Bulstrode Whitelocke, descendant of a distinguished soldier, chronicler, and ambassador in the days of Cromwell; he had entered the Army at the youthful age of fifteen. Another officer named Spry, though eighteen, had already served with the colours seven years.

In the year following its formation the 77th sailed to India, and during two years in the southern parts of that vast country fought in the conquest of Travancore and took part in Abercromby's column over the Ghats to Mysore by way of Coorg. The first Mysore War ended in 1792, by which time the Regiment had helped to secure both Malabar and Coorg. In the same year that the 57th set out for the West Indies the 77th were engaged in operations against the Dutch in Ceylon, and then remained for two years in Cochin. Records of that date show that among the officers of the Regiment seven were English, five Irish, and nineteen were Scottish by birth; while the ranks counted 335 English, 62 Scottish, 73 Irish, and 42 foreign soldiers in their total.

As the eighteenth century drew to its close the 77th fought in the second Mysore War, once again in opposition to Tippoo Sahib, who perished with ten thousand of his men in the siege and storming of Seringapatam. In the summer of 1800 the Regiment served under Colonel Arthur Wellesley in his first independent command, and helped to hunt down the freebooter Dondia Wao. By the end of the following year, however, as a result of the constant and harassing campaigning against the rebels in the jungle country of Madura, the 77th was unfit for further service and was withdrawn to rest at Mangalore, thus following the suit of the 57th, then garrisoned in Trinidad.

Of the Regiment Wellesley wrote in his despatches: "They went into the field in the beginning of 1799, and I may safely say that they have been in camp ever since and have been more harassed than any regiment in the service." Double battle honours of "Mysore" and "Seringapatam" were awarded to the colours of the 77th, though this did not take place until very many years later. After service in Bombay the Regiment returned to England in 1807, after an absence of nearly twenty years and with a record of great distinction. It was at this moment, too, that the 77th was styled the East Middlesex, not that this title had any practical significance, for many of the new recruits came from militia regiments in West Kent, West Yorkshire, and from Ireland.

Two years after the disastrous expedition to Walcheren, where folly and mismanagement combined with the ravages of malarial swamps to undermine both the success of the undertaking and the health of the troops involved, the 77th went in 1810 to Jersey and spent there a year with the 2nd Battalion of the 57th. This was the first occasion upon which the two regiments had met. It was at this time, too, the Prince of Wales's plume, which had been used for some years as the regimental badge, was officially recognised. A boon of a different order was the abolishment in 1808 of the queue, the troops being allowed to wear their hair short.

It was a strange fate that set Dr. W. H. Fitchett, a Methodist parson in Australia, to retell in vivid prose some of *The Deeds that Won the Empire*, but he did it, as he said, "not to glorify war, but to nourish patriotism." Perhaps in 1897 we needed some such stimulus.

Not the least memorable of the stories is that which tells of Beresford's battle of the Fusiliers, twelve miles south of Badajoz, at Albuhera, where the 57th Regiment of Foot, on May 16, 1811, earned undying fame, their first battle honour, and the name of "Die-hards." "Albuhera," wrote Fitchett, "is the fiercest, bloodiest, and most amazing fight in the mighty drama of the Peninsular War"; and Beresford, hardly even a third-rate general, with British troops less than one-third of his half-starved army to manœuvre with, ought not to have fought that day. Wellington had directed Beresford to besiege Badajoz, had warned him that Soult would hurry to its relief, had advised his subordinate to avoid giving battle if possible, but had suggested Albuhera as the best place to fight if the need arose.

The French commander, Soult, brought some 25,000 troops and all his skill to bear on the battle. Both sides fought with amazing courage, and at a critical moment in the contest a fierce second counter-attack was launched by the British. Houghton's brigade, less than 2,000 men in all, swept up the hill, led by Houghton, hat in hand. Up a deep ravine they pushed, and they held the ground at the crest against a column more than four times their number. Colonel William Inglis, commanding the 57th, dressed his thin red line shoulder to shoulder, with the colours in the centre, before he would give his men the order to return the fire, which scourged them at fifty yards range. Houghton was killed. Twenty-three other officers were killed, the colour-bearers were shot down as others came forward to keep the colours flying. The British line, decimated by murderous fire of shell and grape-shot, stood unflinching and held the hill until reinforcements came to turn the tide of battle.

Of the 57th, 430 out of 570 were killed or wounded, and were found with their faces towards the enemy and their wounds in front. It was Colonel Inglis, who had already had a horse shot under him, who, lying grievously wounded near the colours in front of his ranks, shouted to his troops : "Die hard, my men, die hard !"

The sobriquet stuck to the Regiment, whose crest bears, in

commemoration of the battle, a silver laurel wreath and the epitome of heroism, "Albuhera."

Soult gave to the British troops their best testimonial : "There is no beating these troops, in spite of their generals! I always thought them bad soldiers, now I am sure of it! For I turned their right, pierced their centre, they were everywhere broken, the day was mine, and yet they did not know it, and would not run !"

Wellington's view of the battle forms an interesting contrast to the enthusiasm of the French opponent, for he termed Albuhera "a strange concern." "They were," he wrote, "never determined to fight it; they did not occupy the ground as they ought; they were ready to run away at every moment from the time it commenced till the French retired. . . . Another such battle would ruin us."

Beresford, however, lacked no warmth of praise in his despatch to Wellington when he wrote : "Nothing could exceed the conduct and gallantry of Colonel Inglis at the head of his regiment." Inglis, described by Napier as "one of those veterans who purchase every step of promotion with their blood," recovered from his wounds, was eventually promoted Lieutenant-General, and became Colonel of the 57th in 1830, holding that appointment until his death five years later. He was buried in Canterbury Cathedral. It is a fitting coincidence that Inglis, who joined the 57th as an ensign in 1779, should die in the fifty-seventh year of his service. The present headquarters of the Middlesex Regiment at Mill Hill bear his name as a proud memory.

One of the Regiment's treasured possessions in Inglis Barracks is the picture "Steady the Drums and Fifes" painted by Lady Butler. It shows the drummers and fifers drawn up on the right of the 57th Foot, under Colonel Inglis, who is on horseback, on the ridge of Albuhera. Still remembered are the lines that Byron wrote upon the first great action of the Regiment :

> "Even as they fought in files they lay,
> Like the Mower's grass at the close of day,
> When his work is o'er on the levelled plain
> Such was the fall of the foremost slain."

The 77th, who did not land in the Peninsula until 1811, two years after the 57th, joined the Third Division, commanded by General Thomas Picton, who in that same year became the Regiment's fifth colonel. Under him they had already served in Walcheren two years previously, suffering heavily from malaria during that campaign. He had been Governor of Trinidad while the 57th were there twelve years previously. Picton was a flamboyant, picturesque commander whose voice resembled a score of trumpets in volume, whose costume was invariably eccentric. At Vittoria he rode up and down, angry, wearing a blue coat and an unmilitary top-hat, shouting : "Damn it ! Lord Wellington has forgotten us." He sent his division into battle with the characteristic command : "Come on, ye rascals ! Come on, ye fighting villains !" He led them into action, to quote Guedalla, "in a cloud of blasphemy and a top-hat."* Picton was killed at Waterloo one second after he had urged on his troops to charge.

On September 25, 1811, Picton's division held the plateau by El Bodon, some six miles out from Ciudad Rodrigo, which Wellington was then blockading. The French commander Marmont pushed forward with 2,500 cavalry on a reconnaissance, found the position weakly held by a long, straggling line, and attacked. The 77th and the 5th Foot (now the Royal Northumberland Fusiliers) formed one square, the Portuguese troops another, and both repulsed time and again with great steadiness and courage the French charges. The front rank knelt, holding their bayonets towards the cavalry, and all fired volleys into the oncoming horses. Despite continuous enemy shelling, not one British officer was lost. An officer of the 77th who took part in the action wrote : "A shot fell under Colonel Dunkin's horse and covered him with dirt, without hurting him or his horse. Our major had a portmanteau knocked from the rear of his saddle by one of the enemy's nine-pounders, within half a foot of his back; he coolly turned round and said : 'There was nearly an end of poor Jack !'" The British guns were overrun and then recaptured. The position was held by our troops until they were able to rejoin the remainder of the division. General Picton,

* On another occasion he is reported to have beat his horse with a furled umbrella.

speaking to the Regiment during the action, said : "Your safety, my credit, and the honour of the Army all rest with you at this moment," a sentiment that must have occurred in the mind of many a general since that day. Though El Bodon was only a rearguard action, it was hardly less proud a feat for the 77th than was Albuhera for the 57th. Wellington "recommended to the particular attention of the officers and soldiers of the Army an example to be followed in all such circumstances."

During 1813 the 57th took part in the Battle of Vittoria, pursued the retreating French across the Pyrenees into France, fought battles at Nivelle in November and at Nive in the following month, winning honours at each. They were joined in 1814, in the victorious advance towards Toulouse, by the 77th, who had been obliged to recuperate in Lisbon, having been reduced by casualties and sickness to one hundred men fit for duty, after helping in the capture of both Ciudad Rodrigo and of Badajoz. After a year in Canada the 57th spent the winter of 1815 near Paris, and served with the army of occupation in the brigade commanded by Sir Manley Power, who gave his name to the present regimental march. He is supposed to have found the music in a French camp, and caused it to be adopted by the 57th. Another march, "Lass of Gowrie," dates from 1857, and is also played. The 77th, on the other hand, have "Paddy's Resource" as a march past, and this tune was composed by the regimental bandmaster in 1855 in the trenches before Sevastopol. It appears that the Colonel desired a march with an Irish air, because of the high proportion of Irish soldiers serving in the Regiment at the time.

During the next forty years of peace the 77th served in Jamaica and Malta, in Corfu and Canada, while the 57th was stationed in Australia and in various parts of India. When the Crimean War broke out in 1854 the 77th was the first of the two regiments to be engaged, for it saw action at Alma. It is the Battle of Inkerman, however, that is remembered by the Middlesex Regiment with especial pride. This battle occupies one whole volume in Kinglake's *Crimean War*, and Fitchett, in his *Fights for the Flag*, describes it thus :

"It was one of the most distracted, planless, muddle-headed yet magnificent battles in British history . . . an illustration of the chivalrous daring of the British officer and the dogged, unconquerable fighting quality of the British private."

It was a battle with no strategy and with but little tactics; with every man his own general; desperate charges, unco-ordinated attacks, and, ultimately, a glorious victory for the smaller army. Fitchett summed up Inkerman in words that deserve to live :

"The individual courage displayed on the part of the British, the close and deadly quality of their fire, and the resolute daring with which clusters of men numbering a few score threw themselves, again and again, on massed battalions to be numbered by the thousand, *had given a tiny few the victory over the many*."

Four companies of the 77th, under Colonel Egerton, found a huge Russian column winding up a ravine. Without delay they charged the flank of the Russians with fifty men only, broke through them, and fractured the column's spine. When a second enemy column, personally led by General Soimonoff, came up the slopes, Colonel Egerton and his men attacked it. The fire from their muskets, the charge of the bayonets, and the few officers on horseback so alarmed the Russians in the fog of war and weather that, with the prospect of more deadly charges by light and heavy brigades of cavalry, they broke and were pushed down the hillside.

Later on Lieutenant Acton, with sixty men of the 77th, was ordered to attack Shell Hill in company with two other tiny groups of soldiers. The officers of the other regiments refused to bring up their companies on the flank, so Acton called to his own men : "Forward, lads !" But they saw that a task too desperate for three companies was madness for one, and they refused to advance. "Then," said Acton, "I'll go by myself," and off he started. Soon Private Tyrrel ran after him and shouted : "Sir, I'll stand by you." Such is the magical effect of courage that the 77th rushed after him, the two other companies followed suit, and the Russian gunners wheeled round their guns and made off.

Nor were the 57th to be outdone at Inkerman, for it was

their task, two hundred of them led by Captain Stanley, to attack the right battalion of the Russians, firmly planted, massive and undestroyed, on the Home Ridge. Stanley shouted to his men, charging with fixed bayonets : "Men, remember Albuhera !" Then he fell, mortally wounded. But his courageous example and his timely shout sent the two hundred forward, now under the son of Inglis of Albuhera, in a charge that cleared the whole ridge, held by at least an enemy battalion. Listen to Fitchett's comment, in words that were to be used, slightly modified, in a still more fateful hour :

"Where else in the history of battles can we find such amazing examples of the overthrow of the many by the few?"

Both regiments shared in the Siege of Sevastopol the next year, during which Colonel Egerton died, shot through the head at a moment when his men had driven back the Russians. While the French vainly stormed the Malakoff, the 57th and 77th led the right flank assault on the Redan. This failed too. It was during the fighting round Sevastopol that Victoria Crosses were won by Colour-Sergeant James Gardiner of the 57th—he had won the Distinguished Conduct Medal only a few months before, and was the first man to hold both decorations—and by Privates Wright and McCorrie, and by Sergeant Park. A memorable exploit was the capture by the fifteen-year-old Drummer MacGill of an enemy bugle; he dashed into the Russian pits, seized a bugler, and forced him to surrender his instrument as a trophy. The 77th won a battle honour for Alma, the 57th won one for Balaclava, and "Inkerman" and "Sevastopol" were awarded to both regiments as doubly earned honours for the colours.

After the Crimean War companies of the 57th served in Malta and in Aden, but 1860 saw the Regiment transported to New Zealand for the Maori War, a conflict of bush-fighting, attacks on native stockades, and skirmishes that dragged on until 1866. In one such encounter, on September 24, 1863, Drummer Stagpoole won the D.C.M. for rescuing wounded comrades, and only a week later he earned, with Ensign Down, the Victoria Cross. To win both decorations within a week was unparalleled, and "New Zealand" was added to the Regiment's battle honours. After only six years in England the 57th, now the West Middlesex, was abroad in Ceylon, from where it was despatched in 1870 to Durban to fight in the Zulu War against Cetewayo in such remote places as Ginghilovo and Ekowe.

The 77th, meanwhile, had served in New South Wales and in India. The Regiment, leaving there in 1870, was the first to pass through the newly completed Suez Canal. It was in the summer of 1876 that the title of the Regiment was changed to the Duke of Cambridge's Own (East Middlesex), and the Duke's coronet and cypher were added to the badge of the 77th. 1881 saw the end of the independent existence of both the 57th and the 77th, and in this year they were permanently linked as the 1st and 2nd Battalions of the Duke of Cambridge's Own (Middlesex) Regiment. It is noteworthy that during the century and a quarter since it was first raised the 57th had served abroad for eighty-five years. The Royal East Middlesex Militia and the Royal Elthorne Light Infantry became the 3rd and 4th Battalions, thereby completing the regular strength of the Regiment.

The 1st Battalion was in India and the 2nd in England when in 1899 the South African War broke out. The 2nd fought with Buller at the failure of Spion Kop, took part in the Relief of Ladysmith, saw action at Alleman's Nek and Laing's Nek, for which service they were highly praised, and finally helped to clear Natal. Although the 1st Battalion stayed out in India until 1913, the 2nd came home from South Africa in 1903, and stayed ten years before proceeding to Malta a little before the coming of the first World War.

On the outbreak of war in August, 1914, the four regular battalions of the Middlesex Regiment were in readiness. By the end of 1918 no fewer than forty-six battalions were serving at home or overseas. Six Victoria Crosses and eighty-three battle honours were won by the officers and men of these battalions, and the memorial at the regimental depot commemorates more than twelve thousand soldiers who lost their lives during those four years of conflict. The war, as for every other regiment in the British Army, was a story written in blood and mud, in carnage and long casualty lists, in valour and persistence, in glory and in sacrifice. The record of the Middlesex Regiment is second to none.

The 1st and 4th Battalions took part in the retreat from Mons, the former fighting at Le Cateau, the latter losing in killed or wounded 15 officers and 452 other ranks during one action alone, when they held a loop of the Mons Canal throughout one whole day. Though subjected to intense artillery fire, these men beat back the drive of six German battalions before falling back on orders; they were paid the compliment of being cheered as they came out of the line by the other regiments present. Both battalions played a full part in the Battle of the Marne. The 2nd suffered fearful casualties at Neuve Chapelle in March, 1915, and the 3rd hurled back a superior enemy force during the second Battle of Ypres. Loos saw the 1st Battalion again, attacking uncut wire, while the 13th was almost annihilated in its first action, the defence of the *Fosses* there.

It was during the fighting on Bellewarde Ridge in the last days of that September that Second Lieutenant R. P. Hallowes won the Victoria Cross for inspiring gallantry with the 4th Battalion, and his dying words are with justice placed beside those of Colonel Inglis at Albuhera :

"Men, we can only die once. If we have to die, let us die like men—like Die-hards !"

The 2nd Battalion won great fame at the Somme Battle in July, 1916, when in an attack towards La Boiselle, unsupported by their flanking troops, 300 men reached the first German line of trenches, captured this and reached the second line, where the forty survivors of this shattered advance cleared an entrance, only to be obliterated by enemy shellfire. Five men and their sergeant came back from that ordeal.

Mention of the achievements and endurance of the Regiment can only be by selection, but those who fought will remember the 2nd and 16th Battalions at Albert during July of 1916, and Private Ward, the stretcher-bearer who earned the D.C.M. and a bar to his Military Medal. Nor will the Regiment forget how the 12th, having captured Trônes Wood that summer, fought on Thiepval Ridge in the September, and how Privates F. J. Edwards and Robert

365

Ryder won the Victoria Cross on this battered field of action.

No less than eleven battalions were involved in the Battles of Arras in 1917, and, while the 17th suffered grievous losses in Oppy Wood that April, the hard-fought 1st Battalion lost 6 officers and 400 men during one day's fighting in the to-and-fro struggles through Polygon Wood. The Regiment gained a battle honour at Cambrai in November, and Captain MacReady-Diarmid of the 17th won an unsurpassed V.C., holding with but a handful of men a trench for two days, himself killing or wounding single-handed 94 Germans. Finally he drove the enemy back three hundred yards by flinging bomb after bomb, until he was killed, after a feat which, to quote the official citation, "can hardly, if ever, have been equalled in the past."

During the final assault of the German armies in March, 1918, many battalions of the Middlesex Regiment were shattered in desperate fighting; casualties and sacrifices were enormous, yet courage and tenacity never waned, and at last the tide turned again. In the April battle of the Ancre the 2nd Battalion, whose colonel had reported near Arras a few weeks earlier that "the pride of all ranks in the Regiment grew from day to day," lost near Villers-Bretonneux 13 officers and 530 other ranks, so that a mere 39 survived for further trials of the human flesh and spirit. It was a company commander of this same battalion, Captain A. M. Toye, who in the gallant defence of the Somme crossings that March had, though twice wounded within ten days, earned a Victoria Cross on the Eterpigny Ridge. The commanding officer, Colonel Page, had himself, with two men, covered the withdrawal of his headquarters; he left the trench only three minutes before the German troops rushed in; he had fired three hundred rounds, and thereby set a memorable example to his men during a defensive action in which eleven platoons perished, resisting at all costs. As the Colonel wrote afterwards: "The 77th has never fought against such odds with such success except at Inkerman. Thank God all ranks did their duty!" The Battle of the Selle in the final advance through Picardy found the decimated and exhausted 1st Battalion able to muster only ninety ranks, while in Artois, one month before the "Cease Fire," a brigadier and the commanding officer had personally led the remnants of a company into attack.

Far beyond the blood-stained and mud-churned confines of the Western Front the 3rd Battalion won a battle honour at Suvla Bay in Gallipoli, the 2/10th marched with Allenby from Gaza to Jerusalem, and the 1/9th fought in the later stages of the Mesopotamian campaign in the advance on Mosul.

The cost and the sorrow had been great, the heroism and endurance, the determination and spirit worthy to be praised and to be remembered. The traditions of the Regiment had been maintained and enhanced, and further honours added to the colours.

In the prolonged and often desperate struggle of the second World War the Middlesex Regiment fought against all three enemies on fronts as far distant one from another as Dunkirk and Hong Kong. The 2nd Battalion, firing their machine-guns in support of Montgomery's Third Division, fought in France in 1940 under its commander, the future Lieut.-General Sir Brian Horrocks, advanced through Belgium to Louvain, withdrew to Dunkirk, and returned to Britain in the little ships of salvation. Last out then, the battalion under Colonel Weston was among the first to set foot in France four years later on D Day. It fought in Normandy, drove into Belgium, helped at the Escaut Canal bridgehead, and progressed to the Weert Canal in Holland. That October the battalion, by Overloon and Venraij, fired 8,000 bombs and 638,000 rounds. The winter was spent watching the banks of the Maas, and with the early spring in the air Weston's men took part in the final stages of Operation "Veritable" against the Rhine and advanced with the Third Division to Bremen, clearing up resistance by-passed by the Guards Armoured Division. Their last action was a moonlight attack on April 24 against that part of Bremen west of the Weser River.

The 1/7th, which, like the 18th, also fought with the British Expeditionary Force, served as machine-gun battalion to the Fifty-first (Highland) Division from El Alamein to the Baltic, played an active part in the fighting south of Caen, in the capture of St. Valéry and the assault on Le Havre. After a winter beside the Maas the 1/7th saw fighting in the Reichwald battle.

The 2/7th represented the Regiment on the blood-stained beachheads of Anzio and Salerno and supported the First Division in North Africa and in Italy, while the 8th Battalion shared the Thirty Corps' dash to Arnhem, aided the withdrawal of the First Airborne Division, and was the first battalion of the Middlesex Regiment to enter Germany.

The two Territorial battalions, the 1st and 2nd Kensingtons, supported the Seventy-eighth and Forty-ninth Divisions respectively. The former fought over the Catania plain of Sicily, was present at the landing at Taranto, at the battles by the Sangro River and in Cassino, and shared in the drive towards Rome. After refitting in Egypt, in climate sharply contrasted to that experienced by their companion battalion in Iceland, and later in France, the 1st Kensingtons took part in the final offensive to the Po, by way of the Senio and Santerno Rivers. These men were to tread the soil of both Austria and Greece before they returned to their native shores.

If these activities of the Regiment seem to be a sequence of journeys and places, so, too, are they in the memories of those who fought there a sequence interwoven with the myriad details of their life and their companions, their successes and failures, their gains and their losses, their tension and their boredom.

In this brief survey of the Middlesex Regiment's achievements during the second World War pride of mention should go to the 1st Battalion, whose members were killed or captured in the defence of Hong Kong. Such a complete disaster caused the 2/8th to be renamed the 1st in 1942, and this second version supported the Fifteenth Scottish Division in the Normandy landings and in the August drive across the Seine. It reached the Albert Canal, formed a bridgehead on the Escaut, wintered in Holland, and, when the "Cease Fire" was sounded in May, 1945, this battalion was holding another bridgehead across the Elbe.

But what of Hong Kong in the closing weeks of 1941?

368

In company with the 2nd Battalion Royal Scots, two Canadian and two Indian infantry battalions, the 1st Middlesex formed the garrison defending that small and distant colony. Since the outbreak of war the four machine-gun companies had between them manned 110 guns in the beach defence pill-boxes, the battalion being responsible for defending almost the entire coast of Hong Kong Island.

It was in the early hours of December 8 that the Japanese launched their initial attacks, and for the next seventeen days and nights the officers and men of the 1st Middlesex and their companion units were engaged in all but ceaseless fighting against the heaviest odds. After ten days the enemy landed by night on the north-east shore of the island, the most lightly held sector of the perimeter, and both the choice of place and the execution of the landing were only too successful, for their rapid advance brought the Japanese to the summit of such commanding heights as Mounts Parker and Butler and Jardine's Lookout. It is reported that a large number of the enemy troops swam the channel, towing their arms and equipment on floats—no mean feat. The enemy force threatened to split the island; our troops were compelled to withdraw from one line to another, resisting doggedly, worn out by great loss of sleep and intense physical fatigue.

Among the exploits during those searing days and nights the withdrawal of Second Lieutenant Cheesewright and the crews of his five pill-boxes to the Stanley Peninsula, the southern tip of Hong Kong Island, is striking. The party walked in stockinged feet for five hours in darkness, bringing out safely every gun and some ammunition under the very noses of the Japanese, who had already penetrated the area. Or again, how dramatic was the escape of Captain West and his observation post party, who, when discovered in an upper room of their house, fought their way out with hand grenades, killed the enemy officer, and made away to fight again. Also memorable is the defence of Leighton Hill on the northern flank by Captain Man and his composite "Z" Company.

When Christmas Day dawned the situation in Hong Kong had become desperate, for only Stanley Peninsula and the western end of the island still held out. In the middle of that afternoon, the spirit of which was far removed from that associated with Christmas, the General Officer Commanding, Major-General C. M. Maltby, telephoned to the commanding officer of the 1st Middlesex, Lieut.-Colonel H. W. M. Stewart, and announced that he was obliged to make a very grave decision, which would be based largely upon the Colonel's replies. The General asked : "How long do you think you can hold your present line, and what is the state of your troops?" Stewart replied : "I do not think this line can hold for more than one hour with the enemy pressure as it is at present. I could, if not too heavily pressed, hold on till nightfall. After that I fear that it would be difficult, due largely to the sheer exhaustion of the troops. They are very tired." A few minutes later the decision was made. "We are going," said Maltby, "to surrender so as to stop further bloodshed and wholesale slaughter. You are authorised to raise a white flag."

That Christmas night was the first chance of rest for many days. The struggle was over; the battalion had lost 11 officers and 140 other ranks killed in action. Those who had passed through the fire of battle and had survived had now to endure the flames of brutal captivity, from which yet another 200 men were never to return. If Hong Kong seems to figure small in the vast sequence of campaigns and battles, of retreats and invasions, if maybe we hardly noticed these happenings among the black trail of disastrous headlines during those long-ago months, and if, too, we have all but forgotten that Hong Kong saw fighting, then we are wrong. For the brave men who fought there it is "their war," the fount of their most burning memories, the gravestone of their gallant comrades.

Colonel L. A. Newnham, senior staff officer of the fortress headquarters and formerly commanding officer of the 1st Middlesex, wrote to Colonel Stewart after the battle in these striking terms : "From the General down to other ranks of other units there is nothing but admiration for the way the men of your Regiment have fought. They have upheld the traditions of the Die-hards and relived the glories of Albuhera." The Japanese, too, expressed their admiration for the defenders of Stanley Peninsula.

Both during the rigours of fighting and the ghastly conditions and disillusionment of captivity, Colonel Stewart, the magnificent and beloved commander, shone as a tower of strength and energy. When, after ten months of imprisonment in Hong Kong, the Japanese shipped the remnants of his battalion towards Japan in the *Lisbon Maru,* the vessel was torpedoed. The enemy, leaving a few guards on deck, abandoned ship, after locking the 1,100 prisoners in the holds. Stewart's calm prevented panic under these brutal conditions, and he and his men eventually forced their way to the daylight, though many were shot by the waiting guards. When the survivors did at last reach Japan the gallant Colonel died within a few days from—I quote from Lieut.-Colonel Hedgecoe's report—"the effects of his exertions on behalf of his beloved men, and from the knowledge of the cruel fate so many of them had suffered."

Although the Regiment won no Victoria Cross during the second World War, such conduct as that of Stewart and his companions, and of Colonel Newnham, is as high as anything in the rich annals of the Die-hards, and it was fitting indeed that a posthumous George Cross should be awarded to Colonel Newnham. This officer and Captain D. Ford, of the 2nd Royal Scots, were arrested by the Japanese in July, 1943, in Hong Kong, and both officers were interrogated under torture for information that would have implicated fellow-prisoners had it been divulged. It was not. They both tried to concoct a joint story and, having failed to achieve this by tapping Morse signals on the wall of their cells, they confided in an Indian lying in another cell across the passage. This man turned out to be an informer and he betrayed them to the Japanese, who had promised the Indian his life.

The pair were kept in Stanley until the beginning of December, when their belated trial opened. Newnham was extremely ill from malnutrition, and he was suffering with a temperature of 103° at the time. The British officers were condemned to death, but they lay in their cells for a further seventeen days, growing weaker and more gravely ill. They lived without exercise, without hope of reprieve, on starvation rations, not permitted to communicate with a soul. Yet their self-control and their courage were maintained unbroken to the end throughout the harrowing ordeal and strain. On December 18 they were shot by a firing party of Japanese. Colonel Newnham's heroic conduct earned this tribute from General Maltby : "Without any doubt I and quite a number of other senior officers owe our lives to his unequalled bravery under the most terrible physical suffering and mental strain."

And so the war came to an end on the widespread battle-fronts of the world. Those who survived came home to their people, and those who lay on foreign fields lived on in the memories of those who had loved them. Another long chapter of disastrous history had been written in letters of black and red, fresh lustre had been added to the colours of every regiment. In company with the millions of their comrades who fought during these years, and, indeed, from the days of the Peninsular War forward, the officers and men of the Middlesex Regiment, the famous 57th and 77th, had made their contribution to the triumphs at long last of the freedom-loving peoples of the world.

But the Axis War was not the last chance of distinction for the "Die-hards." In the Korean campaigns, towards the end of 1950, the 1st Battalion of the Middlesex Regiment kept up the grand traditions of the past, even in the bitter winter conditions which then prevailed, when the men had only four days of rest in over three months of campaigning, and the temperature dropped to 18 degrees below zero.

Chapter XXV

WILD LIFE IN MIDDLESEX TODAY

ONE of the most momentous of decisions ever taken by those responsible for town planning and building was the refusal of the Corporation of the City of London in 1636 to accept four fresh wards in the suburbs of the Metropolis. This had even more far-reaching effects than the turning down by Charles II and the authorities of Wren's very hastily produced plan (one among four) for the rebuilding of the City after the Fire of 1666. What was wanted was some control of present and future development of London, and very wise hints were given by John Evelyn and Sir William Petty, who between them outlined a scheme for a green belt in 1666 only about two miles from the centre.

The chances then lost did not occur again for more than two hundred years, and in the meantime serious inroads of unplanned building had been made in almost every direction round London. The suburban sprawl almost all round the Metropolis was not as bad as the hideous monstrosities— the back-to-back rows of slums—erected in such towns as Leeds, but it provided problems in London and Middlesex which have never yet been solved.

The work of Ebenezer Howard at Letchworth, the first of the real garden cities, showed how very attractive could be the plan of a convenient town set in the softening surroundings of a green and pleasant countryside. It was really the first attempt to build a separate satellite town and not to enlarge an existing desert of bricks and mortar by creating "radial suburbs following the main roads, arms of an octopus whose body is the town." These suburbs have neither the self-contained life of the town nor the rural amenities of the country, and they often fail to produce the good citizen, seeing that they illustrate only a fraction of his life. As Dr. Vaughan Cornish so aptly puts it : "In a well-planned city the architecture is displayed against a verdant setting; in the country any good architectural feature forms a suitable focus for a landscape of informal lines; but in the unplanned

373

suburb the confusion of these forms produces a state of camouflage, which is the bane of beauty." The serious damage done to the City of London and the wider area administered by the London County Council by the aerial attacks during the Battle of Britain and later have given a chance of wise reconstruction. But this is not so much the case in Middlesex as it is in South-west Essex and North-west Kent, where bomb damage was far more widespread.

It is a thousand pities that there is so little of the charm of the village or the medieval town in most of the never-ending suburbs of London. In fact "the antithesis of the Arcadian scenery of the country parish is that of the national Capital." The spread of London's population between the two World Wars has tended to increase the social impoverishment of suburban areas by increased ribbon development, even along the arterial roads that are centred on London, and whose early miles in so many instances pass through Middlesex. The growth of Greater London during the between-war period has affected Middlesex more than any of the three or four other counties concerned, and a very considerable proportion of the million additions to the population of the Greater London area is to be found in Middlesex.

Dr. Vaughan Cornish, in a special appeal for the restoration of Nature in the modern farm, asks that "every practicable means of smoke abatement be promoted by the authorities; let every householder brighten the view with flowers in window-boxes whose colours are so telling against the background of masonry; and above all let the rebuilding schemes be for the accommodation of no more than the present population but in higher houses occupying less land, and thus leaving space for town gardens and boulevard avenues." Recent visits to Switzerland will have convinced many of us that we have much to learn from the Swiss on all these problems of reconstruction.

Almost every other county in England save Middlesex has most of its acres untouched by suburbia, and even in Surrey and Essex, which have had to submit to London's sprawl, the majority of the county is still unspoiled. True it is that the close-packed suburbs to the north-east, south-east, and south of the City have reached a far higher level of overcrowding and a lower level of design than the corresponding areas in Middlesex, but the areas here which can still be saved are few in number and many problems arise from time to time to threaten the country which still remains.

In reading Eric Parker's parallel volume on *Surrey* one is struck by the fact that much more than half its pages are occupied by vivid descriptions of the countryside, artistic and accurate stories of bird-life, wild animals, forests, moors and wild flowers, a thing which would be quite impossible in modern Middlesex. His introductory chapter complains that a glorious piece of Surrey was sacrificed when Brooklands was created. A far more pathetic series of stories could very easily be told of at least a dozen parts of Middlesex. There are, however, two bright spots in what sometimes seems a completely gloomy prospect. The Green Belt has materialised just in time to save quite a big slice of Northern and Western Middlesex, and the construction of reservoirs in various parts of the county has given a remarkable fillip to the restoration of bird-life.

The problem of a national park for London is not of similar design to that of any other part of the British Isles. London and therefore Middlesex have to be content with a far more modest layout than, say, Dartmoor for Plymouth or Bristol, the Black Mountains for Cardiff, the Lake District for Liverpool and Manchester, the moors and dales for Leeds and Sheffield, the Roman Wall for Newcastle, or the Trossachs for Glasgow. The passing of the Town and Country Planning Act in 1932 gave powers to local authorities to preserve scenic amenities, and it was passed only just in time, because the spate of building which followed the first World War made serious and almost unavoidable inroads on the countryside, especially in counties like Middlesex, which were already seriously over-urbanised. Motor traffic, with greatly increased manufacture of cars and unlimited petrol supplies, disturbed the age-long peace even of remote villages, and there was a serious threat to rustic beauty by sporadic poster advertisements. As Dr. Vaughan Cornish emphasises in his book on the *Preservation of Our Scenery,* the Council for the Preservation of Rural England should have shown even more concern for protecting urban England.

There are special town and country problems in Middlesex today which occur in no other county in England. In spite of the proximity to London and the rapid suburbanisation of Middlesex itself, the county still prides itself on a good deal of open space, which it is straining every nerve to protect. The pathetic cry for more houses is met by the demand that the Green Belt shall be sacrosanct. An outward push to more distant suburbs makes the business man spend time and money which he can ill afford in getting to and from his job in the City. If to remedy these anomalies satellite towns are suggested, where families can live and work without long train journeys, landowners in the threatened area plead for the exclusion of their own pet site from development, and protest that to bring more bricks and mortar into their district would be a civic crime.

There have been many arguments put forward by interested folk as to the good or harm done by birds to crops in this country. But the weight of evidence is enormously on the side of those who regard bird life as an essential feature in town and country alike. As a nation of those who are countrymen at heart, in spite of the sprawling of the hideous town, we are lovers of bird life and expect the birds to breed and multiply without often asking if the conditions are favourable for their survival. The authorities for nearly half a century past have planned for the active protection of birds in the London area. London itself—that is, the L.C.C. area—is governed by the Wild Birds Protection Order for the County of London, 1909, while Middlesex had to wait for a similar order until 1935.

On all sides of the Greater London area the streams and ponds and reservoirs have helped to preserve the bird-life of the district, and of those in Middlesex we should mention the Brent Reservoir between Hendon and Neasden, water in Gunnersbury and Osterley Parks and the Royal Parks, which, both in London or near it, have all been made official bird sanctuaries. The Ministry of Works makes itself responsible for these preserves and publishes an interesting annual report on the birds seen in them. Those in Middlesex include the wonderful oasis in the south-west of the Thames consisting of the gardens of Hampton Court and Bushey Park.

The London County Council protects birds in its open spaces, and Hampstead Heath and Kenwood, with Golders Hill hard by, are either on the fringe of Middlesex or just on the Middlesex side. Even the City of London Corporation is able to come to the aid of birds in Middlesex by preserving as open spaces important areas in Highgate and Hornsey, Queen's Wood and Highgate Wood, and the curiously named Finsbury Park. There are also several private bird sanctuaries in Middlesex : one, the Gilbert White Memorial Sanctuary belonging to the Selborne Society and established in 1901 at Perivale, and two smaller ones at Ickenham and Ruislip. Perivale is rather in the midst of built-up areas, but its actual situation is just on the south side of the Grand Junction Canal not far from Horsenden Hill. Horsenden is a wooded ridge rising to 275 feet, with masses of trees on the north and a magnificent view on the southern side, including the North Downs round about Box Hill. Two big trunk roads recently constructed near Horsenden and the Perivale Bird Sanctuary may have done something to lessen bird life in the district.

As far back as 1911 a full account of the Perivale experiment was published by W. M. Webb under the title *The Brent Valley Bird Sanctuary,* for it is situated quite close to the River Brent. The thirty-five years that have elapsed since then have confirmed the conviction that bird sanctuaries are essential if we are to maintain a prolific bird life sufficiently large to cope with the problems of insect and rodent life. If the Green Belt is to help by keeping large stretches of country free from building and development, it is important to train the public not to interfere with birds, especially during the breeding season. In small private sanctuaries it is possible to provide nesting boxes and food supplies which attract the birds and enable them to produce their families in peace.

Reports of the Perivale Sanctuary in 1946 tell us that it attracts thirty-seven species that breed there regularly and eleven which breed occasionally, while forty visit the place without ever breeding. "Spotted flycatchers, green, great, and lesser spotted woodpeckers, nuthatches, wrynecks, tree creepers, five kinds of titmice and six kinds of warblers, as well other interesting and useful species, can be induced to remain, breed, and ever increase their numbers in a built-up

area." Efforts to preserve the countryside have often gone
hand in hand with schemes for helping to develop bird life,
and in several instances both these aims have been given
remarkable help by the construction of reservoirs for providing large populations with their water-supply and by
making plans for refuse disposal.

It is only natural that the reservoirs constructed by the
Metropolitan Water Board should mainly be in the valleys
of the Thames and the Lea. On the Essex-Middlesex border
there are the twelve reservoirs at Walthamstow, which were
constructed from 1853 to 1897, cover 450 acres at depths
varying from 10 to 34 feet, and the more recent example
called King George V Reservoir, between Ponders End and
Chingford, almost as large, constructed from 1900 to 1913,
with depth of 27 to 32 feet. On the Middlesex-Surrey border
there are a group of reservoirs round Kempton, Hampton,
and West Molesey, considerably smaller in size.

In Middlesex itself there is a big one between Stanwell and
Staines, constructed in 1902, covering 424 acres, with a depth
of from 29 to 39 feet, and a still larger one, called after
Queen Mary, constructed in 1925, covering 723 acres, with
a depth of 38 feet.

The Elstree-Aldenham Reservoir of 65 acres, which supplies the canals with needed water, is on the Herts-Middlesex
border, mostly in Herts, and is safeguarded by the Green
Belt, but a small piece at the southern end is actually in
Middlesex. It was constructed in 1797, thirteen years before
the Ruislip Lake of 43 acres, and twenty-three years before
the Brent Reservoir or Welsh Harp, which was constructed
in 1820 and enlarged to 197 acres in 1851. Elstree Reservoir
is now scheduled for preservation, and a considerable land
area is to be left in its immediate vicinity. In 1931 two swans
bred there, and several pairs of mallards, grebes, moorhens,
and coots are reported from time to time. The flowers have
also increased near the water's edge, and, though one seldom
sees the lesser spearwort, some marigolds, water forget-me-
nots, flowering rush and foxtail grass grow reasonably well.
Before the second World War there was a good deal of
boating and fishing, and these amusements are coming back
rather slowly into fashion.

The Welsh Harp was also called the Kingsbury Reservoir, and as late as 1898 it was possible to commend Kingsbury for its rural character and to claim it as "one of the most charming resorts in the whole country for wildfowl and other birds. The Brent meanders pleasantly through the parish, while the meadows on either hand are intersected with field-paths, lanes, and flowery meadows." In those days, half a century ago, there was a Welsh Harp station on the old Midland (L.M.S.) Railway. Trains stopped there in the summer sometimes for boating, and in the winter for skating, more seldom; and there were two well-frequented inns. Fishing was carried on under "Rules and Conditions of the Fishery" as laid down by the landlord of the Old Welsh Harp. Jack and perch could be caught from June 1 to the end of February, but "bottom fishing" went on all the year round, and bream and carp were common. The charge was 1s. a day for the latter and 2s. 6d. a day with live bait. The annual charge was reasonable—one guinea only. But a great feature of the reservoir was its bird life, and J. E. Harting and Frederick Bond, as well as Mr. Warne, of the Old Welsh Harp, observed and sometimes shot most of the known species of water-birds. These included curlew, tern, snipe, plover, gull, spoon-bill, widgeon, and even the avocet, turnstone, and the bar-tailed godwit. Wild duck and teal were plentiful in the winter-time. For about ten years, from 1868 to 1878, there were very ill-organised races on a course near the inn, and bookmakers had to take prize-fighters with them for protection against assault and robbery. These meetings were held four times a year, and about the same time race meetings were started at Alexandra Park, Ealing, Edgware, Enfield, Finchley, Harrow, Hendon, Uxbridge, and West Drayton. In 1878 a Bill was passed through Parliament prohibiting all horse-racing within ten or twelve miles of London.

A specimen of the carrion crow once met its death by drowning while trying to pick up angler's bait at the Welsh Harp. They used to report starlings in large numbers at this reservoir, and J. E. Harting in 1866 stated that numbers of linnets were to be seen on its shores. Up to 1866 the bird-watchers used to see such birds as squacco heron, night heron, little bittern, ferruginous duck, avocet, grey phalarope, not to

379

mention waders, ducks, and gulls. But times have very much changed. There is building all round the reservoir, though not close to its banks. Hendon, Kingsbury, Cricklewood, Neasden, and Willesden have all advanced tentacles of houses and shops where once were meadows and woodland. The banks are well trodden, factories have sprung up quite close, and the great days of Kingsbury Reservoir or the Welsh Harp as a bird sanctuary are over. Still, even in recent years some birds have come to visit and even to nest there. Two spotted flycatchers were reported in September, 1938, and during the second World War, in 1943, yellow wagtails nested close by, and the red-necked grebe was seen in February, 1943.

The area to the north and west of Ruislip—that is, towards Uxbridge and Harefield—seems to be the part of the county least spoiled, and there is a reasonably good hope that this happy state of affairs will now remain unchanged. Here are the largest woods in the county, there are still rustic lanes and roads, several private parks are well preserved, there is considerable bird life along the Grand Union Canal and in the valley of the Colne. Ruislip Mere, like the Elstree Reservoir, is a canal reservoir of 77 acres, with 14 acres of foreshore and woods and grassland close at hand. To the west are a series of reservations which bring up the total area of open country to 850 acres, including Park Wood, mainly oak and beach, with thick, unkempt undergrowth of fern and bracken; a grass area through which the Pinn flows south towards Swakeleys; Haste Hill and Ruislip Common and Copse Wood. Much of this land has been bought under the Green Belt scheme and has oak trees, hornbeam, and birch. Mad Bess Wood is fir and birch, and Breakspears, associated with our only English Pope, is mainly parkland. This area of Breakspears (572 acres) brings the Green Belt right up to Harefield, which adjoins the county border.

J. E. Harting in 1866 reported water-rails as close in as Kingsbury. Nowadays there are usually some found wintering along the Colne Valley between Uxbridge and Harefield in the ditches, but there is no nesting there today. The small outcrop of chalk in the extreme north-west of the county gives rise to quarries, in which there is a good deal of bird life. Rooks, magpies, and starlings are attractive-looking birds, but the evidence seems clearly to indicate that the rook at least does more harm than good. In Ruislip, in Harefield park and churchyard hundreds of nests in oak and elm trees were reported in the early 1930s, and the damage done to cultivated crops demands repressive measures.

Magpies do some damage to game, but their diet of larvæ and beetles makes them, on the whole, beneficial to agriculture. Starlings have not been greatly affected by the urbanisation of Middlesex, so we are told, but not long before the second World War an immense number of them swooped down on the gardens immediately north of Scratch Wood at Elstree, and it seemed evident that they had found their usual haunts built over. Such an invasion has not occurred in the decade since then. Near Ruislip some thousands were reported between half-past four and five o'clock one afternoon, and such numbers must be harmful. Numbers should clearly be restricted, and in fruit-growing and agricultural districts the eggs should be collected. Autumn migrants should be destroyed, and holes which might serve for nests must be filled in.

In order to preserve the balance of Nature, it would be as well to afford some protection to such birds of prey as kestrels, merlins, and owls. Occasionally to the north of Scratch Wood at Elstree herons are seen flying very high. They pounce down on small ponds which contain fish, and those they see they devour. In those ponds which are natural the fish can find shelter under the weeds, and some of us are lucky enough to find our fish multiplying, not diminishing.

Middlesex has been lucky in its bird historians, and when W. E. Glegg wrote his standard book on *The Birds of Middlesex* in 1935 he gave a bibliography of over 1,300 items dealing with bird life in the metropolitan county, emphasising the importance of J. E. Harting's *Birds of Middlesex*, published in 1866, and owing much to the zeal of Frederick Bond, and controverting Professor Newton's dogma of 1907 that "Rutland and Middlesex are, ornithologically speaking, of small account and may be safely neglected." As a matter of fact, Charles Dixon's *Bird Life of London*, published in 1909, taking a wider view of London than the L.C.C., was able to list 134 varieties found in a rather ill-defined Greater London area, and from that time onwards there have been very definite efforts to discover the extent of the influence of reservoirs on avifauna, and to produce a genuine county ornithology. Aerial photography has provided evidence otherwise almost inaccessible, and, so far from bird life having diminished in Middlesex, it has actually grown to an extent almost phenomenal. W. E. Glegg, writing twenty-six years after C. Dixon, gives this estimate of varieties seen in Middlesex : Residents, which breed and remain all the time, 54; summer residents, which come to breed, 23; winter residents, which come for the winter from colder climates, 19; passage migrants, 13; and casual and irregular visitors, 131; making a total of 240. This compares in a very interesting way with Dixon's total of 134, but it would not be safe to assume that the increase is accurately scheduled and that it is due to the growth of bird life on the reservoirs.

W. E. Glegg reported, just before the second World War, on the changes brought about in bird life by the growth of London and the further urbanisation of Middlesex; and then just after the war was over two important books were added to the growing volume of material on the fauna of Greater London. The first was R. S. R. Fitter's *London Natural History* (1945), which discusses the gradual growth of what Cobbett called the "Great Wen" up to the time of its bursting all reasonable bounds, and includes chapters on the parks and gardens and efforts made to preserve and increase them, and the influence of trade and traffic on the water-supply and artificial reservoirs, on the disposal of refuse and drainage systems, on the influence of smoke and its abatement, of sport which has tended to wander outside the county, and the sometimes subtle influence of the war.

The second is *Birds in a Sanctuary Garden* (1946), by C. Percival Stapley, which discusses the work of the Selborne Society in creating small sanctuaries in private gardens, such as the author's at Ickenham, or larger ones like the Brent Valley Sanctuary near Perivale.

The encroachment of London into Middlesex has spoiled the better aspects of the county, and instead of woods, copses, hedgerows and trees we find waste barren areas with dumps of soil, patches of weeds, and coarse undergrowth, with no gardeners to clear the ditches of rampant growth. As a result

WILD LIFE IN MIDDLESEX TODAY

we get more rats and mice, more flies and other tiresome insects, and far fewer insectivorous birds to eat them up. The bird-lovers claim that it requires only a small area to attract birds, and that a number of compact reserves scattered over the county would serve a far more useful purpose than a few large ones. Some gardens of very ordinary size can be made most attractive for wild birds by nesting boxes and nesting trays of various types and sizes. The ornithologist does his best to persuade the gardener that it is not a sound proposition to assume that "a bird, of no matter what species or feeding habits, on a seed-bed or among the fruit trees, is harmful." It is not fair "to credit birds with an inherent and malevolent desire to seek out and injure whatever man may strive to cultivate." In kitchen gardens netting and other similar precautions are no doubt necessary, but on the credit side one must remember that were it not for the destruction of insect life by birds, universally performed, vegetation be meagre or perhaps non-existent.

There can be no doubt that "the chief utility of birds lies in their insecticidal capacity." A very competent observer has calculated that one pair of blue tits will consume in a year two million caterpillars and grubs as well as innumerable insects' eggs too minute for accurate estimation. Unremitting warfare is waged by many birds against insect life, and without their efforts hedges and trees and undergrowth would suffer most severely. Many, if not most, of the higher types of plants owe their survival to the work of the birds. Seed-eating birds become partly insectivorous during the summer, and, besides, they tend to keep down the growth of ragwort, plantains, docks, and thistles, thus giving the grass a chance of survival. Another benefit bestowed by the birds comes from the destruction they inflict on small invertebrates and on rodents. Willow warblers and spotted flycatchers spend most of the day destroying the former, especially when there is a family to rear, while the owls destroy numberless mice, rats, and voles during the day as well as the night.

"A pair of barn owls has been observed to carry 27 rodents to their nestlings in a single night, and in just over 200 pellets cast by a tawny owl the remains of some 400 rodents and other injurious creatures were found." This ought to stop the

383

objections of those who claim that birds on the whole do more harm than good. Such an argument has very little foundation. "A bird consumes its own weight in food daily. The more active the bird, the more the fuel is required to stoke the fires of energy. Translated into terms of insects, rodents, and seeds of weeds, the daily consumption is enormous, and the potential capacity of birds as pest destroyers an asset of supreme national importance."

Gardeners will vary as to their attitude to birds, and the only kind way to weigh the scales fairly is to approach the discussion without prejudice. The earthworm undoubtedly does good by burrowing, aerating the soil, and also helping fertility by its castings. But the average gardener is glad when he sees the common birds of the garden eating the earthworm, which provides nitrate, potash, and phosphate for the soil by passing it through its body. Birds probably keep the balance in the garden fairly well on the whole, but some few are definitely harmful, others are a mixed blessing and curse, and the best do little but good to growing crops.

A keen ornithologist, with wide experience of bird life in bird sanctuaries, has taken the trouble to assess the good and bad qualities of our commoner birds, and he comes to the studied conclusion that the wood-pigeon is wholly baleful. "No good word can be said for this bird. It is at all times and in all places overwhelmingly harmful. It has no redeeming feature. One is loath to regard any bird as an unmitigated pest, but facts must be faced. The wood-pigeon is a greedy feeder, devouring large quantities of wheat, oats, barley, beans, rye, cabbage, turnip-tops, and roots; the buds of fruit trees and lettuce, and fruit in the form of cherries, currants, gooseberries, and raspberries. Its natural food also includes acorns, beechnuts, hips, haws, and holly-berries, and the seeds of coarse weeds, including goosegrass, wild mustard, dock and chickweed. During the winter, greens suffer particularly from attacks by this bird, whose numbers are then greatly augmented by an influx of individuals from the Continent."

The house sparrow comes high in the list of harmful birds. It has its good points, as it lives mainly on insects while it is breeding, and feeds its young very largely on rose-tree aphides, crane-flies, small caterpillars, and other plant pests;

384

Harrow Weald, Grimsdyke and Manor House

but it disturbs newly sown seed-beds far too much. This may be due to the fact that the fine soil attracts the sparrow as a dust-bath, and then the seeds thus revealed are either eaten or left to rot. In Central London the sparrow is very popular, and in peace-time the average Cockney likes to share his bread with them.

W. H. Hudson, in his *Birds in London,* tells of the three men he saw feeding sparrows in Hyde Park :

" 'I call these my chickens, and I'm obliged to come every day to feed them,' said a paralytic-looking, white-haired old man in the shabbiest clothes one evening as I stood there; then, taking some fragments of stale bread from his pocket, he began feeding the sparrows, and while doing so he chuckled with delight, and looked round from time to time to see if the others were enjoying the spectacle. To him succeeded two sedate-looking labourers, big, strong men, with tired dusty faces, on their way home from work. Each produced from his coat pocket a little store of fragments of bread and meat, saved from the midday meal, carefully wrapped in a piece of newspaper. After bestowing their scraps on the little brown-coated crowd, one spoke : 'Come on, mate; they've had it all, and now let's go home and see what the missus has got for our tea.' And home they trudged across the Park, with hearts refreshed and lightened."

But the sparrows of Hyde Park and of still more Central London like their holidays the same as the rest of us, and they take them in Middlesex at least twice a year. In the spring they leave their local roosts or "chapels" and descend on to the fields in large flocks, stripping the buds from goose-berry and currant bushes, eating young carnation shoots, spoiling crocus and polyanthus blooms, and pulling up all kinds of seedlings. The decrease in house traffic must have reduced the numbers of house sparrows in Central London, and may have sent them into still rural Middlesex.

In the autumn they do serious damage to corn of all kinds, and the rapidity with which they breed makes them a serious menace. True it is that they eat up the seeds of docks, dandelions, chickweed, charlock, and groundsel, but the gardener is right in thinking them a real pest in rural areas. It is wise to destroy all nests near dwellings with their eggs, in order to

Grimsdyke, Harrow Weald

keep down this extremely prolific breeder. Great care must be taken to observe the sparrows accurately, or robins, wrens, buntings, warblers, hedge sparrows may be destroyed by mistake. Any one of these different breeds is of more service in destroying insects than a dozen ordinary sparrows.

Before the Boer War peregrine falcons were killed in Hampstead, Finchley, Highgate, and Harrow, presumably while hunting for pigeons; the hobby used to nest in woods near Wembley, feeding on smaller birds as big as the missel-thrush and on cockchafers and similar insects. It makes no nest, but borrows a deserted cradle from a crow or magpie and then in June lays from three to five brown eggs. By September the family is reared and the move south has begun. Up to 1909 kestrels were reported in Osterley Park and at Acton, Ealing, Hanwell, Wembley, Sunbury, and Finchley, and here again another bird's nest was borrowed or a hole in some building.

The barn owl and the sparrow-hawk used to be frequent in Wembley and Neasden and Dudden Hill, and farther afield at Enfield and Barnet. Frogs, mice, rats, rabbits, and lots of small birds fall victims to the hawk, and somewhat similar food, though on the smaller scale, is usual with the various owls. Writing in 1909, Charles Dixon hoped that the barn owl would be given a better chance by farmers, as it was capable of killing off from thirty to forty mice in a single night, and may be regarded as one of the farmer's best friends. The nightingale is a summer migrant to this country and is perhaps the most popular bird of which the average man is aware. It is a long while since the nightingale actually sang in Berkeley Square, but the song which said so struck a receptive chord in most Cockney hearts.

An early record is in 1703, when the Duke of Buckingham was building his house to the south-west of Piccadilly, and there he found "under the windows a little wilderness full of blackbirds and nightingales." A previous building in the same grounds, Goring House, had been famous for its mulberry trees.

The bird arrives in Middlesex somewhen in late April or early May, and back in 1909 was beginning to desert "spots now given up to the jerry-builder or the domain of squalor and wretchedness." The name is attached to several well-known lanes such as one in Harlesden, where the bird is no longer heard. In Harrison Ainsworth's house near Kensal Rise, Dickens and Thackeray used to accompany their host along the Harrow Road to hear the song of the nightingale. Even by 1909 there were no such birds to be heard in the altered Harrow Road, with its succession of funerals and its many evidences of squalor and poverty. But before the second World War the increase of reservoirs had begun to make a difference. Trees and shrubs, especially when they are close enough together to make a wood, are almost essential for nearly every form of bird life, and where the gardens are small it is not always possible or desirable to have forest trees growing up near the houses. But love of the country still remains. In the *London Bird Report* in 1948 we get confirmation of an increased wild life in reservoirs and on sewage farms. On one such farm near Staines we read of dozens of black-headed gulls nesting all through the war years, while wood sand-pipers, greenshanks, ruffs, orioles, ringed plovers, black redstarts, and greater-crested grebes are occasional visitors, hindered from nesting by fierce carrion crows. The jays, "those shy, cunning crows," as Sir W. Beech-Thomas calls them, have recently been seen at Gunnersbury.

Several journeys by train from Liverpool Street Station during the second World War gave one many glimpses of the love of even a tiny garden which is a characteristic of most, if not all, Londoners. It is a very fortunate thing that all corners of the metropolitan area are reasonably well equipped with parks; even the north-east has Victoria Park and the Hackney Commonlands quite near and Epping and Hainault farther out. The south-east side is most fortunate, starting with Blackheath and Greenwich, and going on to Woolwich, Oxleas, Plumstead, and Bostall. Towards the other points of the compass the Regent's Park-Hampstead oases have been repeated in Hendon, Ruislip, and Harefield, while the south-western commons of Clapham and Wandsworth, duplicated in Wimbledon and Richmond, are repeated by dozens of rescued commons in all the Surrey villages. In London itself, inside the one square mile, tiny glimpses of country still remain : the Tower Moat Garden and Wharf, the Embankment Gardens, the Inns of Court and Chancery, the single tree in Cheapside, immortalised by Wordsworth and spared in the German blitz, Finsbury Circus and Finsbury Square— all of them part of the original Middlesex.

But the problem of preserving a certain rusticity in a built-up area is no easy one to solve. Thinning or pruning is un-popular with many, who fear to lose even a limb or branch of a favourite tree. An enthusiast actually purchased the lease of a house in order to preserve two very poor specimens of the plane tree in a front garden in the Blackfriars Road. Another tree-lover left instructions in her will to remove a tree from Portland Place to a more suitable environment in Hampstead. Even more recently the London and Middlesex Archæological Society was asked to take steps to preserve a 200-year-old elm tree in one of the suburbs which had already lost most of its branches.

It took, however, many years to persuade the authorities to plant trees along the Embankment. Whether they were afraid of damage from fumes and soot and smoke I do not know, but that danger is far more noticed in the eastern parts of London. John Evelyn, early in Charles II's reign, noted in the *Fumifugium* that the westerly or south-westerly winds were the most common, and so the fashionable quarters of London escaped much of the smoke. A very good instance of the damage which factories can produce was given when a gardening enthusiast commented to the caretaker on the sad condition of the trees in St. Giles's-in-the-Fields. "Well, with Crosse and Blackwell's at one end and Nixey's Black Lead Works at the other, it's a wonder there's a living plant left." Now that both these factories have been removed, it would be interesting to discover whether the strong smoke-resisting trees planted in St. Giles's Churchyard have improved in health and appearance.

It is obvious that all kinds of trees will not grow equally well in thickly populated areas where considerable manufac-tures exist and where countless chimneys give forth their smoke. Here again the increased use of electricity has un-doubtedly helped the London and Middlesex trees.

Among the most popular London trees are the plane and the lime, which flourish well, but have ruthless treatment from the loppers. It has been suggested that smaller varieties would avoid the necessity of annual lopping. With "the beautiful flowering thorns, catalpa, the dwarf acacias, the almond, cherries, mulberry, or mountain ash, all this lopping and restraining of noble growth would be avoided." For built-up areas "deciduous are preferable to evergreen kinds; in fact, coniferous species, with perhaps one or two exceptions, should be severely left alone." Thus speaks the expert, and he is probably right.

The efforts of many lovers of the country have, after many years of effort, preserved some thousands of acres to the north-west of London as an open space, and it is a delight to look out southwards from one's garden in Barnet Lane, just at the top of Woodcock Hill, and to feel a sense of deep satisfaction that the town cannot come any nearer on the south side than a mile and a piece away, and that the view of Harrow-on-the-Hill is still outstandingly good, despite the dreadfully ugly gasometer which does its very best to spoil the view. From Stirling Corner to Apex Corner is safe, and beyond one can see the hill on which Hendon Church and its well-planned civic centre stand; farther off the line of Hampstead Heath; and then on the far side of the Thames the stretch of the North Downs from Wrotham and Westerham Hills to the Hog's Back. Scratch Wood, Moat Mount, and Highwood are among the nearby beauty spots effectively preserved, and the many acres attached to Mill Hill School and to the Roman Catholic Institutions in Mill Hill help to swell the areas which have been saved for posterity. It is not uninteresting to realise that from one of the hills which we can see to our south the English Channel is visible. Turn to the north, and St. Albans Central Tower with its wealth of Roman bricks can be seen. Two steps farther north bring the chalk hills of the Chilterns and then the skyline of the Cotswolds into view. It needs only two more turns to reach the Peak and the slopes of Snowdon. More than half a century lived on these northern heights of Middlesex have made them almost sacred in the many historic and personal associations connected with them.

It has required no persuasion to produce a determination to do all in one's power to help in the belated scheduling of a green girdle for London, and it was a great satisfaction to take a Chairman of the London County Council round some of the beauty spots of the Middlesex and Hertfordshire border when the scheme was still being debated, and still more gratifying to be summoned one afternoon, at very short notice, to broadcast the news that the Green Belt was, as far as North-west London is concerned, a *fait accompli.*

CHAPTER XXVI

MIDDLESEX TODAY

THE Industrial Revolution concentrated many industries in the North and the Midlands near the coal-mines, and after a century and more it looks as if that had always been the case. But in medieval times there were many manufactures going on in London, with the City companies regulating hours of work, wages, apprenticeship, and prices. Some workers, to shake off restrictions, went beyond the precincts of the City, and the coming of refugees with important trade secrets made the suburban areas important industrial centres. Many former Middlesex industries have now to be included in London : tailoring in Whitechapel and the East End in general; boots in Shoreditch and Bethnal Green; shirts and ties; furs, boxes and brushes, matches, jams, pickles, sauces, artificial flowers, feathers and mineral waters—all these are done outside the City but inside the County of London.

But there were many maltsters in Enfield in the late fifteenth century, and they had to bring actions against brewers in Southwark for allowing their bills to remain unpaid. Other places where malt was made included Brentford, Chiswick, Isleworth, and Staines. Ale was an important drink in medieval time, and the poor standard of water-supply made ale a universal beverage. In his *Dyetary of Helth,* written before 1550, Andrew Borde says : "Ale for an Englysshe man is a natural drinke . . . it must be fresshe and cleare, it must not be ropy nor smoky. Ale should not be dranke under V dayes olde." The usual allowance for a man in a medieval monastery was one gallon of good ale a day, and often a second gallon of weaker ale; and in the towns the price was 1d. for two gallons, and only half that in the country. Ale conners sampled the fresh brew, and those makers who sinned against the City's regulations had to "play bopepe thorowe a pillery." Beer was introduced from Flanders as early as A.D. 1400, but its use and manufacture were at first largely confined to foreigners. Andrew Borde resented such alien innovations, and complained that in his day it was "moche used to the detryment of many Englysshe men . . . for the drynke is a cold drynke, yet it doth make a man fat." But it had been drunk by English troops at the siege of Rouen in 1418, and was far more popular than Borde would admit. Cider and perry were old drinks in the district, and they became more popular in Elizabeth's reign, being made in many Middlesex villages.

Besides food and drink there were other domestic manufactures in the neighbourhood of London. Tiles and bricks are an early product in the villages on the heavy London clay. In the late fifteenth century John and Agnes Maur made tiles for William Code, of Harlesden Green, at the rate of 11d. per thousand. Brick-making today is mainly carried on in Herts, Bedfordshire, and Essex, but the London Brick Company may suggest by its name that it all began in the Middlesex area.

Soap is an obvious industry for the neighbourhood of a big city, and in addition to the City Soap Works at Wapping there are other factories in Brentford and Isleworth. Three big linoleum factories have been established at Staines, Edmonton, and Ponders End, the latter being a riverside extension of Enfield, which has of recent years become a very busy manufacturing centre.

Copper-mining was important in Tudor times, and William Herbert, Earl of Pembroke, brother-in-law to Henry VIII, employed some of his monastic spoil not only to finance Hawkins and Frobisher, but also to develop copper-working at Cornwall and in Cumberland. Norden reports copper manufacture at Isleworth, where John Brode made brass and copper vessels with some success. A company which was started to acquire his patents, under the Duke of Norfolk, Lord Cobham, and others, seems to have been badly treated by Borde, who caused them great loss and refused to pay his rent. Sir Julius Cæsar and his brother, the Lord Mayor, and his son appealed in 1596, but there is no record of any decision. When Lysons wrote his *Environs of London* 200 years later, he says that "these copper mills still exist, being situated at Baberbridge; they belong to the Duke of Northumberland, and are rented by the incorporated Society of the Mines Royal."

The early industries of Middlesex were thus of a scattered variety, and no problem of an almost insuperable character was presented for some centuries. It must always be recalled that the strict rules enacted by the City companies did not apply in the suburbs, and that there were hardly any regulations dealing with the erection of cottages and houses. When folk at last awoke to the need for planning, most of the damage had already been done. And even then the effort to plan was only spasmodic, and it was not till the 1930s that planning on a really extensive scale was begun. The principal areas where considerable industries occur in Middlesex today are, first, in the Lea Valley, from Tottenham to Waltham Abbey; then in Enfield, close by; along the Edgware Road as far as West Hendon; then the Willesden, Park Royal, Acton, Wembley area, which has spread into Greenford and Perivale; Uxbridge and neighbourhood; Southall and Hayes; the Great West Road, the Bath Road, and the South-west Road. And development has been so rapid that it is an almost impossible task to effect any great improvement in these already built-up areas.

The existence of a Green Belt would have enabled foodstuffs to continue to be grown near the crowded Metropolis, while the earlier construction of satellite towns, mainly self-supporting in food and industries, instead of suburbs whose population worked in London, would have solved so many of our problems which today seem well-nigh insoluble. No wonder that the authorities have now set before themselves schemes which suggest solutions of many problems which have not yet arisen, and have endeavoured to anticipate difficulties by taking the widest possible view of the future.

The North-west London concentration is one of the most important and recent of the industrial areas, to which definite limits must at once be placed. There were a few big firms in Willesden and one or two along the Edgware Road before the first World War. But most of the industrial development dates from after 1919, when disused munition factories came into the market, and five years later, when most of the capital Exhibition buildings at Wembley were turned over to industry. Then came the construction of some arterial roads, improvements in railway facilities, and as a result this north-west area became "London's most popular area for light industry largely manufacturing proprietary articles and semi-luxury goods, including electrical equipment, motor-cars and car accessories, pharmaceutical preparations and household appliances, mainly in small or medium-sized factories." This is mainly new business, but some has been decentralised from the L.C.C. area. Industry has utilised railways and roads; starting from Willesden Junction and Park Royal, the factories have advanced north-west along Western Avenue and the Great Western Railway to Northolt, north along the L.M.S. and L.N.E. Railways to Wembley, north-east along the North Circular Road from Willesden to the group of factories on the Edgware Road.

The Abercrombie Plan deals with an area of over 2,500 square miles, extending 30 miles outward from the L.C.C. boundary, which covers about 120 square miles, itself a tremendous development from the one square mile of the City of London. Four rings are marked out in Greater London, the fourth of which hardly touches Middlesex, and the first of these, an inner urban ring, includes such parts of Middlesex as Brentford, Chiswick, Acton, Ealing, Willesden, Hornsey, Wood Green, Tottenham, and Edmonton. There are some good open spaces in the first two, but Acton, once full of historic houses with rural surroundings, is now a maze of railway lines, a tangle of sidings and engine sheds, with the huge industrial concentration of Park Royal. There is still time to save Ealing and its own green acres, and the policy of decanting its surplus population into Berkshire may solve its problems. Willesden is traversed by London's devious exit, the Harrow Road, a contrast to the straight Watling Street on Willesden's eastern edge. It is hemmed in by four close-crammed metropolitan boroughs, and the founding of factories in disused munition sheds and in the Exhibition buildings at Wembley made its expansion extremely rapid and unorganised. The Welsh Harp has lost most of its rustic appearance, with more factories along the Edgware Road and on the North Circular, but Northern Hendon has been extremely well planned. Much of Hornsey is still unspoiled, but the part towards Tottenham suffers from excessive density of houses and lack of open spaces. Edmonton, too, is a place of many industries, but is lucky in the Lea Valley with its common land and reservoirs. The Metropolitan Water Board proposes a new reservoir to add to those already constructed, and sewage works for all East Middlesex are planned. Wood Green may well be glad that television has saved the grounds of Alexandra Palace.

In the suburban ring London has expanded enormously, and thousands prefer to travel "strap-hanging," and devote hours a day in getting to work. They save on rents, but pay heavily on fares. A rector of one of these dormitory suburbs commented on the financial stringency for some of his parishioners, whose commitments challenged their earnings. The conditions of housing and open spaces are, on the whole, good in Twickenham, Heston, Isleworth, Southall, Hendon, Ruislip-Northwood, Harrow, Wembley, Finchley, the Barnets, Potters Bar, Southgate, and Edmonton.

There are fine open tracts or wedges of country in Hampton Court and Bushey Park; on either side of the Watford and Barnet by-pass roads, enhanced by the 150 acres round Mill Hill School, and the areas along that Ridgeway occupied by Middlesex Barracks, the Research Works, and Roman Catholic seminaries; while the whole of the northern boundary, where Middlesex impinges on Hertfordshire, has been saved by the Green Belt.

In the third ring, that of the Green Girdle, there has always been the risk that the authorities might use the remaining open spaces to provide room for houses and thus seem to solve the problems of suburbia. That was the policy adopted from decade to decade and from century to century in the past, and few were long-sighted enough to realise all the dangers involved. In these circumstances it is perhaps a remarkable achievement for Middlesex to have retained so much open country, so many amenities, and so many great and small, picturesque, and historic buildings in spite of the spread of suburbia. Even if we cannot find as much as we should like in the way of "unspeakable rural solitudes," there is always "the sweet security of streets." Take a walk from South Tottenham Station to the county boundary near Waltham Cross, and in Tottenham you will find All Hallows Church with a fourteenth-century tower and additions of the next three centuries; the High Cross, Homestead Moat, Bruce Castle and the Priory, with several seventeenth-century houses in the High Road. Edmonton has a fifteenth-century church, Pymme's Park and Salisbury House, and several old cottages, mostly of the seventeenth century, and, of course, Charles Lamb's retreat, now preserved as a museum. Enfield town is to the west of Enfield highway, and has retained much of historic interest besides St. Andrew's Church. There is an earthwork at Old Park Farm and four homestead moats outside the town, some attractive houses in Gentleman's Row, the Grammar School, several old inns, Forty Hall, and Glasgow Stud Farm, both scheduled for preservation, and parts of the old vicarage. And then to the north and west of Enfield come the magnificent open spaces of the Green Belt included in the historic name of Enfield Chase.

Another stroll, this time from Finsbury Park Station, goes through Hornsey, with Sir Roger Cholmeley's school and Cromwell House at Highgate; Christ Church and another homestead moat at Southgate; St. James's Church at Friern Barnet, with memories of Thomas Cavendish, who knew Wolsey, and Edmund Duncan, who knew George Herbert; and the Laurence Campe Almshouses, founded in 1612; on to the other Barnet, technically in Herts; back into Middle-sex between Wrotham Park and Dyrham Park to South Mimms, a veritable treasure-house of antiquity. St. Giles's Church has a fine tower, chancel, traceried screen, glass, and monuments, all described so affectionately by Frederick Brittain, biographer of "Q"; there is a motte and bailey castle, probably constructed by Geoffrey de Mandeville; half a dozen sixteenth- or seventeenth-century farms—Blanche, Old Fold, Wyllyott's, Sparrow, Bridge Foot, and Bentley Heath—several good old inns, and the sixteenth-century Knightsland Farm, with fine linenfold panelling and remark-able wall-paintings. Just beyond Mimms we reach the Herts border. Mimms and its adjacent village of Ridge, with the wooded line of its hill, were favourite spots for C. E. Montague, who loved from high ground thereabout to spy the minster church of St. Albans on the skyline, "picked out by its harder lines from the softly modelled woods that it seems to spring from."

In following the great north way and the Watford By-pass
the development seems to have been more rapid, and there is
not so much of historic interest to report. St. Mary's Church
at Finchley has been much rebuilt and bombed; there are two
homestead moats in Finchley, and but little remains of old
Finchley Common, where the Guards marched to resist the
Young Pretender, who never came so far.

Hendon has its church and Norman font, a fine seventeenth-
century farmhouse at Church End, recently rescued from the
despoilers, some old farm buildings, and Copt Hall on the old
road to Mill Hill, and several attractive seventeenth-century
cottages along the Ridgeway at Mill Hill near the grounds
and buildings of Mill Hill School, and houses associated with
Raffles and Wilberforce on Highwood Hill. South of the old
road from Elstree to Arkley there are some magnificent pieces
of Green Belt to mark the county boundary.

Watling Street has almost nothing of historic interest until
the Hyde and Edgware are reached, with their memories of
Goldsmith and Chandos. There are still some picturesque
cottages and almshouses in Edgware or Stanmore, for the
road divides the parishes; and on Brockley Hill are remains
of the Roman settlement of Sulloniacæ, which has recently
given up interesting remains to enthusiastic diggers. The two
churches of Great and Little Stanmore have memories of
Laud and Handel, and there are seventeenth-century farmhouses on the western side of Brockley Hill.

On either side of the Harrow Road there is a lot to explore,
and the starting-point may well be Willesden Junction Station.
Willesden has some pleasantly laid out areas, but there has
not been enough open space left to provide for adequate
recreation. The parish church of St. Mary's is interesting,
and there are some seventeenth- and early eighteenth-century
buildings at the Grove, Oxgate Farm, and the Grange, all in
Neasden, and at Willesden Paddocks. Wembley, besides its
modern stadium, has three seventeenth-century farms—
Hundred Elms, Sudbury and Hillside, and John Lyon's Farm,
where the founder of Harrow School lived. Major Hugh
Braun has recently identified the moot-side of the Hundred
of Gore 1,000 yards north-east of John Lyon's Farm. Forking right from Wembley, we reach Kingsbury, almost entirely

developed in very recent years, but still retaining Blackbird
Farm, seventeenth-century work, and what is probably the
oldest church in the county. Dr. Stukeley, who was so ready
to identify everything as Roman, claimed that the building
was largely composed of Roman bricks from Verulam. The
Kenton road leads to Harrow-on-the-Hill, with Wealdstone
and Harrow Weald not far away. St. Mary's, Harrow, is
certainly one of the finest churches in the county, and there
are the buildings of Harrow School to explore, a homestead moat, parts of Grimsdyke, and some old farms and
cottages.

Pinner has an interesting church; the Headstone Manor,
once the property of the Archbishops of Canterbury; four or
five sixteenth- or seventeenth-century farms close by; and
some attractive old houses in the main street. Northwood is
a well-developed residential area with good gardens and wide
open spaces, but with nothing of historic interest.

There is no obvious through road leading to Ruislip and
Harefield, and so, passing the industrial area of Park Royal
and Greenford, we find a good deal of unspoilt country.
Perivale has an interesting church and rectory, a homestead
moat, an important bird sanctuary, fostered by the Selborne
Society, but its proximity to Greenford factories is a disadvantage. Greenford old village has Holy Cross Church, an
unusual dedication, with the best collection of glass in the
county, with the arms of Eton College and King's College at
Cambridge. There are some interesting memorials to the
seventeenth-century family of Coston. Passing by Northolt
Aerodrome, we come to Ruislip and Eastcote, with a fine
parish church dedicated to St. Martin, two homestead moats,
and a motte and bailey castle, a dozen or more attractive
seventeenth-century houses in the main street, a dozen old
well-preserved farms, and some historic inns.

To the north-west of Ruislip are well-preserved open
spaces before we reach the singularly unspoiled village of
Harefield. Harefield is a repetition of Ruislip, only far more
rustic, with its inns, farmhouses, and seventeenth-century
cottages. Brackenbury, Brakespear, Harefield, and Swakeley
are among the many attractive houses to view. The Colne
and the Grand Union Canal add interest and charm to the

neighbourhood of Harefield and form the county boundaries.

The Western Avenue is one of the latest of the by-pass roads, and is mainly of use in avoiding built-up areas, in providing a convenient approach to Northolt Aerodrome, and in cutting out Uxbridge. To reach Uxbridge we go through Acton, with a rebuilt church, Berrymead Priory, now a club, and the George and Dragon Hotel. Next comes Ealing, well equipped with open spaces, but with little of ancient date save the fittings of the rebuilt church, and Rochester House; then Hanwell, with its mental hospital, several modern churches of conspicuous design, and a huge glacial boulder in Elthorne Park, which marks the southern limit of the Ice Age in England. Southall has its magnificent Tudor manor-house; Hayes has a particularly interesting church and manor-house and another of the homestead moats, of which there are so many in Middlesex. Hillingdon Church is really the mother church of Uxbridge, and there are a number of well-preserved farmhouses and others in the main road of the sixteenth and seventeenth century.

Southall with its highly convenient railway system has been largely industrialised for thirty years or more, starting as far back as 1902, and Ordnance Survey maps published in 1925 show very considerable development northwards to the Uxbridge Road and southwards to the Canal and eastwards to the Brent. Of recent years Hayes has also become a big industrial area, with small working-class houses, twelve to the acre, without any adequate open spaces to relieve the drab monotony. The two towns are full of factories because of the good transport facilities, and most of the firms are large, one multi-storeyed factory employing 12,000 persons. Food, engineering, gramophones, and ancillary trades are the chief industries in Hayes, and the housing problem for the workers has long been acute. It has been suggested that all the houses within a four-mile radius of Hayes and Southall should be taken over for the factory workers and the black-coated folk accommodated elsewhere. Southall-Hayes industry is partly organised in big, prosperous, expanding units; besides the food factories for jam, cocoa, tinned foods, groceries, there are also engineering, heavy motor vehicles, aero engines, bicycles, gramophones, gasworks. The area is less a producer of semi-luxury goods than some of the more modern industrial concentrations in West and North-west London.

To the west of Hayes there is at present an unbuilt-up area before we reach Hillingdon and Uxbridge. On the maps are marked Hillingdon Court, Place, and House, Field Heath and Colham Green, and, though considerable suburban expansion is encroaching, there is still a Green Belt separation. The construction of the Western Avenue between the two branches of the Great Western Railway has opened up a lot of unspoiled country between Northolt and Greenford and between Ickenham and Hillingdon, but it has been extended north of Uxbridge and across the Colne towards Denham, and this has solved, perhaps, some of the Uxbridge problems. The town is an important busy market and shopping centre, with two or three railways and a canal as well as several natural streams. The crowding in the High Street and its adjacent one-way streets will be diminished by the future absence of much through traffic, through the construction of Western Avenue. Most of its industries are constructed near the canal and are associated with it. There are timber yards, furniture and joinery factories, flour mills, and concrete works, all of which find the canal service useful. One of the chief features of Uxbridge is its wealth of substantial and sometimes picturesque inns. To the south there are numbers of glasshouses still functioning. The spread of urbanisation southwards through Cowley to Yiewsley has, as usual, been spasmodic and unregulated. The chief road which joins them is rightly described as "one of the most tortuous main roads to be found in the region." It is vitally important to have any further development carefully scrutinised and regionally planned so as to retain the separate identity of the three townships.

Ickenham was said, before the second World War, to retain at the centre its old-world charm, despite the neighbouring depots of the Royal Air Force. It is still partly true to say that it still looks, from certain angles, like a typical English village, "with its wide-open space at the cross-roads, its pond, its inn, its attractive little church, and its suggestion of a big house (Swakeleys) beyond the tall trees." But through it now runs the Western Avenue, and it is vital that ribbon development along it should be strictly forbidden. Swakeleys Road has been attractively planted with flowers and shrubs down the centre of the roadway, and it is a challenge to other districts which value rural amenities.

Harefield is tucked away up in the extreme north-west corner salient of Middlesex, west of Northwood and Ruislip, south of Rickmansworth and north of Denham. It has a lofty situation, with a village green and a number of parks and farms close at hand. The River Colne and the Grand Union Canal run close by, with a small industrial area round Harefield Mills consisting of some old-established factories, which should not be extended. The district is a most attractive one, and industrialisation should be kept at bay. The council houses already built should be formed into a coherent plan grouped round the existing village centre.

Writing in 1934, Martin S. Briggs, in his *Middlesex: Old and New*, emphasised the need for more open spaces in order to anticipate the suburban development which might well be expected to engulf still more of Middlesex's few remaining country areas. Among his suggestions was the acquiring or reservation as a private open space of the Great West Aerodrome at Heathrow, comprising then 180 acres and belonging to the Fairey Aviation Company. His prayer has been answered, though perhaps not quite in the way he intended, for Heathrow is not an open space in the usual sense of the word. He also comments on another open space : "It can hardly be said that the enormous area reserved for the new Sludge Disposal Works of the County Council at Perry Oaks, south of the Bath Road (250 acres), can be regarded as a permanent place of recreation !"

Starting from Hammersmith Broadway, we approach Turnham Green, with its memories of the Civil War, and Brentford, which, in spite of narrow streets, has considerable charm in the Butts and High Street, where there are numerous seventeenth-century houses. Old England has many ancient associations from prehistoric man onwards. Leaving Boston Manor and Osterley Park on our north side, we go along the new Great West Road, lined mainly with well-planned factories. The Bath Road, which forks off near Hounslow, passes to the north of the Heath, famous for soldiers, then for highwaymen, and more recently for soldiers once again. On the Heath were laid the foundations of the Ordnance Survey, while to the west Harmondsworth Aerodrome has been completely absorbed in the seven square miles of Heathrow, London's airport. At the various corners are interesting villages : Cranford, with two moated areas, the fifteenth-century church of St. Dunstan, a seventeenth-century rectory, Cranford and Springfield Houses; Harlington, with a really outstanding church dedicated to St. Peter and St. Paul, Dawley Manor, Church Farm, and a dower-house, all sixteenth century. These are both on the east side of the airport. On the west is Harmondsworth, with a twelfth-century church, a particularly fine barn, five or six seventeenth-century farmhouses, four old inns—Five Bells, King William, Old Magpie, and White Horse—and two other farms, of which special mention must be made. These are Heathrow Farm, which has been engulfed in the airport, and Perry Oaks, near the drainage works. On the south side of the airport are Stanwell and the two Bedfonts. Stanwell still retains its village green, its thirteenth-century church, with additions in the next century, unusual sedilia, and a monument to Lord Knyvet, who died in 1622 and endowed a school which is still standing and in use today. Knyvet was the magistrate who detected Guy Fawkes in the cellars under the old Houses of Parliament when the letter to Lord Montague had given the Gunpowder Plot away. He was also guardian to James I's daughter, Mary, who died at Knyvet House in 1607. There are several moats near the church, two or three seventeenth-century inns, and Foyle Farm, Foyle Manor, Hammonds, The Hollies, and "King John's Palace." To the south-west of Stanwell are big reservoirs, reaching almost to Staines. Close to the Cardinal's River and the Duke's River are the two Bedfonts, East and West. East Bedfont Church dates from the twelfth century and has a wooden tower and dwarf steeple. In the churchyard are the famous yew trees cut into the shape of peacocks in the year of Blenheim, and made the subject of a dull poem by Hood and some satiric prose by Pope. A shorter poem by Colmer commemorates the yew trees and the landlord of the Black Dog :

402

"Harvey, whose inn commands a view
Of Bedfont's church and churchyard too,
Where yew trees into peacocks shorn,
In vegetable torture mourn."

Due south of Uxbridge are three historic villages. Cowley has St. Laurence's Church of the twelfth and thirteenth centuries. It has a priest's doorway and fragments from earlier times worked into a chancel screen. In the churchyard are buried Barton Booth, the famous Shakespearean actor, and Dr. Dodd, a most successful parson and editor of the *Beauties of Shakespeare,* who was hanged for forgery. Yiewsley has some seventeenth-century farms, the De Burgh Hotel, and the Red Cow Inn of the same date, but a great deal of modern development, which has taken away much of its picturesque antiquity. The third is West Drayton, with a fine church dedicated to St. Martin and possessing a fifteenth-century font with strange carvings and a Communion chalice and paten dated 1507. The original manor-house of the Pagets and De Burghs was destroyed two centuries ago, and only the gatehouse remains. In the village street are some sixteenth- and seventeenth-century inns, and nearby are several old farms, including the Frays, which all date from the fifteenth century. There was for a short time a disreputable race-course at West Drayton, but after a few years of shame it died unwept, unhonoured, and unsung. A recent writer on Middlesex developments laments the loss of the winding lanes and picturesque farms and cottages of these villages, and speaks of the tragic squalor which has overtaken them. It is a curious fact that the villages of Yiewsley, West Drayton, Harmondsworth, Longford, Heathrow, and Sipson have had less encouragement from local historians than any other villages in Middlesex, though just before the Axis war Gordon Maxwell included them in his volume on *Highwayman's Heath.* The village green at West Drayton still retains some of its ancient beauty, but Colham Green is threatened with speculative building, and the back streets of Yiewsley are poor.

In the areas of Feltham, Hanworth, and East Bedfont great chances of wise development have been missed. The Duke of Northumberland's River and other streams should have been treated like Dutch canals, but they have mainly

403

been spoiled by bad planning. In Feltham there are some unplanned industries, including the manufacture of aircraft and
motor components and concrete products. The village has
suffered greatly from uncontrolled mineral excavation. Gravel
working in vast areas of backland has produced an indescrib-
able mix-up of huge pits and ponds, which are an eyesore and
hinder the use of the land for farming. Orderly expansion is
difficult, and the effect of the spasmodic, unregulated gravel
working is to produce clumsy and non-continuous ribbon
development. Large areas of fertile agricultural land have
been spoiled, and not enough has been done to reinstate the
land and to disguise heaps of refuse by careful planting of
trees. Feltham's earlier reputation as a market gardening
centre is reminiscent of Fulham forty years ago, and the value
of having fertile country close to London has been in both
these cases largely ignored. There is now some first-class land
still left which should at all costs be kept.

South of the Staines Road is Whitton, where the Duke of
Argyll in George I's reign had a particularly fine house and a
well-wooded estate which laid him open to satire and imitation. The fine group of cedars raised from seed grown there
are still standing. Nearby is Feltham with three churches, two
interesting Anglican ones and a fine modern Catholic edifice.
The manor-house, barn, and several cottages date from the
seventeenth century. Hanworth figures among the great
houses of the county, while Ashford has two seventeenth-
century farms and a rebuilt church dedicated to St. Matthew.
Littleton was described forty years ago as one of the smallest
parishes in the county, consisting of "big farmhouses, with
spreading barns, old half-timbered cottages, delightful fields
with avenues of big elms, a mansion, a vicarage and a church,
and a few houses of more recent date. To the north lies a
stretch of graceful woods." In 1925 King George V opened
the Queen Mary Reservoir, which has engulfed in its depths
woods and fields and quite half the village. It cost two million
pounds, is one of the largest reservoirs in the world, covering
a larger area than the City of London, the "one square mile."

Our last perambulation is along the Thames, and it is
pleasant to record that a conference was held at Middlesex
Guildhall on Friday, February 28, 1947, to consider the

future of the 136 miles of towpath along the Thames from Cricklade to Teddington. From time immemorial there has always been a path or road along which men and horses could proceed, drawing barges up and down the river. But nowadays the traditional usage has waned, and towpaths are not used for their original purpose. The exact legal position is complicated and it is quite possible for great stretches of towpath to be really private property.

Some ferries have ceased to function and access to considerable lengths of the towpath has ceased. It would be a very good scheme to convert those towpaths into a public riverside walk. No doubt the style of walk will vary with surroundings, but it is to be hoped that there will not be too much asphalt. A considerable portion of the towpath is on that portion of the river that separates Middlesex from Surrey. As *The Times* leader writer comments, "those who, in the future, are privileged to walk the riverside, and see 'sweet Thames run softly,' should be able to see it as free from needless urban tidyings as in centuries past." So from Teddington up to Staines, and presumably from Chiswick to Teddington, will be a riverside walk for the public for ever.

Rudyard Kipling was emphatic as to the origin of the nature of Teddington when he says of the Thames:

> "Up I go, and I end my run
> At tide-end-town, which is Teddington."

But the more prosaic and factual editors of the *Place Names of Middlesex* have other views. The earliest form of the word is "Tedintun," and it seems to imply "Tuda's Farm."

There is more of the Thames bankside which is partly in Middlesex nearer to the mouth than Teddington, and it begins just west of Chiswick. Sir John Squire is one of many to write of this attractive spot, with birds everywhere, "starlings crossing the upper air, sparrows troubling the holly, a thrush intermittently singing behind the upper veils of the ash tree, chaffinches tinkling somewhere unseen." Chiswick Eyot provides a place of refuge for water-rats and for crows; wild duck and gulls swim round its edge. Swans are sometimes able to rear a family of cygnets there, an occasional heron is seen in the reeds, and the swallows come and go at the proper season in their thousands. Chiswick has a fine church dedicated to St. Nicholas, Chiswick House, and a series of attractive seventeenth- and eighteenth-century houses along the Mall.

After the bend of the Thames between Chiswick, Barnes, and Mortlake comes Strand-on-the-Green, a real village street still intact, with spacious Georgian houses and tiny cottages in between, with microscopic gardens abutting on the towpath, which almost disappeared during the floods of early 1947. This flooding of the towpaths and, higher up-stream, of many acres of meadowland inevitably aroused the controversy between those who want to leave the river more or less alone and those who would prefer a "high-water tideless Thames."

"The antiquated and outlived conditions of a tidal river through one of the densest centres of population in the world" seem to call for drastic enquiry, and the supporters of the proposed barrage claim that above the dam the fresh-water lakes would not be stagnant or unhealthy, while below it there would be "no sewage, no flooding, better fire pro-tection, access to 480 wharves above Woolwich at all times, less waiting for the tides," and so on.

This year seventy or eighty small lifeboats broke adrift at Hampton, swirled downstream and piled against a boom protecting the weir and threatening all sorts of serious damage. Rivermen had to stand by so as to lasso the boats if they broke adrift. At Staines the river was full and the tow-paths were awash, with flooded farmland fifty yards wide and here and there what seemed to be islands tenanted by wildfowl. All this, which occurs more or less each year, would, it is claimed, be obviated by the barrage; but against that benefit comes Sir Alan Herbert's complaint *No Boats on the River*. So far it would seem that the Port of London Authority is opposed to the Thames Barrage Scheme, and the river is still available for steamers and water-buses, at the cost, be it said, of serious annual flooding. It is only fair to the river itself to say that the Thames, which engendered London, with its last bridgehead over the river, is not only a great commercial asset, but is also itself one of the chief open spaces of the metropolitan area.

CHISWICK EYOT

Chiswick Eyot was bought by the Brentford and Chiswick
Council in 1934 from the Ecclesiastical Commissioners, but
its history goes back to the dim period of the lake-dwellers,
whose prehistoric homes among the osiers were probably prior
to the first London settlement on the Walbrook.

Half a century ago the Eyot, which was $3\frac{1}{4}$ acres in extent,
partly in London but mainly in Middlesex, was a home for
many swans and a resting-place for herons and kingfishers.
It was until recently covered with osiers used for making
baskets, and the knives employed by the reapers were sharpened on a black whetstone formerly kept at the Red Lion in
Chiswick Mall, now a trophy in the Chiswick Public Library.
The tides on the river and the wash of passing steamers have
swept away the piece of island belonging to London, and
various schemes to protect the Eyot with a concrete promenade
or with wooden stakes and hurdles have all been abandoned.
The backwater between it and Chiswick Mall has silted up,
so that boys can clamber across at low water and they have
flattened down the osiers. Four public bodies—the local and
county councils, the Port of London Authority, and the
Ministry of Town and Country Planning—have washed their
hands of the whole problem, so an appeal has been made to
the Societies for the Preservation of Nature Reserves,
Commons, and Open Spaces of Rural England and to the
National Trust to rescue this island, once occupied by the
Danes in A.D. 879, the nearest Nature reserve to London and
the first island in the River Thames, from the serious danger
of complete disappearance.

But we are still only at Kew Bridge and the "squalid
respectabilities of Gunnersbury," as Sir John Squire calls
them. Next comes Brentford on the northern bank, with the
glorious gardens of Kew on the Surrey side. Brentford has
the Brent River flowing into the Thames, close to Old England, and the possible or even probable place of Cæsar's
crossing. Brentford figures in Tom Hood's verses on *The
Duel* between the "two kings smelling at one nosegay," Mr.
Bray and Mr. Clay, who both fell in love with the same lady,
and also in Thackeray's ballad on *The King of Brentford's*

Testament, where the dying monarch bequeaths with great wisdom the lands "of Chiswick, Fulham, Brentford, Putney, Kew."

Rather over a century ago—to be precise, in January, 1841—the Welsh Harp, down Hendon Way, burst its banks owing to an unusually rapid thaw, tore numerous boats, barges, and lighters from their moorings and drove them towards the Thames, where nearby many houses were flooded. The filth which was so prominent a feature of Brentford has much diminished of late, and the construction of by-pass roads has removed the congestion of traffic. Thomson, the poet, who lived at Richmond, and was therefore a man of Surrey, spoke contemptuously of its opposite number :

> "E'en so, through Brentford town, a town of mud,
> A herd of bristly swine is preeked along,
> The filthy beasts that never chew the cud,
> Still grunt and squeak, and sing their troublous song,
> And off they plunge themselves the mire among."

Many folk will have passed by Brentford without remembering Ben Jonson's promise : "We'll tickle it at the Pigeons," where Shakespeare, too, may have enjoyed himself. The inn, which was famous for the "fat woman," that effective disguise of Falstaff, was pulled down in the late 1890s, and its carving and panelling have completely disappeared.

Between Brentford and Twickenham is a very picturesque bend of the stream, with Kew Gardens and the Old Deer Park on the Surrey side and Syon House opposite. Isleworth, besides Syon, has All Saints' Church, with a medieval tower, three homestead moats, the Ingram Almshouses, dating from 1864, and other period houses and cottages.

Farther south the beauty is continued with Richmond Park and Ham and Petersham Commons in Surrey, Marble Hill and Strawberry Hill on the Twickenham side. If one may believe the old ballad of Marzials, which we all used to sing with such feeling in the 'eighties, it cost "but a penny to Twickenham Town," and the ferryman had all the attractive qualities that one might expect. Having reached Twickenham, either by Richmond Bridge or the ferry, one finds more important old buildings there than in almost any town in

Middlesex. These include Kneller Hall, York House, and Radnor House. Strawberry Hill is now St. Mary's College, and Fortescue House is a school. All these are late seventeenth- or early eighteenth-century work, and there are many others of similar date.

Teddington rebuilt its parish church in the eighteenth and nineteenth centuries and has since then been trying to erect a Thames-side cathedral. Hampton has almost enough houses of real distinction to make it famous apart from Hampton Court Palace. Round the Green are several sixteenth- and seventeenth-century buildings, including the Old Court House, where lived Sir Christopher Wren. Reservoirs on both sides of the Thames above the new Hampton Bridge are not picturesque, but they do at least preserve open spaces; and then there follows a singularly unspoilt reach of the river.

Sunbury has a rebuilt church, but it contains, as many reconstructed churches do, earlier relics. There is part of an old homestead moat at Kempton Park and several houses dating from about 1700. Sunbury has grown from a Thames-side village into a dormitory suburb, and is disfigured in parts by gravel pits.

Upper Halliford is close to the Thames, Lower Halliford actually on its banks. Both retain a great deal of beauty, and the bends of the river hereabouts are most attractive. Shepperton has a church which was rebuilt as long ago as 1614, while its rectory is older. Ivy Cottage and White Cottage date from the sixteenth century, and the barn at Manor Farm is about a century older.

The last few miles of the Thames as it skirts Middlesex are not quite so picturesque and unspoilt as they were when Thomas Arnold, of Laleham and afterwards of Rugby, spoke of them early in the nineteenth century :

"Of the country about us . . . I have explored much, but not nearly so much as I should wish. It is very beautiful, and some of the scenes at the junction of the heath country with the rich valley of the Thames are very striking. Or, if I do not venture so far from home, I have always a resource at hand in the bank of the river up to Staines; which, though it is perfectly flat, has yet a great charm from its entire loneliness, there being not a house anywhere near it; and the river

409

here has none of that stir of boats and barges upon it, which makes it in many places as public as the high road."

Staines possesses a church tower attributed to Inigo Jones, but the church itself was rebuilt in 1828. In the attractive streets of this riverside town are Duncroft House and two inns—the Blue Anchor and the White Lion—and some smaller houses, all of the seventeenth century.

Matthew Arnold, in a letter of January 2, 1848, just a century ago, written on his way from Laleham to stay with the Marquess of Lansdowne at Bowood, writes somewhat disparagingly of Middlesex as compared with Surrey. "Yesterday I was at Chertsey, the poetic town of our childhood, as opposed to the practical historic Staines; it is across the river, reached by no bridges and roads, but by the primitive ferry, the meadow path, the Abbey river with its wooden bridge, and the narrow lane by the old wall; and itself the stillest of country towns backed by St. Ann's, leads nowhere but to the heaths and pines of Surrey. How unlike the journey to Staines, and the great road through the flat, drained Middlesex plain, with its single standing pollarded elms."

Still, in spite of Matthew Arnold, an artist in 1937 called Staines the English Bruges, and justified the comparison by some charming drawings.

A by-pass for Staines like the Western Avenue, which avoids Uxbridge, would be a godsend. If more industry should be suggested, then kindred concerns such as plastics might be added. Boat-building is encouraged, and Staines with its riverside provides recreation for Londoners. Ashford is almost joined on to Staines, with a good shopping centre and accommodation for middle-class folk, and with an unfortunate development on land formerly used for orchards. It has been suggested that Ashford might serve as a residential area for employees in the London Airport at Heathrow. West Bedfont is characterised in a recent report as a "semi-derelict area, with an evil-smelling animal products factory which should be removed to a more isolated locality." Laleham, Stanwell Moor, and Stanwell are attractive villages which should be carefully preserved. Laleham, being on the banks of the Thames, is developing into a recreational centre, and steps should be taken to prevent its war-time timber

410

storage becoming permanent. The other two villages should be preserved as agricultural areas.

At various intervals attempts have been made to form a definite plan, which would include all Middlesex within its scope, for regulating the spread of housing and industry, for preserving what remains of open country, and for concentrating on the satellite town rather than on the suburban dormitory. The London and Middlesex Archæological Society's recent excavations on the Roman-British site at Brockley Hill, with its buried town of Sulloniacæ, have revealed to those privileged to take part in the digging a really wonderful piece of open country, scheduled as a permanent open space, from Elstree, Barnet Lane, and Woodcock Hill on the north, through Scratch Wood, Highwood, Moat Mount, to Watling Street on the east and west, an area of beauty hardly to be equalled anywhere near London, and owing its preservation mainly to the joint efforts of Hendon Borough Council and All Souls' College at Oxford.

THE NORTHERN FRONTIER

Three boundaries of Middlesex are plain and straightforward, and are all rivers—the Thames, the Lea, the Colne. Where the L.C.C. has taken away a large portion of ancient Middlesex the determining factor was the extent of the Bills of Mortality. It is the northern boundary that needs some elucidation. In discussing the irregular outline of the extreme northern boundary we must note that this is evidently a special effort to include Enfield and Edmonton and South Mimms in Middlesex, but to exclude Totteridge, Chipping Barnet, and East Barnet and Monken Hadley. Totteridge belonged to the Bishop of Ely's Manor of Hatfield, the two Barnets to the Abbot of St. Albans, Hadley and North Mimms had been given by Geoffrey de Mandeville to Walden Abbey, and so all these figured, appropriately enough, in Hertfordshire. Friern Barnet was part of the Manor of Whetstone, belonging to the Priory of St. John of Jerusalem at Clerkenwell, and so was included in Middlesex.

Halfway between Waltham Abbey and Enfield Wash the county boundary strikes off westwards from the Lea, between

411

Theobald's Park and Turkey Street, past old Enfield Chase, between Northam and Potters Bar, including South Mimms, but not North Mimms, and then it turns almost due south past Ridge and Dyrham Park to the Arkley Hotel at Barnet. So far five important trunk roads have crossed the county frontier : the Kingsland-Tottenham-Cheshunt Road and its by-pass, the new Cambridge Road; the Great North Road, A1, which forks at Barnet into the old main road to the north; and A6 and the Barnet By-pass.

At the Arkley Barnet corner comes that remarkable enclosure which includes all the Barnets save Friern Barnet, and Totteridge, land which belonged before the Conquest to the Abbot of St. Albans. From the top of Hendon Wood Lane by the Windmill at Grimsgate, Barnet Lane is for a very short distance the county boundary. Then a small piece on the south side of the lane belongs to Herts, and next at Furze Hill Road the south side of the lane is the county boundary once more. Where my house is situated just above Scratch Wood the ditch marks six boundary lines : the County, Hundred (between Gore and Cassiobury), Parish, Petty Sessions, Local Government, and Parliamentary. When I asked the late Sir Montagu Sharp to inspect my six frontiers, he added Grim's Dyke to make a seventh, and Major Hugh Braun, the latest authority on the subject, is inclined to agree. Barnet Gate, which lies along our frontier road about a mile and a half nearer Chipping Barnet, used to be called Grim's Gate; there is a ditch in Arkley which has always been called Grim's Dyke; and the presence of Scratch Wood, in close proximity, called after his Satanic Majesty, as Grim's Dyke and Gate also seem to be, does suggest that Barnet Lane is approximately on the line of the old boundary, though whether it was drawn for protection or hunting or merely property definition has not yet been authoritatively decided.

The county boundary runs along the south side of Woodcock Hill and Barnet Lane, more or less exactly into Elstree village, and there are names in use along it which suggest some association with the abbots and monks of St. Albans, or possibly Westminster; the Priory, Deacon's Hill, Prior's Mead, Abbot's Mead have a distinctly ecclesiastical sound, and some at least are medieval. At Elstree, where the Lane

412

runs into Watling Street (A5), the policeman on point duty does, or did, stand in two counties, four parishes, and four Parliamentary constituencies.

The boundary line leaves a small piece of the reservoir in Middlesex, crosses the Watford By-pass, climbs north-west through part of Bushey Heath, between Bentley Priory and Harrow Weald Common, leaving Oxhey Woods on the Herts side, Pinner Hill in Middlesex, leaving Moor Park and Batchworth Heath in Herts, and then takes a north-west line to include all the Harefield area, and to reach the Grand Union Canal and the River Colne between Mill End, Rickmansworth, and Maple Cross. In part of this last trek we are on the edge of the new Harrow, which embraces Edgware, Stanmore, Wealdstone, and Pinner, which all have as parks and open spaces remnants of elm-set fields, relics of big estates which their owners found too expensive to maintain, and reserves along the edge of streams. Stanmore and Harrow Weald Commons cover 165 acres, and the Middlesex County Council has taken over the late Sir W. S. Gilbert's estate of Grim's Dyke of over 100 acres. Farther south is part of Canons Park, about 50 acres of it, and next to it is the North London Collegiate School for Girls, which has taken over the house on the site of the Chandos mansion with part of the estate.

The Englishman is still at heart a countryman, despite a century or more of town-dwelling, and side by side with his use of the open road there comes his love of the trees, and many of the newer by-pass roads today are beautified by wise planting. At first the wiseacres warned us that trees by the roadside would spread their leaves and cause accidents to cars, but their gloomy prognostications have not been realised. Arthur Young, writing in 1780 in his *Six Weeks' Tour* in the Southern Counties, also objected to trees on the roadside, though for a somewhat different reason. In his view, no road "that ever disgraced this kingdom, in the very ages of Barbarism, ever equalled that from Billericay to Tilbury." And the two defects were just its narrowness, so that "for nearly twelve miles a mouse cannot pass by any carriage," and, secondly, "the trees everywhere overflow the road, so that it is totally impervious to the sun." But for most of us today the wider roads with their tree-lined borders are a source of great delight; and owners of even small gardens plant in them trees which are often far too large for their surroundings, but which delight the heart of the suburban dweller. As tree-lovers we all like that story which "Alpha of the Plough" told of Sir Henry Campbell-Bannerman, who used to take off his hat to favourite trees when he returned from Westminster to Scotland.

CHAPTER XXVII

LAST WORDS

I T is only too true to say that the story of any county of ours is supremely worth telling, especially in such days as these when world problems are constantly demanding our attention and setting us tasks for which most of us can find no solution. But a county is of a size more adapted to the purview of the average man or woman, and it is abundantly desirable that its story should be known to every girl and boy who lives within its boundaries.

Sydney Smith wrote some words of wisdom just about a century ago when he told his contemporaries : "Our sphere of thoughts has hardly any limits, our sphere of action hardly any extent; we may speculate on worlds, we must act in families, in districts, and in kingdoms." And to one who has made his home in Middlesex for more than half a century and has been active in her county Archæological Society for more than twenty years it is a great source of satisfaction to look out from her northern frontier which she shares with Hertfordshire and see more than half the county with a single sweep and to know that what he sees as unspoiled country is guaranteed for all time.

As has already been suggested, for many years past people who wrote about Middlesex usually discussed London and its buildings and its government and life, and then left a few pages only for the rest of the county. Nowadays people sometimes ignore Middlesex in rather a different way. Harold Clunn had a very interesting and extremely well-illustrated book entitled *The Changing Face of the Home Counties,* and, although nearly half the roads that lead to the places of interest described go through Middlesex, there is hardly a line about the county. Another attractive book is *This England,* by W. S. Shears, and out of 700 pages only three are devoted to Middlesex, where all the other counties have nearly six times as much.

In W. J. Loftie's two-volume *History of London* he does
415

devote a whole chapter to Middlesex, and at the end of it exclaims : "It would be but too easy to make a volume about the outlying districts of Middlesex and their eminent inhabitants. There are many temptations to prolixity—there is scarcely a village in the county without its memories of someone who made himself famous in the great neighbouring city. . . . Many of us are better acquainted with foreign countries than with our own. But, granted health, there is no place in the world which has the same interest for an Englishman as the county of Middlesex." Two recent writers in the 1930s, Martin Briggs and Arthur Mee, gave each a well-sized book to our county, and more than justified their decision to do so.

What makes any account of Middlesex almost immediately out of date is the rapidity with which changes take place in a way that is hardly possible in any other county. A glance at an advertisement column in the daily paper will tell you of houses to be sold in Kenton and Northwood. Well and good, for these have been growing suburban areas for some years, with smaller and larger properties for sale. But a further inspection invites those folk who are intending to move to London to come to Whitton, West London's modern suburb, where luxurious houses can be purchased for sums from two thousand to three thousand pounds, and where the journey to London takes only twenty-three minutes. Here, unless great care is exercised, is another serious threat to the rural remains of Middlesex.

Middlesex, as well as London, figures in every metropolitan newspaper, morning and evening, every day. This is only natural, but the wide range of topics included is really rather remarkable. On a single day, in one evening paper, we read that parts of the docks are overgrown with grass and used as a car-park, thus allowing food to go bad and causing shortages in the metropolitan and Middlesex areas. Ballet companies are announcing performances at Golder's Hill and boxing competitions are billed in Clissold Park. The Ministry of Supply is urged by the Councils of Acton, Ealing, Hayes, and Southall to release for housing a 300-acre site at Northolt, at one time used as an ordnance depot, and an Acton school cannot be repaired after war damage owing to shortage of tiles. Another educational problem is the taking of children

416

to school, and the Willesden Council is hoping to solve it by purchasing two twenty-six-seater buses, at a cost of £2,400, for child transport. The stage has never really lost its grip on the popular imagination, and the cinema and television have begun to attract the amateur to try his hand at acting. A Middlesex Drama League has recently been started to interest as many as possible of young folk in the county in depicting its history on the stage, and a small council has been enrolled to ensure that complete historical accuracy is achieved.

An extension of the Central Line Underground from North Acton through three new stations at Hanger Lane, Perivale, and Greenford was opened on June 30, 1947, and will serve North Ealing as well as the suburbs mentioned. It is expected that four million passengers will be carried each year, as the trains will run from Greenford to and from the West End, Liverpool Street, and Leytonstone. Trains will run every six minutes in the peak periods, seven and a half minutes at other times, and ten minutes in the evenings. The line is the joint affair of the G.W.R. and the L.P.T.B., and while these lines are being penned both these railway lines are being absorbed in the national system.

Another indication of the need for a quick eye to detect progress in Middlesex was contained in the *Listener* for August 7, 1947, under the weekly heading "Did you hear that?" A new school for 520 girls and boys in Ruislip between eleven and sixteen was finished in six months owing to quick methods of construction. It has a dining hall, at present used as a gymnasium; an assembly hall, in the making; fourteen classrooms; a science "lab"; a sewing-room; a carpenter's shop; and a domestic science room with laundry attached. A steel framework was fixed up with a metal sheeting roof, and constructional work was possible even in wet weather. There is no plaster on wall or ceiling; doors, windows, and cupboards were prefabricated, and wood-wool and glass-silk deaden sound and conserve heat, thus economising in fuel. Doors are sunflower yellow, radiators are turquoise blue in this one-floor building. The heating arrangements are fitted with thermostatic control, and a regular temperature of 60 degrees Fahrenheit is maintained in winter. Hot-water pipes dry damp overcoats and special blackboards are fitted which minimise labour. If schools like this one can be designed by the county architect, Mr. Lobb, and erected thus quickly from steel, wood, brick, concrete, and glass at £100,000, our educational problem in Middlesex should present fewer difficulties than at first seemed likely.

The Federation of Ratepayers' Associations of Middlesex were recommending in October, 1947, after the Government's insistent demands for austerity, that the Middlesex County Council, which in 1946 had a Labour majority for the first time, should cease all fresh capital expenditure except that of absolute urgency, and that the saving should be passed on to the ratepayers.

An interesting project was the purchase of Franklin House, Northwood, from King's College, Cambridge, with 10 acres of ground, as a memorial to R.A.F. pilots who fought in the Battle of Britain. It is intended to use the house and three army huts as a meeting-place for the youth of Britain and countries in the Commonwealth, and to foster friendship and the community spirit. There should be room for 120 young men, and to help in the residential training courses all kinds of distinguished folk will be asked to come as guest lecturers. The house is to be called the "Battle of Britain" House, and is to be run by the Middlesex County Council and the Northwest Middlesex Youth Committee.

In Middlesex there has recently been established a Federation of twenty-six local associations which have since the end of the second World War enrolled 7,000 former Civil Defence personnel. They are to serve as an essential adjunct to the reserves for the armed forces, "ready at a moment's notice to function with full effect if this country is to withstand the devastating effects of action arising from the use by an enemy of bombs and rockets with atomic war-heads." The Middlesex Federation recalled General Eisenhower's view that "push-button warfare" would bring swift, shattering attacks, and that the first sixty days would decide the issue. The members of the associations within the Federation are convinced that the time limit for our crowded cities, which provide the world's most vulnerable targets for atomic rockets, will give a far shorter shrift, and they recommend the establishment of a national citizen force to answer the call. In reply to these suggestions a scientist wrote that crowded areas like Middlesex would only last a day or two of atomic warfare, and that the one logical aim should be to ensure that atomic warfare does not happen.

An interesting comment on the growth of Middlesex and the danger of a decline of any county consciousness is given by two books written and illustrated by my old schoolfellow, Martin S. Briggs. He produced *Middlesex, Old and New* in 1932 and *Round the Shires* in 1947, and had to lament in the first the tremendous destruction of the country of Middlesex since we were boys together at Mill Hill in the 'nineties. He was then attempting "to rescue, from the apparently irresistible and relentless tide of spreading suburbia, some memory of the old scenes and old buildings which are annually becoming submerged and forgotten, if not actually destroyed." He wanted "to restrict the senseless methods of ignorant land-sharks and jerry-builders," and to prevent thoughtless and indiscriminate cutting down of far too many trees to allow of road widening and speculative building. The illustrated brochures that attracted people to buy their own houses held up a picture of real country, and the folk who bought them realised too late that their purchase was not a solitary one, but that there were many hundreds, if not thousands, of "cosy palaces" and "Tudor homes" whose building had driven the country still farther away. In his second book he prints a drawing of the village pond at Mill Hill in 1905, and comments with pathos on the fact that most of Middlesex is now suburban, while this corner stands out almost alone, unaltered. But this is not the only piece of rural Middlesex surviving by a long way, and the plans made by individual boroughs and rural districts, by the county as a whole, and by national schemes, have done an immense amount to back up and supplement the efforts of individual owners to preserve some aspect of the county against the "spreading of the hideous town," as William Morris called it. He seems to have called it many other things as well, and London deserved most of what he said. In Holbrook Jackson's collection of Morris's lectures and essays, *On Art and Socialism,* he quotes a furious onslaught on the uglification of the commercial cities of his day, which he calls "mere masses of sordidness, filth and squalor, embroidered with patches of pompous and vulgar hideousness, no less revolting to the eye and mind when one knows what it means." Morris goes on to condemn the vulgarity of the hell of big cities and the wretched suburbs that sprawl round them, and claims that the folk of the present are really trustees for posterity and ought to preserve beauty as a precious jewel. At this particular lecture John Ruskin was in the chair, and both these Victorian reformers would have backed the planning of the Green Belt with enthusiasm.

And recent journeys by car or bus through Middlesex make it clear that there is still some pride in the locality in which a man finds himself, and a genuine endeavour to provide a rural home for his wife and children. Just after the second World War J. M. Richards wrote his *Castles on the Ground,* in which he discusses the picture of his home that the ordinary Englishman had in his mind when away at the war, the home which he was fighting to defend, the home which so often was destroyed by indiscriminate Nazi bombing. There are several types of home which reveal the depth of their owner's purpose, one a house standing in its own grounds, with pine trees and rhododendrons and a tennis court. Just a little lower in the revenue scale there is the typical suburban home, with trim garden and dog, with privet hedge, ampelopsis, may, and laburnum, with tradesmen's entrance and rockery. This type he finds in such a suburb as Mill Hill, where the linen-collared suburban dweller lives. And then there is the type of house rather less expensive which he sees in a place like Osterley.

The period between the two World Wars saw nearly four million houses built, and many of them bought by their tenants, and a great number of this total are to be found in suburban and semi-rural Middlesex. Here is a new Suburbia, and in nearly all these homes you will find care and cleanliness both in house and garden. The Hoover and the lawn-mower are among the most treasured possessions. But another thought that comes as one drives or, better still, rides through the newly built-up areas is the remarkable similarity that exists between one suburb and the next, and the lack of any obvious boundary. Few are so lucky as Hendon, which has Hampstead Heath to the south and the Green Belt to the north, the Dollis Brook along much of the east, and Watling Street as a western boundary. It is still comparatively easy to beat the bounds of Hendon, and the local Historical Society tries to do this in part at least every year.

When driving recently along the Watford and Barnet By-pass Road, that runs as a single road from Finchley Road to Apex Corner and then divides into A500 and A555, I was asked by my passenger when the attractive houses with adequate gardens which sprang up along this immensely important highway would become a slum area. It was a very searching question and reflected the anxiety of many who live just inside or just outside the county boundary as to the future of what is now so attractive. It would probably be true to say that the considered answer is "Never," just because the layout is so much better designed than that of other areas which have gone from bad to worse in the past, and because we all have our eyes open to the dreadful possibilities which our knowledge of the past suggests. A recent meeting of ratepayers in a singularly unspoiled area in Middlesex discussed problems of private trading in residential areas, often the thin end of a wedge that brings decline and fall to a hitherto decent suburb. It was unanimously decided to take a very strong line with the local council to aid them in checking this abuse of freedom from the very outset.

If anything was wanted to convince the citizens of Middlesex that they have a county of which they may well be proud, it was provided by the publication in 1937 of the *Inventory of the Historical Monuments in Middlesex,* compiled under instructions from the Royal Commission on Historical Monuments in England. This very handsomely produced volume contains a detailed account of every building in the county worthy of note, with hundreds of illustrations and plans, and it also commends to the King's notice a selection of buildings in the county "especially worthy of preservation." Local patriotism must strain every nerve to see that no ancient or historic building is needlessly destroyed, but especial care must be taken to preserve those specially scheduled by the Commission. These include Grim's Dyke, an earthwork mainly in the parishes of Pinner and Harrow Weald, but possibly extending as far east as High Barnet; earthworks at Enfield and East Hillingdon; a motte at Ruislip; and a motte and bailey castle at South Mimms. Rather more than a dozen parish churches are scheduled : East Bedfont, Cranford, Enfield, Harefield, Harmondsworth, Harrow, Hayes, South Mimms, Ruislip, Great Stanmore, and Hanwell, with Moor Hall Chapel, near Harefield, an old chapel of the Knights of St. John. It is a little difficult to justify the special selection of the Caroline church of Stanmore when Harlington and Hendon are omitted. Perhaps its dedication by Archbishop Laud has won it the preference. Of secular buildings, by far the most important is the royal palace of Hampton Court, with the adjacent Royal Mews.

Others are Boston House at Brentford, Forty Hall and Glasgow Stud Farm at Enfield, almshouses at Harefield, the famous Barn at Harmondsworth, Osterley Park and Syon House, Swakeleys at Ickenham, Cromwell House at Hornsey, Knightsland House at South Mimms, Southall Manor House, the very simple and dignified Schoolhouse at Stanwell, Bruce Castle and the Priory at Tottenham, and York House at Twickenham. But the perusal of this invaluable gazetteer of Middlesex antiquities, and the publication just before the second World War of a county book to celebrate the jubilee of the Middlesex County Council, must have aroused and stimulated a great deal of county pride. It is a great triumph for the county that it has figured so early in these inventories, only *London, Buckinghamshire, Essex, Herefordshire, Hertfordshire, Huntingdon,* and *Westmorland* having preceded it. Local patriotism will no doubt see to it that very many other objects of beauty and historic interest are preserved. Indeed, there has been a very marked stimulus about in favour of preservation, and ill-judged efforts to destroy have aroused a still more determined intention to retain.

Middlesex had its share in the Battle of Britain, a considerable portion of which was fought in the skies above it, and was plotted by the Royal Observer Corps. The various defensive measures designed to protect London were seen to the full in the adjacent country, and the line of Barnet Lane, which joins so many great trunk roads to the north, was to have been part of the last outside defence of the capital had things gone as badly as that. A skeleton force of the R.O.C.

still functions within the county, and reunions of former members take place when all the circumstances are favourable.

An interesting problem to solve is the question whether Londoners who live in Middlesex belong to one or other of the two counties or to both. Are people who work within the sound of Bow Bells real Cockneys, or only those who were born in that limited area? The modern Cockney speech is that of the Middlesex, Essex, and Hertfordshire countryside, and it is exemplified in the exchange of "v" for "w" and *vice versa*. It seems to be generally agreed that Londoners developed a version of the Essex dialect, which was considerably modified towards the end of the nineteenth century by the crowds of folk from the provinces who flooded the metropolitan area.

A very interesting relic of feudal tenure in ancient Middlesex came to an end with the year 1947. The homage jury of the Manor of Fulham, whose last survivor was J. C. Platt, of Hammersmith, elected in 1935, was really a committee of copyholders with the task of ensuring that the customs of the manor should be strictly observed. Fulham and Hammersmith were held continuously by the Bishops of London from A.D. 691 until the Ecclesiastical Commissioners took over more than half a century ago; and the copyholders reaped financial rewards when the manorial common lands were submerged by sporadic building. Here are some of those which very largely disappeared as London advanced : Eel Brook or Hell Brook Common, Fulham Fields, Gaggle Goose Green, Paddingwick or Starch Green, Parsons Green, Shepherd's Bush Green, Stamford Brook Green, Walham Green—which "still show a blade or two of grass among the manor's wilderness of bricks and mortar." Starch Green is the name of a district between The Vale and Uxbridge Road on the north and Goldhawk Road on the south. Eel Pie Common, Parsons Green, Fulham Recreation Ground and Cemetery, Hammersmith Cemetery, Queen's Club, Shepherd's Bush Green, Ravenscroft and Wendell Parks—these are some of the open spaces still preserved; and the present site occupied by St. Paul's School is part of the ancient manor.

Each encroachment on the ancient Manor of Fulham and

hamlet of Hammersmith brought compensation to the homage jury, and their great source of funds came from Wormwood Scrubs. Copyholders were entitled to graze their cattle and their "stint" of hogs or hoggerds on the Scrubs, and the number permitted varied from two for a cottager, three for a tenement holder, and ten for a farmer.

The War Office paid rent from 1812 to 1879 for training the Life Guards on the Scrubs, and compensation was paid by railway companies (now national property) for constructing their lines through the woodlands, which lasted in theory till 1903, when the woodman's cottage was sold. The area extended as far north as Kensington Road, where a small piece of Gibbs Green remained until very recently, just opposite Holland House Park. The compensation thus obtained was used to help the Wasteland Almshouses "for the comfort of aged and decayed householders" in Fulham and Hammersmith, and the homage jury dined together at suitable intervals. Lord Birkenhead's Law of Property Act of 1922 made copyholder tenure come to an end in 1926, but money still came in until 1931. J. C. Platt at the end of 1947 legally divided what was left of the homage jury's funds between two ancient and deserving almshouses, and an interesting historical function has come to an end after a story lasting over twelve and a half centuries.

When we consider the problem of national parks, we have as a rule to think of the Lakes, the Pennines, Yorkshire moors and dales, Dartmoor, Central and South Wales, and the like. But nearer to London small areas can still be saved, and there is quite a deal of wild life in Middlesex, which must be preserved. There is a danger that any county may be suburbanised, and it is vital to ensure that every place where men may live should have green fields and some woodland close at hand. "Nothing rare need greet us here," writes Antony Collett, in his *Changing Face of England,* "only the leaves, and the hawthorn or bracken in its season, and the song-thrush or the skylark in song." But preservation of birds and shy beasts and wild flowers calls for restraint on the part of the townsman : there will have to be areas from which the public with its myriad feet, its bonfires for kettle boiling, its unextinguished matches, its ruthless flower picking, is excluded. Strong efforts must be made to prevent "the subtle and melancholy transformation of country woods and commons into suburban wastes."

Middlesex has at long last secured its Green Belt. It must be shared between picnic-makers, lovers of games, and not least by wild birds and beasts in their natural habitats.

In discussing development and preservation it is important to be clear as to the precise area which one has in mind. Besides Abercrombie's "Greater London," so immeasurably greater than the historic City, there is the London Passenger Transport Area, which is very similar in size, but not quite the same shape. Another area is that controlled by the Metropolitan Water Board, which affects Middlesex only partially, covering most of the south and east of the county, but excluding the north and west from Potters Bar south-west to Staines. The last area is the Metropolitan Police District, again an entirely different area, but including the whole of Middlesex.

The various plans for development have had as one objective the limiting of population, which makes axiomatic the sanctity of the Green Belt. This means that any surplus population may have to be decanted into regions outside Middlesex altogether, and one London borough (Hammersmith), one Surrey borough (Richmond), and five Middlesex ones are planned to send their surplus to Bracknell in Berkshire. Some 20,000 will go as a short-term plan from the boroughs of Southall, Brentford, and Chiswick, but others will follow from Heston and Isleworth, Ealing, and from Finchley, which is so hemmed in by its neighbours that expansion is impracticable. The existence of the planning schemes has already done some slowing up of house-building along the discarded extension of the Edgware Tube to Brockley Hill, Elstree, and Bushey. But restrictions in one area must mean development in another, and it is vital to synchronise policies, so that, if a crowded area is to be closed down or an open space preserved, new houses must at once be made available in some satellite town farther out.

The programme for roads must be planned with effective care so that their construction coincides with their degree of urgency. In the Master Plan it is suggested that among the roads whose construction must have precedence are the Exeter Road, that to South Wales, the Birmingham and Edinburgh Roads, all of which pass through Middlesex. These are all express arterial roads, and in addition the Staines By-pass and the Heathrow By-pass on the Bath Road should be given priority. With the increase of air transport it will be necessary to build an electrified loop from Feltham to Heathrow. The electrification of the existing lines from Hatfield Airport to King's Cross or St. Pancras, and of that from Didcot to Paddington, affects Middlesex not a little.

Such an opportunity for wise, long-sighted planning has seldom occurred before on so large a scale. We have only to look back one, two, or three centuries to see what glorious earlier chances of developing Middlesex on wise lines were blindly thrown away. The story of the Roman Sibyl is being repeated, and there is a modified chance that the wise outlook which has ensured for us a green girdle gives a chance of recovering something from the past and ensuring wise progress for the future. Only we must realise that the chance now offered must be immediately accepted, and this last opportunity of preserving what is left of the rural beauty of Middlesex must be seized without the smallest possible delay.

A SELECT BIBLIOGRAPHY

W. Camden : *Britannia,* 1586. Edmund Gibson's Transla-
lation, 1695.

J. Norden : *Speculum Britanniæ* (Vol. I), 1593. An historical description of Middlesex.

J. Gerard : *The Herball, or General Historie of Plantes,*
1597.

J. Stow : *A Survey of London,* 1598.

J. Bowack : *Antiquities of Middlesex,* 1705.

Daniel Defoe : *A Tour thro' the whole Island of Great
Britain,* 1724.

Anon. : *A Description of the County of Middlesex,* 1775.

W. Curtis : *Flora Londinensis,* 1777-98.

D. Lysons : *The Environs of London* (Vols. II and III),
1792-6; *Parishes in Middlesex* (not included), 1800;
Supplement, 1811.

J. Middleton : *View of the Agriculture of Middlesex,* 1798.

E. W. Brayley and J. Britton : *The Beauties of England and
Wales* (Vol. X), 1814-16.

W. Pinnock : *History and Topography of Middlesex,* 1824.

J. H. Sperling : *Church Walks in Middlesex,* 1849.

W. Keane : *Beauties of Middlesex,* 1850.

London and Middlesex Archæological Society's Transactions,
1860 onwards.

J. E. Harting : *The Birds of Middlesex,* 1866.

H. Tremen and W. T. Dyer : *Flora of Middlesex,* 1869.

W. Lawson : *Middlesex,* in *Collins's County Geographies,*
1872.

W. Hughes : *The Geography of Middlesex,* 1872.

T. Murby : *Middlesex,* in *Murby's County Geographies,*
1874.

J. Thorne : *Environs of London* (2 vols.), 1876.

H. J. Foley : *Rambles in Rural Middlesex,* 1887.

J. A. Brown : *Palæolithic Man in North-west Middlesex,*
1887.

E. Walford : *Greater London* (2 vols.), 1893-6.

H. S. Vaughan : *The Way about Middlesex,* 1896.

W. Andrews : *Bygone Middlesex,* 1899.

W. G. Grace : *"W.G." : Cricket Reminiscences,* 1899.

D. Moul and R. E. Hill : *Picturesque Middlesex*, 1904.
V. G. Plarr and F. W. Walton : *A School History of Middlesex*, 1905.
J. B. Firth : *Middlesex*, in *Methuen's Little Guides*, 1906.
C. G. Harper : *Rural Nooks near London*, 1907.
A. R. Moncrieff : *Middlesex*, in *Black's Colour Books*, 1907.
Mrs. A. Bell : *The Skirts of the Great City*, 1907.
W. Jerrold : *Highways and Byways in Middlesex*, 1909.
J. Tavenor-Perry : *Memorials of Old Middlesex*, 1909.
Charles Dixon : *Bird Life of London*, 1909.
Middlesex : *Victoria Counties History*, Vol. II only, 1911.
G. F. Bosworth : *Middlesex*, in *Cambridge County Geographies*, 1913.
C. L. Kingsford : *The Middlesex Regiment*, 1917.
A. D. Webster : *London Trees*, 1920.
G. C. Turner : *The Old Flying Days*, 1920.
Fred Turner : *History and Antiquities of Brentford*, 1922.
London's Underground : *London's Country*, c. 1922.
W. G. Bell : *Where London Sleeps*, 1926.
G. S. Maxwell : *Just Beyond London*, 1927.
London's Underground : *London Town and Country*, 1928.
C. E. Vulliamy : *Archæology of London and Middlesex*, 1930.
T. Michael Pope : *Middlesex in Prose and Verse*, 1930.
G. S. Maxwell : *The Fringe of London*, 1931.
Sir Montagu Sharp : *Middlesex in British, Roman and Saxon Times*, 1932.
Martin S. Briggs : *Middlesex Old and New*, 1934.
W. E. Glegg : *A History of the Birds of Middlesex*, 1935.
G. S. Maxwell : *Highwayman's Heath*, 1935.
W. W. Druitt : *Harrow, Stanmore, Pinner, through the Ages* (3 vols.), 1935-8.
Historical Monuments Commission : *Middlesex*, 1937.
L.C.C. : *Open-air London*, 1939.
C. W. Radcliffe : *Middlesex, 1889-1939*, 1939.
Arthur Mee : *Middlesex*, 1940.
J. E. B. Gover and others : *Place Names of Middlesex*, 1942.
Sir Patrick Abercrombie : *Greater London Plan*, 1945.
R. S. R. Fitter : *London's Natural History*, 1945.
C. Percival Staples : *Birds in a Sanctuary Garden*, 1946.

INDEX

431

Printed in Great Britain by
Billing and Sons Ltd., Guildford and Esher

G2039